Subjectivation and Cohesion

Historical Materialism Book Series

The Historical Materialism Book Series is a major publishing initiative of the radical left. The capitalist crisis of the twenty-first century has been met by a resurgence of interest in critical Marxist theory. At the same time, the publishing institutions committed to Marxism have contracted markedly since the high point of the 1970s. The Historical Materialism Book Series is dedicated to addressing this situation by making available important works of Marxist theory. The aim of the series is to publish important theoretical contributions as the basis for vigorous intellectual debate and exchange on the left.

The peer-reviewed series publishes original monographs, translated texts, and reprints of classics across the bounds of academic disciplinary agendas and across the divisions of the left. The series is particularly concerned to encourage the internationalization of Marxist debate and aims to translate significant studies from beyond the English-speaking world.

For a full list of titles in the Historical Materialism Book Series available in paperback from Haymarket Books, visit:
https://www.haymarketbooks.org/series_collections/1-historical-materialism

Subjectivation and Cohesion

Towards the Reconstruction of a Materialist Theory of Law

Sonja Buckel

Translated by
Monika Vykoukal

Haymarket Books
Chicago, IL

First published in 2020 by Brill Academic Publishers, The Netherlands

Published in paperback in 2021 by
Haymarket Books
P.O. Box 180165
Chicago, IL 60618
773-583-7884
www.haymarketbooks.org

ISBN: 978-1-64259-594-9

Distributed to the trade in the US through Consortium Book Sales and Distribution (www.cbsd.com) and internationally through Ingram Publisher Services International (www.ingramcontent.com).

This book was published with the generous support of Lannan Foundation and Wallace Action Fund.

Cover art and design by David Mabb. Cover art is a detail of *Two Squares, no. 4*, El Lissitzky's "About Two Squares" on William Morris "Willow" wallpaper, paint and paper on canvas (2008).

Printed in the United States.

10 9 8 7 6 5 4 3 2 1

Library of Congress Cataloging-in-Publication data is available.

For Alex and Christiane

Contents

PART 3
Reconstruction: Subjectivation and Cohesion

PART 4
Self-government

Preface to the English Edition

When the first edition of this book was published in 2007 on the eve of the great crisis of capitalism, it was impossible to imagine how much the world would change over the following decade. In this crisis of the economy, hegemony, politics, gender relations and ecology, the historical formation of post-Fordism came to an end. Naturally, law – the legal form, as I will argue – also entered into crisis. The dialectics of democracy and capitalism, as developed by Marx in his essay *The Eighteenth Brumaire of Louis Napoleon*, unfolded with destructive momentum. The legal and democratic achievements of social struggles are eroding and authoritarian state formations are on the rise world-wide. Executive power is able to free itself from its legal enclosures.

This book was thus written in another era; at a time when I could pursue calmly for five years the question of how the law of those societies in which the capitalist mode of production prevails, presents itself as a system. How can its contradictory basic structure – that it constitutes at the same time a technology of power and a deferral of this very power – be understood? How can the limited emancipatory potential of the legal form be explained?

Today, after ten years of capitalist dystopia, the answers that I believe myself to have found have to meet new challenges: the law at the limits – in the double meaning of the territorial borders of the global North and at the boundaries of the legal form itself.

For the English edition one chapter of the original manuscript has been omitted. This chapter consisted of an empirical investigation into the case law of European fundamental rights, the purpose of which was to empirically deepen the analytical results. This investigation would have required a substantial update, something which the hectic pace of academic practice leaves me no time for. Above all, however, such a study is not necessary for the theoretical reconstruction of a materialist legal theory.

Most of all I want to thank two people: Loren Balhorn of Historical Materialism, who succeeded after ten years in setting everything in motion to finally realise the planned translation project. I also have to thank Monika Vykoukal, and not only for the meticulous translation of the book. In fact together with Marietta Thien of Velbrück Wissenschaft, she made sure that the German version (published by Velbrück Wissenschaft in 2007) was submitted to the translation funding programme Geisteswissenschaft International for German works in the humanities and social sciences, a joint initiative of the Fritz Thyssen Foundation, the German Federal Foreign Office, the collecting society VG WORT, and the Börsenverein des Deutschen Buchhandels (the German

Publishers and Booksellers Association). I am grateful to this funding body for financing the translation of this book. Finally I would like to thank Danny Hayward from the Historical Materialism Book Series for carefully reading the text and Jennifer Obdam from Brill Publishing for her friendly support.

S.B.
Frankfurt am Main, December 2019

Preface

The spectres of law live unrecognised amongst us. Now and again they appear publicly in full daylight: in decisions such as that in the case of *Marbury against Madison* before the US Supreme Court in the year 1803, when the court empowered itself to check the laws of the political sovereign for their constitutionality and where necessary to dismiss them; or again, a century later, during the Weimar Republic in Germany, when the Supreme Court of the German Reich undertook with its *appreciation ruling* of 1923, in a private law dispute, the reappraisal of mortgage debts against the explicit will of the legislature; or, once more, fifty years later in 1973, when the Federal Constitutional Court suggested in the *Soraya verdict* that there was a 'surplus of law' beyond the political constitution, and that it was the task of jurisprudence to 'find' and actualise it; and, lastly, in the jurisprudence on Fundamental Rights of the European Court of Law, which created European Fundamental Rights out of nothing and in doing so suggested that they had always existed.

But the spectres also reveal themselves in everyday legal practices, namely when those who, as enlightened citizens, should know their rights, in reality face what with regards to their legal concerns amounts to a secret science. There have been countless attempts to methodically exorcise those spectres or at least to decrypt them as politics in disguise. But that has not helped at all. We have not rid ourselves of the undead – because they have made themselves comfortably at home in the haunted castle of capitalist socialisation.

A theory of law that argues in the tradition of Karl Marx is often expected to unmask law in one way or another as a mere reflex of 'the economy'. However, the aim of this study is diametrically opposed to this, as it starts with the notion that law is its own 'base'.

Precisely this spectral, self-contained realm of the law was what fascinated and inspired me from the first semester of my legal studies, that is to say, the fact that law has a 'normative self-determination' (Habermas), or a 'specific autonomy' (Kelsen) – that law determines what is law (Luhmann).

How could a materialist theory of law do justice to this fact, without at the same time giving up the claim to reveal all *social* phenomena as such, in the sense of showing them to be based on the material living conditions of human beings? How to do the spectres of law justice, without doing 'living labour' wrong?

With his theory of fetishism, Marx himself mapped out the path towards such an analysis. One only has to think of the table which turns itself on its head, 'and evolves out of its wooden brain grotesque ideas, far more wonderful than if it were to begin dancing of its own free will'.[1] Materialist theory does not deny this 'phantasmagoric process',[2] but traces it back to the relationships between people.[3] Today the most advanced social theories agree that what is specifically social is the dominance of relations over people, and that therefore precisely the notion that society is formed by human beings, that it is humane, misses the concept of 'society'[4] and creates an obstacle towards understanding in social theory.[5]

Understanding what is incomprehensible, that is, the fact that people lose control of their own relations, involves explaining the situation in which law itself becomes its own foundation through social relationships. This is the motivation of my attempt at a 'reconstruction of a materialist theory of law'.

In order to find those spectres, I have enlisted the help of a diverse range of theoretical approaches as well as my analysis of the practice of law. Above all though, my perspective has developed through discussions with people to whom I owe a lot, and whose ideas and critiques can be found in this publication. The present book is a revised version of my thesis, which was accepted in 2005 at the Department of Social Sciences at Goethe University Frankfurt, Germany, with its prestigious tradition. A theoretical practice shared with other critical intellectuals anticipates some of what I conceive of as a different, emancipatory form of the social division of labour; it represents a solitary and self-organised form of the public, coming together with the aim of shared knowledge production. That this was possible is due not least to the two reviewers of the doctorate. Josef Esser provided me a space of freedom within the still feudal structures of German academic life, and provided his support so that our shared approach to materialist theory could also be developed in the field of law. To Gunther Teubner I owe a precise demonstration of the blind spots that are invariably most discernible from another perspective, here that of systems theory. Through him I found a fascinating intellectual habitus, distinguished by its great interest in other theoretical explanations, and able to forgive with magnanimity even 'youthful polemics' against systems theory itself.

Andreas Fischer-Lescano also convinced me, with equal measures of rigour and humour, in varied, exciting discussions, that the Frankfurt School of the systems theory of law could rightly claim to advance a socially critical normative approach.

---

1 Marx 1976, pp. 163–4.
2 Derrida 1994, p. 199.
3 Adorno 1989, p. 147.
4 Adorno 1989, p. 144.
5 Luhmann 2012, p. 6.

The book emerged from a context of state theory outside of academic institutions, associated with Stephan Adolphs, John Kannankulam and Jens Wissel. Our shared conversations over the years, as well as their solidary and original critique, left a significant mark on the publication in its present form.

I furthermore owe Regina Dackweiler my gratitude for her extensive comments as well as her intelligent methodological objections. They saved me from the worst fallacies. I also owe particular thanks to those who tirelessly read the entire manuscript with attention to consistency in terms of both content and language – Oliver Eberl, from the perspective of the radical democratic Kantian theory of law, and Julia König and Dietmar Flucke.

I owe many suggestions to Joachim Hirsch, from whom I learned a lot. Peter Niesen and Eva Hartmann provided convincing commentaries for individual chapters. Bob Jessop, Ingeborg Maus, Marc Amstutz, Rudolf Wiethölter und Hauke Brunkhorst, as well as the members of the Association for Critical Social Research, allowed me to present my ideas publicly and thus profit from their informed objections.

Ultimately it was to Henry Düx – to his committed and impressive practice of law and to the discussions arising from it – that I owe the idea for this study.

I also want to thank Friedhelm Herborth of Velbrück Wissenschaft for his support as well as the careful supervision of the publication.

I alone remain responsible for the spectres of error, which despite all efforts cannot be eradicated.

S.B.
Frankfurt am Main, August 2006

Introduction

In the context of the state examination in law, which ostensibly tests the ability to practice of future legal professionals, it can easily happen that 'Ms. A' and 'Mr. B' conduct the business of 'Company Ltd. X'. Or they may have entered a relationship 'for life'. When it did not go well, 'Mr. B' might have 'damaged the health' of 'Mr. C'. Who are A, B and C? We learn practically nothing about them. They need to be different from each other, otherwise they would all be called 'A'. But what does this difference consist of? While their titles indicate that they are assigned a gender, this is at the same time irrelevant, for the Civil Code only talks about managers, spouses and perpetrators, and tells us above all that they are 'natural persons'. That 'limited company X' is a person too, that is a 'legal' person, leads to further confusion. If 'A' and 'B' were allowed to marry or to share a management role, they are most likely 'of legal age'. However, for 'B' to be punished, he need only be 14 years old, but he must not suffer from a 'pathological mental disorder', a 'profound consciousness disorder' or even 'debility'. If 'A' and 'B' had the fundamental right to freely choose their occupation, they were probably 'Germans'.

What is the relationship between those people? As managers they have to apply 'the care due from a prudent businessman', as 'spouses' they 'hold responsibility for each other', and, finally, as 'perpetrator', 'B' can be 'punished' with a 'prison term of up to five years'. Thereby he is meant to 'be equipped in the future to live a socially responsible life without offending'. Depending on the circumstances, he might have to be 'admitted to a psychiatric hospital' to protect the 'general public'.

Whoever the three 'natural persons' might be, in modern law they are autonomous individuals of sound mind, who initially have so little to do with each other that one can arrange them alongside each other like the letters of the alphabet. They are only connected as the 'general public' through law itself, so that their relationship is one of due care and responsibility. The law thus constitutes them as specific, individual subjects, while it assembles them at the same time into the abstract general.

What would they be without this modern law? One cannot know. One can only analyse how law itself works, and I want to do that in the following. *Subjectivation and Cohesion*, the title of this study, already contains my thesis on how law works. I will develop it over the next three hundred pages. It is the result of my confrontation with the various approaches constituting materialist legal theory.

By 'materialist' legal theory I mean those approaches that argue in the tradition of Karl Marx's critical theory – i.e., that analyse actually existing societies in terms of the structural principles of capitalist socialisation. 'Materialist' is here of course not meant in the pre-marxian mechanical-physical sense of abstract matter. Rather, it is a social category, the materiality of social practice, which is 'the subject and basis of materialist theory'.[1]

In the 1970s one would probably still have called such a theory 'Marxist'. Today this is no longer so easy. On the one hand, the new social movements have made it clear that while capitalist societies are decisively shaped by commodity production, they cannot be reduced to it. Feminist theory, for one, insisted that the hierarchical two-gender system forms a second structural principle, which cannot be deduced as a 'secondary contradiction' from the 'capital relation'.

It is not only concrete social structural principles that cannot be subsumed under Marx's theory; the same can be said of the various authors who refer to Marx. It is well known that Marx himself did not want to be called a 'Marxist'. 'Materialism' thus comprises a greater range of phenomena and theories – hybrid materialities.

However, 'materialism' is at the same time also an antonym in clear distinction to so-called 'idealism', that is, to approaches which do not relate conditions back to social practice, but which postulate that 'those conditions of people, all their doing and carrying on, are products of their consciousness'. That would lead to the demand to merely interpret the existing differently, 'i.e. to recognise it by means of another interpretation'.[2] As an antonym it therefore is always already inherently marked by the problem of the simple negation, the danger of itself being deeply defined by that which it attempts to set itself apart from. Therefore the materialism of Marx aims for a 'constitution of the world', 'and also a constitution of thought, which altogether resides beyond this dichotomy of materialism and idealism'.[3] This can only happen if 'the reproduction of the human species and the satisfaction of human needs will be finally freed from exchange value, from the theme of profit; humanity would then cease to live under the yoke of matter, the complete fulfilment of materialism will be at the same time also its end'.[4]

My subject is thus a materialist theory of law. My aim here is to recall approaches which are now marginalised in the theory of law, and to critically

1 Schmidt 1971, p. 40.
2 MECW, vol. 5, p. 30.
3 Adorno 1974, p. 277.
4 Ibid.

appraise them. In the 1920s as well as the 1960s and 70s they were a part of legal discourse, even though not as a matter of course. However, with the declining power of the student movement, one of its central theoretical approaches also fell by the wayside. Materialist theory, as a genuinely political approach, is more than others connected to social resistance movements. Academic Marxist theoretical works limited themselves more and more to a 'politics of truth', to chaining themselves to the 'power of truth'.[5]

Here it is no accident that materialist theories of society could surmount the 'crisis of Marxism' (Althusser) and continue the discussions productively until today, even as they are marginalised in the field of the theory of law. On the one hand, because legal studies with their *education into the establishment*[6] are not only not particularly welcoming to theories aiming for a radical change of conditions, but indeed to *theories* as such. On the other hand, however, the true subject of this theory, that is law, was one that, when using a misunderstood notion of materialism, did not require any particular study. As a so-called 'superstructure' phenomenon, it did not have its own legitimacy. When at the height of the interventionist welfare state the state then moved to the centre of materialist approaches, law was in addition subsumed under it.

The term 'materialist theory of law' is however inherently always already a social theory. If Marxian materialism means that legal relations are not to be explained through themselves,[7] then a narrow theory, that is, one only focused on law, is to be avoided. It is therefore a theory of a 'Law of Society',[8] which examines the significance of law for social theory or that of society for a theory of law.[9] In the following I am not concerned with law *as such*, but always only with that of capitalist social formations.

After engaging with the current status of research in legal theory in the form of its big frameworks, systems and discourse theory (Part 1), I will reconstruct a materialist theory. In the words of Jürgen Habermas: 'In the present connection, *reconstruction* signifies taking a theory apart and putting it back together again in a new form in order to attain more fully the goal it has set for itself'.[10]

Therefore I will in a first step (the *reconstruction*) describe exemplary theories and critically examine them for their contribution to an updated theory (part 2). In the next step (the re*construction*) I want to use the various reflec-

---

5 Foucault 2003d, p. 756.
6 Wassermann 1969.
7 MECW, vol. 29, p. 262.
8 Wiethölter 2005, p. 65.
9 Wiethölter 2005, p. 73.
10 Habermas 1979, p. 95.

tions for the construction of elements of an updated materialist theory of law (part 3). Here the thesis of the working method of law as 'subjectivation and cohesion' will be at the centre.

Lastly, a materialist approach can hardly stop at an analysis of conditions. A contemporary theory of law has to be a socially critical legal theory,[11] which lives on the demand 'to organise societies in such a way, that history does not only happen to people, but is made by them'.[12] In the last section of the book (part 4), I will therefore turn to the emancipatory potential of law and raise the question of what it offers 'A', 'B', and 'C' – or what a world of 'A and B and C and A and B and C …' without Company Ltd. X – would have to look like.

11 Fischer-Lescano and Teubner 2006, p. 80.

12 Becker-Schmidt 1990, p. 383.

PART 1

Self-reproduction or Self-organisation?

CHAPTER 1

Introduction to Part 1

Before I start with the reconstruction of a materialist theory of law, I will first outline the discursive terrain it is situated in, that is, the controversies between the big concepts in legal theory. Even though legal theory leads mostly something of a shadowy existence within the busy legal subdisciplines, the number of legal theory concepts has grown enormously over the last decades. Feminist theories of law connect with deconstructivist approaches; the US-American critical legal studies movement has by now become an established part of the canon at American law schools and has differentiated itself even in international law. Post-positivist theories of law clash with radical democratic or economic theories, and linguistic or psychoanalytic approaches make the core insights of other disciplines fruitful for legal studies.

Today, this diversity of analytical perspectives has to be acknowledged.[1] When I limit myself in the following to two major paradigms, this provides by no means a comprehensive representation of the 'current state of research'. Instead of a necessarily cursory comparison of diverse approaches my analysis aims to focus in depth on the premises of those theories, and thus to sound out the two opposite poles of legal theory – and in doing so of the phenomenon of law itself; self-organisation versus reproduction of the system. The controversy between the two approaches turns around the question of whether law brings about the democratic self-organisation of society, or whether it simply cannot do so, because law constitutes an independent system unto itself. Those two poles mark – as per the thesis advanced below – the core issues of controversy in contemporary legal theory. This can be retraced in exemplary fashion through the main legal theory works of Niklas Luhmann or Gunther Teubner and Jürgen Habermas. The two theories are not only positioned antagonistically in relation to each other, they form at the same time in dialogue an 'autocatalytic unity, which challenges itself to further theoretical developments and profiling'.[2]

Materialist legal theory has regularly been accused of reducing law exclusively to an instrument for the preservation of power and has to be able to show its relevance in this field of hegemonic discursive confrontation, which itself alternates between domination and freedom.

1 Buckel, Christensen and Fischer-Lescano (eds) 2006.

2 Demirović 2003, p. 338.

CHAPTER 2

The Self-reproduction of the Legal System: Luhmann/Teubner

As the following intends to present the two paradigmatic perspectives on law, it is inevitable that further developments and branches of the two approaches are left out. However, prior to Luhmann's systematic work on law Gunther Teubner in particular had already made an 'independent contribution on the development of the communicative turn in the sociology of law'.[1] It is therefore no longer possible, when discussing systems theory today, to attribute it solely to Luhmann, even though he provided its foundation. The relevance of Teubner is first and foremost in making it productive for the analysis of the trans-nationalisation of law.[2] This will, however, not be at the centre of this chapter, as first of all basic questions of legal theory are to be clarified. Teubner's approach is distinct from that of Luhmann in that he 'cannot content himself with a "cool" systems-theory analysis that merely notes pressure from social problems and records plausibilities'.[3] Instead, he confronts from the outset the challenge of how a social theory that is so very decentred that it no longer knows a place 'where problems, which are relevant for the reproduction of society as a *whole*, could be perceived and dealt with',[4] can nonetheless allow for democratic reflection. Despite all the coolness of systems theory it is still possible for him to adopt a normative critical position. In the following I will first present Luhmann's contribution, and then sketch the main changes introduced by Teubner in the systems theory of law.

1 Niklas Luhmann: Law as a System

The obvious difference between systems theory and materialist social theory consists in that the latter recognises the distinguishing feature of modern societies in their *capitalist character*, whereas systems theory claims to find it in the

1 Calliess 2006, p. 57.
2 Teubner 1997a, 1997b, 2002, 2004; Fischer–Lescano and Teubner 2004, 2006.
3 Teubner 2006, p. 53.
4 Habermas 1994, p. 343.

dominance of *functional differentiation*.[5] The complexity of modern societies is perceived to overcome stratification as the structuring principle of society and to lead to the differentiation of distinct specialist subsystems, which can reduce complexity on a higher level as needed. The legal system is then conceived of as such a subsystem.

1.1 *Autopoiesis*

Luhmann does not ask what law is, but how the legal *system* can be possible. As an 'autopoietic' system it produces all differentiations and designations itself. For only in this way can it create its unity itself.[6] This means, however, that it is not conceived of as autonomous in the strictest sense – even though Luhmann suggests this.[7] Rather, the legal system is from the outset conceived of as a part of the social system, whose 'problem' it solves. The legal system performs society and builds upon its achievements, for example in communication. Society is then 'a comprehensive system of all communication'.[8] The 'autonomy' of the system is not a strict one. Luhmann does not claim that 'law exists without society, without people, without the special physical and chemical conditions on our planet'.[9] What is meant to be expressed is that the system only establishes relations with this environment because of its own efforts; it is therefore 'operatively closed': the legal system acquires its unity only because it reproduces itself through its own operations.[10] This signifies nothing more than the fact that legal communication must be able to connect to previous legal communication. The difference between system and environment is thus produced through the recursive nature of legal operations, where the autopoietic operation of the system represents a banal exclusion of everything that cannot be connected. 'The central theoretical problem is thus transferred from the question of the reproduction of structures to that of the *capacity to connect*',[11] and the core of the term autopoiesis lies in the self-referentiality of law: that law itself defines what law is.[12]

However, for communications to be able to connect to one another, they have to recognise each other as legal in the first place. For this mainly two achievements are important: firstly, the functional orientation of the system

5 Jessop 1990, p. 331.
6 Luhmann 2004, p. 73.
7 Luhmann 2004, pp. 95–96.
8 Luhmann 2004, p. 89.
9 Luhmann 2004, p. 105.
10 Luhmann 2004, p. 73.
11 Stäheli 2000b: pp. 33, 37.
12 Fischer-Lescano 2005, p. 58.

towards a specific social problem, and secondly its 'binary coding'.[13] Only the legal code (legal/illegal) can explain whether a particular communication is of a legal nature. This can only be determined through observation, and on the level of 'observations of the second order'[14] at that. On the first level, one is dealing with the immediate actors, whereas on the second level the attribution to the legal system takes place. Therefore only code-oriented communication belongs to the legal system, as it alone can claim a recursive connectivity.[15] This means that decisions are institutionalised according to the code legal/illegal and are observed by second-order observations according to this code. Luhmann's understanding of the closed nature of the legal system does not go as far as to claim that it exists completely without any connection to the outside and entirely self-referentially. The system is only closed with regard to its norms, which means that it is for instance not accessible for moral norms. It is, however, cognitively open.[16] This allows for the ability of the legal system to learn, for example, with regard to legal consequences, so that one can effectively speak with Dreier of an 'open closedness'.[17]

However, and this is the premise of Luhmann's systems theory, such an openness is always under the autopoietic condition that the individual case is included in the ongoing and continuing decision-making practice. That means that the legal system can acknowledge external factors, but only as internally produced information.[18] It thus produces the corresponding information in an external-referential position: 'the law presupposes that its environment has already structured and reduced its complexity and simply uses the result without, in turn, engaging in an analysis of how this came about'.[19] At least this is how the legal system normally functions, which is decisive for Luhmann. He thus sets himself apart from Carl Schmitt's theorem of exception, as does Franz Neumann (we will discuss this later on). In the state of exception the legal system is considered to be in a 'state of corruption',[20] system-inherent inclusion no longer takes place, but merely random acts, dicta of the political system, so that it ultimately only adheres to dummies of legality. The code is preceded by a distinction, an examination of whether law is to be applied. This 'allows for its

13 Luhmann 2004, p. 93.
14 Luhmann 2004, p. 94.
15 Luhmann 2004, pp. 98–99.
16 Luhmann 2004, p. 108.
17 Dreier 2002, p. 308.
18 Luhmann 2004, p. 112.
19 Luhmann 2004, p. 116.
20 Luhmann 2004, p. 109.

opportunistic adaptation to powerful elites'.[21] This state of exception prevails at times of momentous historical changes and threats as well as in regions 'where the principle of the differentiation of a legal system did not succeed either partially or fully';[22] in other words, at the capitalist periphery.[23]

The 'hardness' of autopoietic systems theory to insist that the 'autonomy remains intact',[24] grows ultimately from the notion that every social system implements social change in its own proper form. Thus the brusque wording – '[A]ppropriately, no social movement and no media campaign can change the law'[25] – quickly appears in a more harmless light, when one adds that changes can simply only take place in the forms of the legal system itself, where it does, for instance, take changes in public opinion into account. Thus Luhmann can eventually conclude that autopoiesis does not block changing views in society, but it merely incorporates a filter 'that allows it to perceive a change of public opinion as a reason to learn – that is cognitively – and not as a direct imposition of new norms'.[26]

1.2 *The Validity of Law as Its Actual Execution*

The system's unity through its changing operations is guaranteed through the symbol of the validity of law. It makes the connection of operations possible, despite constant irritation through the environment, and thus a statement about whether a communication is part of the legal system and therefore counts as legal. In this way the operations refer to their relationship with the system and relate to the context of other legal operations.[27] Validity causes connection, invalidity does not. The fundamental difference with other legal theories consists in the fact that the validity of law is not defined externally, but considered as produced within the system itself.[28] The traditional explanation for the validity of law through reference to a higher (fundamental) norm is rejected as nothing other than a way to stop further reflection, for this reasoning becomes enmeshed in contradictions as soon as one then asks for the source of this norm itself. Luhmann thus radicalises *Hans Kelsen*, who already argued the highest norm purely logically. The only test of validity which Luhmann allows is

21 Ibid.
22 Luhmann 2004, p. 111.
23 See on the legal theory of the periphery in systems theory in particular Neves 2001.
24 Luhmann 2004, p. 116.
25 Luhmann 2004, p. 119.
26 Luhmann 2004, p. 120.
27 Luhmann 2004, p. 126.
28 Fischer-Lescano 2005, p. 56.

the continuous connection of operations; the successful autopoiesis of the system,[29] that is, simply its factual functioning.[30] Legal theorists can be more or less productive in their search for *the* reason for the validity of law, but they cannot provide offers that are convincing across society: 'Only natural law theorists believe in nature as the reason for validity, only discourse theorists in ideal discourses, only Kelsenians in the hypothesis of the basic norm, only Hartians in the *ultimate rule of recognition* [English in original], in *rational choice* only do-gooders'.[31]

Validity, just like money, is in reality only a symbol without intrinsic value, which symbolises the acceptance of the communication, that is the autopoiesis of legal communications.[32] Luhmann pursues a strategy of abstraction, as he proclaims explicitly in multiple passages.[33] An analysis as to *why* a connection is successful and operations can recognise each other as valid is not provided. The theory moves onto a higher level and observes from this vantage point, from 'above', only that *something* is working: 'Whether a norm is a legal one or not can only be ascertained through observation of the recursive network that produces legal norms …'.[34] The 'source of law' is thus nothing but a figure of reasoning within the legal system itself, a way of dressing up a communicative act with a legal meaning in the environment of law. Ultimately the metaphor of the source of law could therefore break up the circular structure of law no more than the attempt to search for the unity of law in hierarchies and in the highest 'values'.[35]

1.3 *Paradox and De-paradoxification*

Accordingly, the legal system is seen to function 'as a closed universe which refers to itself'.[36] One can call this observation Luhmann's central message. In different ways he always comes back to this starting point and tries to explain and secure it with various arguments. However, his real 'point of departure for

29 Luhmann 2004, p. 131.
30 Bolsinger 2001, p. 9.
31 Fischer-Lescano 2005, p. 60.
32 Luhmann 2004, p. 122. In Ernesto Laclau's language of discourse theory one could also say that validity is the empty signifier: one which can temporarily fix the ensemble of discursive moments by producing an outside of the legal system, and thus provisionally expressing the identity of the discourse (Stäheli 2001, p. 201).
33 Luhmann 2004, p. 143.
34 Luhmann 2004, p. 152.
35 Fischer-Lescano 2005, p. 56.
36 Luhmann 2004, p. 290.

the construction of the juridical universe'[37] is only revealed when he turns to the position of the courts. For, like every sub-system, the legal system is also ultimately based upon a so-called 'paradox', which is the 'holy shrine of the system ... [A] deity in many forms'.[38] The code of the legal system is the distinction between legal and illegal, which follows a certain programming, laws, directives and so forth. However, in the final analysis, this distinction is far from unambiguous, if not arbitrary, for the world does not provide any guarantee for logical order and the consistency of deductions.[39] In modern, complex society with its 'acceleration of structural changes',[40] an awareness of complexity emerges, which recognises that the problems cannot be worked through theoretically, but that one has to rely on shortcuts instead. Against one's better knowledge one has to act as though there were something one can rely on, because the pressure to act makes it necessary to cut short the search for knowledge.

For the legal system this means that both the *creation of law* and the *decision-making situation* become paradoxical; systems use guiding differentiations, which they themselves produce, but cannot question without betraying their own identity. It is therefore not possible to question in legal communication whether the difference between legality and illegality itself exists legally or illegally. Moreover, decisions must be made, although they cannot be unequivocal – laws are formulated abstractly and leave gaps as well as undefined legal terms up to general clauses. Nonetheless the courts have to decide *as though* an unequivocal solution existed. They have to do this, and this is at the heart of the autopoiesis of the legal system, because they operate under the interdiction of a denial of justice. 'Contracts need not be concluded and statutes need not be passed ... but courts have to decide every case submitted to them'.[41] In the 'hard cases',[42] in which the legal norms do not lead to an unequivocal decision, courts therefore have to create law and postulate. The institution of legal force then exonerates the decision, contestable as it may be, from any protracted uncertainty.[43] This fact, which can also explain phenomena such as the disintegration of dogmatic guiding principles, formulas for consideration, or the fuzziness in the distinction between legislative processes and jurisprudence, is the reason that the paradox that no *unequivocal* decisions exist, can be 'managed'.

37 Luhmann 2004, p. 289.
38 Luhmann 2004, p. 292.
39 Luhmann 2004, p. 286.
40 Luhmann 2004, p. 291.
41 Luhmann 2004, p. 294.
42 'Hard cases' given in English in the original.
43 Luhmann 2004, p. 288.

Thus, 'even under extreme social tensions "purely legal reasoning" [can] be practiced'.[44] Even the recourse to the presumed 'legal source' only serves as a way to stop reflection here; of hiding the paradox.

The 'castles of global law' are thus 'built on shifting sands'.[45] The fundamental paradox cannot be brought into focus in the everyday operations of law, 'because such work on the foundations would paralyse the operations of law and topple the castles. Instead the operations of law serve to obscure the unstable ground …',[46] a technique which is carried out through legal dogma and theory by acting as though there were a final, legitimate ground for each particular decision.

1.4 *The Function of Law*

After working through the premise of the system, Luhmann goes on to ask which 'problem' of the social system the legal system 'solves'.[47] The differentiation of the functional systems takes place through a reference problem of society, for which they claim exclusive and universal responsibility, and which is constituted through this differentiation. Here functional systems are not derived as structural requirements to secure the continuation of society, that is, in a functionalist manner. Rather, they are considered to have prevailed in an 'evolutionary' manner in communication and can empirically be described in this way.[48]

Luhmann's thesis with regards to *the legal system* is that its function is not social, but temporal; when communication cannot be sufficient unto itself, but, in a temporal extension of its sense, orients itself in relation to expectations, when expectations are communicated, they depend on defining themselves in time, because they have to connect themselves recursively.[49] In order for operations that communicate expectations not to come to a halt, but to connect with one another, 'time binding' is necessary.[50] The relation to the future requires therefore 'a structure of symbolically generalised expectations',[51] that is a system of norms, a legal order. This order stabilises communication so that one can anticipate 'at least on the level of expectations, a still unknown, genuinely

44 Luhmann 2004, pp. 289–90.
45 Fischer-Lescano 2005, p. 21.
46 Ibid.
47 Luhmann 2004, p. 142.
48 Bommes, pp. 73–4.
49 Luhmann 2004, pp. 142–3.
50 Luhmann 2004, p. 144.
51 Luhmann 2004, p. 146.

uncertain future'.[52] Thus law makes it possible to know with which expectations one can find social support: 'One can live in a more complex society, in which personal or interaction mechanisms to secure trust no longer suffice'.[53]

Norms thus stabilise behavioural expectations counterfactually. It does not matter whether the motive for following norms is the threat of sanctions, nor, above all, whether the behaviour *really* follows the norms. Hence all theories which reduce law to a control medium, are hopelessly outdated. 'Norms do not promise conduct that conforms to norms, but they protect all those who are expecting such conduct'.[54] Furthermore, its function is not the regulation of conflicts – this would rather be a social function as it has too many functional equivalents. What is *specific* about law lies in its normative aspect and not in the area of factual activities.

By discounting the social function of law, Luhmann primarily opposes the competing paradigm of Habermas, for whom law has to bear the 'burden of social integration'. In doing so Luhmann does not, however, question the social relevance of law, but only the notion that law can integrate society. The case is rather that temporal connections have social *consequences*. The arbitrary limitation of norms for action achieved through standardisation is 'atoned for' by establishing 'illegality'. Freedom of action is limited in advance on the level of expectations, and those who might wish to contravene this, are in advance expected to learn and adapt. It is, for instance, expected that murderers and thieves adapt, although it is not their own life or property that is at stake. Those are the social costs of wanting to be certain about the future, considering its inherent uncertainty.[55]

Since laws only ensure expectations on a normative level, the problem arises that the norms also have to be valid when they are not realised accordingly. Luhmann again resolves this by evoking the self-referentiality of the system. That 'one' must expect normatively is itself normatively expected in the legal system; this constitutes the reflexivity of law.[56] Therefore institutionally a subsystem emerges within the legal system as a condition for continuously observing the observation of a reliably predictable codification: the organised decision-making system, that is courts, parliaments, etc.[57] The courts form its centre because of their obligation to make decisions while all other legal com-

52 Luhmann 2004, p. 147.
53 Luhmann 2004, p. 148.
54 Luhmann 2004, p. 150.
55 Luhmann 2004, p. 146.
56 Luhmann 2004, p. 157.
57 Luhmann 2004, p. 158.

munications belong to the system's periphery. In the periphery, which is conceived of as 'a zone of contact with the other functioning systems of society', irritations through other forms of functional logic arise.[58]

Since behaviour control and conflict regulation cannot be considered to determine function, Luhmann now ultimately assigns them to the term 'performances' of the system.[59] Thus, after developing through strict derivation the particularity of law, those moments that are not compatible with it, but whose connection with law one cannot deny, are regrouped in the category of 'performance': control and conflict resolution.[60]

2 Gunther Teubner: The Hypercycle of Law

2.1 *Progressive Autonomy*

Already for Luhmann himself 'autopoiesis' was not the same as 'autarchy' in the sense of complete independence from the environment. However, while Luhmann's rigorous wording at least allows for a particular interpretation, Teubner finds clear words to spare himself the polemics of 'the materialist or the bourgeois point of view':[61]

> To allay all suspicion of autarchy, I should like to make it clear that self-production does not imply that all causes are located within the system; neither does it imply that the more important of these ... or even most causes have their origins within the system. Despite what has been said to the contrary, a self-producing legal system is strongly influenced by social, economic, and political factors. Indeed, it is assumed that this will necessarily be the case. What is different, however, is the way in which the environment influences self-producing law.[62]

Furthermore Teubner conceives of the concept of legal autonomy with more preconditions than Luhmann.[63] His goal is an understanding of autonomy and autopoiesis that is differentiated by degrees, whereas Luhmann explicitly rejects this as operative closedness signifies autonomy, and a relational

58 Luhmann 2004, pp. 292–3.
59 Luhmann 2004, p. 167.
60 Luhmann 2004, p. 171.
61 Teubner 1993, p. 34.
62 Teubner 1993, p. 21.
63 See also Calliess 2006, p. 61, note 26.

autonomy cannot exist. While Luhmann himself had worked with this concept before the autopoietic turn, he subsequently emphatically rejected it.[64] By now it was nothing more than the expression of disappointed 'radical Marxist approaches'; '[w]e prefer a concept of autonomy which is backed up by the concept of autopoiesis, that is one which spells out that autonomy is either given or not and which does not allow for any grey areas'.[65]

Teubner on the other hand wants to carefully distinguish between different dimensions of self-reference.[66] Accordingly he distinguishes seven moments of self-reference: (1) the *self-observation* of a system, which he refers to as (2) *self-description* when it is relatively permanent and is used to create order (legal doctrine);[67] then (3) *self-organisation*, which only exists once the system has 'secondary rules' (H.L.A. Hart), that is rules for procedures and for identifying legality; (4) *self-regulation* as a dynamic variant of self-organisation, when the system can be changed according to its own criteria, because it disposes of norms and procedures for changing the law. When self-regulation and self-description are combined in such a way that a context for arguments about the system's own identity emerges, this is the for Teubner particularly important (5) *self-reflexive* form, for example of legal theory.[68] One can speak of (6) *self-production* when a system creates its component parts itself as emerging units, where the internal labour consists in '*extracting and constituting, as it were, new elements from the flow of events, which it then uses by linking them up selectively*'.[69] Self-production is thus not a creatio ex nihilo, but the extraction of units from the 'material substructure', which it uses to construct the system. (7) *Autopoiesis*, finally, demands even more, namely for all system components (elements, structures, processes, boundaries, identity and unity of the system) to be self-produced *and* additionally that this self-producing cycle is capable of maintaining itself. That means that it is interlinked with a second cycle, which serves to make the cyclical production possible by guaranteeing the conditions of its production. Teubner calls this reproduction cycle a 'hypercycle'.[70]

Against this background Luhmann's concept is simpler: when the legal system can reproduce itself though the operations of the system, its unity is preserved. Either this succeeds – or not; autopoiesis is present – or not. Teubner on

64 Luhmann 2004, p. 96, note 47.
65 Luhmann 2004, p. 97.
66 Teubner 1993, p. 16.
67 Teubner 1993, p. 19.
68 Teubner 1993, p. 20.
69 Teubner 1993, p. 21 (emphasis S.B.).
70 Teubner 1993, p. 23.

the other hand insists on a gradual process, which he understands as a cumulative increase in circular relationships.[71] At first legal communications begin to differentiate through the distinction legal/illegal. They then inevitably come across themselves at some point, and are forced to make themselves the subject of legal categories. Law therefore depends on describing its system components with its own categories. It itself determines which preconditions have to be met in order to speak about a legally relevant event. Its self-reproduction is possible from the moment the self-referentially organised system-components are connected with each other in such a way that norms and legal actions mutually produce each other, and that processes and doctrine relate those relations in turn. 'It is only when the components of the cyclically organised system interact in this way that the legal hypercycle becomes possible'.[72] In this way Teubner arrives at three phases in the developing autonomy of the legal system:

> In the initial phase of 'socially diffuse law', the elements, structures, processes, and boundaries of legal discourse are identical to those of general social communication – or, at least, are heteronomously determined by social communication. Law enters the 'partially autonomous' phase when the legal discourse begins to define its own components and use them operatively. Law only becomes 'autopoietic' when the components of the legal system are linked together in a hypercycle.[73]

According to this model, autopoiesis only emerges when the self-descriptions of law develop and practice a doctrine of the sources of law. This doctrine refers the creation of norms to processes of *law-internal* law-making, that is, in modern positivist law 'legal norms can be produced only by way of precisely defined legal acts, be they statutes, decrees, or intra-organizational acts'.[74] Thus circular relations develop: the law only becomes valid through the action of the judge, who in turn has to argue its validity through the law. Teubner thus describes in much greater detail *how* legal communications can connect to legal communications.[75] Luhmann does not concur with this interpretation and claims the

71 Teubner 1993, p. 31.
72 Teubner 1993, p. 33.
73 Teubner 1993, pp. 36–7.
74 Teubner 1993, p. 41.
75 For a variation of this argument in relation to the trans-nationalisation of law, see Teubner 1997, p. 3ff. It is precisely national law which is commonly denied its legal character, as it is centrally based on the monopoly of force, while Teubner develops criteria which instead refer back to the hyper-cyclical ability to self-reproduce.

explanation of the evolution of the legal system for himself,[76] even though he admits that '[T]he arguments ... have also been influenced by' Teubner's critique.[77]

2.2 *The Paradox as 'Dialectic without Synthesis'*

Management of the paradox can be considered the gateway for critical interventions – including for Teubner's theory. Law is based upon fundamental paradoxes. Again and again the hydra of law produces new undecidabilities. In contrast to the often vague discourse about *uncertainty*,[78] systems theory can demonstrate the depth of the problem more clearly. It is able to show that undecidability is not only the result of a coincidentally insufficient formalisation, but that it stems from a fundamental paradox,[79] a real contradiction of the social systems – as Teubner formulates following (and at the same time distancing himself from) Marx. The paradox is not a simple error in the intellectual reconstruction of those systems.

Teubner accordingly holds the view that precisely those circular relationships have to be investigated, which is why he conducts studies addressing the question of *how* the praxis of law deals with them, *how* it is able to transform complete uncertainty into relative certainty and stability.[80] It is not the undeniable critical-destructive potential that drives his epistemic interest in paradoxes; the real fascination lies in the 'productive possibilities of working with them'. For systems theory the paradoxes engendered by self-referentiality constitute not the final punchline, but the starting point. Contrary to the Hegelian thinking in contradictions, the paradox is a 'dialectic without synthesis', an experimental, incremental, wandering creation of orders, indeed the 'worlds of meaning are continually afflicted by their deconstruction', which bring the social relations into a dance – and at the same time it is a 'context of illusion'. De-paradoxification does not promise a solution to the crisis 'but at most its temporary postponement, concealment, invisibilization, suppression, repression. It is only a matter of time before crisis breaks out again'.[81]

76 Luhmann 2004, p. 102, note 58.

77 Luhmann 2004, p. viii, note 3.

78 Thus the central theme of critical legal studies; see for instance Hutchinson and Monahan 1984; Joerges and Trubek 1989; Mangabeira Unger 1986; Frankenberg 2006, pp. 110 ff.

79 Teubner 1993a, p. 6.

80 Teubner 1993a, pp. 10–11.

81 Teubner 2006b, pp. 53 ff.

2.3 *Regulated Self-regulation*

Teubner's decisive 'correction' of the systems theory of law consists, however, in the attempt to conceptualise the systems – contrary to Luhmann – in such a way that they preserve an openness for theoretical reflections on democracy.

Because behaviour control and conflict resolution are from the perspective of systems theory at most performances for which social equivalents exist in other systems, controlling interventions are questionable for Luhmann. If one wants to explain the specificity of law, they cannot be used without expanding the concept of function to such an extent that it becomes imprecise. Therefore Luhmann is profoundly sceptical of any attempt 'to salvage the assumption that there is a social steering through law no matter how limited it is (instead of the self-steering only of the legal system)'.[82] In this way he differs, amongst others, also from Teubner's concept of *reflexive law*.[83] Teubner does not want to resign himself to a mere self-referentiality of systems and is looking for ways out of the dilemma of systemic anarchy. For him reflexive law has a normative and analytical dual character, for reflection in law means 'both empirical analysis and normative evaluation'.[84]

Teubner attempts to implant a normative concept within systems theory which is purely descriptive. This seems justifiable, because within the legal system both dogmatic and legal-theoretical self-reflection are crucial for its reproduction. In doing so he has a decentralised model of reflection in mind, which does not lose the perspective on the 'environment', but transfers it into the subsystems. He thus adopts Luhmann's position in so far as he admits that there can be no control centre. Instead Teubner relies on the one hand on the potential for reflection within the system, and on the other hand on the connection of systems. The versions of this concept vary over the course of his work, but the principle remains. In 1982 he explains in his conception of *reflexive law* that it has to develop norms for procedures which can serve other social systems as premises for democratic self-organisation and self-regulation. It shall not determine the functions of other social systems in an authoritative manner, but 'foster mechanisms that systematically *further the development of reflexion structures within other social subsystems*'.[85]

Teubner goes on to look for those principles which can make a coupling of systems possible. This is at the crux of his foundational work of legal theory, published in 1989. Here he critiques Luhmann's version, writing that the lat-

---

82 Luhmann 2004, p. 165.
83 Ibid., note 43.
84 Teubner 1993a, p. 69.
85 Teubner 1983, p. 275 (emphasis in original).

ter is blind to connections across multiple systems. In consequence systems are isolated, and it is no longer possible to conceive of the over-determination of an event.[86] Teubner counters this with the concept of '*interference*', which emphasises superpositions and overlaps. The legal system is thus genuinely connected with its social environments. Interferences form a bridge that couples the systems through one and the same communicative event, because they use the same 'raw material', that is sense, and they all use, be it in one specialised form or another, communications. Each specialised communication in any social subsystem is always *at the same time* a communication within overall society, so that the subsystems draw elements from the societal communication flow for their specialist communications: 'If this is the case, then it follows that subsystemic and societal elements coincide in a single act of communication. In this way law and society are still linked together'.[87] Interfering systems do not offer each other unorganised complexity, but pre-ordered complexity.[88] Law can therefore regulate society in a limited way by regulating itself,[89] because it becomes reflexive in such a way that it adapts its norms and procedures to the social situation and designs ordering procedures for the protagonists.[90] Direct interventions are actually not possible; rather what we find is indirect control through self-control.[91]

In Teubner's most recent analyses, which are concerned with the transnationalisation of law, the problem of systemic autonomisation multiplies because of the 'fragmentation of global society'. For now one is no longer only confronted with systems, but also with sectorial regulating regimes of laws.[92] The overlapping of two different principles, the territorial segmented and the thematic-functional differentiation, leads to regimes which do not follow an unambiguous logic. Through historical coincidences the functional systems trigger conflicts, scandals and irritations in the legal system, which are answered with the emergence of a non-bilateral regime of rights that crystallises at the point of conflict.

Despite the advanced fragmentation, Teubner, together with Fischer-Lescano, looks for mechanisms of connection between regimes. A starting point can be found in the development of independent secondary standardisations,

86 Fischer-Lescano and Christensen 2012, p. 107.
87 Teubner 1993a, p. 88.
88 Teubner 1993a, p. 89.
89 Teubner 1993a, p. 65.
90 Teubner 1993a, pp. 94 ff.
91 Teubner 1993a, p. 66.
92 Teubner 1997, p. 3; 2000; Buckel 2003, pp. 52 ff.

that is procedural norms about the formation of laws, legal knowledge and legal sanctioning. In this way a mechanism develops which connects reflexive processes of law with reflexive processes of other social spheres, 'auto-constitutional regimes'.[93] Those 'inter-systemic linking institutions' connect occasionally. It is, however, not enough to register and accept factual developments, '[T]hat would ultimately mean to accept the shortcomings of existing networks in regard to theories of democracy'.[94] If one does not want to contribute to the 'justification of a questionable project', this description has to be completed with a normative concept of networks. For this, the approach of self-regulation is again used: social rationality, now on a global level, can *only* be located in the regimes themselves, which have to reflect on other interests and the common good.

3 Critique

Luhmann's systems theory is still heavily criticised by proponents of critical theory. Thus Jürgen Habermas attacked Luhmann's systems theory as 'the height of technocratic consciousness', 'which today allows us to define practical questions from the outset as technical and to thereby remove them from public and open discussion'.[95] Alex Demirović similarly considers Luhmann a systems thinker, only concerned with the preservation of the system and its order.[96] His theory represents a great challenge for the enlightenment tradition and for the social critique that follows it, 'because he dismisses as obsolete exactly this limited humanist model of emancipation and the critique it implies, even critique and emancipation as such'.[97]

It must, however, be recognised that the systems theory of law does not only represent a provocation with regards to critical, but also to traditional theories of law. Like Habermas, Luhmann is also influenced by the linguistic turn;[98] this is not least visible in the turn from structures to processes, and from recognition to construction, as well as finally in the way paradoxes are dealt with. Furthermore, one can note that also within the paradigm of systems theory, advanced and apologetic approaches and moments compete with one

93 Fischer-Lescano and Teubner 2006b, pp. 53ff.
94 Fischer-Lescano and Teubner 2006b, p. 62.
95 Habermas 1971, p. 145.
96 Demirović 2001b, p. 16.
97 Demirović 2001b, p. 18.
98 'Linguistic turn' in English in the original.

another. In particular Teubner's variations can be considered 'critical systems theory', as will be shown in the confrontation with the subject in Section 3.2.

My thesis is that the systems theory approach describes the way social relations become independent as 'systems' – or expressed in terms of value theory: as social forms – rather accurately. The fascination of the theory consists precisely in that it distances itself from common sense (the 'observation of the first order') and names the reification of social relations. Systems theory 'speaks', one could say pointedly, from inside the legal form, by theoretically reformulating the reified procedures. In doing so, however, several difficulties emerge.

3.1 *The New Europe or Switching the Mode of Description*

(Legal-)systems theory and its description of modern society follows the sociological tradition of Karl Marx, Max Weber, Emile Durkheim and Georg Simmel,[99] and develops somewhat self-evidently from it. However, its way of doing 'truth politics' begins with the suggestion that it overturns all conventions that were previously considered certain. Luhmann primarily manages to create this impression by starting his theory at a high level of abstraction. He exponentially increases the problematic characteristics of general concepts, which subsume many different elements and thus unify them according to a logic of identity. By doing so he is able to illuminate fundamental structural principles from the particular perspective of autonomy. At this level of abstraction, he can 'switch' the mode of description in such a way that other concepts in legal theory appear comparatively 'lacking in complexity'. A risk of this strategy is however that the non-identical, the particular, is 'invisibilised' to such a degree that it becomes buried under the rocks of identity.

A closer inspection, however, shows that Luhmann argues in a manner that is far less 'New European' than his 'air of a superior analytical perspective'[100] would appear to suggest.

It would therefore require too much effort to attempt to 'expose' Luhmann's conception of the autonomy of law as illusory,[101] because in principle Luhmann 'confesses' to everything in his texts. An example is the determination of the function's content: the counter-factual securing of expectations, which can make the connection of operations in a genuinely insecure future possible. What is Luhmann's theory doing here, other than representing the theory of 'legal certainty' in new terms? By seemingly creating a counter-position to the

---

99 Bommes 1999, pp. 66ff.

100 Bieling 2001, p. 149.

101 Thus, however, Bolsinger 2001, p. 10.

'social function' of the law, he ultimately nonetheless falls back on a familiar notion, namely – in the words of Franz Neumann – the insight that formal law is 'necessary as a pre-condition of capitalist competition ... for calculability and dependability in the legal system'.[102]

Besides, if the law is highly indeterminate until it is applied (*the* paradox), what then can the normatively expecting person really be so certain about?

Similar considerations apply to the thesis of the legal system's operative closedness, which is Luhmann's core premise. While Teubner shows from the outset that for him this is a matter of the legal system's own dynamism, Luhmann's descriptive mode appears to sketch an autistic planet. Upon closer inspection, however, this planet is reduced to a communication system which only reproduces law through its own language, so that all moments extrinsic to law have to be translated. It really is, similar to materialist approaches, a reflexive process, wherein the practised relations are developed into the legal norms of a legal order.[103] Thus, for example, the practice of exchange is translated into a contractual relationship, the attribution and visibilisation of land ownership as a mortgage, etc.

Moreover, Luhmann concedes, apparently quite incidentally, a kind of 'relative autonomy', when he explains that law needs to have sufficient prospects of being enforced as otherwise one would after all bow to the facts and not the norms. Here the enforcement depends not least on 'the use of physical force' of the 'political system'.[104] What is the central theoretical difference to the 'Old European' Max Weber and his postulate of the state's monopoly of the legitimate use of physical force?

3.2 *Dualism of Subject and Society*

'The objection that systems theory marginalises the human individual in relation to society ...'[105] – this is how Teubner describes the critics' persistent misunderstanding: the 'successful narrative of the "lack of reference to actors" in systems theory'.[106]

Firstly, one has to note that the existence of individuals is actually not denied in systems theory; human subjects *are* 'a necessary environmental precondition for social events',[107] they are as such no less important for the system than

102 Neumann 1957, p. 40.
103 Maihofer 1992, p. 80.
104 Luhmann 2004, p. 140.
105 Teubner 2003, p. 45.
106 Nassehi 2003, p. 84.
107 Kneer and Nassehi 2000, p. 69.

the system itself.[108] What is important, however, is *how* 'human subjects' appear in systems theory, and it is precisely at this juncture that reflections in systems theory take an unusual path with regards to the strategies of the theory, for they dissect the unified subjects into three moments: a 'body-soul unit', as well as into 'organic life and psychic experience',[109] that is to say, into a structurally coupled whole consisting of biological and psychic systems. This whole is only constructed internally during social communication as an individual. Consciousnesses and bodies are therefore 'living, pulsing units in the communication environment'. Something 'extra-communicative' is modelled within law. Communication artefacts are then attributed to actions.[110] Thus, and this is important to Teubner precisely for 'humanist' reasons, there exists a *dualism* of human thought, on the one hand, and social communication, on the other.[111] For a naive equivalence of semantic artefacts and concrete human subjects would be fatal, precisely because it wrongs the latter. Communication is always a social alienation and attribution.

This leads to a further reflection, namely to one on the relationship of communication and consciousnesses or psychic systems. The communication theorem itself is based upon the premise of the radical individuality of psychic systems.[112] Because consciousnesses are opaque for one another, the functional necessity for the emergence of communication arises.[113] Communication is thus the basic articulating unit of a double contingency.[114] But this communication takes on a life of its own with regards to the individual consciousnesses – that is also the reason why 'concrete human subjects' and communicatively constructed persons must not be equated. 'Psychic systems' only participate in communication without creating it, precisely because communication has become self-referentially independent with regards to those individuals; in its 'emerging order' the psychic merely enters:[115]

> That human subjects are not part of society, but face it in insurmountable separation, has an inexorable consequence. Society and consciousness/body are for each other communicatively unreachable. The latter are respectively independent, self-sustaining (psychic or organic) processes.

108 Kneer and Nassehi 2000, p. 70.
109 Teubner 2006b, pp. 171ff.
110 Ibid.
111 Teubner 2003, p. 45.
112 Nassehi 2003b, p. 25.
113 Ibid.
114 Schneider 2003, p. 44.
115 Kneer and Nassehi 2000, p. 69.

> Although both have created communication, they cannot master it. Communication becomes independent of the human subject and creates with regards to individual consciousness its own world of meaning.[116]

Although Teubner assumes, with Luhmann, that functional differentiation represents social progress, he nonetheless considers as one of the main dangers of modern societies those independent communication processes which he calls, in order to underline the issue, the 'anonymous matrix'. The matrix of the economic system, for example, could attack and even destroy human existence. Thus 'sweatshops' are a consequence of 'anonymous market forces'. Against this, resistance – which has to be adequately understood by an updated understanding of human rights – is directed:

> This is the space where bodies and consciousnesses of the individuals ... insist on their 'pre-legal', 'pre-political', and even 'pre-social' (extra-social) 'latent right of their own'. Bodily pain and psychic suffering have to emerge from their speechlessness by introducing the resistance of suffering bodies and souls, for instance in physical violence, as representations into communication.[117]

The representation of this most advanced position of system-theoretical legal theory shows that it absolutely does recognise actors, similarly to post-structuralism with its intention of decentering the autonomous subject.[118] In contrast to post-structuralist approaches, however, splitting the subject into three parts insists on something external to communication, on a separation of communication and 'human subject'. Teubner does not defend a realist position, and for this reason bodies are, for example, not the 'actual reality' in his approach. However, he delineates a strict border between society on the one hand and 'human subjects' on the other. Different contexts are produced within their own respective borders. Although this dualism follows the intention to do justice to each respective logic, it leads to two theoretical problems, which ultimately explain the narration of blocking out subjects.

On the one hand this approach remains despite its postmodern decentring within a traditional subject-paradigm. Foucault had rightly asserted against this idea that the human body was only constructed as a biological entity with the emergence of the modern natural sciences. In order to question the social

116 Teubner 2006b, p. 170.
117 Teubner 2006b, p. 171.
118 See for example Stäheli 2000a.

construct of two sexes, feminist theorists have subsequently demonstrated that a dualism of biological gendered bodies and social gender identity amounts ultimately to a naturalisation of social conditions. The bodily gender must not be understood as 'fundamental core or inert matter' which is confronted with power (or here with communication), but as one of the first consequences of the gender *dispositif*.[119]

> And what is 'sex' anyway? Is it natural, anatomical, chromosomal, or hormonal ... Are the ostensibly natural facts of sex discursively produced by various scientific discourses in the service of other political and social interests?[120]

The body is accordingly no passive medium for which cultural meanings remain external, but itself a culturally generated product.[121] In this respect there is neither a pre-social body nor a pre-social psyche, rephrased in terms of systems theory, there are only 'subjects'. The systemic communications themselves produce that which to begin with they only claim to communicate.

Legal subjectivation (as I will show later on following Foucault) coproduces the modern subject as real lived practice. Isolated consciousnesses, whose isolation precisely creates the necessity of communication, reveal themselves here as historically specific forms of human subjects and lose their character of anthropological foundation.

On the other hand, the dualism of communication and consciousness inflates the independence of systems/matrix. It is a fitting observation that capitalist societies are marked by how 'communication contexts become distant from their organic and psychic infrastructures, from human life and consciousness'.[122] But to deduce from this that human subjects are no longer part of society overextends the argument. It is their social (communicative) practices which first bring this society (communication) about. It is they – as Marx has shown – which become independent with regards to them. Thus, even their independent existences have to be reproduced every day in ordinary activities, they do not detach from them. It is not anonymous market forces that create the inhuman reality of 'sweatshops', but those who act strategically and assume the capitalist commodity form for themselves. While they have to take on their 'laws', they reproduce them in their actions by claiming them for their interests,

119 Bührmann 2004, p. 24.
120 Butler 2002, p. 10.
121 Butler 2002, pp. 11ff.
122 Neves 2000, p. 15.

or to the contrary, by massively questioning them. Thus, the systemic independences have to *pass through practice*, and can be questioned and shifted/moved by it. It is therefore – as I will argue later on – not a question of dualism, but rather a duality[123] of practice and its effects.

The demarcation, the dualism, creates in sum antinomies on both sides, which then have to be broken up with enormous effort. Because society is ejected from the individual and the individuals from society, the theory does not focus on the strategic practice of social subjects. Legal systems theory no longer analyses it on this level.[124] This creates the impression that systems theory is subjectless. From this perspective a class-based analysis, for instance, has to be considered as a false personification of systemic differentiations and rejected, in favour of demonstrating how strategies of classes or other social actors are mediated in systemic processes, have to base themselves upon them and at the same time create or shift them. Precisely this participation is always already assumed on the system level. How hegemonic communication projects actually assert themselves, and in which discursive conflicts, is blocked out: 'Inasmuch as systems theory does not form any hypothesis here, it bases itself consistently on social facts, leaves the idle question of intentions open and focuses instead on communicative events'.[125]

The demarcation produces a similar problem to that in Althusser's structuralism, of 'abstracting the agents, as if there were ... just "place"-holding phantoms'.[126] Elaborate studies of specific conflicts and the differentiation according to forces, factions and alliances become obsolete.

Ultimately, however, the abstraction cannot be consistently sustained. For who programmes the code? Who advances differentiation globally? How are contingency and change ('evolution') to be explained? Therefore the justification for the 'function' of the legal system also remains contradictory; thus Luhmann certainly notes initially that he does not mean by 'expectations' that are to be stabilised the actual state of consciousness of a given individual, but only the temporal aspect of the meaning of communications.[127] But his further explanations are orientated towards concrete subjects. 'One' could thus live better, 'one' would have to adapt, 'one' tries to prepare oneself for the future,

---

123 A duality, however, not an 'action theory complement', which would effectively constitute a categorisation of sociology into micro- and macro-theoretical fields suitable for text books (Nassehi 2003a, p. 84).

124 Similarly Weber 2005, p. 32.

125 Fischer-Lescano 2005, p. 69, note 149.

126 Lipietz 1997, p. 264.

127 Luhmann 2004, p. 143.

etc. At least to establish plausibility he has to briefly set aside the strict separation of society and 'human subjects' at this point. Here evidently the thing itself asserts itself – against the author's intention, similarly to Kant's attempt to explain, unempirically, the transcendental subject that is relieved of all empiricism.[128]

3.3 *The Grand Narrative 'System'*

The unresolved problem of the actors surreptitiously sneaks back into the theory. Thus, there is notably at least *one* basic postulate of systems theory: 'There are systems'. The discourse on the system itself is precisely not re-introduced in comparison to other, non-systemic subjects, but singularly occupies the summit of the pyramid of concepts.[129] The following constructivist deduction only aims to demonstrate *theoretical requirements* to be able to speak of such a system, in this way: *when* operative closedness – *then* the system has to provide its own reproduction – then the legal operations have to connect with each other. What is demonstrated is ultimately a necessity of thinking. That is, the 'grand narrative' of systems theory is called 'autopoietic system'. Thus, ironically, as Andreas Weber notes, 'in subjectless systems theory a subject-logical thinking of a new, subtle kind persists ..., that is in the absolutism of the autopoietic system'.[130] Precisely this system should provide a guarantee for Luhmann against ultimate metaphysical explanations beyond the social. That autopoietic systems produce and reproduce their constitutive elements through their constitutive elements themselves, was precisely meant to cut off the connection to biologistic, ontological or religious premises. Yet this is countered in renouncing a genealogical deduction and implementing the system. Weber assumes that Luhmann intentionally ignores the problem, because he is primarily concerned with excluding the subject from the development of social theory.[131]

However, one has to assume that this forms his hidden normative premise. Before the autopoietic turn this was still readily apparent: 'Our existence depends on functionally differentiated large scale systems of information processing', he states.[132] 'Within them and through them we have to relate to the world'. Certainty only exists as long as they remain operational, and to secure precisely that is the role of law 'and its order is the just'.[133]

128 Adorno 2001, pp. 145–6.
129 Weingarten 2001, p. 303.
130 Weber 2005, pp. 18–19.
131 Weber 2005, p. 37.
132 Luhmann 1974, p. 180.
133 Luhmann 1974, p. 181.

Interestingly, Habermas and the legal systems theorists share this concept of the system, as will become apparent below. It can however already be shown at this point with Habermas' critique of Teubner. He objects that the concept is inconsistent within the terms of the theory itself [*theorieimmanent*], for the common, that is macro-social communication, which all systems use in Teubner, is only objectively identical and precisely not from the perspective of one of the two systems. There is, according to the premises of systems theory, no observer's position which can identify a communicative event as the same.[134] Teubner's suggestion therefore does not sit well with the conceptualisation of law as an autopoietic system; he is upon closer inspection more of an indication of the necessity of a theory of communicative action, 'which distinguishes a "lifeworld" bound to the medium of ordinary language from "systems" steered through special codes yet adaptively open to the environment'.[135]

Habermas thus believes that he 'catches' Teubner in already admitting underhandedly that the necessity of a general language refers to a medium which is not entirely systemic, but encompasses the systems. But this line of reasoning is in turn only necessary for Habermas because he conceives of the functional systems which are differentiated by special codes very similarly (even if for him they are environmentally open) – that is, in such a way that action is also stopped in them. Any possibility of communicative practice therefore has to be transferred into the 'life world' and its vernacular (see further details below).

Both theories grant the systems a problematic subject character. For in this manner the reification of social conditions is explained rather plausibly on the operative level. Subsequently, however, those social conditions and their actors, between whom the relations exist, are abstracted. Because finally only the *product* of human action is 'observed', but no longer the practice itself; also the mode of description is reified, the system acts. In this way the impression that the systems are completely remote and impenetrable is created.

3.4 *'Queer Observations' – Society without Gender*[136]

As the theory spirits subjective practice away from society, it cannot conceive of gendering as a process that structures society. Thus, it is hardly surprising that gender relations are irrelevant in the great works of legal systems theory. The

134 Habermas 1994, p. 54.

135 Habermas 1994, p. 55.

136 The title of Section 4 is a wordplay on queer and quer [oblique] in German. As queer also signifies 'strange', in the sense of crossing norms, the choice was made to retain the term 'queer' in the translation. [Translator's note]

relationship of systems theory and gender studies is according to Ulrike Teubner one of mutual exclusion.[137] A modest number of more recent approaches in gender studies shows that it is considered as a possible subject of discussion, and even relatively parallel to current discourse theory or interactionist feminist theoretical approaches[138] – making the fact that it is blocked out in legal systems theory all the more conspicuous.

But the blind spot is no accident; it rather has 'system'. In a 1988 essay Luhmann directs a polemical lesson at 'women's studies', where he explicitly addresses gender relations: only premodern societies, in particular the stratified ones, had oriented themselves in their character according to differences such as age, social class, or indeed gender, while those distinctions no longer made any 'functional sense' after the shift to functional subsystems:[139]

> Modern society presents a completely changed image, and for precisely this reason the distinction between men and women, provided that it does not have specific relevance for the functional system, that is allows for the creation of families, is now only suited to stimulate social movements.[140]

Luhmann does not deny the empirical effectiveness of the differences, but those are now only 'queer observations', which the functional systems can use on the level of the programme when this 'makes sense', for example in the economic system in the form of (sexist) advertising.[141] The gender category suffers a serious loss of function, when social systems form solely based upon the principle of functional differentiation.[142] Individuals are now situated in the social environment 'and only from moment to moment, only at the moment of their participation in a function specific communication ... included in the various social sectors'.[143] This means then that from the instant that 'no longer hierarchy, but heterarchy, no longer a vertical, but a horizontal order determines the social structure of society', the differences of women and men 'are sooner or later no longer needed'.[144] The functional differentiation thus creates 'effects

137 Teubner 2001, pp. 288–9.
138 See for example Kampmann, Karentzos and Küpper 2004; Pasero and Weinbach 2003; Weinbach 2004a.
139 Luhmann 2003, pp. 26 ff.
140 Luhmann 2003, p. 41.
141 Luhmann 2003, p. 49.
142 Hellmann 2004, p. 22.
143 Weinbach 2004b, p. 50.
144 Hellmann 2004, p. 21.

of symmetry', so that the determinism of the gender stereotypes is made 'lastingly irritated and relativised' by the function systems of modern society. Those cover the stereotypes and are orientated in a more open manner, so that they 'promise *in the long run* the better adaptive capacity and are therefore more successful'.[145]

The attempt to integrate gender relations into systems theory produced a surprising historical teleology, because of the transfer of a question which can only be clarified empirically into a temporal-diagnostic historical dimension;[146] 'in the long run', countered Keynes ironically, 'we all are dead'. This teleology is produced by a short circuit, in which, based on the logic of the socially constructed and contingent nature of a hierarchical relationship, its disappearance is deduced as not only possible but *necessary*. All social artefacts, the function systems included, are contingent. Why then are they considered stable by the systems theorists, whereas gender relations disappear? This stems quite clearly from Luhmann's androcentric perspective. Indeed, he shares this perspective at this point with the Marxist theoreticians whose works were written prior to the 'crisis of Marxism', for there this type of argument became known as the problem of the '*side contradiction*'. Thinking in terms of *side contradictions* is obviously not limited to the Marxian tradition. While they had to realise that patriarchy is not derived from capitalism, but that it is merely articulated with it, systems theorists still believed in the year 2004 that it could not be elaborated based on functional differentiation either. At least the former consider this mode of description to be, by now, at best problematic and at worst downright Old European. As systems theory catches up with the gender discussion internally, it asks instead why it is possible to maintain the gender distinction stably, that is asymmetrically, under conditions where it has become dysfunctional with regards to the *primary* form of differentiation,[147] or if there are '"secret" criteria for inclusion'.[148] Here the answer remains rooted in thinking in terms of side contradictions; the loss in function takes place on the 'macro-level' of modern society, while the gender difference remains a 'secondary effect' on the level of organisation and in particular that of interaction:[149]

> On the level of social structures, the gender difference has lost its structuring function. It remains, however, conspicuously operative in interactions

145 Pasero 2003, p. 104, p. 108. 'In the long run' in English in the original.
146 Knapp 2004, p. 46.
147 Nassehi 2003a, p. 89.
148 Weinbach 2004b, p. 52.
149 Hellmann 2004, p. 35.

> ... The pivotal point of gender inequality is to be found in the production and reproduction of those stereotyped persona.[150]

And with this the circle is closed. For, if gender relations are irrelevant on the social level, then their exclusion, for example in Luhmann's legal theory, is entirely justified. Hellmann also explains Luhmann's lack of interest in gender studies in this way: 'If Luhmann does not accord any greater significance to the problem of gender in social theory, the reasons for this might also be based in social theory'.[151] Gender is only one category besides many others, while Luhmann's research interest was primarily related to social theory, so that 'a lot, which is not directly connected to it, could be disregarded'.[152] Thus he succinctly sums up the gender-specific scientific division of labour and tendency for exclusion, which Gudrun-Axeli Knapp and Angelika Wetterer aptly describe in this way:

> The science of society deals with the major contexts and principal contradictions, it is a matter for specialists of the general; gender questions are subordinate problems, a subject of particular research interests, specialist passions of a self-referential nagging minority.[153]

There is no 'management of the paradox' of side contradictions. If systems theory wants to theoretically open up to gender relations, it has to arrive at a recognition that Marxist theory also had to open up to, that is, that a monotheist concept of society has become untenable. Societies do not come together primarily through *one* single structuring principle, be it the exchange of commodities or functional differentiation. The multifaceted character of the social cannot be united by one fundamental principle that shapes an era. 'There so

150 Weinbach 2004b, p. 75. Christine Weinbach's analysis can show that a person's gender symbolises different, gender stereotypical role clusters and thus performs the mediation of consciousness and communication (Weinbach 2003, p. 165). It thus provides a quite successful theory-immanent contextualisation of the gender question. Her theory only becomes implausible where interactions are meant to have no socially structuring effect, whereas other socially constructivist feminist theories are very much right in starting from the structuring principle of the gender binary. Butler, for instance, begins from the 'heterosexual matrix', which regulates gender categories in terms of social structure (Butler 1990, p. 194). Why the same stereotypes occur again and again remains thus unanswered.

151 Hellmann 2004, p. 33.

152 Hellmann 2004, p. 38.

153 Knapp and Wetterer 2003, p. 7.

no sutured space peculiar to "society", since the social itself has no essence'.[154] Functional differentiation can illustrate *one* structuring principle of socialisation, one that is, however, articulated with others, which are also not 'in the last instance' determined by it in such a way that they necessarily have to lose their independence or distinctive developmental logic.

Historical analysis has shown that, in the transition to modernity, gender difference was not only made unambiguous (in distinction to one-sex-models, for example), but practically naturalised.[155] In this regard the hierarchical gender binary is neither simply a given as part of traditional gender semantics, nor the product of premodern societies.[156] The hierarchical differentiations according to the categories gender, race, nation and sexuality thus have to be analysed independently as structuring categories of socialisation, and only afterwards is it necessary to examine to what extent they are 'irritated' by the function systems. This also brings into view the fact that 'highly complex' capitalist societies encompass alongside heterarchical structuring also equally important hierarchical structuring principles, or, in other words, that functionally differentiated sectors can themselves be stratified.[157] For legal systems theory, this has an important consequence: law can no longer be exclusively traced back to functional differentiation and defined in a gender-neutral manner. The assumption that the totality of society has to be conceptualised in a more pluralist way, can, however, run as a major thread through the entire work. How law relates to the totality of society can be understood as the fundamental problem of the different approaches, which is most visible in its blocking out of gender relations.

3.5 *Subversion in the System*

There is an entirely obvious and conscious gap in Luhmann's legal theory: the strategy of abstraction does not block out just anything; it specifically excludes moments of social power and powerlessness, as though theories of power suffered on principle from an Old European lack of complexity. With them, exactly that part of social reality which deals with the rule of men over men, disappears.[158] Luhmann's systems theory ultimately blocks out capitalist

154 Laclau and Mouffe 2001, p. 96.

155 For an overview see Maihofer 1995, pp. 22 ff.

156 Teubner 2001, p. 298.

157 Knapp 2004, p. 50.

158 Thus also Bolsinger 2001, p. 4: 'For a political theory of law, the term, the validity and the operating principle of law as well as of the legal system, are historically and structurally dependent upon political power structures and struggles between interests over the dis-

socialisation, and racist, post-colonial and sexist conditions, under the term of the complex society. What appears at all times and anywhere in the world as resistant, inevitably has to be excluded by abstraction on the highest level.

But the irony of theoretical historical blind spots resides in the fact that that which they exclude becomes all the more provocatively noticeable; as the 'thundering of hegemony'.[159] Luhmann attempts to rid himself of the political by relegating it to the institutionalised political system and denying it legitimacy everywhere else – even Teubner's models of self-regulation are too much for him. His concept of paradox, however, involuntarily summons up a politicisation of systems theory. Even well-intentioned interpretations reach the conclusion that Luhmann 'takes fright only at the radical nature of the results of his analysis of the paradox'.[160] Urs Stäheli in particular has demonstrated, with a reading of systems theory based on Laclau's discourse analysis, that all systems function as metaphors of the political, because they are founded on an insurmountable indeterminacy.[161]

The political becomes apparent in such moments of a system's history – moments in which it is confronted with the undecidable situations of a paradox. Situations of undecidability are, as Teubner also notes, not logical contradictions, but antagonistic situations. These are undecidable because there is no 'pre-constituted societal signifier for what is law',[162] because it actually has to be permanently created anew in social struggles for hegemony.[163] In the situation of undecidability decisions have to be made *based on power*. They show the contingency of the code: 'The foundation of the code is its success and thus the inextinguishable violence of its instituting'.[164] The technology of de-paradoxification is ultimately the precarious attempt to normalise the daily social appropriateness of legal operations.[165] Undecidability and indeterminacy have to be turned into certainty for the durability of the systemic connection and cannot do without regulating institutions, which Stäheli following Derrida calls 'police' or 'policing functions'.[166] The central problem of every system is the construction of its impossible identity, which becomes pre-

tribution, preservation and shifting of power. Law is always inscribed within the force field of society'.

159 Fischer-Lescano and Christensen 2012, p. 109.
160 Fischer-Lescano and Christensen 2012, p. 103.
161 Stäheli 2000b, p. 265.
162 Fischer-Lescano and Christensen 2012, p. 99.
163 Buckel and Fischer-Lescano 2009, p. 42.
164 Stäheli 2000b, pp. 252–3.
165 Fischer-Lescano and Christensen 2012, p. 99.
166 Stäheli 2000b, p. 236.

carious as soon as undecidabilities reveal the contingency of its previously hegemonic regime.[167] 'Cannot law also be unlawful? The sole protection against such inconvenient doubt is the degree of residual conviction ... The question posed to law as to what is law, is then substituted for by the question of what is plausible within social relationships'.[168] The penalisation of 'software pirating' for example would – if one follows Luhmann's depoliticised version – only be deemed necessary because the lack of normative regulation makes the future of expectations more uncertain. Conversely this means that the future could also be made more certain by permitting it, because then it would also be known what can legitimately be expected. This points to an indeterminacy, which is, however, always fiercely contested and politically decided in actually existing societies.

While Luhmann wants to make de-paradoxifying regulation less dramatic as a mostly rather peaceful, evolutionary process, it becomes clear at exactly this point that it always excludes possibilities in antagonistic struggles and that it is therefore genuinely antagonistic.[169] Precisely the legal decision shows this:

> Indeterminacy 'cannot be overcome by means of a decisionist exercise of power. This impossible distinction marks law to this day: legal decisions embody delay in the giving of the law. Law cannot be identified from the text alone, hence it must be discussed and argued over. However, since the speaking of the law only seldom leads to consensus within non-coercive discourses, a decision must be taken. Yet, because a decision could be decided differently, justification is required. And because even this is not enough, an act of legal implementation is needed. However, postponement is equally not ended by implementation, because there are never any final grounds, only penultimate grounds'.[170]

Ultimately paradoxes are no threat for Luhmann, because they are only produced by the self-observation of a system, leaving the system's reproduction unaffected. However, Teubner's detailed explanation of autopoiesis has just demonstrated that one can only speak of the phase of 'autopoietic law' when the system components of the legal system are connected with each other in a hyper-cyclical manner. Here the self-observation/self-description in dogmatics and theory is very much a vital prerequisite. The momentarily successful

167 Stäheli 2000b, p. 241.
168 Fischer-Lescano and Christensen 2012, pp. 109–10.
169 Stäheli 2000b, p. 273.
170 Fischer-Lescano and Christensen 2012, p. 113.

autopoiesis therefore rather creates a 'deceptively stable base'. For, if the self-description is constitutive for the systems, then it always already influences the system's reproduction: 'That the paradox occurs means that the system temporarily loses its sense of connectivity, or that it is reminded that its fragile modes of reducing complexity can break down'.[171] *Within the legal system lurks thus the subversion of the system*, and this means the political, understood 'as a practice of creation, reproduction and transformation of social relations'.[172]

171 Stäheli 2000b, pp. 277–8.

172 Laclau and Mouffe 2001, p. 153.

CHAPTER 3

Social Self-organisation: Habermas

1 Money, Power, Solidarity

Habermas, with his radically democratic premise, that the 'system of rights' could be the medium of self-organisation of an artificial legal community,[1] represents Luhmann's antipode. He adheres, in the tradition of critical theory, to the possibility of a rationally arranged world which has institutionalised 'the set of necessary conditions for emancipated forms of life about which the participants *themselves* must first reach an understanding'. In the preface of his main work in legal theory, *Between Facts and Norms*, he notes that precisely this democratic self-organisation forms the normative core of the socialist project.[2] Against this background Luhmann's theory has to appear particularly problematic to him, as it does not allow us to conceive of the production of a discursively created rational consensus.[3] Furthermore Habermas criticises all those theories which underestimate the normative presuppositions of legal practices due to a false realism, and which misjudge their normative obstinacy with a certain legal scepticism.[4] This verdict includes Marxist approaches no less than Derrida's deconstructivist reading of law.[5] Habermas' critique is all the more pitiless, because he locates precisely in the legal structures a surviving possibility for 'social solidarity … in need of continual regeneration' in 'highly complex' societies.[6] Why then does Habermas ascribe this potential to law?

1.1 *Communicative Reason*

Habermas already achieved a dialectical perspective in his preliminary studies for *The Theory of Communicative Action*, which he now uses for the analysis of law; with the aim of preserving the practical reason [*praktische Vernunft*] of the philosophy of the subject, he displaces it into the medium of language.[7] In this way he can overcome two central failures of previous concepts of rational-

1 Habermas 1996, p. 111.
2 Habermas 1996, p. xli.
3 Thus also Demirović 2003, p. 340.
4 Habermas 1996, p. xl.
5 Derrida 1991.
6 Habermas 1996, p. xlii. See also Brunkhorst 2002a.
7 See already Habermas 1998.

ity. On the one hand he leaves the horizon of individualistic notions of morality by making language the medium of socialisation.[8] On the other hand, he situates rationality and ideas/ideals in the linguistic telos of understanding itself. Whoever uses language in order to communicate about something in the world also has to engage with pragmatic preconditions of a counterfactual kind: 'In seeking to reach an understanding, natural-language users must assume, among other things, that the participants pursue their elocutionary goals without reservations, that they tie their agreement to the intersubjective recognition of criticisable validity claims, and that they are ready to take on the obligations resulting from consensus and relevant for further interaction'.[9] Thus necessary idealisations are undertaken. On a first level, communicatively acting individuals have to ascribe identical meanings to expressions, even if they are not aware of this. On a second level, the interacting participants must consider themselves mutually accountable, and presuppose that they can orient their actions according to validity claims, which can in the case of critique be backed up with the right kinds of justifications.[10] Ideas or counterfactual presuppositions are thus de-transcendentalised and situated at 'the heart of ordinary, everyday communicative practice', in other words, 'brought down from the transcendental heaven to the earth of the lifeworld'.[11]

Thus, Habermas overcomes the opposition of idea and perceptible reality with a strategy that is very similar to Althusser's. While Althusser had refused to see ideology as a mere reflex of an economic base, and rather found it materialised in social practice and apparatuses themselves (Chapter 7), Habermas conceived of the idea itself as embodied in language,[12] and therefore likewise as being materialised in practice. Normativity is thus not a construct that floats above the 'real world' but a 'counterfactual basis of an actual practice of reaching understanding'.[13] Beyond this commonality Althusser and Habermas differ, of course, in that Althusser speaks of 'ideology' and Habermas of 'reason'.

Against this background, however, Habermas criticises political and legal theory, which are disintegrating into camps that are torn between facticity and validity. While the former lose touch with social reality, the latter screen out all normative aspects.[14] An analysis of social structures always also demands – so

8 Horster 1992, pp. 22–3; Habermas 1996, p. 3.
9 Habermas 1996, p. 4.
10 Habermas 1996, pp. 20ff.
11 Habermas 1996, p. 19.
12 Habermas 1996, p. 34.
13 Habermas 1996, p. 3.
14 Habermas 1996, p. 6.

Habermas concludes – the analysis of normative practice, precisely as a part of those structures. Social interaction is achieved by coordinating the action plans of different actors without the exercise of manifest violence, such that one party's actions 'link up' with those of others. Only in this way can social order even come about, that is to say when language is not only seen as a means to transmit information, but when at the same time the elocutionary forces of speech acts are recognised. It then becomes apparent that they themselves are the primary source of social integration.[15]

No different are the demands made of a legal theory; it has to assume that the underlying tension between 'facticity and validity' constitutes the basic structure of modern law.[16] Those two moments converge particularly in legal validity, that is, the facticity of the state's law enforcement with the legitimising force of a process for creating legislation that claims to be rational.[17] The analysis of law has to combine *external* access to law with a reconstruction from an *internal* perspective,[18] that is, an analysis of its socially structuring function with its own claim to be legitimate law. Habermas assumes with Weber that social orders can only be maintained in the long run as legitimate orders[19] and couples this with Durkheim's insight that the social cohesion produced by norms depends upon democratic will. To those two insights he adds the analysis of the special role communication and language play in this process.[20] Habermas therefore reaches the conclusion that the law's performance of socio-structural integration depends on its performance of normative legitimation, namely on its origin in procedures which assert institutionally the potential of communicative reason as it is embedded in discursive practice.

Habermas succeeds in developing his ideal of communicative reason – the ideal by which he measures existing society – as something already implicit in Adorno and Horkheimer, although he certainly does not share their critical assessment of instrumental reason. Adorno had understood reconciliation in terms of an intact intersubjectivity, which is only brought about in the reciprocity of communication based on free acknowledgement. Thus he himself had developed an 'implicit communicative concept of freedom'.[21]

15 Habermas 1996, p. 21.
16 Maus 1996, p. 825.
17 Habermas 1996, p. 30.
18 Habermas 1996, p. 65.
19 Habermas 1996, p. 67.
20 Hartmann 2006, 2.1.1.
21 Habermas 1981, pp. 685–6.

Habermas is aware that this is most of all a critical assessment and that there exists also, and perhaps predominately, strategic action. Communicative action has a potential which does not necessarily prevail:

> Not all eluctionary acts are constitutive for communicative action, but only those with which speakers connect criticisable validity claims. In the other cases, when a speaker is pursuing undeclared ends with perlocutionary acts – ends on which the hearer can take no position at all – as in relation to imperatives – the potential for the binding (or bonding) force of good reasons – a potential which is always contained in linguistic communication – remains unexploited.[22]

In a very central position Habermas thus, following the linguistic turn [English in original], switches to communication, exactly like Luhmann. But – and this is a crucial difference – this is about communicative action, and not systemic processes. Habermas wants to take account of the assumptions 'that the human species maintains itself through the socially coordinated activities of its members and that this coordination has to be established through communication – and in certain central spheres through communication aimed at reaching agreement'.[23] Therefore practice, even if it is primarily communicative, is of great importance in his theory; society requires the coordination of actions – and this coordination happens through language. Language contains a rationality potential – and it is the language of specific speakers, so that it is not possible to abstract from them.

Modernity thus provides for Habermas, contrary to the understanding of older critical theory, starting points for locating rationality in social practice. They are, however, due to problems modernity creates out of itself, blocked and cannot be exploited.[24]

1.2 *Integration*

While for Luhmann the systems rather have the status of a foundational premise, in Habermas one could ascribe this status to the concept of social *integration*. Both theorists are fundamentally engaged with the question of how the reproduction of the social whole is possible. Interestingly, both theories address law against this background, a premise which a materialist legal theory

22 Habermas 1981, p. 197.

23 Habermas 1981, p. 397.

24 Similarly, but more emphatically in Strecker and Schaal 2001, p. 92.

also has to examine. As Habermas foregrounds the engaged 'actors', he answers the question in a consistent manner from a perspective that is focused on the reproduction of the species.

1.2.1 Dual Socialization

Habermas rejects the idea that society – understood as a holistic whole – is a totality in the Hegelian sense.[25] Instead he conceives three subsystems, two systems proper and the 'lifeworld', from which one has to define the existence of the social whole. He follows the idea that was prepared by Adam Smith, spelled out by Marx in terms of social theory and finally sociologically developed by Talcott Parsons, that modern capitalist societies develop institutional complexes, which become independent of their producers and can as such no longer be immediately understood by them. In Parson's terminology, Habermas conceptualises systems which form in the course of social 'evolution'. Unlike Luhmann, however, he retains a narrow systems-concept[26] which only knows two systems, which both process material reproduction: economy and state.

In his efforts to relate the diverging conceptual strategies of action and systems theory and integrate them with each other,[27] he connects the insights of systems theory with Husserl's concept of the lifeworld and Mead's theory of interaction. In consequence, the basis of the systems still remains the lifeworld, that is the horizon of communicative action, consisting in 'individual skills as well – the intuitive knowledge of *how* one deals with situations – and socially customary practices too – the intuitive knowledge of what one can count on in situations – no less than background convictions known in a trivial sense'.[28]

In the course of their evolution the lifeworld and systems have thus differentiated, as material reproduction, including political regulation, has become increasingly complex, while the rationality of the lifeworld increased, that is, the secularisation and ever more comprehensive questioning of convictions which had been believed to be certain. The crucial difference between the two systems and the lifeworld is that the former operate by means of non-linguistic communication media and control a social intercourse that is largely disconnected from norms and values. The rational potential [*Vernunftpotential*] no longer resides in those reified life contexts,[29] which rather coagulate to Hegel's

25 Habermas 1996, p. 107.
26 Neves 2000, p. 12.
27 Habermas 1987, p. 113.
28 Habermas 1987, p. 135.
29 Following Sohn–Rethel he even speaks of 'real abstraction'; see part 3.

'second nature' and elude the prior knowledge of communicative everyday practice. They are, precisely as in Marx and Adorno, only 'accessible only to the counterintuitive knowledge of the social sciences developing since the eighteenth century'.[30]

1.2.2 Lifeworld

For Habermas the lifeworld as well as the systems – and also law, as will be demonstrated later on – have the function of lowering the ever-present risk of dissensus. His theory of communicative action quite obviously generates a fundamental problem; the mechanism of mutual understanding, on which the entire weight of the theory lies, produces a growing pressure for rationality, in which 'the zones of what is unproblematic shrink'.[31] Therefore the risk of dissensus grows. The lifeworld heads off this risk by embedding communicative action in lifeworld contexts, which 'provide the backing of a massive background consensus'.[32] This is 'a sprawling, deeply set, and unshakable rock of background assumptions, loyalties, and skills'.[33] The lifeworld reproduces itself through three processes; cultural reproduction, that is, the continuity of tradition; social integration through legitimately regulated interpersonal relations and the identity of groups; and the socialisation of the members of the lifeworld, which secures for them generalised competences for action.

1.2.3 Systems

Imperatives of securing existence, that is the material reproduction of the lifeworld, lead with the increased complexity of modern societies to the differentiation of specialised systems. Their specificity lies in that communicative action is suspended here. Instead of through consensus, integration takes place systemically, by way of a non-normative regulation that extends beyond individual consciousness,[34] so that actions are not necessarily coordinated intentionally, that is with the communicative effort of the participants, but objectively, '"behind the[ir] backs"'.[35] This then is the manner in which the steering media of the two systems, power and money, can 'hold off' the

30 Habermas 1987, p. 173.
31 Habermas 1987, p. 183.
32 Habermas 1996, p. 22.
33 Ibid.
34 Habermas 1996, p. 179.
35 Habermas 1996, p. 39.

risk of dissensus. Uncoupling the interaction from lifeworld contexts makes it possible to exert generalised, strategic influence while bypassing processes of consensus-oriented communication, so that the lifeworld context gets devalued.[36]

Habermas calls this development, in Marxian terminology, reification: 'the unleashed functionalist reason of system maintenance disregards and overrides the claim to reason ingrained in communicative sociation [*Vergesellschaftung*] and lets the rationalization of the lifeworld run idle'.[37] He interprets reification as a 'pathological de-formation of the communicative infrastructure of the lifeworld'. Unlike in Marx, however, the development of objectified systems is not in itself an expression of reification, but this occurs only at the moment when the lifeworld does not withdraw from the affected functions, because it is not possible to 'painlessly transfer' those functions to the media-steered systems of action.[38] The internal dynamics of the capitalist economic system can be preserved only insofar as the accumulation process is uncoupled from orientations to use value, and it 'has to be kept as free as possible from life-world restrictions'. The internal systemic logic of capitalism has to be met, even at the cost of *technisising* the lifeworld. However, this is only a practical, not a theoretical postulate.[39]

Habermas thus sees independent development of social conditions much more positively than older critical theory does. One could even say that this is exactly the fork in the road where Habermas leaves the Marxian tradition. He hopes to put the rationally ordered world into practice despite and with the help of those independent developments. For the systemic connections are also a higher and evolutionary advantageous level of integration, a higher level of system differentiation, which opens up new steering possibilities that unburden the actors, and can connect highly complex, global societies and provide them with economic growth.[40] Exactly at this point a turn towards the assumption of systems theory takes place, which considers systems differentiation evolutionary progress. This causes enormous relief:

> The function systems can ignore alien factors and concentrate on the efficient and effective execution of systems imperatives. In the sphere of the lifeworld, discussions, which are as ever conflictual, about economic

36 Habermas 1987, p. 183.
37 Habermas 1984, pp. 398–9.
38 Habermas 1987, p. 375.
39 Habermas 1987, p. 345.
40 Habermas 1987, p. 339.

> allocation and the political self-exposure of society can be discussed freed from the immediate technical tasks, which are now taken care of by subsystems.[41]

The results are in turn – and here we get to the central importance of law in this analysis – translated by law into the rationality of the subsystems, as will be outlined below.

According to Habermas's concept of society '[T]he social-life context reproduces itself both through the media-controlled purposive-rational actions of its members and through the common will anchored in the communicative practice of all individuals'.[42] Thus the three forces of macro-social integration are: money, administrative power, and solidarity.[43]

2 The System of Rights

Against this background Habermas considers law from a 'dual perspective': internally, by reconstructing its normative content, and externally as a component of social reality.[44]

2.1 *The External Perspective: The Socially Structured Location of Law*

For the social location of law in Habermas one has to note first that it is not introduced as a legal system as it is in Luhmann. Rather, it remains a mechanism of the lifeworld, through which the two systems of the lifeworld are 'anchored', that is, institutionalised through private and public law. The reason why Habermas attributes law to the lifeworld is that its potential to bestow legitimacy [*Legitimationspotential*] comes in modernity to bear the main brunt of social integration, which the lifeworld provides in contrast to systemic integration.[45] Again, the problem of dissension is the trigger for this 'functional' necessity of law. For the background consensus of the lifeworld is in complex societies no longer sufficient for successful social integration.[46] The fundamental structure of facticity and validity is noticeable in that, through law,

41 Demirović 2003, p. 341.
42 Habermas 1984, p. 398.
43 Habermas 1996, p. 150.
44 Habermas 1996, p. 43.
45 Habermas 1996, p. 40.
46 Habermas 1996, p. 37.

norms created through consensus-based procedures acquire legitimacy, and their results can be coupled with the potential for sanctions. Thus strategic interactions can be resolved with norms the actors themselves agree on. When action is both strategic and communicative, norms have to take on the paradoxical nature of establishing on the one hand de facto restrictions, while on the other hand still developing socially integrating force. They have to simultaneously bring about de facto constraint and willingness to comply by means of legitimate validity.

The Kantian definition of law, according to which 'the choice of one can be united with the choice of another in accordance with a universal law of freedom',[47] is translated into a theory of integration by way of a procedural turn; counterfactual norms, which have been developed in legitimacy-generating procedures, have a socially structuring effect – this is, yet again, the payoff of Habermas's reflections. Destabilisation resulting from rationally motivated dissent is avoided, because the addressees cannot question the validity of the norms they follow. Through the process of law-making 'the permanent risk of contradiction is maintained in ongoing discourses' and 'transformed into the productive force of a presumptively rational political opinion- and will formation'.[48] In particular, the paradoxically heightened tension between subjective freedoms and coercion requires that the demands for rationality in the process of lawmaking are accordingly high.[49]

The normative self-understanding of law is, however, like all lifeworld components, structurally threatened by the encroachment of systemic imperatives. It also has to process those imperatives, in which often enough 'normatively unfiltered interest positions often carry the day only because they are stronger and use the legitimating force of legal forms to cloak their merely factual strength'. Law therefore remains 'a profoundly ambiguous medium of societal integration'.[50] One could say that Luhmann ascribes greater self-will to the legal system than the discourse-theoretical reasoning, although it is precisely a lack of normative self-will that Habermas decries in Luhmann.[51]

The ambivalent character of law can also be seen in its conceptualisation as a 'transmission belt': because law is the institutionalising medium of systems

47 Kant 1991, p. 56.
48 Habermas 1996, p. 38.
49 Maus 1996, p. 833.
50 Habermas 1996, p. 40.
51 Habermas 1996, p. 2.

in the lifeworld and therefore connected with all mechanisms of integration, it constitutes at the same time a sphere of mediation for Habermas. That is, through law, solidarity, which is rooted in concrete living conditions, is transmitted in abstract form to the relationships of highly complex societies, which have become anonymous,[52] or, in terms of linguistic theory, the legal code brings messages from vernacular language into a form in which it remains intelligible for the special codes of the system: 'To this extent the language of law ... can function as a transformer in the society-wide communication circulating between system and lifeworld'.[53] Habermas thus attributes far greater significance to law than Luhmann. It does not remain limited to its own world, but gains a universal function, which takes on both the burden of social integration, and is also able to switch between different modes of communication. Accordingly, it is much less closed and self-referential than in the systems theory version.

2.2 *The Internal Perspective: The Co-originality of Popular Sovereignty and Human Rights*

For the internal analysis of law, Habermas choses a particular strategy which has led to a range of misunderstandings in the literature.[54] Taking into consideration the theory of democracy, he initially does not propose a normative concept, but tries to reconstruct the paradigmatic background understanding of law, that is, the moral and practical self-understanding of modernity.[55] However, he proposes a new, discourse-theoretical 'reading' of democratic practice until the present.[56] Thus the point is not to immediately present an alternative model to reality, but to interpret democracies up to now as practical realisations of a certain self-understanding of democracy. He now wants to reconstruct this conception in such a way that it can connect with his own concept of communicative reason, in order to make visible the not yet achieved potential of the democratic principle. This typically Habermasian approach, which avoids treating normativity in a vacuum and grounds it instead in social practice, quickly leads to the misunderstanding that he is only concerned with a justification of the existing.[57] As Ingeborg Maus aptly notes, this approach stems, to the contrary, from a democratic intention; Habermas does not want to

52 Habermas 1996, pp. 76–7.
53 Habermas 1996, p. 81.
54 For an overview see Günther 1994.
55 Habermas 1996, p. xlii, p. 82.
56 Habermas 1996, p. xliii.
57 Narr 1994b, p. 94.

explain to the citizens in an expertocratic manner what they should rationally decide, but conversely has to reconstruct the rational from their constitutional practice.[58]

How then does this reconstruction proceed? 'I take as my starting point the rights citizens must accord one another if they want to legitimately regulate their common life by means of positive law'.[59] The socially existing legal form, consisting of subjective rights coupled with coercive force, is the 'product of the disintegration of traditional ethical life' and is in this regard not a normatively justifiable, but simply a really existing principle.[60] Initially it is in no way related to the democratic principle:

> There is therefore for citizens no form of normative necessity to join together in a legal community ... The *decision* to use the historically present legal form in order to legitimately organise collective life with the help of positive law is rather *entirely contingent*. The option of refraining from a legal organization of collective life remains open to all societies. Yet, when a society decides to adopt it, ... it has to accept those qualities of law that result from the functionally complementary relationship to post-conventional morality ... This also prominently includes private autonomy, as the counterpart of coercive power.[61]

Habermas now logically develops the 'system of rights'[62] in a circular process, in which legal code and democratic principle are constituted co-originally.[63] The circular process is meant to make precisely this co-originality possible in the representation. It must not be stopped at any point such that as a result either subjective rights or the democratic principle would have priority over the other. 'That from this perspective subjective right appears as both the "result" and "precondition" of political autonomous legislation, then does not seem to be a "contradiction", but rather the point of the argument'.[64]

The second moment besides the legal form is the abstract *discourse principle*, which is intended to assume the shape of a principle of democracy. Its

58 Maus 1996, pp. 838–9.
59 Habermas 1996, p. 82.
60 Günther 1994, p. 478.
61 Ibid (emphasis in original).
62 'System' here is by no means used in the sense of a functional action system, but merely expresses logical coherence and completeness.
63 Habermas 1996, p. 122.
64 Günther 1994, p. 471.

only purpose is to express the meaning of post-conventional requirements of justification, that is the perspective from which norms of action can be impartially founded in the first place.[65] It is, in principle, the culmination of his reflections on communicative reason. If dissension constitutes the core problem of modern socialisation, where linguistic communication practice in social interaction inevitably raises criticisable validity claims, the institutionalisation of consensual procedures for norm production necessarily follows from this. Hence the discourse principle, which can found both moral and legal norms in Habermas, is given this form: 'Just those action norms are valid to which all possibly affected persons could agree as participants in rational discourses'.[66]

Finally, rational discourse should 'include *any* attempt to reach an understanding over problematic validity claims insofar as this takes place under conditions of communication that enable the free processing of topics and contributions, information and reasons in the public space constituted by illocutionary obligations'.[67]

In *Between Facts and Norms* Habermas has liberated the discourse principle from its moral-ethical one-sidedness. The focus is now no longer on the legitimacy of certain types of arguments, but on the impartiality of the procedures.[68]

When the discourse principle intertwines with the legal form, the democratic principle emerges from this.[69] The legal code as the language in which the legal subjects can realise their autonomy, is coupled with the demand for rational justification. The result are procedures that 'under real conditions of lawmaking where there is simply no way of asking humanity as a whole, enable decisions to be made which "could" measure up to the standards of ideal discourse'.[70] Thus the subjunctive form makes explicit that nevertheless the criteria of ideal discourse are not abandoned despite the limited possibilities of legal institutionalised democratic procedures.[71]

The legal code itself must not be confused with the code of legal theory in systems theory (legal/illegal), but it refers in Habermas to the egalitarian conferring of legal entitlements. It comprises therefore initially three categories of

65 Habermas 1996, p. 107.
66 Ibid.
67 Habermas 1996, pp. 107–8.
68 Niesen and von Schomberg 2002, p. 5.
69 Habermas 1996, p. 121.
70 Maus 1996, p. 855.
71 Ibid.

rights: the right of equal individual liberties, the right of membership in a voluntary association of consociates under the law, and the guarantee of judicial review.[72] But up to now this is – in the thought experiment – only egalitarian juridification. At this juncture is determined whether the legal subjects give over their only virtual authorship to a higher power in the next step or if, on the contrary, they also realise it normatively by allowing each other reciprocal political rights to participate in democratic legislative procedures, whereby they also normatively become the authors of their individual civil liberties. For this, however, they require the discourse principle, whose medium of institutionalisation is again the legal form.[73] Those categories of fundamental rights remain unsaturated until a political legislature interprets and gives them shape in response to changing circumstances.[74] This does not found a dual legality – nothing is given to the legislator, she only implicitly gains liberty rights at the moment she uses the legal code.[75]

There is thus a dialectic, internal relation between popular sovereignty and human rights; it 'lies in the normative content of the very *mode of exercising political autonomy*, a mode that is not secured simply through the grammatical form of general laws but only through the communicative form of discursive processes of opinion- and will-formation'.[76] This is Habermas' development of Jean-Jacques Rousseau's and Immanuel Kant's republican theory of democracy after the linguistic turn. Legitimate right, which is at the same time the social-structural precondition of a durable social formation, presupposes legitimate procedures.

A legal order *is* legitimate to the extent that it equally secures the co-original private and political autonomy of its citizens; at the same time, however, it *owes* its legitimacy to the forms of communication in which alone this autonomy can express and prove itself.[77]

The discourse principle is for Habermas an equally pure a priori, as is the 'only innate human right' for Kant. Both postulate the conditions of legitimacy counter-factually. In Habermas this is the ideal speech situation as the idealist precondition of any constitutional practice which lays claim to reason. 'Regardless of the actual strategic motivations and interests of constitutional

72 Habermas 1996, p. 122.
73 Habermas 1996, p. 123; Günther 1994, p. 480.
74 Habermas 1996, p. 125.
75 Habermas 1996, p. 128.
76 Habermas 1996, p. 103 (emphasis in original).
77 Habermas 1996, p. 409 (emphasis in original).

law-giving and constitutional praxis, a critical standard is established through these principles without which the description of reality would be cynical'.[78]

Finally, Habermas formulates the presuppositions for protecting this system of rights largely from the imperatives of the administrative system. Habermas argues very much in the Kantian tradition that the legal medium already presupposes a political power. For the reciprocal conferral of rights remains a metaphorical event and cannot become permanent unless state power is established with the force of the barracks and put to work.[79] However, he diverges from Kant's concept of rights at a decisive moment, as political power is differentiated into communicative and administrative power,[80] and only the latter poses a problem for the constitutional state. For communicative power, as Habermas formulates following Hannah Arendt, is nothing but the legislating power which emerged in rational procedures from the free processing of themes and contributions, information and reasons, thus corresponding to the discourse principle.[81] Thus it joins forces with law, and power aligns with law, very much in contrast to natural law, where both were opposed to each other. Law is thus the medium which translates communicative into administrative power; and the idea of the constitutional state has to mean that '... the administrative system which is steered through the power code be tied to the lawmaking communicative power and kept free of illegitimate interventions of social power (i.e., of the factual strength of privileged interests to assert themselves)'.[82]

3 Critique

Habermas' legal theory owes its power of persuasion to the nuances of normative and socio-structural perspective and its liberal telos. His attempt to situate law in the force field between communicative action and independent social systems, that is, in the dialectic of acting subjects and social surplus objectivity, is insightful. The following analysis of materialist legal theory will show that its overlaps with the discourse theory of law are considerable, due to their common origin in critical theory. In the following I will therefore concentrate on

78 Maus 1996, pp. 842–3.
79 Habermas 1996, p. 132.
80 Habermas 1996, p. 136.
81 Habermas 1996, p. 147.
82 Habermas 1996, p. 150.

the differences. Here my critique focuses primarily on how Habermas simultaneously over- and underestimates the systems.

3.1 *The Refusal to Think Law as a System*

Firstly, on underestimating the systems: Habermas transfers all his democratic hopes and demands for solidarity to the medium of law. It is meant to achieve the self-organisation of society, stabilise expectations, make the legitimacy of the political regime possible, mediate between system and lifeworld and carry the burden of social integration. Communicative reason is initially embodied in language in general, but then takes – in particular in legal language – a particular shape. And precisely for this reason law itself cannot be a system, that is, no independent mechanism of social integration which takes place behind the back of communicative action. However, just as Luhmann places the systems, Habermas situates the existence of two – and only two – systems and law as a moment of the lifeworld. While he had just criticised Marx's theory of value for falling into a 'monism', which knows only one 'system', namely the economy – suggesting on the contrary that it depends upon a functional supplement through an administrative system of action, which is differentiated through the medium of power[83] – it is not clear why law, in particular in light of its 'internal connection' with political power, could not also constitute such a 'functional supplement'.[84]

In particular Luhmann's representation substantiated the systemic mechanisms of law plausibly, but Habermas does not follow this version, because he sees it as a threat to the potential for solidarity. Interestingly he evaluated law even more ambivalently in *The Theory of Communicative Action*, with the distinction between law as an anonymous, quasi-systemic mechanism, which colonises even the lifeworld, and a law that is still connected to the lifeworld through demands for legitimation.[85] While Habermas thus initially assumed that the description of the legal system in systems theory was at least descriptively adequate,[86] his democratic-theoretical approach in *Between Facts and Norms* led to the rejection of this notion.[87] With the process of legislation, the legal code seems to dispose of an extensive potential which the systems do not

83 Habermas 1987, pp. 343–4.

84 Besides, it must be critically noted that Habermas does not address the development of a materialist theory of the state, and thus cannot clarify that its results are in a rather similar direction and attempt to close this gap in Marx's concept (see part 2).

85 Habermas 1987, p. 360.

86 Nisen and Eberl 2006, p. 11.

87 Habermas 1996, p. 356, note 47; Neves 2000, p. 90.

possess. There, no mechanisms of understanding and no normative feedback seem to exist anymore. But only such a rigid separation, which describes the systemic processes completely detached from communicative action, has then to reach the conclusion that legal relationships cannot take place systematically.

Finally, it is noticeable that the entanglement of law in social mechanisms of power and domination is not sufficiently illuminated and that the connection of law to power is meant to crucially consist in its close relationship to the positive form of 'communicative power'. Or, expressed even more fundamentally: since power and domination are in general not denied in Habermas, but also not discussed, and are at most centred politically in the administrative system, law can also be accounted for relatively harmoniously.[88] This constitutes a significant difference to materialist approaches, which deny that the legal form can be unharmed in an irrational and power-defined world. No matter how severely one considers the difference, it is obvious that law as part of the lifeworld is not burdened with any negative connotations: 'All that is bad seems to come from the outside', objected Alex Demirović to Habermas' social theory, 'but what is not inquired into are the patterns of reproduction through domination of practices attributed to the lifeworld, that is of the family and sexuality, of the form of the subject, of pathological interactions and processes of meaning-making, which have already caused so much devastation in the area of social integration and which only provided [...] the colonisation by the systems with its potential to exert influence'.[89]

The question is how the potential of law, which it undeniably appears to possess in comparison to other immediate forms of domination, could be considered in such a way that it is not 'de-dominated' (Narr) and reconciled, but can be salvaged through its systemic character. In the materialist theory of law, which is reconstructed in Part 3, we will see that this potential can precisely be found in that independence of the law which is also 'co-originally' a reification of human relations.

3.2 *Ghettoisation of the Subjects*

Underestimating the expansion of the systems is at the same time connected to overestimating them, which consists of elevating them to such an extent that (communicative) action is completely halted. This is all the more astonishing as Habermas contended entirely aptly against Luhmann that the latter's elim-

88 Thus also Narr 1994a, p. 330.

89 Demirović 2003, p. 342.

ination of practice and normativity turned towards the affirmative.[90] Upon closer inspection, however, it becomes apparent that in Habermas's conception, action in the proper sense only occurs in the lifeworld. Therefore, law as a central coordinating mechanism also has to be part of this lifeworld. Thus while Luhmann renders the acting subjects irrelevant, Habermas ghettoises them in the lifeworld. In the systems they are mere appendages of the control media, which they can at most use with strategic intent, but that also subjects them to a strict systemic logic. This means that system operations fail once again to be resolved according to the theory of action.[91]

In this manner Habermas's argument is upon closer inspection downright economistic; i.e., it is as though the 'actors' followed the law of value or even the logic of capital. Although he is correct in saying that the media initially 'reach through' conscious action, it would, however, be a 'naturalist prejudice' to consider the economy as a space that is dominated by necessary laws,[92] because this means nothing more than to eliminate politics, which are always-already present. In this sense Nancy Fraser already raised the objection against Habermas that for instance the capitalist economic system too has a moral, cultural dimension:

> However morally dubious the consensus and however problematic the content and status of the norms, virtually every human action context involves some form of both of them. In the capitalist marketplace, for example, strategic, utility-maximising exchanges occur against a horizon of intersubjectively shared meanings and norms; agents normally subscribe at least tacitly to some commonly held notions of reciprocity and to some shared conceptions about the social meanings of objects, including what sort of things are considered exchangeable ...[93]

Also, the systems have to be produced every second by the acting subjects. They are in fact open to their reflexive questioning, albeit under more difficult conditions, and have no final literal character. They are genuinely political. Whether a particular process is claimed to be systemic or not is a question of political definition. Even Luhmann's systems theory raises this in the problem of the paradox: the basic distinction of the systems is highly precarious, it must never be questioned itself, but has to be 'de-paradoxified'. Furthermore

90 Habermas 1996, p. 47.
91 Demirović 2003, p. 342.
92 Laclau and Mouffe 2001, p. 73.
93 Fraser 1989, pp. 117–8; similarly also Maus 1986c, p. 309.

its closedness is itself permanently questioned; in this way, for example, the *Mitbestimmungsgesetz* [Codetermination Act] of 1976 can be interpreted with Ingeborg Maus as a 'lifeworld corridor',[94] because it introduces a political correction to the ostensible economic self-reflexivity. This premise also mitigates the danger which prevents Habermas from conceiving of law as a system.

3.3 *Hegemonic Consensus*

Habermas's theory has a particular advantage in comparison to Luhmann's analysis. By making (communicative) action his focus, he is also under greater constraints to provide arguments and requires more than only *one* mechanism of integration. If the 'actors' are – at least in the lifeworld – more than mere constructions of the systems, then he has to show that the systems depend on them and on their contributions to the shaping of society. Habermas stresses that they have to be 'integrated' through their consent to this society and therefore rejects the conception of the legal system as a self-legitimating circular process: 'This is already contradicted by the evidence that democratic institutions of freedom disintegrate without the initiatives of a population accustomed to freedom'.[95]

Particularly instructive, therefore, are his explanations about the shared pre-categorical background consensus, as well as the intentional mechanisms of consent. He is thus able to show that it is unrealistic to conceive of all social behaviour as strategic action in the utilitarian sense.[96] Each coordination of action has an intersubjective dimension that is based both on shared knowledge and consent. Action that is purely motivated by interest pushes up against its limits in the preconditions for intersubjectivity.[97] Consensus is therefore a crucial precondition for social action.

In the framing of this consensus the absence of politics in his conception becomes, however, noticeable, for it seems possible to determine the 'good reasons' objectively. Admittedly, Habermas notes that reasons are no dispositions for having opinions that can be described naturalistically, but rather the 'currency used in a discursive exchange'.[98] However, his definition of rational discourse suggests that there is a possibility to protect reasons in such a way from social impregnations; that they gain their own dignity via their being undertaken in procedures:

---

94 Maus 1986c, p. 310.
95 Habermas 1996, p. 130.
96 Habermas 1996, p. 337.
97 Hartmann 2006, 2.1.1.
98 Habermas 1996, p. 35.

> These can be seen as arrangements that have an effect on the preferences of participants; they screen the topics and contributions, information and reasons in such a way that, ideally, only the 'valid' inputs pass through the filter of fair bargaining and rational discourses.[99]

Here he is right insofar as interests have to become general to prevail in modern society. He blocks out, however, that those procedural filters do not produce pure practical reason. 'The thought that there could be a state of communication which would be such that the games of truth could circulate freely, without obstacles, without constraint, and without coercive effects, seems to me to be Utopia'[100] – thus Foucault's objection to Habermas. At this point the coercive effects are clearly revealed; they are the filters themselves. They are permeable for certain arguments, which thus at the same time acquire the dignity of 'validity'. Those filters are themselves already socially impregnated. They only let those arguments enter the procedures in which a particular interest has succeeded in articulating its own concern as general. Moreover, the channels themselves are shaped by domination,[101] for the implicit standard for the rationality of communications has a selective and excluding effect.[102]

One must agree with Habermas when he makes consensus a central category of social theory, and connects it to the necessity of the generalisation of interests. The question is, however, to understand this consensus with Gramsci as 'hegemonic' (see Part 2). Such a Gramscian theory of hegemony can in turn learn from Habermas which different technologies of consensus-production can be imagined.

3.4 *Blocking out Gender Relations*

While class relations remain at least rudimentarily present in Habermas, he participates like Luhmann in blocking out the question of gender. Unlike the latter, he at least tries to accommodate feminist theory in *Between Facts and Norms*, after it had reared its head in the context of *The Theory of Communicative Action*. Then Nancy Fraser in particular harshly objected that 'Habermas says virtually nothing about gender' and produces an 'unthematised gender subtext'.[103] Thus his theory becomes 'in important respects androcentric and

99 Habermas 1996, p. 341.
100 Foucault 1991a, p. 18.
101 Hartmann 2006, 2.1.1.
102 Demirović 1997, p. 155.
103 Fraser 1989, p. 114.

ideological'.[104] She based this criticism in particular on the dualistic concept of system and lifeworld, because it assigns the tasks that are socially assigned to women, such as raising children and caring for relatives, to the lifeworld, while the official economy is described as a differentiated system, which functions according to purely systemic mechanisms. He exaggerates the differences, which separate the socially necessary activities in the two areas and ignores 'the fact that in both spheres women are subordinated to men'. He is therefore unable to consider the dimension of male domination in modern societies.[105] This also manifests itself in that the roles of the 'actors' both in the lifeworld and in the systems are not neutral, but gendered roles. Gender identity as a central category is alien to Habermas.[106] This 'gender blindness' ultimately shows in how Habermas uses gender as an ascriptive characteristic and thus cannot adequately look into a central structuring principle of capitalist socialisation.[107]

How then does Habermas react to this criticism in *Between Facts and Norms*? Jean L. Cohen reaches the conclusion that 'he has not only corrected for his earlier "gender blindness" but he has also made what I take to be an extremely important contribution to the "equality/difference" debate ...'[108] How then does Habermas correct his concept and what constitutes his particular contribution to feminist debate?

In his last chapter he turns to political conclusions and demands a new legal paradigm, that is, a new concept of legal communities with regards to the question of how the legal system can be actualised in the perceived context of a given society.[109] In doing so, he develops in contrast to the liberal paradigm of bourgeois formal law and its successor, law as it is materialised in the social-welfare state, a third way: a procedural paradigm of law, in which again the forms of communication are brought to the fore, through which private and political autonomy can be expressed. In this context he turns to the critique made by feminist legal theorists, in particular that of Iris Marion Young (1990) and Catharine MacKinnon (1989). Habermas takes up their critique, that each special legal regulation which is intended to compensate for the disadvantages of women, rests on an interpretation of differences. And to the extent that legislation and adjudication are orientated by traditional interpretive patterns,

104 Fraser 1989, p. 122.
105 Fraser 1989, pp. 119–20.
106 Fraser 1989, pp. 123–4.
107 Dackweiler 1995, p. 66.
108 Cohen 1995, p. 81, note 1.
109 Habermas 1996, p. 194.

regulatory law even consolidates the existing *stereotype of gender identity*.[110] He suggests instead that the difference between the genders needs to be conceived as a relationship involving two equally problematic variables and in need of interpretation. In this way the orientation towards normal masculinity can be avoided.[111]

However, as all his hopes, as shown, are based on legal rights, he does not share a more extensive critique of rights which 'also throw[s] out the idea of realising rights in *any way*' – thus Habermas' interpretation of the feminist approach. Rather, he proposes his discursive model of rights and believes that discussions of gender are also well-placed within the proceduralist paradigm, namely that '*public discussions must first clarify* the aspects under which differences ... become relevant'. He now understands gender identity as a social construction, which also has to be consciously formed. Binary gender as such is, however, not questioned, as the constructions are considered to 'crystallise around biological differences'.[112] He demands instead programmes which articulate the relevant aspects for defining equal and unequal treatment beforehand. Habermas's central concern is that no binding gender identity is socially predefined; neither an essentialist nor an 'androgynous' one. And he offers feminist theorists the parting advice that 'competing views about the identity of the sexes and their relation to each other must be open to public discussion. Even the feminist avant-garde does not have a monopoly on definition'.[113] According to his utopia, all social conflicts, including between genders, must be conducted in rational, legal procedures.

In principle one has to agree with Cohen that Habermas here really provides an ambitious contribution in the theory of democracy to the debate about difference; that is, his suggestion to dissolve all essentialisms by giving them over to public discussions. Yet this suggestion suffers again from an inflated understanding of law. For only when right is not on the side of the power technologies, only when it can assume the procedural guarantees that the potential of action orientated towards understanding can also prevail under power-based social conditions, because the better argument, which could moreover actually be determined, can be institutionalised – only then would it be possible to break up the 'male dominance ... intrinsic ... to capitalism'[114] by means of legal procedures. Only then would a hegemonic discourse be excluded from

110 Habermas 1996, p. 423.
111 Habermas 1996, p. 424.
112 Habermas 1996, p. 125.
113 Habermas 1996, p. 426.
114 Fraser 1989, p. 128.

those procedures, where it could otherwise also secure its power of definition. MacKinnon contests this very possibility because of its approach to *theories of power*: what is crucial is not difference, but its hierarchisation. Hierarchy is a product of power relations and those need to be attacked, instead of being governed by the hope that they could simply be banned from the arena of legal discourse.[115]

But while this problem could potentially still be at least partially solved through certain ways of organising procedures, a fundamental question is raised. Has Habermas really overcome his blindness to gender with this passage? For his fundamental reflections on legal theory continue to treat 'actors', 'addressees', and 'authors' of rights as gender-neutral beings. Habermas remains indifferent to a central criticism of feminist theory; namely that the 'neutral and universal subject of reason' has to be situated in social conflicts and demystified in them as male.[116] Even though Habermas does not engage in philosophy of the subject, but locates reason in communicative processes, he still bases them on those genderless speakers.[117] The subjects are also neutralised in regard to gender, because the social – and that always also means patriarchal – conditions of their production are not considered as a theme. Discourse is seen as an instrument of reflection and for coordinating actions of those subjects and appears external to them, instead of reflecting how the matrix of power and discourse, in this case of right, only brings about that subject capable of speech and action.[118]

Those blind spots are the result of a theorising strategy that still clings to a conception which ignores gender as a structuring category. Habermas' confrontation with feminist legal theorists treats gender relations just as Luhmann does, as one sub-theme amongst others. While the great theory of law continues to deal only with the 'male-human-general',[119] the gender relations that correspond to the hegemonic division of intellectual labour are de-dramatised as a 'special case' – while furthermore the so-called 'feminist avant-garde' is lectured that it has no special right to the critique of those conditions. Nancy Fraser's demand that Habermas's theory be expanded with 'gender-sensitive categories'[120] still awaits its realisation.

115 See also Elsuni 2006.
116 Benhabib 1988, p. 1.
117 Narr 1994b, p. 94.
118 Butler 1992, pp. 13 ff.
119 Dackweiler 2003, p. 88.
120 Fraser 1989, p. 128.

3.5 *Radical Democracy*

Where Habermas is mainly ahead of Luhmann is his possession of a normative perspective that does not limit itself to the self-reproduction of the systems, but looks for a solution, and which allows for social self-organisation in light of the systems. The question is, however, whether Habermas too quickly contents himself at this juncture with socio-cultural preconditions – against the background of a non-systemically analysed right, which is meant to offset the frictions of the systems.

For this purpose the insistence on the inevitability of systemic differentiation appears decisive. The Marxian utopia of a far-reaching self-organisation, that is, of a future association of producers who have brought the conditions of the material life process under their common control,[121] is denounced as a 'future state of affairs in which the objective semblance of capital has dissolved and the lifeworld, which had been held captive under the dictates of the law of value, gets back its spontaneity'.[122]

Habermas has 'checked off' [*'abgehakt'*] this utopia,[123] and attempts instead to enclose and de-dramatise the systems. His theory therefore becomes 'purely defensive' in character, because he 'resigns' himself to leaving the areas it defines as at any rate systemically independent to themselves.[124] This results not only in the loss of a further-reaching utopia of social freedom, but at the same time, as Ingeborg Maus can show by way of the political system, the dangers the systems represent are underestimated. For Kant's and Rousseau's theories of freedom, which still start from the possibility of a free association similarly to that of Marx,[125] systemic independences of this kind were suspect. They considered them accordingly as asymmetries, which referred to the relationship of 'the grassroots of society and the state apparatus', of 'the people' and 'functionaries'. In contrast (thus Maus's critique) the 'discourse-theoretical criteria are geared to those *symmetries* which are linked to the connotations of the "ideal speech situation"'.[126]

This is clearly demonstrated when Habermas believes he can compensate for his adherence to the modern state and its barracked force by dissolving 'the state's physical coercion … through symmetrical relationships by deriving all political power from the communicatively generated power of the cit-

121 Habermas 1996, pp. 46–7.
122 Habermas 1987, p. 340.
123 Narr 1994b, p. 96.
124 Maus 1986c, p. 313.
125 Habermas 1996, p. 44.
126 Maus 1996, p. 870.

izens'.[127] However, this by no means solves, and at best covers up, the problem of 'how the remaining risk of violence in contest with power can be resolved, in particular since the state apparatus undeniably holds the monopoly on the use of force', while communicative power is characterised by how 'no one can actually "possess"' it.[128] The asymmetries, that is, the opposition of a 'people' of nonfunctionaries to the state's monopoly on the use of force, have to form the basis of radically democratic reflections, because otherwise the separation of communicative and administrative power 'has to face up to the harsh resistances of a brittle reality', to the extent that the results of public discourses can actually be maintained at the boundaries of administrative systems that have taken on a life of their own, and there emerge separate circles of communicative power on the one hand, and of 'what in the eighteenth-century was still called the "force" of the state', on the other.[129]

For this reason Maus also insists on an 'empirical consensus',[130] because it cannot be determined democratically who should decide, whether the discursive requirements are met, and this then again falls into the hands of administrative power. She considers a narrowly defined self-interested orientation of the participants as sufficient and counts on fair procedures – not on practical discourses.[131]

Habermas believes that Marx only criticised the hidden class relations in the systemic condition, and completely overlooks the crucial aspect, the 'socio-philosophical' critique that actors are dispossessed of their own conditions, that their own practice coagulates into a second nature, which they can no longer understand. That is the decisive reason a materialist theory cannot content itself with an (however pragmatic) evolutionary differentiation of the system: because the democratic-theoretical aim of *genuine social self-organisation* can only mean that the participants can communicate across *all* social areas, for example also about whether they want to temporarily 'free' certain processes from communicative action. It cannot be allowed that only scientific 'avant-gardes' can recognise and analyse the systems, in order to then decide in an expertocratic fashion to leave it at that.

This means that Habermas's conception of democracy needs to be expanded by also applying the concept of procedures to the systems.[132] Even Luhmann's

127 Maus 1996, p. 872.
128 Maus 1996, p. 874.
129 Maus 1996, pp. 876–7.
130 Maus 1992b, p. 129.
131 Niesen and Eberl 2006, p. 19.
132 Thus also Maus 1986c, p. 316; Rödel, Frankenberg and Dubiel 1989.

legal theory carries with its theorem of the paradox a subversive moment, against its author's will, which shows that the continued existence of the systems is a priori precarious. It is therefore necessary to find a mode which can initially procedurally bring about *social* knowledge amongst the non-functionaries regarding the mechanisms of independence [*Verselbständigung*], and then retain it over time, in order to give them a chance to decide whether systems are an evolutionary advance. Democracy must not be reduced only to the processes of opinion formation and decision-making, but has to comprise all those social processes which could otherwise counteract its results.

CHAPTER 4

The End and the Beginning

It must be stated clearly that the two discussed approaches are distinguished by complex, finely intertwined analyses to which legal theory owes crucial insights. Neither submits to the positivist self-limitation of microsociology or 'middle range' theory [English in original], but both 'aim for everything'[1] – although systems theory in particular could give the impression of dissolving society in subsystems. However, Luhmann rightly insists that he wants to undertake 'a theory of society rather than of any particular special sociology'.[2] In consequence it becomes a problem for both of them how this society can be reproduced. They therefore confront in their legal theories in different ways the problem that capitalist societies can no longer guarantee their unity a priori. Whereas Luhmann wants to solve this under the category of the 'system', Habermas negotiates the issue with the more classical term 'integration'.

At the same time those approaches constitute the two paradigmatic perspectives on law/rights. Thus, legal systems theory finds a remarkable way to illustrate the autonomisation of social relations. Legal communications connect to each other to form the network of legal discourse, which only allows arguments immanent to law and seals itself off from the non-legal environment. This stops instrumentalist arguments which consider law as a mere reflex of a base, whatever it may be like, or as an immediately accessible object for political actors. However if this happens nonetheless at any point, one can show with Luhmann that the exception already occurred in the law, and that means its erosion, which only leaves dummies of legality. In its normal mode, however, the law abstracts precisely from all that cannot be transformed into legal communication and develops a certain 'logic of its own', which initially eludes individuals and can no longer be immediately understood by them. 'From this perspective, Luhmann's systems theory can perhaps be considered as a still affirmative, but also perfectly adequate description of the condition of absolute reification of social conditions'.[3]

With regards to this reification of the law, Habermas makes the necessity of social mechanisms for consensus clear; modern capitalist societies, which are characterised by the existence of developed civil societies, depend very

1 Adorno 2003, p. 143.
2 Luhmann 2004, p. vii.
3 Demirović 2001b, p. 26; also Maus 1986a, p. 59.

much upon democratic 'self-misunderstandings'; and legitimation in the sense of a social consensus even of the dominated is a necessary condition for the successful connection of communicative operations with each other. Even if his concept of system and lifeworld remains too dualistic, a very much crucial insight is nonetheless owed to Habermas: the existence of different consensus technologies, which are either oriented towards communicative agreement or towards the avoidance of communication. In this respect he analyses law in its normative substance as a utopia of democratic theory, focused on the self-organised society.

Each approach is correct in its objection to the other: neither is law a procedure that runs purely systemically, and which can do without social hegemonic consensus, but nor can it be normatively elevated, as is the case in Habermas. It *should* be the medium of self-organisation; but it cannot achieve that precisely because of the independence Luhmann demonstrates.

A materialist theory of law, which starts from this point and with this 'baggage', therefore has to look for the 'de-paradoxification'; of this paradox: How then does law become *simultaneously* independent, systemically sealing itself off, *and yet* in possession of a limited potential for emancipation? How is it *simultaneously* a 'technology of power' *and* a moment limiting domination? How is it *simultaneously* based upon consensus and on the immobilisation of this consensus? It has to be possible to carry the criticisms that have been raised along this arduous and contradictory path, while at the same time elaborating the problems behind them in another 'descriptive mode'. This applies most of all to the elimination or ghettoisation of subjects and the blocking out of the gender relation, as well as the complete marginalisation of relations of power. In contrast to the two big paradigms 'which are consolidated on the basis of a strong conceptual arsenal',[4] however, the reader now has to brace themselves for the arduous journey into the tangle of reconstruction and construction of what, in the Marxist tradition, has been elaborated concerning law over the last hundred years.

4 Neves 2000, p. 9.

PART 2

ReConstructing Materialist Legal Theory

CHAPTER 5

Introduction to Part 2

> The Marxist theory of law ultimately has to prevail in confrontation with competing bourgeois theories. To what extent it does so cannot yet be decided. For this purpose, the knowledge of this science – the examination of the attempts made thus far – is too negligible.[1]

∴

Let us begin by *re*constructing the materialist theory of law. Following Habermas' definition, the first step will consist in analytically 'unpicking' previous theories. This means their premises are presented and critiqued in order to test which insights and limits they provide for an updated legal theory, always within the framework of the issues outlined in part 1. At the same time, the theories will also be confronted with each other. The next chapter will then provide a reflection on the results and bring them together in a new 'construction'. In the representation of the theories I follow a chronological order, which allows me to trace the development of questions and problems as well as their various updates. In this I will limit myself solely to exemplary approaches – a comprehensive review of all of them is not possible here. The selection is, however, intended to reflect the range of discussions.

Let us start the representation with the 1920s, when for the first time a wide-ranging debate about the relationship of law and social structure in capitalist societies took place in Germany. Of course, a materialist legal theory might be expected to start with Karl Marx. However, if this were possible, many 'attempts at deduction' would probably not even have been undertaken, many arguments about interpretation never fought. Marx had no explicit, comprehensive legal theory, such as for example Kant's or Hegel's, any more than he possessed a theory of the state, whose function he planned to dedicate a separate study to.[2] While many passages where he addresses law can be found, such as in the

1 Reich 1972a, p. 18.

2 See MECW, vol. 42, p. x; Korsch 1970, pp. I–II; Negt 1975, p. 31; Harms 2000, p. 168; Reich 1973, pp. 7, 15; Balbus 1977, p. 575.

Critique of Hegel's Philosophy of Right, On the Jewish Question, or the *Critique of the Gotha Program*, they are not based upon a systematically developed legal theory.

In consequence, Marxist-oriented jurists and theorists of the state[3] have subsequently begun to make use not of Marx's words, but of his method, his political and economic analyses, or his historical studies in order to approach the perspective of law. They thus embarked upon the journey towards a materialist theory of law. This is the path I will retrace and then take anew.

The next stage is represented by the historic period of the 1970s, which was again shaped by social conflicts and debates, here now predominately about the role of the state. This is another heyday of Marxist legal theory. This time, however, two different directions emerge: on the one hand an Italian and French current based upon Althusser's structuralism and Gramsci's concept of hegemony, and on the other hand the Hegelian-Marxist tradition of critical theory. Their relationship remains somewhat unreconciled until now. As I consider this controversy no longer fruitful, as will be demonstrated in greater detail, I will attempt to represent the two strands separately in their differences, but bring them back together in the following chapter on reconstruction. Even more decisive for legal theory was, however, the so-called 'crisis of Marxism' at the start of the 1980s, as Althusser also called it.[4] In doing so he above all demanded a confrontation of Marxism with the history made in its name since the Russian October Revolution, as well as a consideration of the new social movements, whose politics can no longer simply be subsumed under the Marxian matrix. Finally, he pointed out the deficits of Marxism until then in relation to the sphere which Marx had called the 'superstructure', that is, the areas of state, law and ideology, which are seemingly merely derived from the 'economic base'. In doing so Althusser did not consider the crisis as an end point, but precisely as a possibility to revitalise theory through the challenges of the new social struggles and to liberate it from dogmatic strictures.[5] Both (post)structuralism in France and critical theory in Germany stand for an undogmatic and fruitful approach to this issue. That legal theory, however, has nonetheless not recovered from this crisis, is the main motivation for the present study. The dialectic of 'facticity and norms' might really make law an 'even "stranger" matter than a commodity'.[6] It was very tempting to undervalue

3 The lack of female theorists is particularly striking.
4 Althusser 1978.
5 See also Laclau and Mouffe 2001.
6 Maus 1995, p. 829.

its independent significance compared to political economy and the state. An understanding of the facticity of norms makes high demands of any legal theory.

Moreover, it is a precarious subject for any social order which claims to overcome its inherent violence to understand that 'law is at the intersection of emancipation and violence'.[7] Marxist legal theory, however, which at its beginnings dedicated itself to the deconstruction of idealist legal theory, and mainly fought the notion of law's social independence, neutrality and freedom from domination, had to expect important obstacles:

> Law traditionally appears to be sceptical of anything that gives itself revolutionary airs. On the other hand Marxists have also contributed significantly to this (mis)understanding, when they understood law … solely as an ideology of domination and denounced it accordingly.[8]

Therefore Pashukanis already noted that 'there is very little Marxist literature on the general theory of law', and that 'hence Marxism is just beginning to conquer new territory'.[9] Even up to the 1970s, those active at the time pointed to this statement by Pashukanis and applied it with certain modifications to the situation at the time: 'The legacy of Marx and Engels still awaits its scholarly exploration on the territory of legal theory';[10] or, less optimistically: Marxist legal theory is 'the stepchild of Marxist theoretical development'.[11] Even in 1992 Andrea Maihofer still harboured an 'unease' with regards to Marxist legal theory thus far. Not only had it ended in a theoretical dead end, it had also become increasingly irrelevant. This was all the more tragic as it 'could be a productive alternative in the contemporary legal theory debate and an important critical corrective'.[12] The problem goes so deep that none of the aforementioned authors still engages in materialist legal theory. Either they have said goodbye to legal theory or to the materialist approach – a development which is somewhat atypical compared to other subject areas. It appears to be a delicate undertaking to attempt to combine those two moments. But precisely this is the aim of this study. In order to do so, however, central deficits have to be overcome.

---

7 Negt 1975, p. 31.
8 Harms 2000, p. 11.
9 Pashukanis 2003, pp. 37–8.
10 Reich 1972b, pp. 154, 197, 3.
11 Negt 1975, p. 31.
12 Maihofer 1992, p. 9.

Those are the following:
- Marxist legal theory has often argued functionally and reduced law to the reproduction of capitalism.
- This was not infrequently coupled with the failure to conceive of the materialist 'primacy of existence' (Charim), that is, the precedence of the material context of reproduction, in a non-economistic manner.
- This almost invariably also leads to a failure to consider other structuring principles for legal theory, such as the hierarchically structured differences (gender, race, sexuality), and thus manifests itself in class reductionism.
- Very similar to systems theory or to the democratic-normative legal theory of Habermas, materialist theories, including Foucault, have ignored practice and its actors.
- Moreover, the role of the nation state in relation to law was overestimated in such a way that legal theory was reduced to a subsection of state theory.
- Accordingly, almost all theories failed to grasp a central mystery of law, namely its relational autonomy, that is, its counterfactual facticity.
- And finally, they very rarely had an answer to the fundamental question as to what role law plays for a strategy of emancipation.

The main deficit of the materialist approach in legal theory consists, to sum up, in that its social theory does not do justice to the complexity of relations of domination.[13] As has been shown in the first part, the approach shares this difficulty with other legal theories. To think the 'relative autonomy of relations of power', repudiating the idea that power has a single source, and instead starting from an intersection of relations of power[14] – this will be a central concern of this reconstruction. This critique of the described approaches will *highlight* – as was already the case in part 1 – how gender relations are conceptualised/ignored, because criticism by women and gender studies of the androcentric perspective of the major theories is extensive, and because they also addressed their own constraints in relation to other relationships of domination. I am aware of this methodological limitation. A multidimensional intersectional critique is not possible in the context of the present study. It would require a more extensive research design, namely one that in the tradition of feminist theory depends upon 'fantasies of collective work, cooperation, and knowledge exchange in numerous subject areas'.[15]

13 Engel, Schulz and Wedl 2005, p. 12; Knapp 2005, p. 75.
14 Engel, Schulz and Wedl 2005, p. 12.
15 Knapp 2005, p. 77.

The following *re*construction will develop the deficits noted above and test how far they can be overcome. Their unfulfilled potential will thus become apparent, and although it could not unfold due to the crisis of Marxism, it lives on in the legacy of those theories.

CHAPTER 6

Foundations: The 1920s and 30s

The period between the two world wars, which saw the Russian Revolution, the global economic crisis, and the rise of National Socialism and the constitutional changes it brought, led in Germany to numerous discussions of methodology and general reflections on law. These also involved Marxist theorists.

1 The Constitutional Theories of Neumann and Kirchheimer

At the time social-democratic legal theorists (Otto Kirchheimer, Ernst Fraenkel, Franz Neumann, Otto Kahn-Freund, Martin Drath, Hans Mayer, Hugo Sinzheimer, Herman Heller) were primarily engaged in a debate about the Weimar Constitution – in opposition to Carl Schmitt's theory.[1] This debate led to the general thesis that the Weimar Constitution was the legal expression of a class compromise between the working class and the bourgeoisie,[2] which had to be pursued as a legal strategy for transformation[3] to support an extensive restriction of private property and the socialisation of the means of production.[4] In the following, the two Marxist authors and their contribution to this discussion will be presented.

Franz Neumann and Otto Kirchheimer worked at the Institute for Social Research, although they were never really integrated in the circle of the old Frankfurt School. The two lawyers were mainly tasked with legal services there.[5] The relationship of the Horkheimer circle to Kirchheimer and Neumann is described by Wiggerhaus as 'a provisional arrangement, courteous and aloof'.[6] This cannot primarily be explained by the fact that both authors took up partially social-democratic reformist positions; mainly it arises from the fact that the question of law – as was typical for the non-dogmatic left in Germany – remained a void for the old Frankfurt School,[7] so that one can even speak with

1 Luthardt 1976, p. 11.
2 Perels 1973, p. 36.
3 Bast 1999, p. 59.
4 Thus for example Hermann Heller, see Maus 1986b, p. 175.
5 Söllner 1978; Wiggershaus 1995, p. 234.
6 Wiggerhaus 1995, p. 236.
7 Maus 1995, p. 826.

Maus of their 'legal nihilism'.[8] This relationship of the old critical theory to Neumann and Kirchheimer still reproduces itself today (also outside Germany),[9] for example when they are relegated to a footnote in an article about critical theory and law, with the argument that their theories 'do not necessarily represent an application of the larger Frankfurt School approach to critical theory'.[10] But they are also denied recognition in the bourgeois mainstream: 'That the theorist who in emigration wrote the most important ... analysis of the NS-system [Neumann, S.B.] is practically unknown in the Federal Republic and at the same time receives little academic attention, is a stain upon this Republic and at the same time symptomatic for its spirit', concluded Jürgen Seifert in 1984.[11]

Neither Neumann nor Kirchheimer could have recourse to a materialist *legal* theory: 'The German Marxist movement has somehow failed to produce significant achievements in the fields of legal and state theory ...', Neumann wrote in 1935.[12] They were therefore both, as far as legal theory was concerned, significantly influenced by bourgeois theorists, Neumann by the tradition of Max Weber, Kirchheimer by Carl Schmitt. Those different starting points led them in part to greatly divergent positions.

Their shared inquiry was historically specific, as it was concerned with the theory of the constitutional *state*. The question of an adequate theory of democracy and a new concept of the rule of law was the order of the day at the beginning of the Weimar Republic,[13] while the question of the form of law itself was not addressed. Evgeny Pashukanis is the first theorist to raise this question, with the publication of his *General Theory of Law and Marxism*.[14] This had consequences for the development of their theories: while bourgeois theory and philosophy can refer, for example with Kant and Hegel, or with Kelsen and Ehrlich, to long discourses about the question of what law is, the materialist theorists had to fend for themselves.

From the legal theory perspective, the question of the constitutional state is an aspect of how the state's violence is bound to legal norms. In order to adequately respond to this, it is generally necessary to firstly clarify the significance of the law and in particular its materiality. If it is considered purely an

8 Ibid.
9 Scheuerman 1997 is an exception.
10 Whitehead 1999, p. 721, note 96.
11 Seifert 1984, pp. 9–10.
12 Neumann 1978, p. 134.
13 Staff 1985, pp. 7–8.
14 Thus also Neumann 1938, p. 135.

ideology or even exclusively a phenomenon of the superstructure, the question of its binding effect is obsolete. Only when capitalist law is considered to have its own materiality can it also have independent, non-derivative effects on other areas. To use a description by Luhmann, referring to 'other sociological analyses of law', the analysis of society's influences on law or conversely assumes that 'the law is already constituted as something that is more or less susceptible to the influences of society. *However, the more fundamental question as to how law is at all possible in society* is then neither questioned nor answered'.[15] This means that firstly *the legal form* itself needs to be analysed. However, such considerations are not the focus of Neumann's and Kirchheimer's theories, but remain somewhat implicit.

1.1 *Franz Neumann*

For Neumann the modern state is as such a constitutional one, as its constitutive elements are sovereignty and freedom,[16] or, as he later puts, force and law.[17] In contrast to liberal notions of the rule of law or to Habermas' thesis that administrative power could be subordinated to communicative power, Neumann disputes any possible reconciliation of the two principles. They are in irresolvable contradiction,[18] and the liberal understanding that power can be dissolved in legal relations is thus illusory. It is therefore not surprising that Habermas 'for obvious reasons' cannot base himself upon Franz Neumann.[19] Accordingly, the legal theorist of the Frankfurt School is no longer mentioned in *Between Facts and Norms*.[20]

The contradiction – in principle based upon bourgeois statehood – that both the monopoly on violence and also the general law are fundamental coordinates of the bourgeois legal system,[21] is the starting point for the history of the decline of the constitutional state for which Franz Neumann became known. At the end of this history is the National Socialist German 'state', whose statehood he rejects, calling it instead a 'regime'. Instead of a 'realm of law' and a

15 Luhmann 2004, pp. 72–3 (emphasis S.B.).
16 Neumann 1936, p. 2.
17 Neumann 1957, p. 101.
18 Neumann 1957, p. 102.
19 Thus Ingeborg Maus in agreement 1995, p. 826.
20 Contrary to the 'early' Habermas, who included in parts of his theory in *The Structural Transformation of the Public Sphere* Neumann's analysis of the degeneration of the constitutional state, in the context of the Neumann Rennaissance of the time (Fisahn 1993, p. 189).
21 Neumann 1957, p. 102.

unified coercive machinery, it merely disposes of individual measures and various competing authoritarian bodies.[22]

Neumann laid out his concept of law by drawing on the definition developed in the liberal tradition,[23] that is to say, that law differs from other social norms (in particular morality) mainly in its coercive power, namely in that it is ultimately secured through the monopoly of force.[24] Accordingly the 'state' is a sovereign institution which exercises the highest legal force, which means that it has the historic right to enact laws and individual norms,[25] and also the power to enforce them.[26] Neumann stresses that this is a 'legal power', not a natural one as conceived by Carl Schmitt with his notion of the exception. When the abnormal becomes the only and decisive element, this cannot explain legal reality under normal conditions.[27]

Constitutionality or rule of law [English in original] means first and foremost the prevalence of the general law, the lawfulness of administration and judiciary, and the existence of formal, rational law. State intervention has to be predictable, calculable and under the control of independent judges.[28] According to Neumann the suggested contradiction of the modern constitutional state is revealed precisely in its ambivalence, which he aims to show in three aspects of bourgeois law.[29] For besides its protective function, which is safeguarded by legality, it also has a concealing function, as it hides the 'real conditions' of class society,[30] that is, the rule of the bourgeoisie. Invoking the rule of law makes it superfluous to directly acknowledge this actual ruling power.[31] Thirdly, law in the constitutional state also makes the exchange processes in a competitive economy predictable, which serves in particular the ruling class.[32] Its ambivalent relationship to the constitutional state, which haunts materialist legal theory like no other problem, stems, for Neumann the class theorist, ultimately from the fact that it is a creation of the bourgeoisie,[33] which requires

22 Neumann 2009, p. 468.

23 The act of defining itself references Max Weber: 'We wish to define law …' (Neumann 1936, p. 15); see also e.g. Kelsen 1981, p. 87.

24 Neumann 1936, pp. 15–6.

25 Neumann 1936, p. 41.

26 Neumann 1936, p. 43.

27 Neumann 1936, pp. 45–6.

28 Neumann 1936, p. 347.

29 Neumann 1936, p. 407.

30 Ibid.

31 Neumann 1936, pp. 492–3.

32 Neumann 1936, p. 407.

33 Neumann 1957, p. 118.

sovereignty in order to destroy local and particular powers and establish a uniform administration and judiciary, as well as to secure civil liberties for its economic freedom.[34] The atemporal element, which also guarantees a certain measure of freedom and security for the working class,[35] that is to say the third function, is rather an unintended side effect. In his essay 'The Change in the Function of Law' Neumann calls it 'ethical', as it guarantees a minimum of personal and political freedom that is only formal, but nonetheless contains at least guarantees of negative freedoms. Hegel, who recognised the inadequacy of a merely formal and negative determination of the concept of freedom with the greatest clarity, had already warned earlier against underestimating this determination:[36] 'The generality of the law and the independence of the judge contained both elements transcending the functions of obscuring the actual distribution of power and the maintenance of calculability'. The rationality of law also benefits to a high degree the poor and workers.[37] Precisely this possibility of transcending bourgeois law was the theoretical starting point of social-democratic legal theorists: If the bourgeoisie uses law to secure its economic freedom (and in England also its political freedom), it cannot prevent other classes from also referring to it, as it is after all founded in the *generality* of the law.[38] The hopes for a peaceful transition to socialism are based on this; merely negative formal freedom at least always preserves the consciousness of the unfulfilled utopia of positive freedom and equality.[39] But according to Neumann – following Marx's analysis of Bonapartism here – it is precisely this 'ethical' moment which the bourgeoisie is willing to sacrifice when it threatens its economic domination. This is the central point of the history of decay. Wiggershaus therefore reaches the conclusion that '[t]here could only be hope if something similar to the liberal constitutional state could be recreated, but with a ruling class which would recoil with horror from the fascist solution'.[40]

1.2 *Otto Kirchheimer*

In marked contrast to this is Otto Kirchheimer; for him, the bourgeois constitutional state is hardly more than simply an instrument of the bourgeoisie. The

34 Neuman 1957, p. 101.
35 Neumann 1936, p. 510.
36 Neumann 1957, p. 118.
37 Neumann 1957, p. 121.
38 Thus also Fishan 1993, p. 71.
39 Neumann 1936, pp. 377–8.
40 Wiggershaus 1995, p. 226.

difference lies in Carl Schmitt's influence on him. His doctorate was submitted to Schmitt in 1928[41] and constitutes, as Wiggershaus pointedly observes, a 'kind of radical left-wing answer to Schmitt's critique of Weimar parliamentary democracy'.[42] The merely formal democracy, the formal constitutional state, the merely technical law, are shaped by actual social class struggles: they are all the expression of an equilibrium.[43] This is obviously an application of Marx's historic analysis of conditions before 1848 in France, which concludes that the democratic institutions are means of 'weakening the conflict between capital and labour, and of creating a harmony between the two extremes, but not of transcending them both'.[44] The former arms of the bourgeoisie against the feudal system[45] experience in this situation a change in function.[46] For, when the constitution is not based on any general shared 'values', the state becomes nothing but a form to actualise class antagonisms,[47] and the mechanism of the constitutional state ensures that governmental power has as little real decision-making power as possible. Decisions are wrested from the respective social distribution of forces and removed into the 'sphere of law'. All 'power-decisions' are circumvented by 'juridically formalising' the disputed issue. This is the 'real era of the constitutional state':

> For this kind of state consists exclusively in its laws. Decisions are felt to be bearable only because they appear colorless and nonauthoritative, and because they seem to emanate from independent judges freely deciding on the basis of their conviction. Thus, the paradox has arisen that the value of the decision lies in its character as a legal ruling handed down by a generally recognised legal authority, while on the other hand it embodies only a minimum of decisional content. The state lives off the law; yet it is no longer law [*Recht*], it is only a legal mechanism, so that those who think they are guiding the affairs of the state actually wield only a legal machinery ...[48]

Kirchheimer thus here distinguishes law from the mere 'legal mechanism'. Law is thus a substantive decision, while the legal mechanism is the technique to

41 Kirchheimer 1969, pp. 3–21.
42 Wiggershaus 1995, p. 230.
43 Kirchheimer 1969, p. 4.
44 Marx 2002, p. 45.
45 Kirchheimer 1969, pp. 3–4.
46 Kirchheimer 1969, p. 7.
47 Kirchheimer 1969, p. 8.
48 Kirchheimer 1969, pp. 6–7.

make decisions seem non-authoritative, give them the appearance of neutrality and leave them to seemingly independent third parties, who appear removed from political conflicts. At stake is the 'transposition of things from actuality into the legal-mechanistic',[49] of political conflicts into the institutional framework and a terminology of legal process with its own momentum, where they are dealt with according to the autonomous rules of the legal machinery.[50] Kirchheimer rejects the 'legal mechanism' for two reasons. On the one hand it suggests a neutrality that is not actually the case, on the other there are no longer any substantive decisions made as a result, and the state machinery declines into an administrative apparatus.

This understanding can be illustrated once again by Kirchheimer's positive description of Russian law at the time. Here the judiciary is the organ of the workers. There is a break away from the idea of the judiciary as an independent third party above the parties in the conflict. That rulings are made in the name of specific values is openly visible. Soviet judges are practised in 'revolutionary consciousness'.[51] The law is furthermore not one for eternity, but is temporally limited: 'Soviet law does not stand in need of a special *clausula rebus sic stantibus*[52] since it is itself the law of the *clausula rebus sic stantibus*'.[53]

1.3 *The Relationship of Law and Social Structure*

The central difference between Neumann and Kirchheimer lies in their respective conception of the relationship of social structure and law. Both start from class constellations as the determining social conditions. For Kirchheimer, political and legal structures can at best make them processable. Therefore, the bourgeois constitutional state does not contain any genuine moment of freedom either. The 'concealing function' Neumann describes appears to be the only one for Kirchheimer. For him there is no ambivalence, while Neumann assumes a greater autonomy of the legal field. In the following, this relation will therefore be examined more closely once again.

49 Kirchheimer 1969, pp. 7–8.

50 Teubner 1993b, p. 510.

51 Kirchheimer 1969, p. 17.

52 'Things thus standing'. General legal principle of civil law since Roman law, whereby the legal consequences depend upon the fact that the fundamental circumstances do not change. This provision was only posited in the Federal Republic of Germany with the Civil Procedure reform in 2002 (§ 313 German Civil Code); previously it was established through case law as 'absence of valid subject matter'. This played a particularly prominent role in rulings of the Supreme Court of the German Reich in Kirchheimer's time.

53 Kirchheimer 1969, p. 18.

Neumann assumes a 'total interpretation of all social phenomena'. 'Political, religious and mental ideas as well as family relations are realities to which the legal norm is equally subjected'.[54] Law is a dependent moment of a totality, but 'may develop relatively independently of social reality'.[55] Accordingly, legal norm and reality do not always match. One can change without the other – in which case one can speak of a 'change of the function' of the legal norm.[56] Only in this way can the coercive character of the law ultimately be explained, which is necessary because of the general non-conformance of 'all citizens' in a society (even in a socialist one).[57]

Beyond those general considerations, Neumann's materialist perspective is also visible in his methodological approach: he attempts to do justice to the concept of totality by way of parallel legal, economic and political descriptions. Both in *The Rule of Law* and in *Behemoth* he adopts this division. In doing so he makes clear that no sphere can be considered independently of the others. While Kirchheimer refers mainly to Marx's political writings, Neumann, who is much more influenced by Weber than by Marx,[58] reveals his connection to Marx primarily in his acknowledgement of the economy's central importance. This can also be shown in his historic analysis. Thus, law can also be completely abolished when social power relations change. In relation to National Socialism his book on the constitutional state ends with the conclusion: 'That law does not exist in Germany, because law is now exclusively a technique of transforming the political will of the Leader into constitutional reality'.[59] In his examination of National Socialism he radicalises this result with the thesis of the decay of rational law. The latter is designed for the liberal era, namely free competition, the existence of a large number of more or less equal competitors and the freedom of the commodity market. Here freedom of contract and the calculability of administrating justice are essential requirements.[60] With the removal of those elements in favour of 'organised state capitalism' and a monopoly economy[61] the general

54 Neumann 1936, p. 26.
55 Ibid.
56 Neumann 1936, p. 28.
57 Neumann 1936, p. 30.
58 Perhaps rather by Harold Laski and Karl Renner (Söllner 1980, p. 371).
59 Neumann 1936, p. 581.
60 Neumann 2009, p. 443.
61 Here Neumann addresses – similarly to Richard Löwenthal at the same time, or to the social-democrat and communist theory of imperialism during the nineteenth and early twentieth century (Hilferding, Kautsky, Bernstein, Luxemburg, Renner, Bucharin, Lenin) – capitalism's immanent transition from 'pure capitalism' to monopoly capitalism (Löwenthal 1977, pp. 26 ff.).

law also disappears in favour of the command of the leader and the general principle.[62] General norms are nonsensical:

> The individual, irrational norm is calculable for the monopolist, for he is strong enough to do without formal rationality. The monopolist cannot only do without rational law, it is often even a shackle ... for rational law can after all not least also protect the weak. The monopolist can do without the help of the courts, for his command is a sufficient substitute.[63]

The transition from competitive to monopoly capitalism thus undermines from Neumann's perspective the economic basis of the legal order based on the general law.[64]

Law is accordingly a specific phenomenon of the bourgeois, rational state and differs from a 'mere technique' or 'mere ideology' in its relative autonomy. When this is dissolved, power relations can no longer be described as legal.[65] As social power cannot be dissolved in legal relations, the suspension of law in favour of brute force is always a possible general tendency.[66] The contradiction of force and freedom is then dissolved in favour of the former.

Kirchheimer's perspective is about the 'tensions between political and social reality and the standard text of the constitution'.[67] Under the impression of a dwindling balance of forces, Kirchheimer's perspective on the constitutional state changes. He no longer criticises its formality, but rather attempts to reveal its dependence on the underlying social conditions, which led to its decline in the Weimar Republic: the bourgeoisie had constituted itself as a uniform class in 1930 and thus completely changed the basis for the constitutional system. Its position of power then steadily increased, so that it no longer depended on reaching compromises.[68] As the Weimar Constitution encompassed different value systems side by side (bourgeois-liberal principles, but also social fundamental rights), a programme that brought the entire population together was missing from the start. This had consequences under the changed conditions, as the possibility of its implementation depended on the strengths of the dif-

62 Neumann 2009, p. 445.
63 Neumann 2009, pp. 446–7.
64 Thus also Scheuerman 2002, p. 80.
65 Neumann 2009, p. 530.
66 Neumann 1957, p. 110.
67 Luthardt 1976, p. 12.
68 Kirchheimer 1976a, p. 92.

ferent interest groups.[69] Furthermore the precarious political and economic situation of the Great Depression represented for Kirchheimer an 'objective problem', which 'threatened to even bring the democratic governance of a state to the brink of collapse'.[70] Thus he opposed the 'conceptually realist' perspective of Carl Schmitt, who had asserted that the difficulties stemmed from specific inconsistencies within the Weimar Constitution.[71] Here Kirchheimer's materialism becomes visible: a change in the organisational designations of a constitution cannot change anything significant about the social structural relationships:

> Democracy as the legal order, which follows reality as its shadow would at the next step of implementation of law and reality only be a shadow of democracy.[72]

Here too law and political-economic 'reality' are presented as dependent upon each other.[73]

Kirchheimer holds, in particular because of the importance he ascribes to class struggle, a pessimistic view of the Weimar Constitution. Thus, he takes great care to disabuse social democracy and labour unions of the notion that they can achieve a socialist society via the bourgeois institutions. He accuses them of believing in a peaceful transition instead of fighting.[74] This notion is based on incorrect facts, such as 'for Marx himself the political world was never more than a reflex of economic development'.[75] And precisely this 'economic development' which is dominated by the class difference runs counter to the legal principles of popular sovereignty and the supremacy of the parliamentary legislature. At the moment, when the legality principle of the ruling class has become a problem, parliamentary democracy is also 'synchronised with the social status-quo-conditions'[76] and that via the mechanism of 'two-step legality'.[77] Thus, for example, the Supreme Court of the German Reich gave itself the judicial competence to investigate duly passed laws and thus placed itself outside the legal framework. 'The destruction of the Weimar Democracy

69 Kirchheimer 1969b, p. 54.
70 Kirchheimer 1976b, p. 101.
71 Ibid.
72 Kirchheimer 1976b, p. 106.
73 Kirchheimer 1969b, pp. 73–4.
74 Kirchheimer 1969a, p. 10.
75 Ibid.
76 Blanke 1984, p. 166.
77 Carl Schmitt's terminology is used against him (Schmitt 2004).

thus stems – and this is Otto Kirchheimer's central thesis – from the *structural incompatibility of capitalism and democracy …*'[78]

In the post-war period in particular Wolfgang Abendroth, Jürgen Seifert and Joachim Pereis took up the concepts of Neumann and Kirchheimer.[79] Abendroth rephrased the thesis of incompatibility in such a way that 'the separation of the political and the economic command creates a state of tension, which cannot be maintained over time in an only formally democratically organised state'.[80] He interprets the welfare state principle of the fundamental law against this background – against conservative constitutional theory – as the recognition of the historic insight that 'the belief in the immanent justice of the existing economic and social order is dispelled',[81] and that this legal order is rather 'put at the disposal of society'.[82]

1.4 *Critique*

Kirchheimer's and Neumann's writings have to be 'primarily seen in the historical context of the debates on constitutional theory and political strategy of their time'.[83] While Pashukanis and Stucka wrote their works in the time immediately after the Russian Revolution – thus Pashukanis briefly served as a 'people's court judge' in 1917 and his main work, published in 1924, was even used as a teaching resource in Soviet legal studies[84] – the social-democratic legal theorists in Germany had to address a bourgeois constitutional compromise between the working class and the bourgeoisie, and in particular the rise of National Socialism. Kirchheimer and Neumann had to make assertions about legal issues, without being able to first discuss the question of the 'concept of law', and without addressing the methodological problems mentioned above. Karl Korsch recognised in this a typical phenomenon of Marxist legal theory.[85] It thus[86] 'went straight past this main problem of a Marxist legal critique and … simply logically presupposed the form of right as law (collective will, legal norm) as it presents itself in the contemporary reality of the capitalist state as an unmediated phenomenon'.[87] Just as bourgeois economists of the pre-

78 Blanke 1984, p. 167 (emphasis in original).
79 Ibid.
80 Abendroth 1968, p. 129.
81 Abendroth 1968, p. 119.
82 Abendroth 1968, pp. 121, 127.
83 Luthardt 1976, p. 10.
84 Harms 2000, pp. 14–5.
85 Korsch 1930.
86 An example is Karl Renner.
87 Korsch 1930, p. IV.

Marxist period had focused on analysing measures of value and in doing so overlooked what was specific about the value form, Marxist legal theory consciously and categorically refrained from any analysis of the legal form itself even a full century later.[88]

1.4.1 Kirchheimer's Schmittianism

However, the above-mentioned omission clearly leads to theoretical difficulties. In particular, with Kirchheimer the idealisation of a quasi-proletarian law of feelings is apparent. The positive reference to a 'revolutionary sense of justice' with its obvious echo of the 'sound popular instinct',[89] as well as the positive reference to the clausula rebus sic stantibus, that is, the provision of arbitrariness,[90] that what yesterday was still legal can already tomorrow be retroactively illegal, represents an uncritical reference to a totalitarian understanding of the state. For after all it was the Russian state apparatuses which were not tied to anything beyond the mediating legal form, except their 'feeling', and were meant to be freed from any bond. Also his critique of the mere 'legal mechanism' was based on a tradition of authoritarian top-down expertocratic justice, where the state apparatus defines for each individual in material provisions what happiness and justice are, precisely by way of the 'values' Kirchheimer privileged.[91] Evidently Kirchheimer thus wants to clarify his view that a socialist society can only be arrived at through class struggle and not through a reliance on law, on a 'lawyers' socialism' (Engels). But in this representation, he is taken in by a flawed understanding of immediacy. He is not able to illustrate the difficult dialectic of the achievements of the bourgeois legal order and its simultaneous moments of domination and repression. Franz Neumann had from the outset a significantly deeper insight into this issue.[92]

Moreover, the description of the political as a 'reflex' relationship is questionable. As a Marxist Kirchheimer assumes a connection of politics and economy. This is, however, somewhat incidentally assumed, rather than explained.

The disadvantage of addressing legal issues without an analysis of the legal form becomes clearly apparent here. Especially his observation that decisions on power are wrested from the distribution of forces and 'transposed' into the

---

88 Ibid.

89 The German term 'gesundes Volksempfinden' is NS terminology. [Translator's note]

90 On the problem of legal methodology see Rüthers 2005, and for a classic 'application' of the dangers of the provision, Kaufmann 1911.

91 This is incidentally a surprisingly matter-of-fact use of a traditionally connoted term for a Marxist, which – as Adorno (2000a, p. 78) aptly notes – does 'not by accident … call to mind economics and the market' and is itself an expression of reification.

92 For Neumann's critique of Kirchheimer, see also Neumann 2009.

sphere of law, for example, could already give indications for an analysis of the legal form. Teubner, for one, puts forward the argument that Kirchheimer was the first in the Marxian tradition who recognised the parallelisation of the legal form and the commodity form: 'The momentum of a social subsection in its expansion on the entire society is the aspect of Marxian theory Kirchheimer creatively pursues in the relationship of politics and law'.[93] It should however be mentioned that in Kirchheimer this happens – unlike with Pashkunanis – rather unconsciously. This is revealed when he denies precisely the legal character of the legal mechanism. He is unable to consistently recognise the relative autonomy of the legal through the transposition into the legal, for law and power can no longer be distinguished in his conceptualisation: law as such becomes a clausula rebus sic stantibus: the immediate effect of socio-structural conditions. Its relative autonomy is only recognised by Neumann.

1.4.2 Neumann: Relative Autonomy

Franz Neumann theorised the 'relative autonomy' of the law independently. Thanks to his more complex understanding of totality, and by engaging with bourgeois discourse, he is able not to dismiss law simply as a mere reflex of the 'economic base'.[94] In this respect one has to explicitly disagree with Ingeborg Maus, who accuses Neumann of giving 'too little consideration to this machinery's self-interest as a factor in its own right', so that the freedom-securing dimension of law remains 'a strangely foreign, theoretically unqualified aspect' in his theory.[95] Neumann insists that the two elements of coercion and freedom cannot be reconciled. He stresses the element of domination in the law more strongly than do, for example, the approaches of Habermas or Maus.

The reason the 'ethical function' can nonetheless appear as an unsubstantiated element lies in how it is derived. Neumann's explanation of totality and relative autonomy takes up only about half a page. The concept of totality is operationalised as a model of three spheres, which isolates the spheres of politics, economics and law not just analytically, but also factually, and places them alongside each other. While Neumann refers formally to Marx and Hegel

93 Teubner 1993b, p. 509 (emphasis in original).

94 Thus also Scheuerman 2002. Today's common prejudice that Neumann's theory was economistic, such as in the form of a monocausual determinism from monopoly capitalism to National Socialism and the decay of the constitutional state, is therefore incomprehensible.

95 Maus 1996, p. 827.

and their concept of totality,[96] he does not actually apply it to his own work. Ultimately, he remains attached to an abstract concept of totality, that is, a summary one. He therefore deduces the three functions of bourgeois law from the liberal history of ideas, and not from an analysis of capitalist social structure.

Moreover, the relationship of structure and action remains unexplained, as he ties the legal form to 'economic interests' ('free competition' requires the general law, 'monopoly capitalism' does away with the constitutional state) without again strategically connecting them to structures in turn. Further analysis will show that concepts of totality are central for legal theory, because the role of the law has to be explained in this overall context.

Even if Neumann thus does not entirely succeed in describing the articulation of relationships, it can nonetheless be noted that he worked out the central significance of this 'independent moment' of bourgeois law. This is an achievement for materialist theory – one that will have to be frequently referred back to in response to economistic shortcuts. In particular, in the discussion about the internationalisation of law, for example, its insight remains central in order to be able to distinguish between legal and non-legal moments. Only when this 'relative autonomy' from social power relations is given can one speak of law. When someone already equates factual action with law, such as Michael Hardt and Antonio Negri, they omit this special feature. It is no accident that to do so they have to fall back on Carl Schmitt.[97] Capitalist relations of domination, which do not even use the form of law, are ones of brute force. This difference is lost in an understanding of law that is too general.[98] Neumann therefore speaks in the context of National Socialism of a social form 'in which the ruling groups control the rest of the population directly, without the mediation of that rational though coercive apparatus hitherto known as the state'.[99]

After all, to point out the obvious, it was until this historical moment in no way customary to even acknowledge relations of domination beyond the class antagonism. Marxist legal theory meant first and foremost the analysis of the class struggle and the field of the 'economy'. Here how the bourgeoisie took over an old relation of domination in its state formation (Gramsci) and undermined the battles of the sexes that occurred there, was entirely blocked out. Neumann and Kirchheimer share this androcentric blindness to gender relations not only with Luhmann and Habermas, but also with all subsequent Marxist theorists.

96 Neumann 1936, p. 26.
97 Hardt and Negri 2000, pp. 16–5.
98 See Buckel 2003.
99 Neumann 2009, p. 470.

1.4.3 Conclusion

The two legal theorists of the Frankfurt School embarked upon a difficult path and in doing so at the same time only first opened it up for their successors. Both stressed the necessity of always considering law in relation to the social structure and especially the balance of powers ('class compromise'). In contrast to systems theory, strategically acting protagonists are from the outset brought into a relation with the evolution of law. It is the new bourgeois class which historically asserts specifically capitalist law for its way of life and mode of production. Even if this component is not sufficiently conveyed structurally, it nonetheless leaves an important starting point for further theoretical development. Neumann and Kirchheimer furthermore stress in different ways that one can only speak of law when it is relatively independent, that is, 'relatively autonomous' of those power relations when they are 'transposed' into the legal. In this, they insist that social power relations are not entirely dissolved in law, but can even come into conflict with it. Their version of the 'primacy of being' reaches the conclusion that such a contradiction determines or dissolves the legal relationships. Therefore, capitalism and democracy cannot be reconciled from their perspective. One can see that Neumann and Kirchheimer also shift between the dialectical poles of coercion and freedom. They raise in a radical manner those questions which will also be time and again at the centre of materialist legal theory later on, even though they do not always answer them satisfactorily. Their questions, however, will serve as the guiding thread of the subsequent discussion:

1. How does the relationship of law and society, and in particular political economy, have to be conceptualised?
2. What explains the 'relative autonomy' of the law, which allows one to attribute an 'ethical function' to it that also protects the weak?
3. How do power relations materialise in law, and what enables legal technique to 'wrest' political decisions from this immediate relationship?
4. Does law have an emancipatory potential that transcends society, or is this impossible, because social relations slip away from their actors?

2 Evgeny Pashukanis

A methodological break in materialist legal theory is first made by Evgeny Pashukanis. He no longer concerns himself with immediate interests and their analysis, merely producing a theory 'which explains the emergence of legal regulation from the material needs of society, and thus provides an explanation of the fact that legal norms conform to the material interests of particular social classes. Yet legal regulation itself has still not been analysed as a form, despite the wealth of historical content with which we imbue it'.[100] If law always only serves to enforce interests, it remains unclear why this even has to take place in legal form? A materialist general theory of law has to analyse 'the legal form as such'[101] – and do so based upon Marx's analysis of the commodity form in *Capital*. Engaging with the 'legal form as such' means, in contrast to a mere history of institutions or a content analysis of norms, a general legal theory. Pashukanis considers his own work here only a 'modest contribution',[102] 'at best a stimulus and material for further discussion'.[103] As a stimulus it found fertile ground indeed. Whoever expressed themselves in future about Marxist legal theory had to engage with Pashukanis' analysis of the legal form. Pashukanis thus became a remarkable author, one whose theory inspired critical debates about law for decades. The contradictions he left are paradigmatic for material legal theory. They will therefore be described here in detail.

The General Theory of Law was understood as the development of the fundamental legal concepts (legal norm, legal relationship, legal subject). Their 'sociological roots' as well as their historical contingency and relativity were to be revealed.[104] The most general and abstract definition is 'law as form'.[105] It is neither only ideology – for it 'reflects' an objective social relation and is its abstraction or mystified form of perception –[106] nor an eternally valid precondition of human existence, as proponents of natural law claim.[107] The judicial factor only attains complete distinctness with the advent of bourgeois-capitalist society.[108] The legal form is a 'specific set of relations which [human beings] enter into not by conscious choice, but because the relations of production compel them to do so. [One] becomes a legal subject by virtue of the same necessity which transforms the product of nature into a commodity complete with the enigmatic property of value'.[109] Only when this abstract form, which

100 Pashukanis 2003, p. 55.
101 Pashukanis 2003, p. 54.
102 Pashukanis 2003, p. 35.
103 Pashukanis 2003, p. 37.
104 Pashukanis 2003, p. 34.
105 Pashukanis 2003, p. 68.
106 Pashukanis 2003, p. 74.
107 Pashukanis 2003, pp. 68–9.
108 Pashukanis 2003, p. 58.
109 Pashukanis 2003, p. 68; note: terms in brackets have been changed to gender-inclusive language from the original translation. In the references below this will be indicated by the note 'translation modified' after the reference.

in its purest shape exists in bourgeois, commodity-producing society, is then clarified, can one reach the 'historically concrete'.[110] This is how Pashukanis describes his programme.[111]

Pashukanis' presentation of law does not follow a logical linear course, but is fragmentary – something that has rarely been taken into account until now. Therefore, an attempt to systematically reproduce his line of argument will be made below, in order to subsequently present the criticisms raised.

2.1 *Dispute*

The first 'answer' to the question of the legal form is rather abruptly 'anticipated'.[112] After the assertion that law finds its most complete shape, its 'hardest core', in civil law,[113] the conclusion is reached without any further intermediate step that 'therefore the conflict of private interests' is a basic prerequisite for legal regulation: 'This is both the logical premise of the legal form and the actual origin of the development of the legal superstructure. Human conduct can be regulated by the most complex regulations, but the juridical factor in this regulation arises at the point when differentiation and opposition of interests begin'.[114] Civil law is then juridical thought that has become 'flesh and blood', because its doctrine is nothing more than 'an endless chain of deliberations for and against hypothetical claims and potential suits'.[115] On a closer reading, one notices that Pashukanis has here the dispute (in court) in mind as the typical and unproductive expression of an individualistic, not collectively organised society.[116] Inevitably 'separate subjects, each of whom represents [their] own private interest' face each other here. For example, 'doctor and patient

110 Pashukanis 2003, p. 71.

111 The first steps in a Marxist analysis of the legal form made by Pyotr Ivanovich Stuchka and Pashukanis came to an abrupt end with Stalinism (Reich 1972a, p. 10). Thus Stuchka initially became a persona non grata, losing positions and recognition, while Pashukanis undertook a self-denying reversal in 1930/31, which leads Reich to speak of the 'other Pashukanis'. At the centre of his analysis was no longer the legal form as such, but instead he began to separate bourgeois and socialist law, in order to legitimate the latter as a 'special law of the transitional period', which 'was radically different from the law of bourgeois-capitalist society' (Pashukanis 1972, p. 111). He was, however, nonetheless arrested and eventually disappeared in 1937 in unexplained circumstances – he was probably murdered (Harms 2000, p. 18; Reich 1972b, p. 155). In the following, therefore, only *The General Theory of Law* will be considered, as it was not yet characterised by scientific opportunism.

112 Pashukanis 2003, p. 82.

113 Pashukanis 2003, p. 80.

114 Pashukanis 2003, p. 81.

115 Pashukanis 2003, p. 80.

116 Ibid.; Pashukanis calls this the 'atomised economy' (Pashukanis 2003, p. 85).

are thereby transformed into subjects with rights and duties, and the regulations which govern them are transformed into legal norms'.[117] Under certain conditions social relations thus take on a legal character.[118] This is the provisional answer to the question 'as to whether a social relation *sui generis* is to be found whose inevitable reflex is the legal form. In what follows, we shall try to establish that this relation is the interrelationship of the owners of commodities'.[119]

2.2 *The Primacy of the Legal Relationship*

The necessary social relationship is then firstly defined as 'the economic relation of exchange'.[120] '[I]n other words, the existence of the legal form is contingent upon the integration of the different products of labour according to the principle of equivalent exchange' and not according to 'needs and abilities'.[121] This 'must be present for the *legal relation* of contracts of purchase and sale to arise'.[122] The 'fundamental condition of existence of the legal form', which is 'rooted in the very economic organisation of society'[123] is the source of the legal relationship, which comes into being only at the moment of dispute. 'The legal differentiates itself from the economic and appears as an autonomous element through legal proceedings'.[124] Law is thus understood as a 'reflexive' reaction to a material social reality. For Pashukanis the legal norm thus exists on an even more abstract level. He objects to the classic concept that the normative 'superstructure' produces the legal relationships. Rather, the legal relation that comes into being through dispute is the cell-form of the legal fabric:[125] '[t]he succession of subjects linked together by claims on each other, is the fundamental legal fabric which corresponds to the economic fabric, that is, to the production relations of a society based on division of labour and exchange'.[126] It has primacy over the norm:[127] Objective law or law as the epitome of the norms guarantees and safeguards the relation but it in no way creates it.[128]

117 Pashukanis 2003, p. 82 (translation modified).
118 Pashukanis 2003, p. 79.
119 Pashukanis 2003, p. 82.
120 Pashukanis 2003, p. 93.
121 Pashukanis 2003, p. 63.
122 Pashukanis 2003, p. 93 (emphasis S.B.).
123 Pashukanis 2003, p. 63.
124 Pashukanis 2003, p. 93.
125 Pashukanis 2003, p. 85.
126 Pashukanis 2003, p. 99.
127 Pashukanis 2003, p. 87.
128 Pashukanis 2003, p. 89.

Here Pashukanis constructs a hitherto unfamiliar and extraordinary base and superstructure scheme: the base is formed by the material relations of exchange. When the thus interconnected subjects come into conflict, a legal relationship emerges organically; this makes the contradiction expressed in the dispute processable. As civil law it is, however, still directly connected to the base, but not genuinely abstract. The political superstructure, on the other hand, which constitutes a later, *conscious* social form to assert the general interest, is something artificial.[129] For this reason, the system of civil law is simple and clear, while constitutional law teems 'with far-fetched constructs which are so one-sided as to become grotesque'. 'Constitutional law is only able to exist as a reflection of the private-law form in the sphere of political organisation, otherwise it ceases to be law entirely'. It is a 'reflection', because it also deals with disputes – of an administrative or parliamentary nature.[130]

2.3 *Guardians of Commodities*

Having now presented both the dispute as a constitutive moment of law as well as the resulting legal relationship, Pashukanis ends his 'deduction' by specifying this relationship as one of commodity owners.[131] The legal form emerges with the beginning of commodity exchange, which reaches its full development with the onset of the capitalist mode of production, for only then does it acquire 'universal significance'.[132] The reified social context in the production process requires for its realisation a particular relationship between people with products at their disposal.[133] Here he follows Marx's wording in *Capital*:

> It is plain that commodities cannot go to market and make exchanges of their own account. We must, therefore, have recourse to their guardians, who are also their owners ... In order that these objects may enter into relation with each other as commodities, their guardians must place themselves in relation to one another, as persons whose will resides in those objects, and must behave in such a way that each does not appropriate the commodity of the other, and part with his own, except by means of an act done by mutual consent. They must therefore mutually recognise in each other the rights of private proprietors.[134]

---

129 Pashukanis 2003, p. 104.
130 Pashukanis 2003, pp. 103–4.
131 Pashukanis 2003, p. 114.
132 Pashukanis 2003, p. 45.
133 Pashukanis 2003, p. 112.
134 Marx 1976, p. 178.

Pashukanis's central argument is that the social connection of people, that is, their shared production and reproduction, becomes independent of them. This unconscious socialisation therefore 'presents itself ... in ... absurd form[s]: ... as man's capacity to be the subject of rights'.[135] Because the individual subjects cannot recognise each other as social[136] and meet each other's needs, but instead exchange commodities, with reciprocal human needs only serving as commodities for exchange value, their shared relationship becomes independent in the form of the commodity economy, where the individuals become legal subjects. Their function is precisely to exchange those goods. Not only are social relations thus reified in commodity producing society, but as a result the subjects are reduced to character masks, that is to mere 'personifications of economic relations' for their bearers.[137] The legal subject 'follows with absolute inevitability from ... the commodity'.[138] The transformation from the biological to the abstract legal subject thus takes place against a background of material conditions and in no way arises as a human invention from reason: 'In reality, of course, the category of the legal subject is abstracted from the act of exchange taking place in the market'.[139] Just as under conditions of commodity production, concrete human labour is dissolved into abstract human labour, '[A]ll concrete peculiarities which distinguish one representative of the *genus homo sapiens* from another dissolve into the abstraction of [the human being] in general, [the human being] as a legal subject'.[140] The abstract agent of circulation, the 'legal subject', now supposedly acquires a will, which makes them absolutely free and equal.[141] This is the birth of legal fetishism.[142] In sum, his argument is that the possibility of a dispute between sovereign, formally equal individuals, which is inherent in commodity exchange, requires a specific form of social regulation. It has to formalise the method of dispute resolution, without weakening the sovereignty and equality of the guardians of commodities: '*that form is law*'.[143] Pashukanis's central discovery was thus the *existence*

135 Pashukanis 2003, p. 113; and as 'the value of commodities' in the production process (Ibid.).

136 In the sense of Hegel's '*self-determining universality*': 'When the will has universality, or itself as infinite form, as its content, object [*Gegenstand*], and end, it is free not only *in itself* but also *for itself* – it is the Idea in its truth' (Hegel 1991, § 21, p. 52).

137 Marx 1976, p. 178.

138 Pashukanis 2003, p. 42.

139 Pashukanis 2003, p. 117.

140 Pashukanis 2003, p. 113 (translation modified).

141 Pashukanis 2003, p. 114.

142 Pashukanis 2003, p. 117.

143 Mieville 2005, p. 7 (emphasis in original).

of a further form besides the commodity form. For this reason, the term 'commodity form of law'[144] is in this crucial aspect misleading.

Pashukanis questions the eternal validity of law, for when the relation of equivalence as a form has been overcome, the juridical factor will also disappear from social relations – a proletarian law cannot exist as such.[145] Pashukanis thus shares with Marx and Lenin the so-called thesis of the 'withering away of law'.[146]

The concept of commodity exchange has rightly been described by Harms as Pashukanis' 'core theorem'.[147] It is therefore also used to explain criminal law, which is very different from civil law: the approach to 'crime' is also interpreted as an exchange of equivalents, in the sense that the contract relationship is retroactively and involuntarily determined in a certain proportion between crime and retribution. The appropriateness of a punishment is thus a question of equivalence – of abstract, temporally measured labour – and not one of punitive damages.[148]

2.4 *The State*

Just as in classic legal theory, the function of the state also plays a central role in Pashukanis, and a very traditional one with regard to legal validity. 'The political superstructure, particularly official statehood is' – as we have already learnt in the context of the legal relationship – 'a secondary, derived element',[149] merely the 'reflection and correlate of the subjective legal claim'.[150] Accordingly public law, the law of the state, is also something ephemeral, because the legal form develops from isolated private interests. This 'primacy of private law', as Pashukanis's position could be called, stands in an unresolved, if not even contradictory relationship to his simultaneous claim that the state is indispensable as a 'guarantor of peace', because legal intercourse does not 'naturally' presuppose a state of peace. However, this is necessary when exchange becomes a regular phenomenon.[151] Despite this almost liberal contempt for the state, Pashukanis even paves the way with his approach for several later materialist theorists of the state (see B.III).

Pashukanis begins his explanation with the by now famous question:

---

144 Cutler 2005, pp. 531–2.
145 Pashukanis 2003, p. 33.
146 Harms 2000, p. 56; Negri 2016, p. 35.
147 Harms, p. 60.
148 Harms, p. 62.
149 Pashukanis 2003, p. 91.
150 Pashukanis 2003, pp. 99–100.
151 Pashukanis 2003, pp. 134–5.

> Why does class rule not remain what it is, the factual subjugation of one section of the population by the other? Why does it assume the form of official state rule, or – which is the same thing – why does the machinery of state coercion not come into being as the private machinery of the ruling class; why does it detach itself from the ruling class and take on the form of an impersonal apparatus of public power, separate from society?[152]

The answer consists is that the *form* of the state is also based upon the exchange relation. The commodity exchange presupposes formal equality and freedom, equivalent exchange and competition. If coercive power were monopolised by one capitalist, those principles would be dissolved due to his particular market position: 'Exchange value ceases to be exchange value, the commodity ceases to be a commodity, if exchange ratios are determined by an authority situated outside of the internal laws of the market'.[153] Coercive force can therefore not figure as a social function, as it is neither abstract nor impersonal. Rather, it has to appear as coercion emanating from an abstract collective person, exercised not in the interest of the individual, but in the interest of all parties to legal transactions.[154] However, 'the life of the state consists of the struggle between various political forces, between classes, parties', etc. Those are 'the real mainsprings of the machinery of the state'.[155]

2.5 *Critique*

Pashukanis interprets Marx's theory as an attempt 'to penetrate the secrets of social forms and to reduce all social relations to [the human being itself]'.[156] This is visible not least in that he breaks down abstract law into legal relations. He stays faithful to Marx's method by interpreting human history not as a history of things or individuals, but as the relations between persons or classes.[157]

Antonio Negri already pointed out in 1972 that Pashukanis is 'among the first (and unfortunately also the last) Marxist theorists of law' to have developed the Marxian standpoint.[158] Andrea Maihofer makes a similar argument that Pashukanis was one of the few to 'critically enquire into the conditions under

152 Pashukanis 2003, pp. 139–40.
153 Pashukanis 2003, p. 143.
154 Pashukanis 2003, pp. 143–4.
155 Pashukanis 2003, p. 147.
156 Pashukanis 2003, p. 84 (translation modified).
157 MECW, Volume 16, p. 476.
158 Negri 2016, p. 12.

which social relations are organised legally, and not, for example, with political force or technically'.[159] Despite the difficulty of grasping the concept of the legal form, it is clear that it is primarily a concept of the law as a specific form of regulating social relations.[160] Pashukanis has thus left the field of mere ideological critique – which even today remains often the only terrain of critical legal theory – not by pursuing the ideological role of law, which he considered self-evident, but the 'objective social conditions' which the law illustrates.[161]

Nonetheless there has been wide-ranging critique of Pashukanis for decades. In what follows I will present this critique according to its four main points: the reduction to the sphere of circulation, the fetishising of private law, economism, and the critique of the 'withering away' theory.

2.5.1 The Reduction to the Sphere of Circulation

The main critique of Pashukanis was sparked by his 'core theory' that law 'derives' from commodity exchange. The commodity form of capitalist societies requires legal subjects who dispose of those commodities, he argues. Thus – according to the critique – law is, however, derived from the sphere of circulation. 'For a "Marxist"' this is a rather odd overestimation of 'circulation' – thus Karl Korsch in 1930, who inaugurated this strand of critique.[162] Korsch's review also made Pashukanis' work known amongst Marxists in the German-speaking world.[163] In 1975 Oskar Negt took up this critique and further clarified: Pashukanis mistakes the position of Marx's analysis of the sphere of circulation within the overall argument of the first volume of *Capital*: 'It is not the general fact that all owners of commodities have to consider each other as equal in their economic transactions and recognise each other, that bourgeois law is based upon', he objects, but the underlying special exchange relation between wage-labourers and capitalists. The sphere of exchange is therefore always already mediated by production. Within this theme, Negt became known for the so-called 'product-mediating exchange' in which law developed.[164] This critique was presented even more forcefully by Burkhard Tuschling in 1976,[165] and it was also the dominant one in the Anglo-Saxon world.[166]

159 Maihofer 1992, p. 26.
160 Ibid.
161 Pashukanis 2003, p. 47.
162 Korsch 1970, p. XI.
163 Harms 2000, p. 71.
164 Negt 1975, p. 48.
165 Tuschling 1976, pp. 12–3; 1977, p. 269.
166 For an overview see Mieville 2005, pp. 91ff.

This objection with regard to the sphere of circulation is a classic Marxist argument, and one that is mainly raised against *bourgeois* theorists. It states that bourgeois theory develops its categories from the surface of social reality, which veils precisely its 'character', namely the exploitation taking place in the 'hidden abode of production'.[167] To bring up this fundamental objection against a Marxist is serious, and therefore it is precisely this debate which endured for decades in the reception of Pashukanis.

Upon closer examination the question is the following: the circulation sphere of pure commodity exchange *necessarily* produces the bourgeois concepts of freedom and equality, for its practice really is that of equivalent exchange: 'The sphere of circulation … was indeed a very Eden of the innate rights of man. It is the exclusive realm of Freedom, Equality, Property and Bentham', Marx writes polemically.[168] The surface of society is here not a false, veiling one, but that society's necessary expression. Without the exchange of commodities the realisation of surplus value would be impossible. Its isolation, however, makes it untrue. That being and appearance are disjoined in capitalist society is not a mysterious process, but the result of social practice; of, as Pashukanis puts it, the 'reification of the social context', which structurally obscures insights into social relations. Society can therefore not be immediately recognised, the first impression – what 'common sense' perceives – is not the whole. If essence and form of appearance were to coincide – thus Marx – any science would be superfluous.[169] But what takes place in the background of circulation, 'which is not visible in the circulation itself'?[170] The creation of surplus-value in production. The consumption of the commodity labour-power is completed, as in the case of every other commodity *outside* the sphere of circulation.[171] Marx has described this dialectical relationship by stating that capital cannot arise from circulation, but that it is equally impossible for it to arise *apart* from circulation.[172] This 'paradox' reveals itself, upon dialectical observation, as a real social process: 'It takes place through the mediation of circulation because it is conditioned by the *purchase of the labour-power in the market*; it does not take place in circulation because what happens there is only an introduction to the valorisation process, which is entirely confined to the *sphere of production*'.[173]

167 Marx 1976, p. 279.
168 Marx 1976, p. 280.
169 Marx 1981, p. 956.
170 Marx 1976, p. 268.
171 Marx 1976, p. 279.
172 Marx 1976, p. 168.
173 Marx 1976, p. 302 (emphasis in original).

At this juncture the meaning of the objection to the deduction from 'mere' circulation becomes apparent: 'Circulation, therefore, which appears as that which is immediately present on the surface of bourgeois society, exists only in so far as it is constantly mediated'.[174] Only through the abstraction of this mediation do individuals become equal and free. 'Its immediate being is therefore pure semblance. *It is the phenomenon of a process taking place behind it*'.[175]

The real appropriation process first occurs in the real production process, which is preceded by that first formal transaction in which capitalist and worker confront each other *purely* as *commodity owners*, relate to each other as buyer and seller. For this reason, all the vulgar economists … remain stuck at that first formal transaction, precisely in order to swindle away the specific relation.[176]

It was against this background that Korsch, Negt and Tuschling want to point out that, if law is meant to be derived from the commodity form, it cannot be derived from circulation alone. Antonio Negri, writing in 1973, draws attention to such a 'sort of reduction' in Pashukanis' writings.[177] Pashukanis excludes a very particular form of exchange: the specific exchange between the commodities labour-power and capital.[178] However, Negri rather emphasises the ambivalent character of Pashukanis's main work, which he himself already described as fragmentary. Ultimately it becomes apparent, despite all the ambiguity, that Pashukanis believed that the completed form of the capitalist market forces a qualitative jump in the legal form. 'It is the whole that qualifies the parts; the phenomenon of exchange now lives only within the dynamics of exploitation and cannot be separated from it'.[179]

But what is the meaning of those ambiguities? Has Pashukanis really overlooked the sphere of production, the holy grail of Marxism? What are the consequences for law that circulation is mediated by production, or rather that the whole determines the parts? And why in fact does not only surplus-value, but also law, have to systemically arise from the sphere of production?

Andreas Harms objects that the element of mediation that goes beyond equivalent exchange remains alien to law:[180] 'Surplus-value may well arise from the sphere of production, Pashukanis does not argue against that either. Law,

174 Marx 1993, p. 255.
175 Ibid.
176 MECW, Volume 34, p. 153.
177 Negri 2016, p. 16.
178 Negri 2016, p. 14.
179 Negri 2016, p. 16.
180 Harms 2000, p. 121.

however, only does its concept justice through circulation, precisely because it leaves out production'.[181] It must be recognised that the legal form remains limited to exchange, forming a factual abstraction from the social relation of capital.[182] He believes that Pashukanis was perfectly aware of the totality of capitalist society and that he equally consciously related law precisely to exchange, because it shares the real abstraction of the exchange process. But what is the consequence of real abstraction? According to Josef Esser, it is specific to the character of capitalist commodity production that the fetish of the legal subject mystifies the underlying class relation, and that the antagonism of the production sphere, along with factual inequality and unfreedom, can no longer be recognised in law.[183] In the introduction to the English edition of Pashukanis' main work, Chris Arthur strengthens this understanding: the objection concerning the sphere of circulation is misleading,

> for it is precisely one of the interesting features of bourgeois exploitation that it inheres in economic relations that *do not* achieve formal legal expression. Formally speaking, Pashukanis is *correct* to refer law only to social relationships based on commodity exchange ... The monopolisation of the means of production by the capitalist class is an *extra*-legal fact ...[184]

Bernhard Blanke also argues that the categories of freedom and equality, which are owed to the simple circulation of commodities, belong constitutively to the concept of capital: 'They already contain the contradiction between the formal equality of commodity owners and their content of inequality in the production context'.[185]

The extensive and long-lasting controversy about Pashukanis' supposed derivation from the sphere of circulation is a classic sign of a dogmatic narrowing of the overall issue, which is exemplary for the impasse Marxist legal theory had reached. For instead of asking the question of how law is connected to myriad social relations (and not only economic ones), a conflict about the relationship of production and circulation rages. This is particularly unfruitful, because circulation and production are only partial aspects of the social *reproduction process*; this 'includes both the circulation process proper and the

181 Harms 2000, p. 122.
182 Harms 2000, p. 164.
183 Josef Esser 1975, p. 155.
184 Arthur 2003, p. 30 (emphasis in original).
185 Blanke 1975, p. 428.

actual production process. These form the two great sections of its movement, which appears as the totality of these two processes'.[186] Marxist theory's fixation on production over the last century has led to the most peculiar blunders, and not least that of excluding generative reproductive labour, which in patriarchal societies is predominantly carried out by women.[187]

The main problem emerging in this discussion lies in the difficulty of grasping antagonistic capitalist society in its *totality* and thus of conceiving a partial moment such as law so that it contains the determinations of that totality as such, and not only of one moment. It is doubtful that this issue has been satisfactorily resolved in what has been represented thus far. The relationship of circulation and production may have been put into the appropriate perspective. But has the *analysis of the legal form* really been exhausted, as Karl Korsch demanded?[188] A first indication to the contrary is the basic fact that neither Pashukanis nor his successors bothered to develop what was meant by such a form-analysis *before* going on to describe law's 'function' for or its 'reflex' out of the commodity form. Pashukanis' method itself remains rather more schematic, as he merely juxtaposes the commodity form with the legal form.[189] As the following critiques will show, this lack of a form analysis leads to further confusion and reductionism.

2.5.2 Civil Law as Primary Law

Closely connected to the 'circulation-allegation' is the critique that was already raised by Hans Kelsen: that 'all law is private law' for Pashukanis, and that 'public law is a mere ideology of bourgeois jurists'.[190] This is no less true for criminal law, whose differentia specifica is not at all developed. Pashukanis has not actually overlooked this possible objection. To the contrary, he took care to note that private law is the 'ratio scripta of every commodity-producing society'.[191] He assumed that it represents at the core 'law as such', of which the other areas of law are only variations, for in the commodity-producing society the most diverse relations 'approximate the prototype commercial relation'.[192] In particular the principle of equivalence becomes generalised, as he aims to show in the case of criminal law. But in this he was not really convincing. Thus Norbert

186 Marx 1993, p. 620.
187 See Beer 1990.
188 Korsch 1970, p. 11.
189 Ibid, p. 10.
190 Kelsen 1955, pp. 95–6.
191 Pashukanis 2003, p. 82.
192 Ibid.

Reich wrote in 1972 that 'if one wants to truly understand Pashukanis' work in legal theory, one must not forget that Pashukanis did not really present a general legal theory here, but a *theory of civil law*'.[193] This is due to Pashukanis' understanding of the relation of commodity owners to each other as the fundamental one – the relation that generates, and is the source of, law. The theory of civil law is thus brought about by the reduction of the legal concept to the commodity form.[194] Antonio Negri criticised around the same time the 'privatistic mythology' in Pashukanis' work. This is the most disappointing aspect of his concept ('This may well be the case!'). The claim that the idea of subjection to an external norm-setting authority has nothing to do with the legal form, misrecognises that 'in its highest stage, capitalist development' brings forth just such a kind of public law – a public law that affords to bourgeois law only a dialectical autonomy.[195] His 'polemic against state controlled normativity' overreaches, as it lets the antagonistic rifts of bourgeois society disappear under the organising element of private law: 'The private is thus exalted in a radicalism of the founding functions of the juridical order that is purely illusory'.[196] Here the connection of the two points of criticism becomes clear. The state form is for Negri the expression of the fundamental social antagonism. A society based on exploitation cannot only reproduce itself based on the laws of the market and can therefore not be reduced to private law either. In this respect ignoring state law (in the sense of public and criminal law) is illusory.

What leads to this surplus of civil law in Pashukanis? What shines through here is first of all the Marxist notion that civil law is closer to production than public law, because 'in it the relations and reciprocal demands of materially producing subjects are recorded'.[197] In addition one must not forget the historical context here. For a similar, although not Marxist, idea was articulated in 1913 by Eugen Ehrlich, who is considered a founder of the sociology of law, when he responded to Kelsen and legal positivism that legal norms established by the state are insignificant in comparison to 'living law', the legal relations of people and the law of jurisprudence.[198] Furthermore, in the methodology of civil law the theory of *free law* was gaining ground for its doctrine of judicial

193 Reich 1972b, p. 155.
194 Harms 2000, p. 110.
195 Negri 2016, p. 19.
196 Negri 2016, pp. 14–5.
197 Negt 1975, p. 38.
198 Ehrlich 1913; see also Kelsen 1915; Teubner 1997a.

interpretation, which aimed to liberate judges from the fixed letter of the law. This was grounded in the understanding that statutory law as such remained incomplete.

In addition, Pashukanis continued to oppose the rationalist illusion of theories shaped by the Enlightenment: that capitalist societies could actually self-regulate autonomously through the conscious establishment of norms. Ultimately, however, it must be noted that in overestimating the opposite position he fell victim to a widespread cliché, namely that it is possible to separate the public and private sphere, the state and the market, beyond the level of analysis; in this respect one has to agree with Negri. Only in this creation of absolutes, which has to assume a self-regulation of the market, can one area of law have precedent over another. In this historical partition of private and public law into separate legal matters which previously coexisted side by side – as occurred in Prussian Common Law, for example – lies the risk of ignoring their shared context. Thus neoliberal theories already pronounce the 'society of private law'.[199] In this context Klaus Günther pointed out that there are certainly good reasons to read modern theories of natural law and rationality as though 'private law was there "first", that is, functionally and temporally before public law as the law of bourgeois society'. Those interpretations, however, stay silent on the fact that private autonomy was, for instance in Kant or Locke, always connected to the force of coercive power.[200] This abstraction from the totality of society thus leads not only here, but also in Pashukanis, to a 'privatistic mythology'. Furthermore, ignoring public law shows its weaknesses especially in the era of the welfare state. For it is its establishment in particular that has led to an enormous public juridification of seemingly private spheres – one that Pashukanis could not imagine for historical reasons.

The critique, however, clarifies one thing above all: similarly to the problem of the sphere of circulation (significantly, private law is *the* ideal type of law for the circulation sphere) the lack of a form analysis also shows its negative consequence here. This is also apparent in the next point of critique.

2.5.3 Economism

Without a form analysis, the impression is easily created that what matters is to derive law from the commodity, in the sense of deriving the so-called 'superstructures' from 'the economy'. Law then appears to be reduced to a mere 'reflex', an ideology of 'true' reality, without its own momentum, without

---

199 Mestmäcker 1991.

200 Günther 1992, pp. 474–5.

the relative autonomy evoked by Franz Neumann. Thus, Pashukanis seems to entangle himself in contradictions, because law simply cannot be a necessary real 'function' of commodity exchange and at the same time a mere reflex, a mere mystification of market operations. Kelsen in particular interprets the theory of the commodity guardian as an economic one, when he alleges that 'Pashukanis imitates Marx's economic interpretation of political phenomena by reducing, in the field of jurisprudence, legal phenomena to economic phenomena ...'[201]

Tellingly, this critique is mainly picked up by another theoretical tradition, which I will present in the second part of the following chapter. This approach, which goes back to Louis Althusser, rejects the analysis of the commodity form for reasons of principle. Thus Nicos Poulantzas takes up Althusser's classic separation into a 'young' and a 'mature' Marx, and only acknowledges the latter and rejects the former as still determined by Hegel und Feuerbach.[202] The central objection is that the various levels of society are conceptualised as though they were produced by a creative subject of society, a centre or an essential being – and that this could be traced back to Hegel. Every level is thus simply nothing but the expression of the central subject, which gives it its meaning. With Marxists, Hegel's 'absolute spirit' is merely replaced by the 'economy' or the 'social class' – the principle, however, remains, so that one can speak of a simple 'reversal'.[203]

This fundamental dilemma concerning Hegel is the reason that Pashukanis too can only understand law as the immediate reflex of the economic base[204] and thus succumbs to a purely instrumentalist conception of the superstructure: 'Like a mere appendage law contents itself to follow the twists and turns of the economic base more or less faithfully'.[205] Because law is actually nothing other than the reflection of the base, in principle Pashukanis also cannot establish his own legal theory, for accordingly law as a specific object of scientific research cannot exist.[206] Neither could the individual social classes be analysed in their specificity, nor their relations between each other, for: 'One can only speak of relations between two terms, when both as such *exist* in and through their relation and *their relation is based on their specificity and*

201 Kelsen 1955, p. 89.
202 Althusser 1968, p. 31 ff.
203 Poulantzas 1972, p. 184; Althusser 1968, p. 68.
204 Poulantzas 1972, p. 181.
205 Poulantzas 1972, p. 182.
206 Ibid.

autonomy'.[207] In Pashukanis' expressions such as 'mystification' and 'illusion', Poulantzas recognises the theory of the young Marx, for whom the levels of the superstructure (thus also law) were understood according to the model of 'alienation': that is as false and deceitful phenomena, 'whose only function it is to disguise the nature of social reality, which consists of human beings as such – the concrete individuals'. They are, in other words, nothing but mere ideology. 'This is the "humanist" conception of Marxism, which continues to cause harm amongst Marxist researchers even today'.[208] In the mid-1990s Jens Christian Müller-Tuckfeld and Andrea Maihofer reassert this thesis of 'Pashukanis's economism'[209] or that of a 'legal theory without analysis of law'.[210]

This critique of Pashukanis effectively points out an insufficiently complex and not problematised understanding of the relation of 'base and superstructure'. The reduction of law's function to that of making commodity exchange possible through legal subjects, the mythology of private law and the partial talk of 'reflex' are attached to a one-dimensional determining logic. It is, however, noticeable that the critics do not really make an effort to acknowledge the ambiguities of Pashukanis' approach, and to engage more extensively with his intended goal.[211] Poulantzas and Müller-Tuckfeld get by without representing his theory at all, while Maihofer subjects Pashukanis to something of a hermeneutics of reckoning, which does not live up to its claim of taking the 'theoretical significance of an author like Pashukanis'[212] seriously – although this significance is nonetheless universally recognised. As soon as 'Hegelian Marxism' is diagnosed, Althusser's verdict is pronounced.

That Pashukanis, for example, defined himself against a 'hopeless subjectivism'[213] which believed that the law or the state only exist in the imagination of individuals, and insists on their materiality ('What a pity that the practice of the political power struggle radically contradicts this psychological view of the state, confronting us at every step with objective material factors'),[214] is ignored. This is much too facile a way to deal with Pashukanis. Poulantzas mentions him in the same context as his colleague Stucka, without developing the significant difference between the two, namely Pashukanis' specific innovation that law has to be deciphered by way of an analysis of form. The commodity

207 Poulantzas 1972, p. 185 (emphasis in original).
208 Poulantzas 1972, p. 186.
209 Müller-Tuckfeld 1994, p. 188.
210 Maihofer 1992, p. 28 (emphasis in original).
211 Thus also Harms 2000, p. 138.
212 Poulantzas 1972, p. 181.
213 Pashukanis 2003, p. 77.
214 Ibid.

form as such is equated with the 'economy' in a most problematic reductionism that was already developed by Kelsen. Only in this way can the strong assumption of 'economism' and essentialism even be preserved with regard to Pashukanis. For his notion that the analysis of the commodity form had not been used at all for the study of the 'legal superstructure'[215] was more centrally focused on the 'reified social context', the fetishistic manner in which human beings organise their social relations. That Poulantzas and his successors can misunderstand Pashukanis as economistic is connected to the lack of a form analysis.

2.5.4 The Withering Away Thesis

Finally, his suggestion that the law would have to 'wither away' was attacked. Here what is at stake is the significant question, already addressed by Neumann, of to what extent law has emancipatory potential. Pashukanis is even more sceptical than Neumann of this hope that we have gotten to know through Habermas. With his concept of the withering away of the law Pashukanis, picks up directly from Marx and Lenin.

In Marx's analysis of the Social-Democrats' Gotha Program, the foundation of the 'withering away' thesis is laid: Marx accuses the social democrats of remaining attached to bourgeois law in their programme with the use of the term '*equal right*', for the principle of equivalence forms the basis of the commodity-exchanging society.[216] This was not surprising, as law can never be higher than the level of development of a society. An idea that makes sense at one particular time, can at another become 'obsolete verbal rubbish'.[217] In a higher phase of communist society it would not make sense to think in those categories, for

> after the enslaving subordination of the individual to the division of labour, and thereby also the antithesis between mental and physical labour, has vanished; after labour has become not only a means of life but life's prime want; after the productive forces have also increased with the all-round development of the individual, and all the springs of common wealth flow more abundantly, only then can the narrow horizon of bourgeois right be crossed in its entirety and society inscribe on its banners: From each according to his abilities, to each according to his needs![218]

215 Pashukanis 2003, p. 39.
216 MECW, Volume 24, p. 86.
217 MECW, Volume 24, p. 87.
218 Ibid.

It only makes sense to talk of '*equal rights*' in bourgeois society, whereas a communist one is based upon a principle other than commodity exchange – thus bourgeois law also loses its significance.

The term '*withering away*', on the other hand, comes from Friedrich Engels, who talks in *Anti-Dühring* of the withering away of the *state*: at the moment when the state really represents all of society, it renders itself superfluous: 'State interference in social relations becomes, in one domain after another, superfluous, and then dies out of itself; the government of persons is replaced by the administration of things, and by the conduct of processes of production. The state is not "abolished". *It dies out*'.[219]

It falls to Lenin to connect those ideas in 1917 in political practice as well as theoretically. In his text *State and Revolution*, which contains the programme of the October Revolution, he above all addresses the question of how the *transition* from capitalist to communist conditions could be possible. If in Engels we already see that the state cannot simply be abolished, Lenin also suspects that it is impossible to simply abolish social practices. People would rather have to gradually '*become accustomed*' to new habits.[220] The coercive apparatus of the state, which is necessary in bourgeois society to oppress the exploited part of the population, would become unnecessary in a communist society, which is no longer based on exploitation and want. 'With the removal of this chief cause, the state will inevitably begin to "wither away"'.[221] The metaphor of 'withering away' is connected to a particular concept of development. Lenin thus assumed that the 'machine for the suppression of one class'[222] was still necessary during the transition, because in the 'lower phases of communism' (socialism), defined as a 'transitional state' 'freed from capitalist slavery, from the untold horrors, savagery, absurdities, and infamies of capitalist exploitation', people[223] do not become different subjects from one day to the next – particularly the old ruling class. The goal is, however, the 'higher phase of communism', which Marx speaks of in the above quotation, in which people have learned to observe 'the elementary rules of social intercourse that have been known for centuries and repeated for thousands of years in all copybook maxims ... without force, without coercion'.[224]

'Bourgeois law' does not stop in the first phase either. It is significant that for Lenin and Marx it was already out of the question to speak of proletarian

219 MECW, Volume 25, p. 268.
220 Lenin 2014, p. 127.
221 Lenin 2014, p. 129.
222 Lenin 2014, p. 128.
223 Lenin 2014, p. 127.
224 Ibid.

law in this transitional phase, for this cannot exist any more than can a communist state. State and law are in his understanding capitalist forms and as such remain only significant during the transition.[225] Bourgeois law thus has the role of functioning as 'regulator (determining factor)' in the distribution of goods and labour amongst the members of society,[226] because this would not yet work without rules of law (and this is a defect): '[f]or if we are not to indulge in utopianism we must not think that, having overthrown capitalism, people will at once learn to work for society *without any rules of law*. Besides, the abolition of capitalism *does not immediately create* the economic prerequisites for *such* a change'.[227] In bourgeois law, which is designed to regulate the distribution of labour and products, the state is also presupposed, 'for law is nothing without an apparatus capable of *enforcing* the observance of the rule of law'.[228] The economic preconditions for the withering away have been noted by Marx: all-round development of the individuals and their productive forces, co-operative wealth, 'i.e., when people have become so accustomed to observing the fundamental rules of social intercourse and when their labor has become so productive that they will voluntarily work *according to their ability* ... There will then be no need for society, in distributing products, to regulate the quantity to be received by each; each will take freely "according to his needs", without any control over the labor of the individual citizen, any quantity of truffles, cars, pianos, etc'.[229]

It seems as though Pashukanis had a similar idea in mind with the replacement of law by merely 'technical regulations', that is, rules of such a kind that they do not have to proceduralise the dispute, but only resolve organisational issues. In contrast to Neumann, Pashukanis thus connects with a Marxist tradition which stresses the *historical* character of social forms and thus denies that 'law' is an eternally valid category, if only to regulate – as Franz Neumann argues – the eternally existing quarrels between people. Law in general is for Pashukanis connected with the bourgeois capitalist society. The laws of antiquity and of feudalism were only embryonic predecessors of law, which reaches its peak under capitalism. If law still persists in a supposedly socialist society, it is a remnant[230] or residue[231] of the still commodity-producing society.

225 See also Reich 1972b, p. 156.
226 Lenin 2014, p. 132.
227 Lenin 2014, p. 118 (emphasis in original).
228 Lenin 2014, p. 137 (emphasis in original).
229 Lenin 2014, p. 135.
230 Reich 1972b, p. 157.
231 Düx 1972, pp. 352–3.

Pashukanis's withering away thesis has been criticised from various perspectives. Thus Norbert Reich reproaches Pashukanis that this 'fundamental critique of law' could only be achieved by reducing the concept of law to the society of commodity exchange.[232] He basically repeats here his criticism of the seemingly narrow concept of law, which is only adapted to civil law: 'With this, however, little is achieved, for other areas of social life remain which also have to be regulated by norms, albeit not by legal norms'.[233] But Reich's critique fails to reach its target, because Pashukanis – as has been shown – only continues the approach of Marx, Engels and Lenin; and Lenin in particular did not only limit law and the state to guaranteeing civil laws, but understood them as forms that are intended to 'hold down' the subaltern in a historical situation of capitalist exploitation and want.

Andreas Harms, on the other hand, problematises the 'historical teleology of Marxism'[234] that is expressed here: 'Pashukanis also seems to believe in an immanent reason of history which lets law first reach full maturity, before it withers away …'[235] Antonio Negri, meanwhile, notes that the question of the transition was also central for Pashukanis. Not a reason of history [*Vernunft der Geschichte*], but only class struggle would lead to the withering away. Pashukanis has this concept of the opening up of a path towards transition.[236] This is 'a process of proletarian estrangement interpreted by the struggle against any form of institutional actualization of the relations of force between the classes that confront themselves. There is no alternative use of law that can replace this process of struggles'.[237]

Harms argues moreover[238] that the concept of technical regulation does not remove the problem of coercion: 'In this case, however, not following technical regulations, just as not following a legal norm, is also a reason for the state to intevene' – unless there is consensus in society. Ultimately Pashukanis seems unable to completely liberate himself from the idea that, even in a far-away future, enforceable and general regulations will be necessary. 'Thus, Pashukanis is unable to produce a transition from a critical reconstruction of the legal form to an intellectually coherent anticipation of a social formation without abstract formalised rules'.[239] Apart from the fact that it is an astonishing demand to

232 Reich 1972b, p. 157.
233 Reich 1972b, p. 158.
234 Harms 2000, p. 144.
235 Harms 2000, p. 145.
236 Negri 2016, p. 37.
237 Negri 2016, p. 41.
238 Harms 2000, p. 147.
239 Harms 2000, p. 149.

expect an author to anticipate a future society in which today's contradictions are resolved, this critique of Pashukanis also seems flawed to me. The objection would apply to Franz Neumann, who considered the dispute in need of regulation as the fundamental precondition of any society. However, Pashukanis assumes on the contrary that social conditions will change in such a way that people are able to organise their relationships without legal norms. That they, to paraphrase Lenin, are able to work for the common good and to recognise it as the condition for their freedom. Perhaps Lenin's term 'habit' is more appropriate than that of 'technical regulation'; but both imply that an enforcing apparatus must no longer be necessary.

Jens Christian Müller-Tuckfeld finally refers in the context of the withering away thesis to 'orthodox Marxism',[240] in order to criticise the notion that law is merely an external coercive force. However, if legal norms are not external to the subjects, but inscribed in their practices, it would be naive to imagine that law can wither away in a different society because the state has been abolished. Law and state would then have exclusively repressive components. Reflections about ideological mechanisms of power, such as those undertaken by Althusser and Gramsci, or about disciplinary and biopolitical mechanisms of power in the spirit of Foucault (more on this below) were still alien to Marxists. How the political subject, the working class, becomes hegemonic, that is, how it can make its aims universal, was ignored in favour of the idea that the repressive apparatuses simply had to disappear.

One must, however, not overlook that such concepts only emerged later in the history of theory and that the withering away thesis was certainly also an undogmatic moment in Pashukanis' theory, because it at least articulated the notion that there are no everlasting social relations. Withering away is precisely not identical with 'destroying', but contains the elements of a gradual redundancy. Significantly, under Stalinist persecution it was precisely the withering away thesis that Pashukanis was made to revoke. He now wrote about his earlier assumption that communism and law are incompatible that

> this is without a doubt also a grave formal mistake ... For [this] prevents from being addressed the question of Soviet law as a particular law of the transition period – a law that is fundamentally different from the law of bourgeois-capitalist society.[241]

240 Müller-Tuckfeld 1994, p. 187.
241 Pashukanis 1972, p. 111.

His early insight that the legal form and the commodity form go together had to be given up politically at a time when the State Marxism of the Soviet Union no longer wanted to know about it, because while it had abolished private property, it had not done away with the commodity form.[242]

The withering away thesis contains at the same time a model for the transition to another society. In its principal considerations it has a rather emancipatory outlook. The model of transition remains, however, problematic, as it wants to retain the contradictory institutions of state and law for a certain time – and thus dominance, coercion and oppression. That the practice of Real Socialism has disproved the transition thesis is almost banal. Which theoretical alternatives could have been imagined is, however, much less so.

2.5.5 Summary

With the second Marxist approach in legal theory a further element was added to the analysis of power relations. While Neumann and Kirchheimer referred rather to the political writings as well as to the surplus value and class theory of Marx, Pashukanis started from the first chapter of the first volume of *Capital* and thus with the analysis of the commodity form and the theory of fetishism. Marx himself, who had connected both moments in *one* theory, assumed that *class struggle* takes place *mediated through the commodity form*, and that both moments are thus connected.[243] But neither the critical theorists nor Pashukanis make this connection. The questions that remained unanswered in the last chapter, in particular about the totality of capitalist societies as well as the 'relative autonomy' of the law, also represented gaps for Pashukanis. He provides, however, a different answer to the question of law's emancipatory potential. Instead of locating it in its potential 'ethical function', he situates law altogether as part of a strategy of power which must be overcome. The withering away thesis is the final consequence of the form analysis. That is to say, precisely that analysis which, according to the understanding reached here, Pashukanis actually only called for, but did not provide it. The 'reified social context' is demonstrated in the commodity exchange without basic reflections that could make clear that this is a structuring principle of society, and not only an 'economic' fact. Pashukanis had this in view; in this respect the charge of economism, as well as that of a reduction to the sphere of circulation and to private law, does not apply. However, he could not realise this in his execution,

242 See also Düx 1972.

243 More extensively Buckel 2006, pp. 119 ff.

which remained fragmentary due to the historical circumstances in which he worked, so the critique of what he actually achieved nonetheless contains valid points.

Pashukanis' unfulfilled potential thus lies in a further continuation of his work from this point. How Marxist legal theorists of the 1970s attempted to solve this problem will therefore be analysed in the next step. Afterwards I return to the alternative approach in the tradition of Althusser and Gramsci, which also reached its endpoint in the 1970s.

CHAPTER 7

Renaissance and Crisis of Marxism Since the 1970s

In the context of the student movement and the euphoria over reforms of the 'social-democrat era', legal theory in the undogmatic Marxist tradition was revived during the 1970s. Of particular importance were the two collected volumes edited by Hubert Rottleutbner (1975) and Norbert Reich (1972), as well as the 1971–3 issues of *Kritische Justiz*. Alongside this there was a temporary renaissance of a (at the time still called Marxist) left-wing legal theory in West Germany, and also French, Italian and US-American debate. Authors such as Joachim Pereis, Norbert Reich, Wolfgang Abendroth, Thomas Blanke, Wolf Paul, Oskar Negt, Ulrich K. Preuß, Nicos Poulantzas, Burkhard Tuschling, Umberto Cerroni and Toni Negri or Monique Chemillier-Gendreau, Isaac D. Balbus and Sol Picciotto engaged here with the issues raised by Pashukanis, or Franz Neumann and Otto Kirchheimer. They took particularly great interest in the activities of the state, its room for manoeuvre and steering potential.[1] This was due to the expanding Keynesian welfare-state and the 'illusions of the social state'[2] it created, but also to the early crisis of the Fordist formation. The concentration on the 'capitalist state' was not least visible in the scale of the 'state derivation debate'.[3] This was also the time when the independent significance of law was relegated to the background: considered an aspect of the state, it was frequently subsumed under it. Until now it has not escaped from this embrace.

The discussions at the time were at first attempts to bring 'fragmentary approaches'[4] into a 'systematic engagement with the questions of the development and effects of legal norms or legal-political strategies'.[5]

As an example I will pick out two theory strands with different initial premisses from this debate. They are suitable for different reasons. The first strand develops Pashukanis' approach further. On this basis, the ideas it presents can be examined as to whether they succeed in filling out the 'blind spot' of the legal form analysis described above. The second strand (associated with Nicos Poulantzas and Michel Foucault), on the other hand, is of interest because it

1 Rottleuthner 1975, p. 7; Picciotto 1982, p. 169.
2 See Müller and Neusüß 1970.
3 See also Kannukalam 2000.
4 Perels 1971, p. 239.
5 Rottleuthner 1975, p. 7.

explicitly rejects this starting point and instead picks up from Louis Althusser and Antonio Gramsci.

After the awakening of the 1960s, the start of the next decade brought the so-called 'crisis of Marxism'.[6] With the crisis of the Fordist welfare-state and the emergence of multiple social struggles, in particular the new women's movement, but also the ecology movement and the atypical forms of social struggle on the capitalist periphery, social conflicts expanded to encompass a wide field of issues. Thus 'the very wealth and plurality of contemporary social struggles has given rise to a theoretical crisis', which calls into question the centrality of the working class, the role of *the* revolution as the transition from one type of society to another and the idea of a completely homogenous collective will[7] as well as the primacy of 'economic laws' in Marxist concepts. While theory based upon Marx was as a whole challenged to engage in continuous self-examination, and was successful in doing so in many areas, one must note that legal theory did not survive the crisis: for at its end there was no longer a living Marxist legal theory. The following discussion will show at which points the crisis can be theoretically defined.

In this context Michel Foucault's work becomes particularly significant. On the one hand it is marked by a critical engagement with Marxism, and on the other hand his interest in knowledge relates to social phenomena which allow for the expansion of the theoretical field: 'madness', 'deviance', and 'sexuality'. His objections and theoretical shifts lend themselves therefore to a reformulation of Marxist legal theory.

1 The Tradition of the Legal Form Analysis

1.1 *Production-Mediated Exchange*

1.1.1 Presentation

The renewed Marxist debate on the function and nature of the legal concept kicked off with discussions in the journal *Kritische Justiz*. The most prominent contribution was made by the 'academic spokesman of the neo-Marxist left in the 1970s',[8] Oskar Negt. According to Harms, it is mainly Negt who made the concept of 'Marxist legal theory' known. His concept was introduced as early as 1972 and has stimulated debate ever since – a main manifestation of this can be found in Rottleuthner's essay collection (1975), both as statement and

6 Althusser 1978.
7 Laclau and Mouffe 2001, p. 2.
8 Harms 2000, p. 115.

counter-statement. Negt's approach was, however, again not at all a systematic contribution, but *his ten theses* rather reflected a new beginning.

As has already been described with regard to the critique of Pashukanis, his own intervention consisted of bringing the sphere of production into the debate. Here it was central for him that the term 'production' not be understood in a narrowly 'economistic' way. Production should not be assimilated to an instrumental approach to working material, instruments and organisation, but be identical to the production and reproduction of real life at a historically specific stage of development of the forces and conditions of production, ideas, concepts, and consciousness, that is, of lived relations that are based upon the material activity of individuals: 'With the production of material goods individuals produce and reproduce at the same time the conditions which define the rules and limits of their actions and behaviour ...'[9]

The legal form can be explained from this context. The basic theorem is thus: bourgeois law is not based on the general fact that all commodity owners consider each other in their economic transactions as equal and have to recognise each other as such, but rather on the underlying special exchange relation between wage labourers and capitalists. The exchange process wherein law develops is 'production-mediated exchange':[10] 'Not all commodities, nor the movement of goods mediated by contracts, but only the commodity labour power is therefore the reference point to derive and explain law'.[11] The consequence of this new definition of the derivation's location remains, however, unclear.

Only with Burkhard Tuschling's *Rechtsform und Produktionsverhältnisse* (1976) is this undefined connection explained. He starts from Negt's thesis and takes it further. For in Negt it remained a 'merely methodological demand'.[12] In capitalism, law expands from a social subsection to a system that regulates all social relations. From this it follows that the field of law's development and regulation cannot be that of circulation (this applies only to pre-capitalist societies) but the 'capitalist production process'.[13] This process is characterised by labour power itself becoming a commodity. Tuschling's central thesis is therefore that capitalist commodity exchange fulfils the decisive function of this production method, namely 'the combination of producers and means of pro-

9 Negt 1975, p. 45.
10 Negt 1975, p. 48.
11 Negt 1975, p. 52 (emphasis in original).
12 Tuschling 1976, p. 13.
13 Tuschling 1976, p. 9.

duction'.[14] The central contradiction of capitalism thus has to take the form of a process, that is, become communicable and thus reproducible in order to make capitalist production possible.[15] Law has to be derived from this 'totality', not from a partial moment.[16] The specific contribution of law is that it regulates and guarantees that the services that buyer and seller of the commodity labour power expect are in fact delivered: realisation of the means of production, replacement of the equivalent of the commodity labour power as well as of a surplus value that exceeds it. The results of the production process are thus organised legally: 'The law guarantees that in the case of conflict the constitutional state's instruments of power can be used, in order to safeguard by way of sanctions … the relationship of the separation of the producers from their means of production that is reproduced and thus newly put in place at the end of the capitalist production process'.[17]

By 'totality' Tuschling understands the contradictory relations of capitalist society, which can be considered as relations of production, as class relations, or precisely as legal relations. Law is thus only 'a legal aspect of this totality' or nothing but '*the same relations of individuals to each other and to the means of production*, only seen from a different angle …'[18] The relations of production are the totality, which differentiates into 'relations of production and law'.[19] With regard to form analysis this means that Tuschling understands production as the content and law as its form.[20] This content is the basic structure of capitalist society, which represents the natural core of any positive law.[21]

1.1.2 A Mania for Foundations

Maihofer argues in relation to Negt's intervention that his theses are nothing but a 'more precise' definition of the point from which the origin of law can be derived. How law originates is, however, by no means more precisely defined by this.[22] Harms argues similarly: 'Although he differentiates himself from Pashukanis, Negt's arguments in this context are similar to Pashukanis'.[23]

14 Tuschling 1976, p. 15.
15 Tuschling 1976, p. 16.
16 Tuschling 1977, p. 271.
17 Tuschling 1976, p. 37.
18 Tuschling 1976, p. 32.
19 Tuschling 1977, p. 274.
20 Tuschling 1976, pp. 27, 88, 99.
21 Tuschling 1976, p. 94.
22 Maihofer 1992, p. 33.
23 Harms 2000, p. 117.

Maihofer's central objection is directed at how Negt's particular emphasis on production is a vehicle for the notion that production brings forth all social relations from itself as a, so to speak, godlike source of all social existence.[24] Rather, production as socially determined has to always already be thought within particular ways of production, practices and forms of consciousness.[25] This critique does not seem convincing with regard to Negt, because he defends the same idea with a different terminology, and Maihofer criticises him for precisely the misconception Negt seeks to clear up. When applied to Burkhard Tuschling, however, the criticism hits the mark. For the specificity of Tuschling's theory consists in how it brings the critique of Pashukanis – virulent to begin with – to a head. But this also means that the immanent problem of this critique is revealed very clearly: the creation and appropriation of surplus value in production is seen as the crucial element of capitalism; therefore, law also has to be connected, rooted in it. Not only law, *all* social relations are based upon this fundamental problem, are an expression of the subject 'capital'. Society can thus not be recognised as multi-dimensional and overdetermined by a diversity of contradictions, but has to be reduced to a 'fundamental contradiction',[26] from which everything can be derived. Besides the fact that this argument is economistic, it also points to a more basic methodological problem, which is ultimately expressed in economism; to an ontological idea of society: 'the … assumption that every conceivable existent thing can be reduced' to the fundamental.[27] What Poulantzas and Maihofer thus label Hegelian thinking of the simple contradiction is no less criticised by the Hegel-following Adorno. He calls such a notion a 'mania for foundations'[28] and means by this 'the belief that everything which exists must be derived from something else, something older or more primordial'.[29] This 'cult of the notion of originality' contains the claim that the first and earliest was truer, better, and deeper.[30] This original is in Tuschling 'capital as subject of domination'.[31] But from where can it ultimately be 'derived' that law regulates the 'core' of capitalism? Why not only secondary aspects? Why 'regulation' and 'guarantee' at all? Those premises are obvious choices, which are only hidden by how they seemingly lead back to

24 Maihofer 1992, p. 35.
25 Ibid.
26 Maihofer 1992, p. 15.
27 Adorno 2001, p. 16; 2018, p. 17.
28 Adorno 2001, pp. 15–6.
29 Adorno 2001, p. 16.
30 Adorno 2018, p. 17.
31 Tuschling 1976, p. 47.

the fundamental. But the social is an infinitude, 'not reducible to any underlying unitary principle'. The idea of an original centre of the social therefore no longer makes any sense.[32] In particular when Tuschling himself admits that law precisely abstracts from relations of inequality, the argument becomes contradictory, if it is *at the same time* derived from this particular aspect.[33] The aspect that goes beyond the equivalent exchange can just as well remain alien to law, as Harms argues.[34] Furthermore Tuschling misrecognises the double meaning of simple circulation.[35] It is not merely the *historical* precondition of capital, 'pre-capitalist'; it is likewise the precondition of capital within the bourgeois mode of production.

1.1.3 Totality

In the mania for foundations we encounter yet again a questionable concept of totality. '[H]ow this totality can be grasped in one fell swoop, without its aspects being developed out of each other'[36] – this remains Tuschling's secret. This is only possible because Tuschling understands by totality, not diversity and the inherent momentum of its aspects, but simply the examination of a single relationship from all angles. Everything is in principle 'capital'. 'Concrete totality' is rather visible in the mutual dependence of the individual parts, which can differ from each other so much as to even form polar opposites.[37] Law has its own density and is not only the expression or outward form of production. And it is precisely this claim that Tuschling cannot live up to. While he thus completely denies the independence of its aspects, Neumann on the other hand struggles with the merely abstract totality of their addition. How to understand society as a totality and consider law in relation to it emerges more and more clearly as the main challenge of the various theoretical strands.

1.2 *On the Relationship of Law and State*

After engaging with those who adhere to the 'derivation of law', I will now turn to the 'school of state derivation'. 'Pashukanis' Status as a patron saint of this school is widely accepted, whatever one thinks of the school itself …'[38]

32 Laclau and Mouffe 2001, p. 139.
33 Bader 1977, p. 292.
34 Harms 2000, p. 121.
35 Reichelt 2002, p. 165.
36 Bader 1977, p. 290.
37 Adorno 2000a, pp. 43, 61.
38 Mieville 2005, p. 122.

1.2.1 The Value Form

The materialist theorists of the state who followed Pashukanis did not succumb to the mania of foundations. Instead of seemingly radicalising Pashukanis at this juncture, they attempted to apply his insights to state theory. The internal changes in function, which emerged with the development of capital, did not change anything about the legal form, as this form is a functional requirement of capitalism and does not simply disappear with the development of class structures. The principle of the equivalent exchange is broken up, but the exchange relations remain in their form relations of equivalence.[39]

Because of their symbiotic engagement with law and state this representation cannot neglect those authors, although they 'actually' wanted to explain the political form and commented on the legal form somewhat in passing. While this always already includes the problem of making mutual dependence a premise that is not historically variable, but a priori given, they nonetheless also contributed – without losing sight of this – a series of important insights to the analysis of the legal form. From the 'state derivation debate' – which started with the text by Müller and Neusüß in 1970 and involved amongst others authors such as Elmar Altvater, Joachim Hirsch, Flatow and Huisken or the 'Projekt Klassenanalyse' who initiated and developed it – Blanke et al and Esser will here be selected as those authors for whom law, and Pashukanis's analysis, gained a special significance.[40]

Their initial thesis was that Pashukanis was the only one to recognise thus far that the 'primary function' of the state was concealed in the commodity form.[41] The separation of politics and economics (and thus the development of politics as a field of its own) had its origin in the commodity.[42] The commodity form was 'the specific capitalist form of socialisation'.[43] Blanke, Jürgens and Kastendiek as well as Esser proceeded methodologically in such a way that they developed the three central forms – value-form, legal form and state form – one after the other and building upon one another. The basic form here is the value-form as developed by Marx, while the legal form comes from Pashukanis. Both approaches want to show in this way how the state 'has to be explained through particular requirements of capitalist society'.[44]

39 Blanke, Jürgens and Kastendiek 1974, pp. 74–5; Blanke 1975, p. 422.
40 See Esser 1975, Note 91.
41 Esser 1975, p. 69.
42 Blanke 1975, p. 419.
43 Esser 1975, p. 151.
44 Blanke 1975, p. 417.

The value-form Marx described is characterised by the 'domination of the purely factual connection' and the absence of physical force.[45] The development of bourgeois society is associated with a gradual 'depoliticising' of the economy (giving up rule of force [*Faustrechts*], robbery, etc.). *At the same time*, however, it requires an entity which guarantees this process.[46]

The value form becomes the necessary form, because general abstract labour, which makes the social exchange of commodities possible in the first place, cannot present itself as such. It is precisely abstract labour – '*labor sans phrase*', which according to Marx is the basis of value – which produces a contradiction: because value is something purely social, a result of labour cannot indicate the exchange value it contains. Then it would not be exchangeable. It therefore requires an expropriation, an independent representation. The money form has according to Esser this 'necessary function' of expressing the exchange value.[47] Marx thus discovered that the commodity-producing society makes a particular function necessary, which presents itself in the form of money. But with this, according to Esser, the derivation of the money form is not yet achieved. He addresses the critique of critique of the derivation merely from circulation by distinguishing functions based upon whether commodity production is simple or capitalist. From the moment human labour power itself takes on the commodity form, it produces surplus value in the production process. The money form then transforms into the capital form. In this form, the specific capitalist relations of domination are expressed: the 'domination of reified capital over value-producing living labour'.[48]

1.2.2 The Legal Form

Both approaches now take up Pashukanis' theorem of the commodity guardian for the legal form: the second necessary function presents itself as the legal subject.[49] The purely factual connections become independent of each other in two different ways: firstly as the relation of things (the commodities) to each other, expressed in value as the reified form of the social character of

45 Blanke, Jürgens and Kastendiek 1974, p. 70; Blanke 1975, p. 420.

46 Blanke, Jürgens and Kastendiek 1974, p. 70; The two different Marxist tendencies of state theory described agree on this point. Poulantzas also notes that the capitalist state with its monopoly on the use of force constitutes the pacification of the territories that were fragmented by feudal wars. The separation of state and economy was accompanied by a centralisation of physical violence in the state (Poulantzas 2000. p. 80). Foucault also argues this (Foucault 1978).

47 Esser 1975, pp. 151–2.

48 Esser 1975, p. 152.

49 Esser 1975, p. 154.

human labour,[50] and secondly as the relation of individuals (for the *realisation* of value). And this second relationship now constitutes the legal form just as it does in Pashukanis. For value to be able to realise itself, the conscious actions of human beings are necessary – because as mentioned above, the commodities cannot bring themselves to the market. Out of those intentional relations a system of legal relations emerges at the moment when they are agreed upon and regulated. The individual thus becomes a legal subject.[51] Those actions are of course not free rational activities, but purely functional actions, executed through character masks or agents of circulation. Law is here the essential form which leads them to act functionally. The social context asserts itself as reified coercion, which however requires individual actions.[52] The change in the legal form noted by Esser in expanded capitalist production takes place in a different way for the legal form than in the transformation of the money form to the capital form. While there it is a case of the transition from one form of expressing exchange value to another, the transformation here consists in a mystification: the specific legal subjects of capitalism, wage labourer and capitalist, stand in a class relation to each other and precisely that is mystified in the legal form, in which both appear as equal and free legal subjects.[53]

1.2.3 The Political Form

The next step in this line of argument consists then in deriving the state form from this legal function. At this juncture, which is decisive and new for both approaches, the authors take different paths, but they arrive in principle at the same result: the political form develops from the necessity to secure by implementing the legal form the continuous production of commodities through an extra-economic coercive power.

Blanke et al stress that commodity exchange takes place on the basis of the contract. This could not exist without coercion,[54] so that '*enforcing the law of value … constitutes enforcing the law of right*'.[55] Equivalent exchange involves the necessity of guaranteeing the equivalence of exchange conditions.[56] The security of the law (both substantive legal certainty as well as certainty of enforcement) necessarily produces, in the view of Blanke et al,

50 Blanke, Jürgens and Kastendiek 1974, p. 70.
51 Blanke 1975, p. 421.
52 Blanke, Jürgens and Kastendiek 1974, p. 55.
53 Esser 1975, p. 155.
54 Blanke 1975, p. 421.
55 Blanke 1975, p. 421; Blanke, Jürgens and Kastendiek 1974, p. 72 (emphasis in original).
56 Blanke, Jürgens and Kastendiek 1974, p. 71.

the 'extra-economic coercive force'.[57] Esser stresses following Pashukanis 'that the legal relations of the legal subjects of a commodity producing social formation do not "by their nature" imply a state of peace. This state of peace becomes necessary, however, when commodity exchange is meant to proceed smoothly according to its immanent principles'.[58] The political form therefore has the necessary function of guaranteeing continuous commodity production. In order to safeguard this, it has to adopt a 'particular' form, that is, one that is separated from the immediate class relations, for:

> this commodity production can only function, when all commodity owners face each other on the market as free and equal and possessing an autonomous free will. This ability to function is however significantly diminished if one or more of those commodity owners were to monopolise the coercive force for continuous commodity production. The freedom and equality of all would be abolished in favour of whoever has the monopoly over the use of force; the equality of the equivalent commodities would be destroyed. Thus the necessity for the function of force to be the monopoly of an entity that is not involved in the commodity exchanged has been proven.[59]

The modification of the political form on the level of capitalist commodity production consists in the fact that the continuity of the exchange is not maintained as it is on the simple level in the name of all, but reproduces the class-specific relations of domination. As in the case of the legal form, a mystification process also takes place with the political form: because of the equivalent exchange in the sphere of circulation it appears as a class-neutral entity.[60]

Thus one can then ultimately ask how the relation of state and law is conceived when the former is necessary for securing law. Only Blanke, Jürgens and Kastendiek speak to this: they assume that extra-economic coercive force thus has to start with the two central forms of social relations, the money and the legal form. The attempts to exert influence therefore do not take place directly without mediation, but are mediated through the basic forms. The 'extra-economic force thus "regulates" externally through the enforcement of norm-adequate conduct the factual reproduction relation'.[61] The relation of

57 Blanke 1975, p. 421.
58 Esser 1975, p. 155.
59 Esser 1975, pp. 156–7.
60 Esser 1975, p. 158.
61 Blanke 1975, p. 430.

state/politics and law is thus a congenial and close one. The basic form of politics is even defined as 'the debate about and the determination of legal relations ...'[62] Politics is the 'struggle over law and over the entity that guarantees law', the form in which class struggle expresses itself in the context of the bourgeois state.[63] Accordingly, the purely formal rights to freedom and equality also harbour a danger for the bourgeois system: namely as points where class struggle breaks into politics. Similarly to Negt and Neumann, Blanke et al assume that the bourgeois constitutional state has a double effect: law as a purely functional requirement *and* as a relation that transcends this.[64] It is, however, not clear here either why it is meant to have this dual character.

At this juncture one can also add a reflection by Tuschling which, in contrast to his suggestion on derivation, is a good continuation of Blanke et al. He thus stresses that the connection of state and law is not fixed; there are no effective connections. The state could temporarily detach itself from the formal system; in this he concurs with Neumann's and Kirchheimer's analysis of the constitutional state. The reason is that the relation of the individual to the generality (of the state) is again not constituted legally: 'The relation between the guaranteeing power and those, whose rights it is intended to systematically guarantee, again cannot be legally regulated and guaranteed; it remains a relation of force ...'[65] In other words, there is no coercive force that in turn binds the state to law.[66] Tuschling calls this dilemma, in contradistinction to normative approaches, 'non-reflexive'.[67] This fact shows up empirically in miscarriages of justice and in planned breaches of the law in totalitarian systems, but also in normal times in the final decisions of the highest courts. Minority opinions are declared 'unlawful'. With this institutionalisation of the highest courts, which no one can oversee anymore, their decisions, no matter how they turn out, become 'law'.[68] In Luhmann's words: courts are the institutions of deparadoxification.

1.2.4 Critique

In comparison to the legal theory debate, it can be noted that the form analysis 'faction' in the discussion on state derivation – a faction considered to have the

62 Blanke, Jürgens and Kastendiek 1974, p. 52.
63 Blanke, Jürgens and Kastendiek 1974, p. 74.
64 Blanke, Jürgens and Kastendiek 1974, p. 78.
65 Tuschling 1976, p. 81.
66 Tuschling 1976, p. 79.
67 Tuschling 1976, p. 81.
68 Ibid.

most advanced position in this discussion of the state –[69] has benefited from more wide-ranging debate. It is true that it cannot move beyond Pashukanis as far as the legal form itself is concerned, except perhaps for the clarification of the relationship of circulation and production. However, it does succeed in developing the idea behind this approach further by *methodologically* establishing the relationship of the different forms more precisely than Pashukanis himself. He must have had a similar concept in mind, but his fragmentary approach, which constituted rather a continual engagement with and distinction from bourgeois legal theories, could not deliver this. According to this insight, the value form can be considered as the methodological model that operationalises the reified social process. The legal form has to be reconstructed in a similar manner.

1.2.4.1 *Reductionism and Functionalism*

Yet *how* this is to happen still remains unclear, as the state theory approaches hardly provide further suggestions. Their arguments are predominantly reductionist and functionalist. Pashukanis' main weakness, of reducing law to the smooth circulation of commodities, endures. 'The legal form is therefore nothing else', Reich has written of Pashukanis, 'but the juridical mediation of commodity owners' relations … Legal form means contract; the complexity of the legal concept is not recognised'.[70] The single most fundamental metaphysical assumption of the theories presented thus far[71] consists in the idea that certain 'functions' become necessary in commodity-producing society, which then take on certain forms. 'Smooth' commodity exchange requires both the subjects to bring the commodities to the market and a state of peace. In this way, an ideal capitalist world is logically assumed in which the 'necessary' solution is always already found. Contingency, social struggles and the failure of functional solutions cannot be contemplated. But this theorem is in particular grounded in the notion, as Alain Lipietz appositely demonstrates,[72] that 'everything is made for something', whereby reproduction serves as the final reason for all functions. Only a subject can have a goal; but society is not a subject[73] but rather a myriad of contradictory relations. If at all, one can at most

69 Holloway and Picciotto 1978, p. 20; Kannankulam 2000, p. 128.

70 Reich 1973, p. 16.

71 Poulantzas also uses this circle, as we will see later on. In addition the 'definition of functions' of systems theory also remains similarly functionalist. The functionalist reasoning is a typical phenomenon of the 1960s and 1970s, when a euphoria for control mechanisms was convinced that relations could be constructed through state intervention.

72 Initially as a critique of Althusser's structuralism.

73 Lipietz 1997, p. 253.

speak of an ex-post functionalism and thus stress the logical coherence of various forms after the fact. To me the strategy of saying goodbye to functionalism as a whole and speaking instead of 'effects' appears, however, more promising. For such a shift, the theory of Michel Foucault provides some ideas.

1.2.4.2 *Blindness to Gender as a Structural Category*

The functionalist approach also makes another gap obvious – one which Marxist theory shares, as has been shown in the preceding chapter, with both systems theory and Habermas' discourse theory: namely its blindness to the structural category 'gender'. 'Structural category' means that the hierarchical gender relation is neither random nor particular, but a structurally present and institutionally anchored systemic factor in social formation.[74] This blindness is decisive for the crisis of Marxism. When the value or commodity form is meant to be *the* form of socialisation of bourgeois society, and everything has to be derived from it, then all social relations beyond the organisation of labour as a social activity to satisfy needs remain invisible. The legal form which is developed in this way serves to guarantee the exchange of commodities and remains limited to it in the way it operates – that is, it is not situated in relation to the totality of social relations. Even though it might be assumed that the legal form develops at the moment of commodity production, the question of how this specific socialisation is connected to other, in part also older forms of domination, should at least be addressed. Feminist critique has done enough to call attention to the fact that commodity production does not only comprise production and distribution, but also presupposes reproduction.[75] This means that the possibility of social reproduction also necessarily includes those processes which guarantee the lives of individuals.[76]

> The particularities of capitalism – its dependency on unpaid labour for the reproduction of labour power, and its separation of home and workplace – have combined patriarchal gender relations and the capitalist structure. As historical structures, capitalism found at hand family households that, by means of pre-capitalist patriarchal structures and gender segregation, established both the responsibility of women for reproductive activities and the lower esteem of women's labour to which that responsibility is tied.[77]

---

74 Becker-Schmidt 1990, p. 392.
75 Beer 1990, p. 266.
76 Becker-Schmidt 1990, p. 391.
77 Kohlmorgen 2004, p. 40.

But blindness to gender relations could also develop because capitalism is *logically* conceived as gender-neutral, although *historically* this is not the case. Similarly to systems theory, this approach, albeit 30 years earlier, jumped to the conclusion that socialisation is based upon a single principle from which all relations, including domination, are derived. However, the gender relation in particular shows that there exist forms of domination – such as sexual exploitation and violence – which can in no way be derived from commodity production, or only at the price of a crude economism. Because of this monism, when they looked into the mystification of class relations through law the state theorists did not even consider whether there might not be other relations of domination made to disappear under its formal freedom and equality.

1.2.4.3 *The Symbiosis of State and Law*

It is also problematic that engaging with the legal form, while essentially completely adopting its 'derivation' from Pashukanis, becomes something of an alibi. For further considerations did not seem appropriate for the legal form, given that it is only the backdrop against which the state can develop, as well as the form it has to use in its expression. Law is nothing without the coercive force it guarantees. That the law of value leads 'necessarily' to the law of right and the latter requires the state for its own realisation – this is the ultimate rationale here. Joachim Hirsch rightly objected that it is not the legal form that creates the state form, 'but the particularity of capitalist reproduction of class relations ... a particular formal determination of class violence and the particular form of bourgeois law', so that both cannot be mutually derived from each other.[78] This shows that *legal theory* is not recognised as its own field by the state theorists. Law was used as a vehicle to then reach the actual subject: the state. It therefore seems as though it would be sufficient to fall back on Pashukanis for the question of law.

1.2.4.4 *The Illusory Legality of the State's Activities*

Finally, the assertion of Blanke et al that besides the money form the state's central form of action is the law has to be criticised. The authors certainly reach the correct conclusion, that even the most unjust regimes still give themselves the appearance of legality. In principle, however, one has to concur with Hirsch's critique that this leads to the untenable thesis that the state's exercise of violence is consistently legal.[79] Against this, the non-reflexivity described by

78 Hirsch 1976, p. 146, Note 11.
79 Hirsch 1976, p. 147, Note 11.

Tuschling can show that legality is only a moment and that boundless regulation is its co-original compliment.[80] Indeed, in Blanke et al the force of public law that cannot be derived from the exchange relation necessarily appears as a deus ex machina that cannot be systematically explained at all.[81] But this critique does not go far enough either. For the legal fetishism of this perspective does not end with the addition of extra-legal violence. It rather consists precisely in that state activity as a whole is reduced to the duality of legal/illegal. This would remain within the same paradigm – in Foucault's words, the juridical discourse[82] – according to which the rule of the state is exercised on an external and repressive basis. As though it were enough to establish a legal norm and equip it with the power of sanctions in order to mechanistically force the exchange agents to engage in 'norm adequate' behaviour. 'Objective force' and individual actions are conceived in a way that is too one-sided. While individual actions are necessary – legality does not enforce itself – actions no longer have any independence here. Power is outside the subjects and the actions of the state are, accordingly, exclusively repressive. At this point the French-Italian approach, which will be covered below, introduces the categories of the 'integral state', of 'hegemony', of 'ideological state apparatuses', and of 'government' as well as of 'discipline' and 'bio-politics'.

1.2.4.5 *The Relationship of Form and History*

Finally, the main critique of the debate on derivation in form analysis as a whole must be borne in mind. One could call it the critique of abstract academicism. The entire approach is fundamentally a-historical, in that history always only appears as an external moment and any empirical review is postponed for later. In particular this has been pointed out by John Holloway and Sol Picciotto, as well as Bob Jessop.[83] Instead of a 'conceptually informed understanding' of empirical reality, a logical deduction is carried out.[84] Joachim Hirsch traces the concentration on abstract-categorical problems and the concomitant academisation in the 1970s back to the particular socio-political situation in West Germany, that is, a period of relatively 'undisturbed' capital accumulation in the Fordist formation and the ideological integration of the working class.[85] This specific situation led to the limitation of theory to purely

80 Hirsch 1976, paraphrasing Preuß.
81 Ibid.
82 Foucault 2000, p. 46.
83 Holloway and Picciotto 1978, p. 22; Jessop 1990, p. 58.
84 Holloway and Picciotto 1978, p. 26.
85 Hirsch 1976.

objective 'structural laws', because the practice of (class) struggle appeared to be missing from reality.

The advantage of this approach is that it avoids any rash assumptions of instrumentalisation (law as the instrument of the ruling class) and provides a theoretically rigorous explanation. A categorical state derivation is therefore not wrong or superfluous, but a fundamental precondition of any analysis.[86] '"State derivation" begins to be theoretically questionable when the epistemological scope of this approach, which lies in its specific level of abstraction, is not correctly assessed'.[87] For it is then no longer possible to determine how the coercion into a form translates in practice. 'In their abstraction the state derivation debate can often only refer to seemingly blindly functioning "economic laws", which ensure that the "correct" politics are pursued'.[88] Struggles, however, cannot be understood as external reactions to purely technical laws; rather the historical process of capitalist development has to be decrypted as the movement of (class) struggles.[89] Those social struggles always contain a certain degree of autonomous movement,[90] and are not merely subjective realisations of objective constraints, brought together by a metaphysical world spirit. What matters is thus a 'categorically guided investigation into the concrete mediating relation between the social formation's objective structural and movement principles and the class struggles that advance the historical process'.[91] Picciotto values a perspective where class relations are embedded in the law itself.[92] Classes must not be conceived of as external moments.[93] This leads to an ahistorical, abstract structural analysis, which continually postpones the historical investigation until a later point in time.

It is therefore crucial to both accurately distinguish between the levels of abstraction and to plausibly explain in the course of describing them more concretely the relationship of general structural principles and concrete social formations with their institutions and balance of powers.[94] Today's materialist legal theory has to meet those demands. It is not sufficient to emphasise, as Moishe Postone still did in a text published in 1993, that the reflections on form analysis constitute only abstract preconditions of modern capitalism, and that

86 Hirsch 1976, p. 102.
87 Hirsch 1976, p. 101.
88 Kannankulam 2000, p. 128.
89 Hirsch 1976, p. 128.
90 Hirsch 1976, p. 130.
91 Hirsch 1976, p. 103.
92 Picciotto 1982, p. 170.
93 Picciotto 1982, p. 171.
94 Thus also Jessop 1990, p. 58.

'they do not represent an attempt to analyse directly, without any mediations, a more concrete level of social reality on the basis of the most abstract categories'.[95] If this conclusion is actually correct, it must also have consequences. Otherwise the quite correct insight that the 'impersonal and seemingly objective character' of capitalist domination distinguishes this socialization decisively from previous ones,[96] is questionably escalated to consist, 'on its most fundamental level', not 'in the domination of people by other people, but in the domination of people by abstract social structures',[97] that is to say 'a form of abstract social domination'.[98] Such erroneous one-sidedness would lead form analysis to join systems theory in taking the undialectical side of merely systemic domination. According to Marx, however, it is people who make their own history – even if not under circumstances they choose for themselves.[99] In this sense, people certainly do rule over people – but simply not in the immediate class-reductionist manner that Postone rightly seeks to distance himself from.

1.3 *On the Concept of 'Form Analysis'*

It is notable that the legal form approaches barely address the underlying question of what actually is to be understood by the concept of the form. 'Form analysis' can, depending on the theoretical approach, actually mean different and even completely divergent things. The commodity form of capitalist society might still be the common starting point, but what is meant by this needs to be interpreted. At the latest this becomes clear with Tuschling, for whom form meant the same thing as 'mere form', an abstract shell, a form of expression. What is essential is the content.[100] This shows again the idea of an intrinsic reality, which only projects schematic shadows onto the surface like in the 'allegory of the cave'.

The state theory approach, on the other hand, explicitly wanted to focus on a form analysis. Thus, on the one hand, the authors wanted to pick up from the *social theorists* who in principle (that is independently of questions of the state or the law) worked with the Marxian form analysis (such as Backhaus, Reichelt or Rodolsky),[101] in order to, on the other hand, pursue it further towards an

95 Postone 1993, p. 21.
96 Postone 1993, p. 3.
97 Postone 1993, p. 30.
98 Postone 1993, p. 31.
99 Marx 2002, p. 19.
100 See also Maihofer 1995, p. 244, Note 19.
101 Blanke, Jürgens and Kastendiek 1974, p. 63, Note 31.

analysis of the state with Pashukanis and his category of the 'form'.[102] By *forms* they understood the fixed, alienated, seemingly factually determined and ahistorical conditions which subjects of capitalist society necessarily have to enter into (commodity, money, capital, wage labour, profit, etc.). Those are meant to be stripped of their ahistorical character through analysis and decrypted as results of human activities: 'We call this approach in the following simply *form analysis*'.[103] Although this is finally a step in the right direction for developing Pashukanis further, in order to correct his central deficit – it is still nothing more than that. For *why* those 'fixed conditions' develop, and how the process of reification takes place, is not explained. Instead the continuation of Pashukanis' project consists mainly in undertaking this analysis as a structural analysis of the 'necessary requirements' of capitalist commodity production. Today the form analysis approaches are by and large marginalised and have gone 'out of fashion', certainly *also* due to their bad abstraction. As their underlying idea, which Joachim Hirsch will later call 'social forms', remains undeveloped,[104] renewed engagement, starting in a more general manner, is worthwhile.[105]

Isaac Balbus's essay is the first real attempt at carrying out legal form analysis beyond the thesis of the commodity guardians. He probably succeeds in doing so because he only 'discovered' Pashukanis' text after completing his own,[106] and was thus able to change the perspective from the functionalist question of law's *function* for commodity exchange to the question of the manner in which the legal form *functions*. Balbus was the first who did not ask which deficits in the master plan of commodity production law mediates, but rather which form human relations adopt when they present themselves as legal ones. Tellingly Balbus is also more careful as far as the relation of forms to each other is concerned, and conceptualises it as homologous.[107] Homology means a resemblance between two situations, but in contrast to analogy only with regards to their genesis, not to their 'function'. According to this both forms have significantly similar characteristics, but cannot be derived from each other. Rather, they both stem from the same historic development.

102 Blanke, Jürgens and Kastendiek 1974, p. 63.
103 Blanke, Jürgens and Kastendiek 1974, pp. 64–5.
104 See also Esser, Hirsch and Görg 1994.
105 Similarly also Harms 2000, p. 173.
106 Balbus 1977, p. 577, Note 5.
107 Balbus 1977, p. 573.

1.3.1 The Homology of Commodity Form and Legal Form

The similarity between the commodity and legal form consists in their 'movement from the concrete to the abstract', that is from concrete to abstract labour, from inequality to equality. Thus the commodity form stems from concrete human needs and creative labour, but conceals this nature in such a way that people necessarily forget this origin:

> The commodity form, in other words, is an economic form that necessarily functions independently of, or autonomously from, the will of the subjects who set it in motion. Thus the fetishism of commodities: the masking of the link between commodities and their human origin gives rise to the appearance, the ideological inversion, that commodities have living, human powers. Products appear to take on a life of their own, dominating the very human subjects who in fact bring them into existence but who no longer 'know' this. Commodity fetishism thus entails a profound reversal of the real causal relationship between humans and their products: humans, the subjects who create or cause the objects, become the object ...[108]

The way social labour thus becomes autonomous from the worker finds its *parallel* in the legal form. While the products of social labour take on the commodity form, in the capitalist mode of production human beings take on the form of individual citizens. The concrete subject with its qualitatively different human needs or interests, which is like no other, is at the same time the object of exchange, and only exists to represent and to be represented by others. Thus qualitatively different subjects become what they are not: equal. This relation of equivalence is made possible by the law.[109] The legal form is thus an abstraction of the qualitatively different needs of subjects and their activities: 'The "blindness" of the legal form to substantive human interests and characteristics thus parallels the blindness of the commodity form to use-value and concrete labor, and if the commodity-form functions to "extinguish" the "memory" of use-value and concrete labor, so too the legal form functions to extinguish the memory of different interests and social origins'.[110] Balbus calls this homologous principle 'the common mode of substitution'.[111]

108 Balbus 1977, p. 574.
109 Balbus 1977, p. 575.
110 Balbus 1977, p. 576.
111 Ibid.

1.3.2 Abstract Commonality

The shared historic development of the forms is according to Balbus rooted in the kind of sociality that arises under capitalist conditions: legal individuality means under capitalism the abstraction from any qualitative determination and difference, that is, ultimately, nothing other than the individualism and egotism of the commodity exchanging person. The individual exchange agents are necessarily indifferent to the reciprocal needs of others, those serve merely as means for one's own 'private' interests. The individual is not able to act as a *social* individual, aware of the inextricable connection between its development and the development of everyone else.[112] The 'Hegelian Marxist' understanding that dominates here, according to which human beings are always already socialised and as such are the condition (and precisely not as in Kant the 'limit') of the freedom of the respective other, are contrasted with the really existing particularist socialisation, in which exactly this 'inextricable connection' is denied and de facto (really) abstracted from. Under those conditions society also has to take on an illusory character. The 'concrete particularism' of capitalist society, that is the selfish homo economicus, causes a solely 'abstract commonality', that is to say one which, while it is social, has to be externally imposed (through laws, obligations, the state), while only a 'concrete communality' would make it possible 'that individuals act as social individuals who are bound by neither interest nor obligation but rather by the *concrete universal of social need*'.[113] For Balbus such a socialisation is only thinkable if capitalist society is transcended, according to Marx's idea of a 'higher phase of communist society' (see above).

1.3.3 Legal Fetishism

The consequence of the legal form, and this constitutes the specific *formal character* of this development, is legal fetishism:

> The legal form is normally not called into question, I would argue, because the form itself ordinarily precludes the possibility of performing this critical operation. The calling into question of the legal order presupposes individuals who conceive themselves as subjects evaluating an object which they have created and over which they have control. It is just this presupposition, however, which is nullified by the perverse logic of the legal form; this form creates a fetishised relationship between individu-

112 Balbus 1977, p. 578.
113 Balbus 1977, p. 580.

> als and the law in which individuals attribute subjectivity to the law and conceive themselves as its objects or creations.[114]

The reification of social conditions to forms is accordingly the main reason for the atomisation of those conditions, up to the point of making it impossible to recognise this very development. This is for example manifested in theories of the absolute autonomy of the law or in everyday notions that the law is essential for every kind of human society – beliefs which Balbus calls a 'homage to the God-Law'.[115] When society is understood as a result of law and not the other way around, law as the result of a specific kind of society, it is no longer problematised and the illusion is created that law has an actual life of its own: 'Commodity fetishism and legal fetishism are thus two inseparably related aspects of an inverted "topsy-turvy" existence under a capitalist mode of production in which *humans are first reduced to abstractions, and then dominated by their own creations*'.[116] It is only possible to understand the forms by decoding them.[117]

1.4 *Conclusion*

Thus far the study has made it clear that the direction Pashukanis first started out in, of making form analysis useful for legal theory, left open questions. Independently of the fact that a theory necessarily always produces gaps, the thesis advanced here was, however, that a key factor in this was that he only claimed to undertake a form analysis. The path towards a form analysis remained blocked in the 1970s, in particular due to the idea of the derivation of forms. It is only Balbus who succeeds in taking this route, inspired by the striking resemblance of the abstraction and replacement between the two forms. The *commonality* which this 'general mode of substitution' points to is the manner of *socialisation*. Following Balbus I will attempt in my own analysis to develop this approach further. First this requires, however, one further essential correction: the subjects whose particularity is abstracted from appear in Balbus as pre-existing units of first nature, which are deformed in their naturalness by social forms. Such a subject also served as the basic element of legal theory in Pashukanis. This understanding requires a correction via approaches which instead start from the production of those subjects. In particular, differences have to be mapped out as socially produced. This constitutes above all the ori-

114 Balbus 1977, p. 582.
115 Balbus 1977, p. 583.
116 Balbus 1977, p. 584 (emphasis in original).
117 Balbus 1977, pp. 584–5.

ginality of Michael Foucault. At this point the form analysis can be productively connected with (post)structuralist legal theory.

2 The Franco-Italian Theory Strand

2.1 *Introduction*

The theorists presented thus far argued more or less within the lineage of Marx interpretation that sees Marx in the tradition of Hegel. As has already been noted with regard to the critique of Pashukanis, the second line of materialist legal theory starts from the notion that Marx breaks so radically with Hegel that such an interpretation is untenable. The difference between the two theoretical strands stems precisely from those diverging interpretations. This difference will therefore be clarified now, before the Franco-Italian theoretical strand is presented. This is especially necessary because it involved a political-theoretical decision that plays a crucial role for the question of law's significance in society as a whole.

2.1.1 Critical Theory versus Poststructuralism

The difference in the concepts of the two theories stems from their respective historical and political contexts of the 1960s and 1970s. Louis Althusser's Hegel-intervention took place against the background of the situation of the communist parties at the time.[118] He proclaimed the above-mentioned 'line of demarcation', beyond which he wanted to banish those ideas that are '"liberal" and "ethical" in tendency' and rediscover the themes of 'freedom', 'the human person' and 'alienation' by referencing Marx's early writings, to the realm of the unscientific.[119] The 'humanist Marxists' thus identified, and they also included real-socialist theorists and politicians, are Althusser's real intellectual and political opponents. However, building upon this, a dualism between critical theory and poststructuralism developed which had little to do with the starting situation, and which continues to this day. Although both tendencies polemicised in Germany as well as in France against a certain idea of the state as upheld by the dominant parliamentary social democracy or socialists/communists,[120] with both reaching similar results despite their different theoretical references, a 'differentiation' into two theory camps occurred.

118 Kannankulam 2000.
119 Althusser 2005, pp. 10 ff.
120 Kannankulam 2000.

Undoubtedly Marx used Hegel in his early writings differently from how he did in *Capital* and *Grundrisse*. Also Alfred Schmidt asserts that Marx's early engagement with Hegel did not yet establish a clear materialist position on absolute idealism, but that Marx engaged at a more mature age in a second study of Hegel.[121] Only the further conclusion, that he had stepped out of 'the shade of Hegel'[122] in such a way that not only 'humanist Marxism', but any Hegelian Marxism had become untenable, marks the end of commonalities.

Hans Georg Backhaus, for example, counters this with the thesis that one must note a 'striking continuity in Marx's thinking from his dissertation until his last economic work'.[123] What is in turn understood by Hegel's philosophy, and thus the premise of the statements on continuity and discontinuity, also depends on whether it is referenced in the form of the critical theory of, for instance, Adorno, Horkheimer or Marcuse, or rather of Kojève. While legal theorists following Althusser appear to believe that the mere mention of the Hegel problem is enough to dismiss for instance Pashukanis, the other side has become enflamed with something of a Marx-mythology, which suggests that Marx's method remains a dark secret, that value theory therefore remains misunderstood until now,[124] and that the 'only authentic form of Marx's value theory' was never published by Marx.[125] The politically engaged Marx, of all people, is here banished to the sphere of esoteric secrecy and politics of truth.

The increasing one-sidedness of both tendencies is more an expression of social marginalisation than the sign of a productive dispute. I therefore join the position that considers a dialogue between those theories indispensable, 'which does not get carried away in flattening the certainly important differences of the two, but which also sees that both harbour differently developed potentials of social critique, which can productively mutually enrich and illuminate each other, as soon as concrete social critique is undertaken'.[126] This can in particular be demonstrated for legal theory. I will therefore engage in the following with this central difference.

2.1.2 Totality …

All theories presented thus far have an implicit concept of totality and have shown in various ways that the question of *how* the different social spheres are

---

121 See Reichelt 1973, p. 75.
122 Althusser 2005, p. 116.
123 Backhaus 1997, p. 11.
124 Backhaus 1997, p. 16.
125 Backhaus 1997, p. 13.
126 jour-fixe-inititative-berlin 1999, p. 11.

mediated together is very much decisive for a materialist legal theory, because this assigns law its position. To begin with, both theory strands have in common that they assume in the tradition of Marx that law cannot have a history of its own,[127] but always has to be seen in the context of society as a whole. The difference only consists in *how* this whole is conceptualised. Concrete totality in a reading of Marx inspired by Hegel means that all individual elements depend upon it. Totality thus forms a structure beyond the accumulation of individual moments, but it cannot be logically abstracted from them, but rather contains all concrete single moments as the condition of its own possibility.[128] This can be expressed in a circular model: the entire cycle can only function if there are independent moments. Something can only connect to itself if it goes through something else. This other can be so different as to be the opposite. Nonetheless each of the moments contains determinations of the starting point.[129] 'The form of the total system', thus Adorno, 'requires everyone to respect the law of exchange of he does not wish to be destroyed'.[130] This exchange relation contains the antagonism which could 'at any time bring organised society to ultimate catastrophe and destroy it. The whole business keeps creaking and groaning on, at unspeakable human cost, only on account of the profit motive and the interiorization by individuals of the breach torn in society as a whole'.[131] In consequence society is a precarious whole that connects through a particular moment. Socialisation follows a fundamental dynamic, that of accumulation, which has to assert itself 'creaking and groaning' through exchange. This means that all social relations of power and domination, whatever independent significance they may have, are always mediated and connected by this dynamic. Thus Joachim Hirsch writes, for example, as a rationale for why the *capitalist* form of socialisation has to be the starting point:

> In reality there is a whole range of other social differences in relations of domination, exploitation and subordination; based on gender, religion, culture, or region. Those can neither be simply 'derived' from capitalist class relations nor would they disappear with it. They are actually most of the time older than capitalist society itself ... The reason for making the capitalist form of socialisation the starting point for an analysis of the state, is therefore not that those differences constitute insignificant

127 MECW, Volume 5, p. 36.
128 Adorno 2000a, p. 59.
129 Daniel 1983, p. 121.
130 Adorno 1989, p. 149.
131 Ibid.

> or even subordinated 'side-contradictions'. To the contrary, nature and gender relations, and sexual or racist oppression are inseparably interwoven with the capital relation and it could not even exist without them. *Decisive is, however, that the capitalist form of socialization is the context of material reproduction and as such determines the social structures and institutions in which all those social antagonisms are expressed and connected.*[132]

Socialisation understood in the tradition of critical theory implies the 'tendency of developing capitalism to enter all thinkable life-areas and life-forms of social reproduction',[133] and cast all moments of the totality in its light. In this tradition law would therefore have to be developed from the context of the material reproduction of capitalist socialisation. Precisely this is attempted by Pashukanis and also by his successors when they derive law from the moment they have identified as central, namely commodity production.

Also Regina Becker-Schmidt takes up this concept of socialisation from critical theory, but corrects it with regard to the conception of gender relations in a way that assumes a 'double socialisation'.[134] Upon closer inspection, however, we see that with this she departs from the already represented concepts of totality, for now at least two dynamics have been identified that will leave their mark on all moments: the dynamics of accumulation and gender relations. For law, this means that it cannot be enough to relate law only to commodity production. This is no accident, for precisely at the point where capitalist socialisation and gender relations fracture, the difficulty of mediating different structuring principles of totality together in social theory becomes apparent.[135]

2.1.3 … Or a Complexly Structured Whole with One Dominant?

Althusser's concept of the social totality is primarily opposed to the vulgar Marxism of Stalinism.[136] This has to be stressed, because – as must have become clear – critical theory does not assume a single, realised contradiction 'which exteriorises and interiorises the economic *ad infinitum*'.[137] It is therefore possible to find some common points despite the differences in their derivation.

132 Hirsch 1995, p. 25 (emphasis S.B.).
133 Becker-Schmidt 1990, p. 384.
134 Becker-Schmidt 1990, p. 390.
135 Dackweiler 1995, p. 94.
136 Lipietz 1993, pp. 104–5.
137 Lipietz 1993, p. 107.

Firstly, unlike critical theory, Althusser depends in his concept of the whole on Marx's base-superstructure model, which he interprets as a 'metaphor':[138] the structure of a society is constituted by different instances which relate to each other in that they are articulated by a specific determination. He thus arrives at three instances: the economic (base) as well as politics and ideology as the two instances of the superstructure.[139] In doing so he imports the term 'instance' from the Lacanian variant of Freud's psychoanalysis, which considers the psyche as an apparatus of multiple instances.[140] Here every instance is independent. There is no privileged place of social activity, no single social dynamic, but only economic, ideological, theoretical and political practices.[141] The whole is always already given as a complex entity in the sense that it is constituted by diverse, independent contradictions and not an original unity. This is the crucial point at which Althusser seeks to set himself apart from Hegel.[142] The instances cannot be derived from a uniform principle, and there is no inner unity of the social whole. This is the sense of understanding it as an 'apparatus'.[143] With the apparatus no inner, substantive connection is imagined, but only an external organisation; not an intrinsic centre, but only a changing hierarchical structure. The apparatus cannot bring the difference of the elements into one identity; it can only organise their encounter, but it cannot unify them. This unity remains a complex, de-centred one.[144]

Therefore critical theory and Althusser's Marxist structuralism at first seem to differ significantly on this point. Indeed, both theories share the idea of independent moments or instances. But while critical theory assumes a unifying principle (socialisation through exchange that is driven by accumulation) as a privileged place of the social whole which makes an inner unification possible, Althusser appears to assume a complex whole, in which the different instances of society are only articulated externally. Yet with a closer look at the hierarchisation of the instances, the differences between the two versions increasingly dissolve.

For Althusser does not leave it at that, but adds that within the whole there is a dominant structure, which is its unity.[145] It is 'the general light tingeing

138 Althusser 1984, pp. 8–9.
139 Althusser 1984, p. 8.
140 Charim 2002, p. 24.
141 Charim 2002, pp. 25–7.
142 Lipietz 1993, pp. 104–5.
143 Charim 2002, p. 41.
144 Charim 2002, p. 42. See also Part 3, Institutions.
145 Lipietz 1993, p. 105.

all other colours and modifying them in their specific quality'.[146] Althusser interprets the metaphor of base and superstructure in such a way that the economic base ultimately dominates.[147] Indeed, the general validity of economic determination is denied, because its hour never comes. Moreover, conditions are always 'overdetermined', and also the instances of the superstructure can be determining. But an echo of the privilege of economics can be found in its pre-eminence in the chorus of different determinations.[148]

Although a different instance can be dominant in a particular social formation (for example religious ideology), the determining position of economics consists in the fact that it ultimately decides, as the 'conductor', which parts the respective instances (itself included) play in the matrix of structural positions, for it guarantees the 'primacy of being'.[149] This primacy follows the formulation in *The German Ideology* that people have to be able to live to be able to 'make history'. Thus the 'production of the means to satisfy these needs' becomes 'the first premise of all human existence'.[150] Economics is for Althusser no longer so much the foundation in a spatial metaphor, but rather the highest judgement; it occupies different practices with its dominant role, so that one has to assume a 'complex causality': the practices/instances are only determined as such (by way of the determinant).[151] The instances thus have 'relative autonomy'.[152] Here Althusser uses the same term as Neumann. 'The degree of the instance's autonomy is determined by their dependence upon the whole'.[153]

Andrea Maihofer, following Althusser, develops what this means for law. In particular, law cannot be derived from a moment: 'A historically specific law is thus in fact some kind of "result" of a multitude of social reasons'.[154] The dominance of the economic sphere means that it defines fundamental structuring characteristics for law. But law only takes note of them in its own way. It is thus merely interwoven with or rooted in it, and not its realisation, just like 'it is hardly possibly to say of a tree or a spring that they are functional elements of the earth'.[155]

146 MECW, Volume 28, p. 43.
147 Althusser 1984, p. 9.
148 Charim 2002, p. 28.
149 Charim 2002, p. 34.
150 MECW, Volume 5, p. 42.
151 MECW, Volume 5, p. 35.
152 Althusser 1984, p. 9.
153 Charim 2002, p. 39.
154 Maihofer 1992, p. 151.
155 Maihofer 1992, p. 152.

If the spheres of the superstructure do not constitute dependent moments, then they can also no longer merely be forms of false consciousness that cover up a material reality. Althusser instead assumes that ideology and law have a material reality of their own in practices and social institutions.[156] Applied to law this means, according to Maihofer, that the legal relation of commodity exchange, for example, has to be understood as a historically determined type of action and consciousness, which has taken shape little by little in the social practice of exchange and which was gradually reflexively developed and transformed into the legal category of the contract: 'Law is the historically determined way in which this relation is practiced, felt and known', nothing but a 'specific mode of existence'.[157] With the concept of the 'mode of existence', which Maihofer relates in her later writings to gender relations,[158] she aims to make explicit that law has its own materiality in practices. It is not solely a form of consciousness, but a complex connection of different historically formed ways of thinking and feeling, bodily practices as well as social conditions and institutions: 'a historically determined manner of *existing*'.[159] Only in bourgeois society, that is in one of independent, isolated, free and equal individuals, their relations to each other are predominantly lived, practised and felt as intentional relations of free and equal individuals, and thus as legal ones.[160]

2.1.4 … Or Incomplete Totality?

The difference between the two concepts of the social whole is furthermore only relative. Indeed, the two approaches conceptualise the combination of the relatively autonomous moments/instances differently: one as an immanent, fractured connection, the other as an external, forced unification. But ultimately the unity that is produced is, in parallel to its conception in systems theory (see above), the result of *one* structuring principle, which is here the theoretical privileging of 'material reproduction'. In one version this consists in assuming a specific dynamics of unification through exchange-mediated accumulation, in the other it consists in the ultimate determination of all social relations, no matter how overdetermined they might be, through the requirements of economic structuring. It can thus be said that the *materialist* moment of both approaches lies in the mentioned 'primacy of being', which, regardless of how it is mediated, occupies a privileged social position.

156 Althusser 1984, pp. 36 ff.
157 Maihofer 1992, pp. 188–9.
158 Maihofer 1995.
159 Maihofer 1995, p. 85.
160 Maihofer 1992, p. 218.

Ernesto Laclau's and Chantal Mouffe's change to discourse theory ultimately also says goodbye to such a privilege. The authors assume that Althusser has to be radicalised.[161] His idea of overdetermination has to be thought through rigorously, that means, ultimately without determination.[162] Economics itself is no homogenous medium which is moved by some kind of 'laws', but a field of struggles which knows no other 'laws of motion' besides those that stem from a field of antagonistic forces. The economic space also constitutes itself based upon a *political* balance of powers; 'what sense does it then have, to speak of economics as ultimately determinant?'[163]

This argument also applies in the same way to critical theory. Here too the dynamics of accumulation and exchange are ultimately politically and ideologically overdetermined. We will see in Foucault, as Marx had already described in the chapter on 'Primitive Accumulation',[164] that neither the subjects of exchange nor the commodity of labour power are originally given, but that they must first be politically constituted and continually reproduced. The same applies to the dynamics of the 'accumulation of capital', which does not occur automatically, but which is always enmeshed in struggles over hegemony. It therefore appears consistent that Laclau and Mouffe conclude that there cannot be a simple basic principle that fixes the field of differences. 'The incomplete character of every totality leads us necessarily to abandon as the terrain of analysis the premise of *"society"* as a sewn up and self-defined totality'. Altogether, one can only speak of a partial limitation of the field of contingency.[165]

2.2 *Nicos Poulantzas*

Up to now Poulantzas has only been considered as a critic of Pashukanis. In what follows his own approach to legal theory will now be presented. This intention is, however, confronted with a difficulty. Poulantzas developed his theoretical tools in the course of his research three times, and as such one can speak of three different phases in his thought. For legal theory it is decisive that he only addressed questions of legal philosophy explicitly in his early phase, up to his dissertation, which was characterised by its combination of existentialism and Marxism.[166] His legal theory critique of Pashukanis dates,

161 Laclau and Mouffe 2001, p. 97.
162 Laclau and Mouffe 2001, p. 99.
163 Laclau 1982, p. 10.
164 Marx 1976, Chapter 26.
165 Laclau and Mouffe 2000, pp. 97, 111 (emphasis in original).
166 Jessop 1985, p. 26.

however, from his second phase,[167] which is completely rooted in the tradition of Althusser's structuralism;[168] but this consists in his adopting almost word-for-word well known concepts of Althusser's. As described above, this mainly serves to show that the different social instances – and thus also law – have their own dynamics. This can hardly be seen as a special personal contribution on Poulantzas's part. Only when he begins to turn to state theory – still completely within Althusser's conceptual framework – and introduces other elements into his theory, in particular ones from Antonio Gramsci, does Poulantzas's theory begin to take the form that will prove him an original thinker, as is exemplified by the book *State Theory* from this third phase. Along the lines of West German form analysis, it is no longer centred on law, but on the capitalist state.[169] Law is now only of secondary interest. Today Poulantzas is therefore mainly known as a state theorist. But as Bob Jessop has already pointed out, in the history of his reception there has been a notable neglect of the enduring significance of Poulantzas's legal education. Poulantzas did not only obtain his first academic degree in law, but he also went to Germany and France after his dissertation in order to undertake further research in legal theory. His early academic contributions were almost exclusively in the fields of legal theory and legal philosophy.[170] But also when Poulantzas started to engage with the state, his analysis of the state's institutional structure remained in many ways influenced by legal theory.[171] Indeed, this legal theory orientation is one of the three source of Poulantzas's theoretical and strategic innovations identified by Jessop (besides French philosophy and Italian Marxism).[172] I will therefore proceed firstly by addressing briefly the feature of legal theory that also fascinated Poulantzas throughout his life, namely the '*autonomy*' of law, in order to then ask how he could connect this with his relational approach (Jessop). From this combination the somewhat implicit insights for legal theory contained in the third phase can be developed.

167 Jessop 1985, p. 50.

168 Poulantzas 1972.

169 'Who today can escape the question of the State and power? Who indeed does not talk about it? The current political situation, not only France but in the whole of Europe, is certainly one reason for its topicality', he writes already at the start of his book on the state (Poulantzas 2000, p. 11).

170 Jessop 1985, p. 322.

171 Jessop 1985, p. 323.

172 Jessop 1985, p. 313.

2.2.1 The Autonomy of Law

Poulantzas shares his fascination with the autonomy of law with Hans Kelsen and preserves it in his later terminology, most notably in the concepts of 'relative autonomy' and 'class unity'.[173] This 'continual subterranean influence'[174] makes him in principle inaccessible for economistic or voluntaristic interpretations that see in law nothing but a phenomenon of the superstructure.

Poulantzas works through the Neo-Kantian legal theory of Kelsen, just like most Marxist legal and state theorists of the previous generation.[175] Kelsen's *Pure Theory of Law* – a theory which conceptualises law as an independently existing order with enforced coercive norms of its own, and which treats research into the roots and effects of law as a meta-juridical concern[176] – has always been met with the protests of Marxist theorists, who argue that it neglects exactly those material social conditions that are the basis of any legal development. Kelsen insists on the 'specific autonomy of the system of norms', which comes to stand in fundamental opposition to being.[177] Poulantzas, similar to his predecessors, sought to overcome the 'bourgeois antinomy of what is and what ought to be' in such a way that law is neither independent of social reality, nor only its reflex. His concept during this first phase is the 'internal-external dialectic'[178] which goes back to Sartre. Kelsen is the first legal theorist to rigorously consider the particularity of the capitalist legal form, that is to say its 'inner logic'. Most Marxist legal theorists, adopting a ideology-critical approach, overlook this.[179] Poulantzas on the other hand, beyond the critique of Kelsen, takes on a lot of this insight in his early model and also in his later concept of 'relative autonomy'. He assumes that it is crucial to research the internal logic of the legal system (and in particular the principles of abstractions, universality, formalism, and codification as a basis for the changeability of norms)[180] which Kelsen calls 'logic of norms' – but also at the same time the external relations of this system:

> *Internally* it is necessary to investigate how the juridical system reveals a specific axiomatisation, hierarchisation of powers, and logical coherence

173 Thus also Jessop 1985, p. 323.
174 Jessop 1985, p. 26.
175 See Adler 1964; Klenner 1972; Pashukanis 2003; Reich 1978; but also Ehrlich 2009.
176 Kelsen 2005, p. 1.
177 Kelsen 1981, p. 80.
178 Jessop 1985, p. 40.
179 Buckel 2007.
180 Jessop 1985, p. 36.

> such that superior norms validate inferior norms ... *Externally* it is necessary to show how this system is related to the exploitation of oppressed classes through the repressive power of the state. Continuing this dialectical method it is also necessary to show how each juridical norm or institution that is engendered by economic imperatives at the base is then integrated into its distinctive place in the legal universe and thereby overdetermined by the legal order as a whole.[181]

This means that Poulantzas accepts Kelsen's formal logical approach in so far as he historicises it and marks it as a specific feature of modern law.[182]

2.2.2 The Relationship of Forces: The Influence of Antonio Gramsci

In order to grasp Poulantzas's later approach it is important to clearly understand just how crucial Antonio Gramsci's theory of hegemony is for him.[183] Poulantzas integrates this theoretical element already in *Political Power and Social Classes* (1978) in his analysis of power. In his later writings he no longer primarily combines it with the Althusserian theory of instances, but with moments of Foucault's analysis of micro-powers.

2.2.2.1 *Relations of Production as the Basis of Power*

For the Marxist Poulantzas, the relations of production and the social division of labour form the basis of power. Relations of production does not mean an economic structure,[184] but political, ideological and economic conditions. In the assertion of the relations of production in the rights and powers of classes, which result from the positions of those classes, political and ideological relations of domination and subordination are always already present. They are not external to the field of economics: Whoever assigns the means of production to certain purposes and in this way disposes of the products, whoever starts the means of production, whoever rules over the labour process and can appropriate the surplus product, exercises power.[185]

Those rights and powers are in turn woven into a net of relations and struggles; they are therefore not static, but permanently contested. Poulantzas

---

181 Poulantzas 1964, pp. 290–4 quoted in and translated by Jessop 1985, p. 40 (emphasis S.B.).

182 Jessop 1985, p. 45.

183 Jessop 1985, pp. 53, 59.

184 Poulantzas 2000, p. 14.

185 Poulantzas 2000, pp. 26, 35.

thus succeeds in his later work in letting go of the 'determination in the final instance' and actually assuming a complex totality similar to Laclau and Mouffe.[186]

Poulantzas argues, moreover, in a manner reminiscent of Foucault's idea that power exists only in its exercise: that it is not a thing and cannot be owned. This is no accident, for in principle Foucault thus reformulates a Marxian insight in such a way that power circulates – that it only functions as a chain, and spreads over networks.[187] Therefore classes do not exist for Poulantzas prior to the political class struggle which they enter retroactively. They only constitute themselves at all through a class struggle that encompasses the entire way of life.[188] The starting point for Poulantzas's approach is – with a 'remarkable similarity to Foucault' – a relational theory of power.[189] Mechanisms of power such as the state or law are neither a thing nor a subject, but strategic locations within power relations, within relationships of forces. However, Poulantzas engages almost exclusively with class relations. And precisely for this he could take up Gramsci's theory of hegemony, which had also been developed in the context of analysing class domination.

2.2.2.2 *Hegemony*

Thus 'relationship of forces' is the key concept of Gramsci's *Prison Notebooks*.[190] Poulantzas adopts his (and Neumann's) primacy of struggles[191] for the analysis of society. They concur that the position in the production process generates an objective social relationship of forces.[192] Thus a mechanistic or structuralist concept is rejected, according to which one 'always awaits the great evening' and refrains from organising the counterforces,[193] or reduces the subjects to mere carriers of structures, as was typical in the tradition of Pashukanis. For Gramsci, not only are economic positions central, but so too is the political relationship of forces, that is, the degree of cohesion, self-awareness and organisation of the different social classes[194] as well as the military relationship of forces.[195]

186 Laclau and Mouffe 2001, p. 140, however, do not recognise this parallel, as they equate 'relations of production' with 'economic base'.
187 Foucault 2003c, p. 29.
188 Demirović 1987, p. 27.
189 Jessop 1985, p. 129.
190 Buci-Glucksmann 1981, p. 80.
191 Poulantzas 2000, p. 40.
192 Gramsci 1996, pp. 178–9.
193 Buci-Glucksmann 1981, p. 87.
194 Gramsci 1996, p. 179.
195 Gramsci 1996, p. 180.

Against this background the concept of hegemony emerges. Its purpose is to clarify how domination is exercised in advanced class societies. Gramsci adopted the term from Russian Social Democracy, where it appeared in the 1890s and subsequently became one of the most widely used terms of political analysis. The Third International then internationalised it.[196] In this version the term mainly describes the task of the proletariat to take up the political leadership of the other exploited classes in the class alliance, by not only pursuing its own particularist economic goals, but the struggle of all those who are exploited.[197] Gramsci took on this understanding by stressing time and again, for example in the context of the southern question in Italy, that any isolation in trade unions of the working class from the exploited masses had to be rejected. But Gramsci's true originality rather lies in the extension of the term into, in Poulantzas's words, a way to account for 'the political practices of the dominant classes in developed capitalist formations',[198] their effective domination, which requires concessions and universality.[199] Of course the two moments of the concept of hegemony belong together. Below I will nonetheless concentrate in particular on the second meaning, because Gramsci thereby succeeded in developing a crucial feature of the form of domination in bourgeois societies.

As Litowitz correctly notes, in particular one historical phenomenon required an explanation: How could it happen that those people who were exploited by capitalist socialisation, were often its strongest supporters and even agreed voluntarily to their own exploitation? It seemed as though the ruling class succeeded in spreading its worldview via social institutions and popular culture and in retaining in this way a form of leadership.[200] Hegemony is in this sense a form of domination, albeit one characterised by how it retains even the support of the dominated and powerless, and is thus reliant upon consent.[201] It is therefore neither only the 'dominant ideology' nor legitimacy in the sense of Max Weber, but the setting in motion of mechanisms which ensure the assent of the masses to a class politics that in addition relies on violence. Furthermore, it cannot be equated with internalised obedience, either, as consent signifies active approval.[202] For hegemony does not appear as coercion, but has a universalistic goal.[203] The recourse to forms of coercion rather sig-

196 Anderson 1976, pp. 26 ff.
197 Anderson 1976, p. 31.
198 Poulantzas 1978, p. 137; thus also Anderson 1976, p. 35; Cox 1983, p. 163.
199 Litowitz 2000, p. 522.
200 Ibid.
201 Bieling and Steinhilber 2000, p. 102.
202 Priester 1981.
203 Buci-Glucksmann 1981, pp. 63–4.

nifies a crisis of hegemony. In contrast to direct domination, hegemony thus means a contradictory process of generalising interests: 'If particular interest groups want to assert themselves, they can hardly do this by force alone, but have to experience a catharsis in that they have to take other interests into account and accept compromises'.[204] The different respective forces pursue particular, in part competing interests. In order to be successful, however, they have to cooperate with each other, accept compromises and form alliances. If those alliances are stable over a longer period of time, they form a 'hegemonic bloc'.[205]

Here (material) concessions to the dominated play an important role: 'Undoubtedly the fact of hegemony presupposes that account be taken of the interests and the tendencies of the groups over which hegemony is to be exercised, and that a certain compromise equilibrium should be formed – in other words, that the leading group should make sacrifices of an economic-corporate kind'.[206]

Gramsci developed this particular form of domination in comparison to the situation in Tsarist Russia:

> In the East the state was everything, civil society was primordial and gelatinous; in the West, there was a proper relation between state and civil society, and when the state tottered a sturdy structure of civil society was immediately revealed. The state was just a forward trench, behind it stood a succession of sturdy fortresses and emplacements ...[207]

In bourgeois societies there exists thus alongside the state apparatus, which retains the monopoly on coercive force, a resistant structure – civil society.[208] The organisation of assent takes place in this società civile, that is, in those social institutions which are commonly called private: publishers, universities, churches, associations, trade unions, mass media.[209] From the perspective of legal theory it is of course of particular interest that law (in Luhmann's words the periphery of the legal system) therefore also has a civil society component. For although it is codified and enforced by the state, legal practice produces amongst the members of society also certain ideas and views of the right life,

---

204 Demirović 2001a, p. 61.
205 Bieling and Steinhilber 2000, p. 105.
206 Gramsci 1991, p. 161.
207 Gramsci 2011, p. 168.
208 Gramsci 1991, p. 235.
209 Kramer 1975, p. 84.

in particular with regards to what law is, that manifests in corresponding behaviours in everyday life.[210] For Gramsci, law accordingly has to be understood more broadly – similarly to his idea of the state, which is not part of this discussion: 'Law thus becomes (like schools and other institutions and endeavours) a tool bound to a particular purpose', for the organisation of behaviours and habits.[211] This aspect of law requires sanctions, but also produces just as much a collective pressure in the direction of certain behaviour patterns.[212] It allows for a non-repressive function of control by mandating a way of life as 'legal'.[213]

It is, in the words of Foucault, productive – which shows the similarity of the two theories in their rejection of the repression hypothesis. From the perspective of critical legal studies,[214] Duncan Kennedy emphasises the significance of this Gramscian thought for legal theory. It is possible to show that law, with its prestige and claim to universality, produces an important effect for maintaining ruling class hegemony. This prestige is communicated through the influential, professional, technical and intellectual sector, which manages the legal system.[215] The argument here is also very similar to that with regard to the extended state – defined as 'hegemony protected by the armour of coercion'[216] – so that one can speak of an 'extended law': this is not only state repression as conceived in its potential for sanctions, but beyond that and perhaps most of all hegemonic in the sense of a 'tool' for generating consent through practices of everyday life.

Even if one can note that in general any form of domination depends in one way or another on its recognition by the dominated, the hegemonic form of politics only becomes dominant at the start of modernity.[217] For only now are formally free working subjects produced whose assent really matters, and whose relations are constituted as 'relations of will'.

When the generalisation of a way of life to a compact unity across classes that comprises thought and feeling succeeds, Gramsci speaks of a 'historical bloc', which is represented by a group of terms that are binding for collective life, developed by 'organic intellectuals' and spread throughout society.[218] One

210 Kramer 1975, p. 94.
211 Gramsci 1991, p. 246.
212 Gramsci 1991, p. 242.
213 Litowitz 2000, p. 530.
214 See Frankenberg.
215 Kennedy 1982, p. 36.
216 Gramsci 2011, p. 75.
217 Thus, with different connotations, also Laclau and Mouffe 2001, p. 138; Anderson 1976, pp. 46–7.
218 Demirović 2001a, p. 61.

can only speak of a historical bloc when the entire social order reproduces itself as a relatively coherent ensemble of institutions of force and consent over a longer period and includes a particular social way of development.[219] Fordism is the classic example for such a concrete historical social formation.[220]

2.2.2.3 *The Organisation of Hegemony*

Poulantzas now attempts to make the theory of hegemony fruitful for a materialist state theory, not so much by relating to the 'extended state', but rather by developing the idea of the 'hegemonic bloc'. Poulantzas goes further than Gramsci in that he insists that the capitalist mode of production of the competing bourgeois class fractions makes it impossible for them to pursue an immediate common interest. Due to its division the economically dominant class is not able to organise its long-term interests. It thus undermines the conditions of its own existence. Therefore the theory of hegemony also has to be applied to the relation of class fractions to each other. One of the fractions or classes has to play a hegemonic role. If this unification is possible, a 'power bloc' is created,[221] with 'bloc' intended to express, as in Gramsci, a certain coherent stability. The power bloc is more than a tactical alliance in a field of class struggle; it is a long-term organic relation, extending across economic, political and ideological fields. While rivalries and conflicts continue, they have to be pursued by a hegemonic fraction. It has to unite the power bloc by the transformation of its own economic interests and by advancing the general interest of the dominant classes and fractions in continuous economic exploitation and political rule.[222]

Poulantzas' terminology is close to Gramsci's. For, as Karin Priester has shown, strictly speaking Gramsci does not analyse the bourgeois state but the 'state formation' *process* of a class. A class does not take state power, but becomes the state.[223] This process consists of various stages:[224]

> Hegemony is *at first* limited to the intellectual and moral *leadership* within a system of alliances, but has to be expanded when reaching state level. Hegemony now, because it is no longer a question of the leadership amongst allies within a bloc, but of dominance within society as a

219 Bieling and Steinhilber 2000, p. 105.
220 See in greater detail Buckel and Fischer-Lescano 2007.
221 Poulantzas 1978, p. 141.
222 Jessop 1985, pp. 66–7.
223 Laclau and Mouffe 2001, p. 69.
224 See Gramsci 1996, pp. 178 ff.

> whole, has to include besides the still important pole of consent/leadership also the pole force/domination. The 'integral state' as the synthesis of this process is for Gramsci nothing other than the expression of the ideational collective will of a class that has gained state power …[225]

Poulantzas' 'power bloc' is therefore in principle a continuation of this intellectual and moral leadership within the system of alliances. Once a power bloc becomes hegemonic and unified under the aegis of one fraction (which therefore also cannot assert its interests in their pure form), this results in an unstable balance of compromises.[226] Only afterwards does Poulantzas actually expand on this. For he actually assumes that the generalisation of interests as well as social hegemony require the state apparatuses for their realisation, and that classes do not exist prior to and independently of the state, but that the latter is always already present in their formation.[227] Poulantzas maintained this view since his work *Political Power and Social Classes*; he merely elaborates on it in his state theory:

> With regard to the dominant classes, and particularly the bourgeoisie, the State's principal role is one of *organization*. It represents and organises the dominant class or classes; or, more precisely, it represents and organises the long-term political interest of a *power bloc*, which is composed of several bourgeois class fractions (for the bourgeoisie is divided into class fractions), and which sometimes embraces dominant classes issuing from other modes of production that are present in the capitalist social formation … The State constitutes the political unity of the dominant classes …[228]

The state is necessary as the 'cohesive factor' in order to maintain a society that is split into classes and class fractions.[229] Poulantzas practically defines the state through this general function.[230] The unity of the power bloc, but also the unity of the social formation as a whole has to be organised through the creation of a balance of compromise between the classes. This also includes

225 Priester 1981, p. 62.
226 Demirović 1987, p. 64.
227 Demirović 1987, p. 26.
228 Poulantzas 2000, p. 127 (emphasis in original).
229 Poulantzas 1978, p. 1987.
230 Jessop 1985, p. 61.

the disorganisation of the dominated classes. The state prevents them from overcoming through political organisation the isolation that results from the production process.[231] This disorganisation is made possible through a process that Poulantzas calls 'individualisation' or 'isolation effect' – one that has fascinated him since his critique of Pashukanis. The state establishes an atomisation and division of the political body into so-called 'individuals', juridical-political persons and free subjects, and represents their unity at the same time as 'the people-nation'.[232] It thus sanctions and institutionalises this individualisation by transforming the social-economic monads into juridical and political individuals-persons-subjects.[233] In a double movement, the modern state therefore creates individualisation and at the same time constitutes its unity and homogenisation. It totalises the divided monads and incorporates their unity in its institutional structure.[234] The isolation effect thus affects not only the dominated, but all those involved in capitalist socialisation. Yet while the state enables the long-term organisation of the dominant classes for their interests, it sanctions the atomisation of the 'popular masses'. It allows for their division and reassembles them in a new way. In contrast to Gramsci, consent therefore does not emerge directly as a positive one, but is at first negative, brought about through the destruction of unified class or popular interests.[235] The monads thus produced are only 'positively' included through a national-popular consent once they are unified.

What then are the mechanisms that make it possible for the state to function at the same time as a cohesive factor and enable it to produce the isolation effect?

Poulantzas gives two answers. While he mainly holds legal mechanisms responsible (for the production of legal and constitutional subjects) during his 'middle' phase, he later adopts Foucault's thesis, that it is the discipline of normalisation that above all plays a significant part in the formation of subjects.[236]

2.2.2.4 *Relative Autonomy*

However, for the state to even be able to fulfil this role, it has to have 'relative autonomy'. Poulantzas takes this category, which had already surfaced in a

231 Poulantzas 1978, p. 188.
232 Poulantzas 2000, p. 63.
233 Poulantzas 2000, pp. 65–6.
234 Poulantzas 2000, p. 72.
235 Demirović 1987, p. 71.
236 Poulantzas 2000, pp. 69–70.

similar form in Franz Neumann, from Althusser. Althusser had claimed that in the connection of 'base' and 'superstructure', the latter had a relative autonomy from the base.[237] For Poulantzas this is ultimately rooted in the separation of the political from the economic under capitalism, which forms the basis for the peculiar institutional structure of the capitalist state. The specific autonomy of the political space in capitalism is accordingly an effect of the complete separation of the immediate producers from all means of production.[238] Neither in the market, where they from now on have to sell their labour power, nor in the production process, are they subject to a direct political force. 'The capitalist does not at the same time manage the business of politics'.[239] While Poulantzas stresses that the political in a wider sense is present in the economic, he insists at the same time that the political in a more narrow sense, that is, the institutional form of political domination, is differentiated under capitalism into a system of political administration. He thus dialectically arrives at the succinct phrase that 'the capitalist separation of State and economy was never anything other than the specifically capitalist form of the State's presence in the relations of production'.[240]

And only this specific institutional structure of the state makes the unity of the power bloc and the unity of the social formation possible.[241] For only this can make 'long-term uniform hegemony of the power bloc' over the dominated classes possible, for example by imposing material compromises on the power bloc or individual fractions.[242] If the state did not have this 'minimal autonomy ... i.e., if it were nothing but the political "space" of the collision of opposed interests', the potential for social conflict would not be domesticated, but only further sharpened.[243] In contrast to Gramsci, Poulantzas thus developed by referring to Althusser the idea that the state is a 'special apparatus',[244] a structure, which becomes independent of a mere balance of powers because it has its own opacity and resistance: 'To be sure, change in the class relationship of forces always affects the State; but it does not find expression in the State in a direct and immediate fashion. It adapts itself exactly to the materiality of the various state apparatuses, only becoming crystallised in the State in a refracted

237 Althusser 1984, p. 9.
238 Poulantzas 2000, p. 18.
239 Demirović 1987, p. 51.
240 Poulantzas 2000, p. 167.
241 Jessop 1985, p. 56.
242 Jessop 1985, p. 130.
243 Esser, Fach and Väth 1983, p. 15.
244 Poulantzas 2000, p. 12.

form that varies according to the apparatus'.[245] The state thus has a 'material framework',[246] a specific inertia,[247] which justifies speaking of apparatuses.

'Apparatus' is again a term Poulantzas adopts in this characteristic form from Althusser, whose state theory distinguishes between repressive and ideological *state apparatuses*.[248] Here the apparatuses have a crucial significance, for in Althusser's attempt to free the term ideology of an idealistic usage, according to which ideology is false consciousness and thus only exists in people's minds, he advances the thesis that 'ideas' have a material existence,[249] and reaches the conclusion that ideology always only exists in an apparatus and its practices.[250] Therefore 'apparatus', and this is all that matters in this context, makes the materiality of practices, their autonomy and unity apparent. However, Althusser does not consider this unity as an inner, substantive unity in the Hegelian sense, but as an external organisation.[251] 'The apparatus is that "unity" of autonomous elements, of which each in turn is itself the complex "unity" of its sub-elements', a de-centred unity of units,[252] which is only unified by external force.[253]

Adopting the concept of the apparatus and the idea of relative autonomy constitutes one of the main remnants of Althusser's theory in Poulantzas' work. Poulantzas thus observes that the state is no monolithic unit; it is rather the case that the class contradictions that are inscribed in the structure of the state take 'the form of internal contradictions between, and at the heart of, its various branches and apparatuses, following both horizontal and vertical directions'.[254] The state is accordingly not a top-down uniformly organised apparatus based on a hierarchical, homogenous distribution of power centres, which are secured by legal regulations (constitution, hierarchy of norms). The legal appearance does not correspond to the reality of the state's practices. Entirely following the relational theory of power, Poulantzas claims that the contradictions in the power bloc pervade the bureaucracy: 'Rather than facing a corps of state functionaries and personnel united and cemented around a univocal political will, we are dealing with fiefs, clans and factions: a multipli-

---

245 Poulantzas 2000, pp. 130–1.
246 Poulantzas 2000, p. 12.
247 Wissel 2007, p. 75.
248 Althusser 1984, pp. 16 ff.
249 Althusser 1984, p. 39.
250 Althusser 1984, p. 40.
251 Charim 2002, p. 41.
252 Charim 2002, p. 42.
253 Charim 2002, p. 60.
254 Poulantzas 2000, pp. 132–3.

city of diversified micro-policies'.[255] State politics is according to this the result of their clash and not the successful implementation of a global plan.

'In locating the State as the material condensation of a relationship of forces, we must also grasp it as a *strategic field and process* of intersecting power networks'.[256] Despite the diverse micro-policies, Poulantzas insists on the unity of the apparatuses, for otherwise the relations of power alone would simply be reflected. His solution to this dilemma of micro-diversity and macro-necessity[257] consists in assuming certain dominant decision-making centres, mechanisms and modes, which only become permeable for certain interests.[258] Unity thus does not depend on the formal unity of the legal code, but on the capacity of the dominant apparatus to truly exercise power. No rational, coherent global project is formulated, but a strategic causality without a calculating subject develops.[259] Poulantzas's concept can then be summed up with the concept of the state as the '*material condensation* of a relationship of forces'.[260] Starting from the relationship of forces, the state or the law are not a thing, but a relation, a balance of powers between classes, which is, however, always at the same time also more, a material condensation, an apparatus with relative autonomy.

2.2.3 The Law

Let us consider now more closely what Poulantzas's reflections on state theory signify in relation to law. In his chapter on law he develops two main functions: the cohesion as well as the consent function.

Firstly, regarding cohesion – modern law is a central technique in the process of cohesion. It is distinguished by its '*axiomatic system*, comprising a set of *abstract, general, formal and strictly regulated norms*'.[261] This abstract structure leads to its specific functioning; it thus organises social differences as a unity:

> [The law] constitutes the framework wherein agents who are totally dispossessed of their means of production are given *formal cohesion* ... The formal and abstract character of law is inextricably bound up with the

255 Poulantzas 2000, p. 135.
256 Poulantzas 2000, p. 36.
257 Jessop 1985, p. 127.
258 Poulantzas 2000, p. 137.
259 Jessop 1985, p. 128.
260 Poulantzas 2000, p. 129.
261 Poulantzas 2000, p. 86 (emphasis in original).

> real fracturing of the social body in the social division of labour – that is to say, with the individualization of agents that takes place in the capitalist labour process.[262]

It represents the unity of the subjects as people and nation and is involved in the fragmentation of the agents by drafting the code the differentiations are inscribed in. The sanctioning of differences and their simultaneous homogenisation is the source of the law's universality.[263] 'The law thus forms a link between the atomised individuals and the unity of society'.[264] Accordingly it is a mode for the regulation of differences and co-originally a unifying ideological entity.[265] In the second of those ways of working, it replaces religion as the dominant ideology of feudalism, by taking on the role of the social imaginary.[266]

Concerning the dominated classes, the law assigns them on the one hand a position which they have to take up; it incorporates them into the political and social network. At the same time, it constitutes 'an important factor in organising the consent of the dominated classes' by assigning them rights and enabling and sanctioning material compromises.[267] In relation to the dominant classes it also plays the role of a formal framework for cohesion. It takes up the strategic function of making calculations possible (as described by Franz Neumann). The axiomatic systematisation of the law makes a certain foresight possible, which is based upon a minimum stability of the rules. Furthermore, changes in the law can only take place within its own set of rules. In the organisation of the power bloc the law is used for a specific distribution of power and regulates the relationships between the individual fractions within the state. 'By thus giving order to their mutual relations within the State, it allows a changed balance of forces in the ruling alliance to find expression at state level without provoking upheavals'.[268] Bourgeois law is thus the 'necessary form of a State that has to maintain relative autonomy of the actions of a power-bloc in order to organise their unity under the hegemony of a given class or fraction', and to 'organise the structure of the compromise equilibrium permanently imposed on the dominant class by the dominated'.[269]

262 Ibid. (emphasis in original).
263 Poulantzas 2000, p. 87.
264 Adolphs 2003, p. 87.
265 Ibid.
266 Poulantzas 2000, p. 88.
267 Poulantzas 2000, pp. 83–4.
268 Poulantzas 2000, p. 91.
269 Ibid.

Here we are already dealing with the production of consent, which in Poulantzas always implies a certain organisation of violence:[270] The law organises consent, for in principle all social groups can legally gain power through parliament.[271] The relative autonomy of the state in turn manifests itself not least in its ability to fall back on the monopoly on force to implement certain measures. Here Poulantzas very explicitly distances himself from Foucault by stressing that even in modern societies political power remains based on physical violence.[272] The constitutional state is precisely not the opposite of terror and violence, because law is always present in the constitution of power, and the constitutional state unlike pre-capitalist states retains the highest monopoly on violence: the monopoly of war. Therefore the law is an integral element of the repressive order.[273] Legality veils this basic connection by making the role of physical violence in the state invisible. In this regard, law also has, for Poulantzas as well as for Neumann, an ideological effect. It forms the code of organised public violence, or constitutionalised violence.[274] Although it intervenes less when relations of domination are regulated, it is instead at the same time inscribed into the mechanisms of consent, as using techniques of consent already presupposes the state's monopoly on violence, even if it is not directly exercised.[275] Poulantzas thus stresses that the state does not only manage life, but also still remains directly involved in managing death, and furthermore always retains the means for actions which are not subject to any legal sanction.[276] The monopolisation of legitimate force by the state thus remains the decisive element of power, even when this violence is not exercised directly and openly.

Here Poulantzas follows again in the tradition of Franz Neumann, whose *The Governance of the Rule of Law* he used in particular for his book about fascism[277] and whose class analysis is somewhat closer to his than the form analysis of Pashukanis. In contrast to Neumann, however, he does not assume that a central function of the law is to hide real inequalities, but that it rather serves to organise them.

---

270 Adolphs 2003, pp. 82 ff.
271 Adolphs 2003, p. 85.
272 Adolphs 2003, p. 72.
273 Poulantzas 2000, pp. 76–7.
274 Jessop 1985, pp. 120–1.
275 Poulantzas 2000, p. 80.
276 Jessop 1985, p. 122.
277 Poulantzas 1974.

2.2.4 Critique

While the form analytical approaches of the 1970s noted for the most part basic structural principles of the capitalist mode of production, but offered little in the way of an analysis of concrete social formations, the particular characteristic of Poulantzas' approach was that it connected the capitalist state and its laws from the outset to the history of political struggles.[278] This appears particularly incisive as he attempts to conceive of the relationship of forces in the Gramscian tradition and also considers their reification and condensation as constituted in apparatuses. He thus provides an extensive reformulation of his earlier intuition of the internal-external dialectic – or, from a Foucaultian perspective, his own attempt at a Marxist state analysis with the micro-physics of power.[279] In the following the four central problems of this approach for an updated materialist legal theory will be discussed.

2.2.4.1 *Class Reductionism, in the Last Instance*

Poulantzas's strength in comparison to more structuralist theories also leads to his central weakness, his focus on class struggles, which is due to the fact that he locates power in the relations of production. In contrast to his earlier phases, when he completely denied powers that are not class-based,[280] Poulantzas acknowledged in 1978 that power relations are not exclusively based on class relations and can certainly also stem from other aspects than the social division of labour. Therefore they are also not simply their consequence. Here he had mostly gender relations in mind.[281] Nonetheless Poulantzas could not entirely free himself of class reductionism, for he established something that one could call a 'class character in the last instance': although the class division is not exclusively the terrain of the constitution of power, all power in class societies has a class character.[282] This is initially not problematic, just as one can say that in a patriarchal society all power produces the matrix of a hierarchical gender-binary. However, when this leads to the conclusion that both the state and the law can be explained exclusively by the socialisation of classes – and this is what happens with Poulantzas – his theory no longer does justice to the diversity of relations of domination. The material condensation of the power relation is on closer inspection nothing but a condensation of *class* relations.

278 Poulantzas 2000, p. 24.
279 Lemke 2019, p. 117.
280 Jessop 1985, p. 76.
281 Poulantzas 2000, p. 43.
282 Poulantzas 2000, pp. 43–4.

This also explains why Poulantzas refers in his analysis of the state exclusively to class relations and the dominant fractions of capital and the 'popular masses'. He thus ignores both other social structuring principles and furthermore also reduces capitalist relations to the production process and the social division of labour.[283]

Apart from the Marxist debate at the time, this is not least due to Gramsci's concept of hegemony, which focuses on class relations. Laclau and Mouffe have tried to show that the hidden essentialist core of Gramsci is the 'economic base', so that hegemony ultimately has an ontological basis and every social formation is structured around a simple hegemonic centre. Thus the constitutive logic of the economic space is not itself hegemonic, but unified by 'necessary laws' in a naturalist manner.[284] Therefore the hegemonic subject can only be a class.[285]

This critique does not apply to Poulantzas in the same way, as he stressed precisely that the political and the ideological are always already present in the economic, and that a purely economic space therefore cannot exist. For this reason he ultimately also rejects the separation of the different spaces into 'instances' as in Althusser's topological image of exteriority.[286] The moments permeate each other rather than producing a structural matrix.[287] In this respect Poulantzas is actually furthest away from such essentialism. Laclau and Mouffe state in almost identical words what Poulantzas describes at the start of his state theory, namely that 'the space of the economy is itself structured as a political space'[288] and has to be considered as a 'field of struggle'.[289] An ultimate determination by the economy thus no longer exists in Poulantzas – at most he defends the 'primacy of being', which is however always already politically, ideologically and culturally permeated. It therefore remains all the more incomprehensible why the balance of powers is nonetheless only conceived of as one between classes and not as one of articulations, that is of a 'practice, which establishes a relation of elements in such a way that its identity is modified as a result of an articulating practice'.[290] When a plurality of social spaces is assumed, hegemony cannot start from a privileged point: 'The hegemonic

283 Wissel 2007, p. 85.
284 Laclau and Mouffe 2001, p. 69.
285 Laclau and Mouffe 2001, pp. 137–8.
286 Poulantzas 2000, p. 17.
287 Jessop 1985, p. 116.
288 Laclau and Mouffe 2001, pp. 76–7.
289 Laclau 1982, p. 10.
290 Laclau 1982, p. 141.

formation, as we understand it, cannot be derived from the particular logic of a single social force'.[291]

An updated materialist legal theory has to abandon this classism.[292] Even if Poulantzas is correct in assuming that a central characteristic of the state is its cohesive role, because the state apparatus unifies and organises the monads and fragmented fractions that are created by the relations of production, this can hardly lead to the conclusion that only class relations are inscribed in the state and legal apparatuses. The gender relation is much older than the capital relation. It is very decisively constituted and reproduced by the state.[293] In particular the struggles of the women's movement have thus inscribed themselves in law.[294] Ultimately, the constructions 'race', nation or sexuality can also hardly be conceived of without their regulation through state and law.

Litowitz, who attempts to make Gramsci fruitful for legal theory, also criticises his insistence on classes as the sole source of oppression,[295] and pleads for a radical decentring. This results, however, in a solution which abandons Gramsci's and Poulantzas' crucial insight completely, namely the insight that struggles (in a wider sense) have primacy. Instead he shifts to the hegemony of a code.[296] The legal system is accordingly a blueprint which allows for a limited terrain, a legal framework within which everyday operations can take place.[297] But with this simple inversion the very progress made in relation to purely structural theories is again undone, that is, the insight that struggles are the motor of history, and that hegemony and political leadership are also the results of strategic actions. It is thus important not to leave classes behind in some kind of postmodern overkill, but to think with Poulantzas against Poulantzas; and that means expanding the idea of the relationship of forces.

2.2.4.2 *The Failure of 'Relative Autonomy' as a Concept*

The most delicate aspect of Poulantzas's approach is his confrontation with the 'relative autonomy' of the state apparatus. His line of argument on this point remains in part functionalist: because the state secures the long-term hegemony of the bourgeois class, it requires relative autonomy. This devel-

291 Laclau 1982, p. 184.
292 See also Scherrer 2003, pp. 109–10.
293 See on this Pühl and Sauer 2004, p. 169.
294 See for example Dackweiler 2002.
295 Litowitz 2000, p. 533.
296 Litowitz 2000, p. 540.
297 Ibid.

ops in the capitalist mode of production with the separation of politics and economics through the lack of property *and* the dispossession of the direct producers.[298]

Poulantzas argues quite convincingly that relative autonomy is a necessary precondition for the capitalist state apparatus. He can also show that it is expressed in the presence of all social classes in the state, and that the state can therefore not be the instrument of one class alone. Upon closer examination relative autonomy is, however, not convincingly derived, but stated in the style of Althusser. Tellingly Franz Neumann faced a similar problem with his 'relative independence', which he could not solve either. The materialist legal theorists share in this respect a fascination for the 'inner logic' of the law and the political noted by Kelsen, or, if one prefers, for the autopoiesis of the systems, but tend to presuppose rather than account for them.

Poulantzas rightly insists on the materiality of the political in the legal apparatuses, but he only suggests that it has to be there in order to wrest compromises from the power bloc or produce the atomisation of the subaltern. This 'almost magical' 'hyper-functionalism'[299] inevitably leads to the question: which metaphysical being was it that imbued the reified apparatuses with the interest in organising the power bloc, as well as the knowledge of the necessity of doing so?

Buci-Glucksmann and Therborn moreover assume fundamental changes in the relationship of forces and an epistemological break in the context of Keynesianism.[300] It is simply this Fordist shift within capitalism that leads the state to surpass the field of the bloc in power. The expansion of the state that takes place there is not limited to its unification of capital.[301] The strictly classic organisation model of the political field, in which the working class exists outside the state's institutionalisation as a counter state and is not anchored in the state apparatuses, has thus become obsolete (and this supports once more the first critique).[302] This leads to the result, however, that as soon as 'the institutional framework is no longer only created by the bourgeoisie and no longer external to the workers ... the problem of hegemony becomes *for all political forces* the problem of constructing an inevitably composite power bloc'.[303] This insight shows that *both* the extension of the concept of the 'rela-

298 Poulantzas 2000, p. 18.
299 Esser, Fach and Väth 1983, p. 17.
300 Buci-Glucksmann and Therborn 1982, p. 113.
301 Buci-Glucksmann and Therborn 1982, p. 115.
302 Buci-Glucksmann and Therborn 1982, p. 116.
303 Buci-Glucksmann and Therborn 1982, p. 120 (emphasis in original).

tionship of forces' *and* another basis for relative autonomy, which must not serve as a functionalist addendum to the concept of the 'power bloc', are necessary.

This problem applies no less to law: If the law is one of the most important techniques of cohesion, then its relative autonomy plays a central part in this. The law cannot only be the simple expression of the relationship of forces, but it has to be 'relatively' removed from those immediate struggles, to be able to organise compromises, concessions and submissions. Jessop also believes that Poulantzas fails to clarify the concept of relative autonomy in the course of his work. Class struggles were meant to introduce an element of contingency, but also to argue that in the long run the capitalist state always only preserves class domination – even if this is the result of numerous and diverse micro-policies.[304]

> Nowhere did Poulantzas satisfactorily explain how the state's relative autonomy guarantees bourgeois political domination, despite the contingencies of the class struggle ... This suggests that the concept of relative autonomy is at fault and Poulantzas should have abandoned it along with other Althusserian notions. He rightly insisted on the institutional separation of the political and economic reigns in capitalist societies ... But he erred in assuming that somewhere in the state there is something which can somehow guarantee bourgeois class domination. Instead he should have taken seriously his own idea that the state is a social relation. For this clearly points towards a detailed, conjunctural analysis of the contingent necessity of political class domination (or its absence) as the complex resultant of state forms and class forces.[305]

In contrast to Jessop, however, I do not believe that the concept as such has to be abandoned. For relative autonomy does not have to guarantee a certain form of domination a priori; it can just as well be the unintended product of reified social relations, and thus gain a certain density or materiality. How can Poulantzas otherwise explain the 'material condensation' of the relationship of forces? Instead, what is needed is an explanation of the conditions that enable its development. In order to do this, one would actually have to start from the concepts of the form-analysis tradition. Poulantzas, however, expli-

304 Jessop 1985, p. 131.
305 Jessop 1985, p. 136.

citly distances himself from them.[306] At this point it becomes clear that the two seemingly so very different theoretical strands could actually become fruitful for each other.[307]

2.2.4.3 *The Hegemonic Production of Unity*

Poulantzas assumes that besides a certain measure of autonomy, the institutional unity of the state apparatuses is the basis for exacting short-term economic sacrifices from the dominant classes, in order to secure their political domination in the long-term. The specific institutional structure of the state makes the unity of the power bloc actually possible.[308] Unity in a more narrow sense means preserving the state system itself as a form of political domination, and thus above all its capacity to use constitutionalised force and to reproduce its own institutional system in order to ensure compliance with its policies. This has in other contexts been described as the state's interest in self-preservation (Offe), or as the material self-interest of the state apparatus.[309] Unity in a wider sense implies, however, that its political function is performed successfully: that social cohesion is made possible.[310] Poulantzas is here obviously influenced by Neumann's analysis of National Socialism, where Neumann describes the non-state as the competition between state apparatuses up to the decay of the nation state itself.[311]

But what ensures the state's unity, when social contradictions are after all inscribed in its apparatuses and the latter come into conflict with each other? While Poulantzas assumes in his earlier writings that this is made possible by the 'specific cohesion of an autonomised legal-political superstructure',[312] he subsequently distanced himself from this notion. Not the organisational matrix of the state, but the *factual* power of certain apparatuses should now secure unity, with the dominant branch organising the hegemony of the subordinated apparatuses. However, also this later version of unity remains unconvincing. The plausible presentation of the contradictory micro-policies of the enmeshed apparatuses makes it hard to grasp how the state is meant to be unified through the domination of one apparatus. Here Poulantzas rather appears

306 Poulantzas 2000, p. 86.

307 Thus also Wissel 2007, p. 88. John Kannankulam (Kannakulam 2006), on the other hand argues that Poulantzas, despite his assertion to the contrary, tacitly integrated the form analytical approach in his theory.

308 Jessop 1985, p. 56.

309 Esser, Fach and Väth 1983, p. 17.

310 Jessop 1985, p. 350.

311 See Bast 1999, Buckel 2003.

312 Jessop 1985, p. 68.

to fall back on Althusser's concept of instances, where one of the instances is always the dominant one. It is moreover striking that Poulantzas also fails to explain what is meant to ensure that the 'managers of the state' (that is the civil servants and politicians) do not, because of the materiality of the apparatuses themselves and the externality of the political (to the economic), pursue their own corporative interest or simply the state's interest in self-preservation at the cost of its global role.[313]

The question of the unity must, however, be resolved, because, whether they are organised on the level of the nation state or supra-nationally, the legal apparatuses are also part of a contradictory ensemble, a 'flexible institutional totality',[314] and their relation to the totality of the regulatory instances as well as their contribution to the production of cohesion has to be clarified.

Firstly, it must be noted that the state does not exist as a completely constituted, internally coherent, organisationally pure and operationally closed system, 'but as an emergent, contradictory, hybrid and relatively open system'.[315] Therefore no inherent substantial unity *qua* institutional ensemble (that is qua *formal* unity) can exist,[316] but it can only – thus Jessop's proposal – be mediated through a hegemonic project. Hegemonic projects are political projects which succeed in presenting themselves as solutions to pressing social problems. Within them, material interests, strategic orientations, discursive and cultural meanings, ideological convictions and feelings converge.[317] Also the state's managers have to be successfully integrated though this political 'cement'.[318] For the nation state, Jessop speaks of national-popular political projects[319] or of state projects. Those projects are made possible institutionally through specific coordinating procedures and of course ultimately only against the background of a corresponding social base.[320] This means that the substantive unity of the state is just like the unity of the power bloc not given as such, but that it has to be produced from the outset through a hegemonic practice. This can of course also fail, as particularly visible when the state's personnel or that of one particular branch becomes alienated from it.

The autonomous legal structure, which was Poulantzas's first attempt at an explanation in the context of the 'internal-external-dialectic', cannot be

313 Jessop 1985, pp. 350–1.
314 Pühl and Sauer 2004, p. 169.
315 Jessop 1990, p. 316.
316 Ibid.
317 Bieling and Steinhilber 2000, p. 106.
318 Jessop 1985, p. 350.
319 Ibid.
320 Jessop 1990, p. 316.

completely abandoned. If relative autonomy can be 'saved', the law's relative autonomy certainly offers alongside and together with hegemonic projects a second set of explanations, which establish in particular how this unity can gain a certain stability despite constant challenges.

2.2.4.4 *Overestimating the State*

Alongside the functionalist concept of state and law, another parallel to form analysis is obvious in his methodological overestimating of the state. Alex Demirović rightly argues that in Poulantzas the state becomes the only guarantor for the reproduction of society as a whole.[321] Bob Jessop also speaks in this context of Poulantzas' 'enduring politicism with its one-sided concern with the state system'.[322] For Gramsci's theory of the extended state remains ignored,[323] and with this his insight that 'bourgeois society (società civile) reproduces itself in the manifold private initiatives as the dominant order, thus contributing to social reproduction and in doing so extending the state by adding the consensual and voluntary dimension'.[324] Gramsci's thesis stresses that there is no privileged location for the reproduction of a social formation.[325] This historical overestimation of the state leads to law now only being considered of secondary importance. Here too it can always only be seen as a technique of the state apparatus. By thinking with Poulantzas against Poulantzas, this narrowing could be overcome by an expanded field of vision that can include other techniques of cohesion. Here law would be an excellent candidate.

2.3 *Michel Foucault*

Calling on Michel Foucault for a materialist legal theory might seem surprising, as he has a problematic relationship both to Marx and Marxism as well as to law. But precisely this constellation makes him interesting for dealing with central problems in Marxist theory. In particular because he rejects several of its premisses, he reveals potential alternative solutions for the problems encountered thus far. However, this does not mean that I am following the dominant tendency here and consider Foucault's concept of power a successful

321 Demirović 1987, p. 60.

322 Jessop 1985, p. 141.

323 Poulantzas only integrates this approach in a particular sense, that is, in his critical adoption of Althusser's concept of the repressive and ideological state apparatuses (to which he further adds an economic one).

324 Demirović 1987, p. 60.

325 Ibid., see also Lemke 2019, p. 118.

way to *overcome* Marxist social theories by way of a poly-form, multi-centred concept of power,[326] but to the contrary: as a critical *continuation* of *a contribution to the critique of political economy* under the conditions of *the crisis of marxism*.[327] In order to make the theories accessible to each other, Foucault's analysis of power, however, has to be first reconstructed independently of his remarks on law. It will therefore have to be examined in greater detail than the preceding approaches, as Foucault's reflections have to be shown to be compatible with those of Marxist theories in that they conceive of the same phenomena in a relatively parallel manner, although both start from different premisses.

Foucault's reference to Marxian theory is very clearly shaped by the historical context, that is both by the development of the French Communist Party and by his acquaintance with Louis Althusser as well as more particularly by the political struggles of the years around 1968.[328] His notorious critique of Marxism took place in *The Order of Things* and was fiercely attacked by Marxists. In contrast to Althusser, whose *Reading Capital* he, however, did not know at the time,[329] he claimed that Marxism had not really made a break from the depths of occidental knowledge, but had rather been a tempest in a teapot: 'Marxism exists in nineteenth-century thought like a *fish* in *water*: that is, it is unable to breathe anywhere else'.[330]

The reactions against Foucault's position over time were of course no less polemical. Criticism was in particular directed at Foucault's alleged wilful mangling of Marxist theory: 'What Foucault does is to "use" Marx to set up a negative pole against which to elaborate his alternative. The Marx that emerges is somewhat one-dimensional: rigid, determinist, economist, with a narrow conception of power as repression, and viewing the state as a unitary agent and the instrumental bearer of the interests of the ruling class'.[331] Poulantzas' critique took the same path: Foucault 'directs his fire either against his peculiar caricature of Marxism or against the Marxism of the Third International and the Stalinist conception that a number of us have been criticising for a long time now'.[332] He could thus present his own findings as overcoming Marxism, something that Poulantzas comments on almost bitterly: 'Some of us did

326 Rehmann 2003, p. 63.
327 Thus also Lemke 2019, pp. 34 ff.
328 Hunt and Wickham 1994, pp. 33–4; Dosse 1998a, pp. 147 ff.; 1998b, pp. 93 ff.; Lemke 2019, pp. 34 ff.
329 Dosse 1998a, p. 491.
330 Foucault 2005, p. 285.
331 Hunt and Wickham 1994, p. 34.
332 Poulantzas 2000, p. 146.

not wait for Foucault before proposing analyses of power with which his own investigations now concur in certain respects – although we cannot but rejoice at this development'.[333]

In the works succeeding *The Order of Things*, Foucault attempted to partially soften his critique and quite clearly came close in many places to the Marxian approach. The parallels are in part so obvious that Poulantzas, despite his polemics, attempted to overcome the crisis of Marxism by integrating Foucault.[334] He thus writes: 'On this precise question, then, Foucault's elaboration has considerable value, since it furnishes a materialist analysis of certain institutions of power. Not only does it sometimes concur with Marxist analyses – a point which Foucault is careful not to see, or state – but in a number of respects it may even enrich them'.[335] Poulantzas notes entirely accurately that Foucault can very much be considered as belonging to the materialist tradition. For he starts like Marx from the materiality of practices and attempts to dissolve reified social ontologies again in social relations. From this perspective many of his critiques, for example that of the idealist concept of law, are very much parallel to the Marxian critique. Works like *Discipline and Punish*, but also his later lectures or his lectures at the Collège de France on the history of governmentality, could easily have the heading or at least the subtitle *History of Political Economy*. All he cares about here is to avoid a subprocess of society being singled out and removed from its connections with the other processes. Forms of knowledge, ways *of subjectivation*, discourse and bodily practices are just as much 'rooted' in the relations of production, as is the manner in which commodities are produced.[336]

When looking at his statements towards the end of the 1970s, it is noticeable that Foucault rebelled first and foremost against a particular historical development of Marxism. For Marxism was no longer an oppositional theory, but a 'manifestation of power'.[337] It thus presents itself in a traditional manner as a 'science', which considers its declarations to be true and intends them to exert force. Moreover it cannot exist without a political party or without a state, whose philosophy it has become,[338] and finally it plays a part in the 'imaginary historical eschatology'.[339] He was particularly opposed to the Com-

333 Ibid.
334 Jessop 1985, p. 80.
335 Poulantzas 2000, p. 67.
336 Foucault, 2000, p. 87.
337 Foucault 2003b, pp. 753–4.
338 Balibar 1992, p. 52.
339 Dosse 1998a, pp. 147–8.

munist Party, of which he was briefly a member:[340] as an 'impoverishment of political imagination' through the monolithic bureaucratic will of a ruling elite, which constitutes a class as its subject. This Party has come to determine the history of Western Marxism: a hierarchical organisation, reminiscent of a monastic order.[341]

In sum one can take up Balibar's view that '… in ways which were constantly changing, the whole of Foucault's work can be seen in terms of a genuine struggle with Marx, and that this can be viewed as one of the driving forces of his productiveness'.[342] Furthermore the entirely accurate argument has been made recently that a 'secret dialogue' between Foucault and Poulantzas took place in their late works on state theory.[343] This politics of secrecy came from Foucault, even though his engagement with Poulantzas is obvious. The similarity between the concept of the state as a 'material condensation of relationships of forces' and the 'governmentalisation of the state' are striking: both are a microphysics of the state.

What holds for his approach to Marx applies similarly to Foucault's treatment of law. To begin with he, much like Poulantzas, did not produce a legal theory.[344] This had, however, a methodological reason, as his analysis of power aimed above all to attack the so-called 'juridical concept of power'. Some authors therefore reached the conclusion that Foucault theoretically removed law from modernity and could offer at best a critical perspective, a 'negative utopia' on modern law.[345]

As will be shown below, although he did not offer a systematic theory of law[346] (a phenomenon one encounters more often than not in the context of materialist legal theory), Foucault can nonetheless make a contribution to the line of questioning developed here. This consists on the one hand in his attention to the limited character of law as only *one* technology of power, and on the other hand in that he exposes the role of legal practice in the constitution of the modern subject. Thus a gap in form analysis can be filled. This rather indirect relation to law, however, makes it necessary to first present Foucault's general theory of power before addressing law. For only in this way can it be shown that the charge of legal nihilism stems from a misunderstanding of his *social theory*.

340 Foucault 2003b, pp. 77–8.
341 Balibar 1992. p. 39.
342 Adolphs 2007.
343 Hunt and Wickham 1994, p. viii; Tadros 1998, p. 100; Litowitz 1997, p. 65.
344 Litowitz 1997, p. 81.
345 Biebricher 2006, p. 139.
346 Foucault 2009, pp. 247–8.

2.3.1 'The Moving Substrate of Force Relations' – The Problem of Power

That Foucault situated law in the context of his analysis of society is already apparent in that it is one technology of power amongst others. What does power mean in this context? It is noticeable that Foucault speaks of 'THE power' so often that it seems as though the very theorist who opposed all ontologies supported a substantialist analytics of power. But upon closer inspection this thesis cannot be maintained: 'the power' turns out to be rather something of a short-hand for a much more complex idea, which is very similar to the concept as we find it in Poulantzas, Gramsci and Marx.

2.3.1.1 *Power Comes from Below*

'I am well aware that there are those who say that in talking about power all we do is develop an internal and circular ontology of power ...' Thus Foucault countered criticisms of his analysis of power,[347] while throwing back the accusation of ontology at his critics. For it was they who derived all power from universals like the state, instead of recognising and analysing power as an independent phenomenon.[348] He refused to derive power from the 'economic infrastructures' or institutions just like 'anecdotal' histories about generals or kings, namely about people in power,[349] and that is the labyrinthine question: Who has power?[350] Power should be analysed as an independent phenomenon where it unfolds in its practices. The subject of analysis is thus power relations and not power itself,[351] the multitude of relations of force as well as the interplay that transforms those relations of force in continual struggles.[352] Thus he could rightly sum up his premise in his 1978–9 lecture on the history of governmentality:

> ... I repeat it once again, that power can in no way be considered either as a principle in itself, or as having explanatory value which functions from the outset. The term itself, power, does no more than designate a [domain]* of relations which are entirely still to be analysed ...[353]

The condition for the possibility of power lies accordingly not in a place of origin, 'not in a unique source of sovereignty', from which all relations would have

347 Ibid., Lemke 2019, p. 49.
348 Foucault 1977, p. 14.
349 Foucault 2003, p. 28.
350 Foucault 1982, p. 788.
351 Foucault 1978, pp. 92–3.
352 Foucault 2008, p. 1 86.
353 Foucault 1978, p. 93.

to be derived, but in 'the moving substrate of force relations'.[354] If Foucault speaks nonetheless of POWER, then it is only to express the overall effect of all those contested force relations, their concatenation to systems and finally their institutional crystallisation, such as in the state apparatuses and in 'social hegemonies'. POWER is thus the name for a complex strategic situation.[355] Major dominations are the 'hegemonic effects' or 'terminal forms' that are based on those confrontations and are by no means given entities.[356] One can see here that the distinction of power and domination, even if the French language includes both power and domination in the term *pouvoir*, does not significantly differ from the sociological definition in Max Weber. The latter had described power as the more general process, as the 'possibility of imposing one's own will upon the behaviour of other persons can emerge in the most diverse forms'. Domination, however, designates the successful, actual power to issue commands.[357]

The foundational location of power in power relations (in the machinery of production, in families, etc.) also makes clear that neither 'the caste which governs, nor the groups which control the state apparatus, nor those who make the most important economic decisions direct the entire network of power that functions in a society ...'[358] A strictly relational concept of power,[359] one that Poulantzas quite obviously followed in his late work,[360] makes it impossible to consider power something that can be possessed. The 'ruling class' appear rather as managers of relations than as *in power*. Power exists only in relational practices, which articulate themselves to power formations and draw all their effectiveness from the material conditions.[361] This polymorph process only takes on the contours of a multiform and anonymous power when it reaches a certain level of dissemination.[362] It can thus be noted that by power Foucault always means 'a general matrix of force relations at a given time, in a given society',[363] and thus the opposite of an a-historical ontological essentialism of power.

---

354 Ibid.
355 Foucault 1978, p. 94.
356 Weber 1978, p. 942 ff.
357 Foucault 1978, p. 95.
358 Ibid.
359 Jessop 1985, p. 80.
360 Balibar 1992, p. 52.
361 Charim 2002, p. 112.
362 Dreyfus and Rabinow 1983, p. 186.
363 Foucault 1978, p. 94.

2.3.1.2 *Power Comes from Everywhere*

The similarities of Foucault's analysis of power to the analyses of Marx, Gramsci and Poulantzas are obvious, including even the deliberate use of the term hegemony. Moreover, the idea of a concatenation of power relations is very close to Poulantzas' 'material condensation' and differs at the same time from the systems concepts of Luhmann and Habermas: with Foucault 'systems' have to be analysed as effects of hegemony, which are based on relationships of forces.

A crucial distinction from Marxist concepts consists, however, in Foucault's attempt to overcome the narrow concept of the 'force relation', which in the other three authors remains limited to the relations of production (although in a wider sense). In *The Will to Knowledge* Foucault starts at exactly this point a dialogue with the Marxists of his time. Power relations do not form the 'superstructure', but the base, as they are the immediate effects of the inequalities arising in social relations. Those inequalities in turn constitute the internal conditions for those differentiations. They are thus not external to economic processes, knowledge relationships or sexual relations.[364] Power is everywhere and produced at every point, not because – as Foucault stresses – it embraces everything, but because it comes from everywhere. It is rooted in the 'system of social networks',[365] that is, in the 'power relations that exist between the sexes ... between adults and children, in the family, in the office, between the sick and the healthy, between the normal and the anormal ...'[366] As has been shown, the relations of production were for Poulantzas also more than only economic relations. They were co-original political, ideological and economic relations and also present in each other. He could, however, conceive of the power relationship this led to only as one of the rights and powers of classes as they result from their positions. Other power relations were ultimately determined by them. Foucault's at first seemingly conspiratorial assumption that power comes from everywhere, ultimately constitutes an attempt at correcting this classism.

2.3.1.3 *Power is Productive*

Similarly to Gramsci, Foucault assumes that power in bourgeois capitalist societies cannot rest solely on prohibition and violence. What he termed, to great confusion in the literature, the 'juridical notion of power',[367] was coupled with

364 Foucault 1978, p. 93.
365 Foucault 1982, p. 793.
366 Foucault 2003a, p. 673.
367 Foucault 1978, p. 86.

the existence of a feudal absolutist society and was no longer a sufficient explanation for modern forms of power. It is rather the rise of a new type of power, one which no longer traverses social relations from top to bottom.[368] *Juridical* notion, because it is based upon the model of the law with the licit and the illicit, which constitutes the subject as a subject by 'subjecting' it, as someone who obeys.[369] This notion, according to which power is only repressive and coercive, is only a minuscule part of the spectrum of possible effects of power and reduces the most diverse forms of domination to the imperative of obedience, without making the fact of obedience itself the subject of analysis.[370] This so-called 'repressive hypothesis' is an insufficiently complex concept, a 'simple little machinery' based upon the idea of a rebellious energy which only has to be throttled. Power, however, is always already present, where desire exists, not only in a subsequently exerted repression.[371]

In contrast to Rousseau and Kant's Republican theory, whereby modern law is identical to self-legislation, it represents for Foucault the archetype of a feudal power that is simply based upon assuming the statement of the law and the operation of taboos. If society today was still actually based on this, one would have to note that this power is 'poor in resources, sparing of its methods, monotonous in the tactics it utilises, incapable of invention, and seemingly doomed always to repeat itself'. Its force is limited to saying 'no', and it is furthermore unable to produce, only to set limits.[372]

This was once an accurate representation of power. It adequately describes the end of the Middle Ages, when the monarchy and the state apparatuses developed and could position themselves as powers that introduced order on the basis of law in the midst of particular forces.[373] The representation of power, however, has remained caught up in this system until now, and thus under the spell of the monarchy. This is the target of Foucault's famous sentence that '[i]n political thought and analysis we still have not cut off the head of the king':[374] a transitory form of power becomes power as such. Although many of its elements have persisted, it has, however, been completely penetrated by rather new mechanisms of power. Power has to be understood as a productive form which offers a rich repertoire of technologies. His best

368 Lemke 2019, p. 96.
369 Foucault 1978, p. 85.
370 Lemke 2019, p. 90.
371 Foucault 1978, p. 81.
372 Foucault 1978, p. 85.
373 Foucault 1978, pp. 86–7.
374 Foucault 1978, pp. 88–9.

known example of such a productive form of power is disciplinary power, which increases the forces of the human body and produces a subjected and 'docile' body.[375] Foucault pursued his intuition about the productivity of power throughout his work as a whole. Thus towards the end of his work he even reached the position that the formerly ideal types of disciplines are still conceived of in a manner which is too 'repressive'.

2.3.1.4 *The Microphysics of Power*

Foucault's analytics of power are in particular characterised by his attempt not to focus on the great forms of power, which are associated with the repressive apparatuses, but to concentrate on the 'capillary' mechanisms of power, in order to arrive at a minute analysis which does not always already assume that relations of power and domination function almost automatically. He thus examines 'its capillary forms of existence, at the point where power returns into the very grain of individuals, touches their bodies, and comes to insert itself into their gestures and attitudes, their discourses, apprenticeships and daily lives',[376] and even reaches 'the most tenuous and individual modes of behavior'.[377]

However, this does not mean that the great strategies of power are ignored, but rather that they have to implant themselves in the micro-relationships. The small mechanisms, which have their own techniques and tactics, are invested, colonised and inflected by increasingly general mechanisms and forms of overall domination.[378] In other words: the myriad, often minimal and dispersed processes converge with each other – until the contours of a general method gradually emerge. They constitute thus meticulous, often minute techniques, a '... "micro-physics" of power', 'small acts of cunning endowed with a great power of diffusion'. This concept of power is of course above all intended as a departure from Hegel's 'Cunning ... of the Greater Reason that works even in its sleep and gives meaning to the insignificant'. He is rather focused on the 'attentive "malevolence" that turns everything to account'.[379]

When Foucault under the heading of governmentality finally dealt with the state after all, that is, with the apparatus of power he had refused to investigate for a long time, he stressed that there is no break between micro- and macro-

375 Foucault 1995, p. 138.
376 Foucault 1976b, p. 10.
377 Foucault 1978, p. 11.
378 Foucault 2003, p. 30.
379 Foucault 1995, p. 139.

for example in that one could exclude the other. If the state is conceived of on the basis of human, reflexive practice, both forms of analysis can be connected.[380]

2.3.1.5 *No Master Plan – No Headquarters*

Despite all the struggles, relationships, and practices the analytic of power appears unable to deny its structuralist origins. Foucault had, however, explicitly defended himself against being labelled a structuralist: 'I have been unable to get it into their tiny minds that I have used none of the methods, concepts, or key terms that characterise structural analysis', he writes in *The Order of Things*.[381] Nonetheless it can be shown that Foucault's analysis ultimately shows a surfeit of structure or objectivity, as is very much common in materialist theories. This, however, does not stem from a concept which employs predetermined structural frameworks, but rather from the jungle of entangled powers.

Foucault had important reservations with regards to all approaches that were based upon some kind of guiding invisible hand, or on powerful coordinating agents (such as a 'ruling class' or the state). On the other hand social changes should not be the results of chance either,[382] but rather the result of strategic action. When asking in greater detail, however, *who* is taking action, it turns out that the actors play a rather marginal part. Although he does not deny that intentionally acting subjects exist, the diversity of the power matrix makes it impossible for them to straightforwardly realise their intentions. This is also how the seemingly paradoxical sentence has to be understood, that 'the aims [are] decipherable, and yet it is often the case that no one is there to have invented them, and few who can be said to have formulated them'.[383] Foucault continues to use the terms strategy and tactics, but does so in a transposed, impersonal manner. When the micro-practices connect with each other and can only develop into larger formations of domination following constant repetition and mutual support, the intentions remain implicit and disappear in the 'great, anonymous, almost unspoken strategies which coordinate the loquacious tactics whose "inventors" or decision makers are often without hypocrisy'.[384] Therefore there can be neither an overall plan to coordinate the strategies nor a central authority to guide their dissemination.[385]

380 Foucault 2009, p. 358.
381 Foucault 2005, p. xv.
382 Hunt and Wickham 1994, p. 28.
383 Foucault 1978, p. 95.
384 Ibid.
385 Charim 2002, p. 112.

'Power relations are both intentional and non subjective ... they are imbued, through and through, with calculation: there is no power that is exercised without a series of aims and objectives. But this does not mean that it results from the choice or decision of an individual subject; let us not look for the headquarters that presides over its rationality; ... the rationality of power is characterised by tactics that are often quite explicit at the restricted level where they are inscribed ... tactics which, becoming connected to one another, attracting and propagating one another, but finding their base of support and their condition elsewhere, end by forming comprehensive systems'.[386]

Will and calculation thus play their part in the result of power struggles, but the overall effect eludes the intentions of the actors. Therefore functionalist arguments are also out of the question. For there is no system, no inherent logic of stability, only practices which are given their shape and direction by the political technologies of power.[387]

2.3.1.6 *Technologies of Power*

The coupling of different practices, which support and transform each other, and are strengthened and sedimented through repetition, thus leads to anonymous strategies. This results in techniques, or, speaking of larger formations, technologies. Power is a technology. Techniques are ways of working, methods or forms of production, which are not strongly attached to the content and thus relatively independent practices, which regulate sequences.[388] Here Foucault does not describe how something occurs *in order to reach* a specific goal, but *how* power operates. Techniques define how an activity has to be carried out.[389]

Technologies emerge within specific concrete contexts. They respond to concrete problems and offer particular solutions.[390] The term was traditionally reserved for operations bearing on nature, but Foucault consciously broadens it to exercising dominion over human beings, because technology does not remain external to human beings.[391] Hereafter attention must be paid to the fact that Foucault most often argued on this level of abstraction of power technologies. They are his main research subject.

Power technologies are for Foucault the material base, the actually operating forces. This also means that *social* relations of power precede the institutions.

386 Foucault 1978, pp. 94–5.
387 Dreyfus and Rabinow 1983, pp. 187–8.
388 Charim 2002, p. 111.
389 Charim 2002, p. 114.
390 Lemke 2019, p. 72, Note 33.
391 Lemke 2019, p. 88, Note 7.

Foucault therefore argues against a shortened politological approach, which finds its starting point in the institutions, against what he called 'institutional-centric'.[392] What matters is to move outside the institution, because it can be understood on the basis of something external insofar as it is connected up with a global project: the technology of power.[393] The density of the institution itself can hide this under certain conditions, for 'an important part of the mechanisms put into operation by an institution are designed to ensure its own preservation'. This entails the risk, especially in power relations between institutions, of deciphering functions, which are essentially reproductive.[394] Furthermore, one risks discovering quickly the origin of power in the institutions as they act predominately through regulations and apparatuses. If the analysis starts from this point, one can end up giving them a privileged position in the analysis of power and hence again discover only the coercive side of power.[395] The technology of power crystallises in institutions, but it has its anchorage outside them.[396] What matters is therefore, as Gudrun-Axeli Knapp notes in agreement, not to choose the internal perspective alone.[397]

Beyond technologies of power and the institutions they crystallise in, Foucault works with the category of the *dispostif*. A *dispostif* is an extensive 'bundle of power relations'[398] or points of contact, where modes of behaviour converge that are dispersed throughout social space as a whole.[399] The one he covers in the greatest detail is the *dispositif* of sexuality. The *dispositif* provides an answer to the question as to how a pattern of coherent practices can be explained without recourse to a constituent subject or objective laws.[400] In sum, it is a conglomerate of discursive and non-discursive moments, a 'thoroughly heterogeneous ensemble consisting of discourses, institutions, architectural forms, regulatory decisions, laws, administrative measures, scientific statements, philosophical, moral and philanthropic propositions – in short, the said as much as the unsaid'.[401] This ensemble develops as an emerging, strategic answer to a historic '*urgent need*'; therefore a strategic imperative provides the matrix for the *dispositif*. Here again the antifunctionalist perspective is notice-

392 Foucault 2009, p. 116.
393 Foucault 2009, p. 117.
394 Foucault 1982, p. 791.
395 Ibid.
396 Ibid.
397 Knapp 1992, p. 310.
398 Lorey 1996, p. 64.
399 Ott 1998, p. 49.
400 Dreyfus and Rabinow 1994, pp. 150–1.
401 Foucault 1980, p. 194.

able. Different, even opposing strategies are condensed in a *dispositif* to solve a 'problem' in a concrete historic situation. It can then, however, complete itself with other strategies, and support an entirely different process, for the heterogenous elements are overdetermined and produce unintended effects.[402] There is no realisation of a plan, pursuit of a logic, or maintenance of a system.

Foucault's best known example for unintended effects is the 'failure' of the prison system, which in fact starts out by producing the very delinquency it is supposedly meant to prevent. This could then, however, be again strategically reinvested and productively used. Instead of confronting claim and reality, what matters is to distinguish between rationalities, technologies and effects.[403] The *dispositif* is thus an attempt to explain the whole of coherent practices in a non-functionalist manner.

2.3.2 Governmentalised Technologies of Power

In the following individual technologies of power will be distinguished, because Foucault means to demonstrate that law is *only* one technology of power amongst many. In his later works Foucault actually updated the previous technologies and adapted them anew: 'Well, I think I was wrong. I was not completely wrong, of course, but, in short, it was not exactly this',[404] he wrote about his earlier concept. Therefore it will be interpreted here from the perspective of his late work.

In contrast to what Nancy Fraser or Michael Hardt and Antonio Negri maintain, Foucault does not stop at the discovery of the 'disciplines' and thus at the 'fordist [sic] mode of social regulation',[405] or can only discuss its crisis.[406] With the concept of the 'government' his by now published *Lectures at the Collège de France* on the history of governmentality[407] introduce a very much post-Fordist technology. Susanne Krasmann therefore assumes rightly that the 'new regime of power, which Gilles Deleuze sketched in 1990 as the society of control ... was indeed analysed by Michel Foucault with a concept of power, which he detailed in particular in his lectures at the Collège de France: the concept of government'.[408]

---

402 Foucault 1980, pp. 195–6.
403 Lemke, Krasmann and Bröckling 2000, p. 22.
404 Foucault 2009, p. 48.
405 Thus, however, Fraser 2003, pp. 160, 166.
406 Thus Hardt and Negri 2000, p. 23.
407 Foucault 2008, 2009.
408 Krasmann 2003, p. 67.

In principle Foucault is interested in the development of the 'population'. In *Discipline and Punish* he thus maps out a technology of power that can meet the challenges of the population explosion in the context of industrialisation, and which is directed towards strengthening the force of the individual body. In *The Will to Knowledge* a second technology of power is added, which is directed towards the 'life' of the population, now understood as a 'species'. From this perspective it already becomes clear that an adaptation to such global phenomena as 'a global mass that is affected by overall processes' requires more complex organs for coordination and centralisation than he had previously envisioned for the disciplines in the limited framework of institutions. This means that the state becomes the focus.[409] In his later concept of *government* he then addresses population from the perspective of conducting men.[410] For the first time his interest is not focused on the body alone, but also on the more comprehensive processes of subjection.

At the same time Foucault turns to the state itself. This is inevitable, when 'the management of a whole social body', its 'whole scale',[411] is to be analysed. He wonders whether governmentality can be understood as some kind of 'general technology of power' that represents the outside of the state apparatus.[412] The state in contemporary societies is not simply one of the forms or spaces of the exercise of power, writes Foucault now, but all other forms of power relation refer to it. Of course not because they are derived from it, but because power relations have been progressively governmentalised, so that they have been elaborated under the auspices of state institutions.[413] The readjustment of the technologies of power shows in particular in that Foucault now insists that he has always looked into the presence and effect of the state's mechanisms. For what else is the organisation of madness, of clinical medicine or of the disciplines ultimately? – 'The problem of bringing under state control, of "statification" (*étatisation*) is at the heart of the questions I have tried to address'.[414]

It can thus be noted that with the increasing 'statification' or 'governmentalisation of the state',[415] with the technology of power that inscribes itself in the apparatuses of the state, governmentality expands its sphere of influence

409 Foucault 2003c, pp. 242–3.
410 Foucault 2009, p. 76.
411 Foucault 2008, p. 186.
412 Focault 2009, p. 120.
413 Foucault 1982, p. 793.
414 Foucault 2008, p. 77.
415 Foucault 1991, p. 103.

and thus overdetermines the others or has a preeminent position.[416] This is the perspective from which various technologies of power will now be presented.

2.3.2.1 *The Juridical Technology of Power (Law)*

The first technology of power leads Foucault to distance himself initially from the classic understanding of the state, namely that of sovereignty. This differentiation has led to myriad misunderstandings, not least in relation to law. In the following I will attempt to map out what Foucault was concerned with in those reflections.

The classic meaning of sovereignty is tied to the territory: *sovereignty over a territory*.[417] Therefore according to the juridical theory of the sovereign, which may well have been appropriate for the absolutist states, the relation of the prince to his principality remains fragile, for the bond between them is only one of violence, family heritage or treaty. There is no essential connection between the two and therefore the relationship is continually under threat from external as well as internal enemies. The target of this power is thus the *territory* including its inhabitants. The traditional problem of sovereignty consists in conquering new territories as well as holding on to conquered territory.[418]

Sovereignty and law are here always closely linked, because since the Middle Ages power in occidental societies has always articulated itself through law. This seems initially surprising, considering that for Enlightenment philosophy monarchic power is on the side of injustice and not that of justice, while the democratic juridification of political power is, in contrast, an achievement of modernity. According to Kant the transition to the democratic nation state is determined by the replacement of the territorial principle by that of the union of individuals. His writings were in particular directed against the practices of contemporary absolutist states, which treated the people inhabiting a territory as mere adjuncts of its ground. Democratic law was a new constitutive moment in the development of the nation state's identity.[419] Foucault on the other hand considered the law as a traditional and seemingly outdated form of the juridical monarchy, even if it could be democratised.

He emphasised that one must not overlook the 'fundamental historical trait of Western monarchies: they were constructed as systems of law, they

416 Ibid.
417 Foucault 1991, p. 93.
418 Foucault 2009, p. 64.
419 Maus 2006, p. 467.

expressed themselves through theories of law, and they made their mechanisms of power work in the form of law'.[420] In doing so, the great institutions could implant themselves precisely because they succeeded in presenting themselves as agencies of regulation, arbitration and demarcation, that is, as an organising power of the diversity of prior competing feudal powers.[421] The great forms of power could thus insert themselves as a principle of law, enforce their laws by acting through mechanisms of interdiction and sanction, and establish peace as the prohibition of feudal or private wars – which is to say, in the words of Max Weber: monopolise the legitimate use of physical force. Roman law was thus decisive for the reactivation of a juridical edifice at the height of the Middle Ages, as a technical and constitutive instrument for authoritarian, administrative and ultimately absolute monarchic power. Even though this juridical edifice escaped from royal control in later centuries and was ultimately turned against royal power, the limits of that power were always the issue at stake here.[422] Royal power thus progressively reduced the complex interplay of feudal powers and formed something like the keystone of a system of justice, buttressed by a military system.[423]

Foucault can therefore easily be read as though he holds the view that this form of power no longer plays a role and has been replaced by productive technologies. For legal theory this implies, however – and important theorists such as Alan Hunt and Garry Wickham and also Nicos Poulantzas understand him in this way – that Foucault holds the view that not only sovereign power, but at the same time also law, disappear in modern society. This would of course be a contradictio in adiecto for a legal theory and under the current conditions of increasing juridification also downright counterintuitive.

However, Foucault encouraged this interpretation through his writing style and his orientation towards criminal law. But ultimately this is a misunderstanding. For this, let us firstly again review Foucault's in part apodictic propositions: What does he understand by juridical practices?

> ... the manner in which wrongs and responsibilities are settled between [people], the mode by which, in the history of the West, society conceived and defined the way [one] could be judged in terms of wrongs committed ...[424] [That is] the system of the legal code with a binary division between

420 Foucault 1978, pp. 87–8.
421 Foucault 1978, pp. 86–7.
422 Foucault 2003c, p. 26.
423 Foucault 2008, p. 8.
424 Foucault 2000, p. 4 (translation modified).

> the permitted and the prohibited ... This, then, is the legal or juridical mechanism ... the archaic form of the penal order, the system we are familiar with from the Middle Ages until the seventeenth or eighteenth century.[425]

If Pashukanis can be accused of having written a theory of civil law, one could accuse Foucault of having limited himself to criminal law. Criminal law is at once the most repressive legal terrain and also one that is monopolised by the state. The connection of sovereignty and the right to punish up to the death penalty is completely associated with the repressive character of power. This fixation on the penalising form of law is now combined with statements which amount to saying that the juridical is regressing in comparison with pre-seventeenth century societies and that the functioning of the norm is made possible at the cost of the juridical system of the law,[426] or that 'our historical gradient carries us further and further away from a reign of law that had already begun to recede into the past at a time when the French Revolution and the accompanying age of constitutions and codes seemed to destine it for a future that was at hand'.[427] In this context the demand to free oneself from the 'juridico-discursive' understanding of power,[428] or to abandon the juridical model of sovereignty,[429] actually appears at first glance like a daring underestimation of the significance of law and the state's monopoly of force in contemporary societies. And it is precisely this charge Poulantzas brought forward against Foucault.[430]

Because institutionalised political power recurs less often to violence under regulated relations of domination than in pre-capitalist times, the illusion can arise that modern power is no longer grounded in physical violence.[431] In particular Hunt and Wickham reproach Foucault for this attempt to sketch law as an essentially pre-modern phenomenon.[432] His view could be summed up as the 'expulsion of law from modernity'.[433] Foucault's inclination to marginalise law is in sharp contrast to the main tendency of twentieth-century thought,

425 Foucault 2009, pp. 5–6.
426 Foucault 1978, p. 44.
427 Foucault 1978, p. 89.
428 Foucault 1978, p. 82.
429 Foucault 2003c, p. 265.
430 Poulantzas 1978, p. 77.
431 Poulantzas 1978, p. 80.
432 Hunt and Wickham 1994, p. 44.
433 Hunt and Wickham 1994, p. 56.

which accords law a central role in modern society. His concept therefore rather corresponds to a common simplified view, which equates all law with criminal law.

Carol Smart, who similarly to Hunt and Wickham, but from a feminist perspective, follows Foucault, argues in line with this:

> In fact much of Foucault's genealogy de-centres law as the prime historical agent or mode of control. Rather he focuses on newly emergent forms of regulation and surveillance and constructs for us a vision of the disciplinary society in which law's place diminishes with the growth of more diverse forms of discipline ... The status of law in modern societies is therefore somewhat uncertain in Foucault's account ... However, I am doubtful that law is simply being superseded, nor can we assume that it remains unchanged – a relic form pre-modern times.[434]

In this sceptical interpretation,[435] as Victor Tadros entirely accurately observed,[436] the potential of Foucault's work for law in particular is, however, lost. The 'fundamental misunderstanding'[437] consists in equating the term 'juridical' and 'law'. By 'juridical' Foucault rather means to describe 'any form of power, which attempts to prevent a certain type of action through the threat of legal or social sanctions'.[438] The law appears in this juridical model as the basic form power shows itself in.[439] The individual becomes the subject of natural laws or initial forms of power. What Foucault seeks to distance himself from might better be described as a kind of 'juridical idealism', that identifies all power as emanating from sovereignty.[440]

In principle Foucault wanted to grasp with this a very similar problem to Gramsci, namely that the focus on technologies of power in the form of violence ignores a whole series of other forms of power which have long ago gained ground in the niches of the law. In short, power and domination in modern societies are not limited to the dualism of law and violence, and from this perspective a significant aspect of modern power relations is missed. The historical

434 Smart 1989, p. 14.
435 Munro 2001, p. 553.
436 Tadros 1998, p. 76.
437 Tadros 1998, p. 79.
438 Tadros 1998, p. 78; in agreement i.e. similarly: Krasmann 2003, p. 90; Munro 2001, pp. 556 ff.; Ewald 1991, p. 138.
439 Foucault 2003c, p. 265.
440 Balibar 1992, p. 55.

background against which monarchic juridical power developed has until the present day encouraged the idea that law is the preeminent form of power.[441]

In sum, Foucault's critique of the juridical model of power is *not* concerned with playing down the significance of *law* in modernity, but with critiquing an exclusive or essential *interpretation of power in terms of law*: violence, interdiction, censoring, coercion.[442] Hence: 'We must construct an analytics of power that no longer takes law as a model and a code'.[443] Even in one of his last lectures in 1981–2, Foucault still insists that the increasing juridification of Western culture 'has led us to take law, and the form of law, as the general principle of every rule in the realm of human practice'.[444] And precisely this general principle is only a superficial appearance, only one part of the real power relations. On this point there is a parallel to Neumann's 'veiling function of the law'. But this in no way means that modern law has become irrelevant.[445]

Furthermore, he rejects a chronological sequence of power technologies, according to which for example law has been replaced by disciplines and biopolitics. Rather, sovereign power still continues to play a decisive role after the eighteenth century: 'I would say that, on the contrary, the problem of sovereignty was never posed with greater force than at this time'.[446] However, this does not mean either that a *sovereign or juridical model of power* is appropriate. The old modalities imply the new ones. The juridico-legal system does not lack a disciplinary side, even if it appears less important.[447] Neither are the juridico-legal structures cancelled out by mechanisms of security, on the contrary:[448]

> So, there is not a series of successive elements, the appearance of the new causing the earlier ones to disappear. There is not the legal age, the disciplinary age, and then the age of security. Mechanisms of security do not replace disciplinary mechanisms, which would have replaced juridico-legal mechanisms. In reality you have a series of complex edifices in which, of course, the techniques themselves change and are perfected, or

441 Foucault 1978, p. 88.
442 Lemke 2019, p. 96.
443 Foucault 1978, p. 90.
444 Foucault 2005, p. 112.
445 Furthermore, a look at Foucault's political practice shows the practical significance he granted law; thus he focused at the end of the 1970s and the start of the 1980s on human rights, such as in the case of the extradition of the RAF-defender Klaus Croissant by France to Germany in 1977 (Dosse 1998b, p. 337).
446 Foucault 1991, p. 101.
447 Foucault 2009, p. 6.
448 Foucault 2009, p. 7.

> anyway become more complicated, but in which what above all changes is the dominant characteristic, or more exactly, the system of correlation between juridico-legal mechanisms, disciplinary mechanisms, and mechanisms of security.[449]

A complex analytics of power thus has to assume a 'system of correlation' of techniques and mechanisms, wherein one of the techniques can be dominant as is the case with governmentality in the era of the modern nation state.

2.3.2.2 *Disciplines*

Foucault's attempt to expand the analytics of power begins – as it does in Marx – with a general attack on the liberal ideas of bourgeois democracy and formal legal equality. While those base themselves, 'blissfully unaware',[450] upon the freedoms of the law, beneath the legal form a very different technology of power has already implanted itself as the complement of formal legal equality:[451]

> For a certain bourgeois liberalism to become possible at the level of institutions, it was necessary to have, at the level of what I call 'micro-powers', a much stricter investment in bodies and behaviours. Discipline is the underside of democracy.[452]

While in the theory of the contract the contractual practices of subjects are always already self-explanatory and appear practically natural, Foucault makes clear that they are on the contrary the product of individuals who have been subjected to habits, rules and orders beforehand.[453] The introduction of an explicitly codified and formal egalitarian legal framework blinds one to the 'dark side of this process':

> The general juridical form that guaranteed a system of rights that were egalitarian in principle was supported by these tiny, everyday, physical mechanisms, by all those systems of micro-power that are essentially non-egalitarian and asymmetrical that we call the disciplines. And although in a formal way the representative regime makes it possible, directly or indir-

449 Foucault 2009, p. 8.
450 Tadros 1998, p. 91.
451 Lemke 2019, p. 71.
452 Foucault 1985, pp. 2–3.
453 Foucault 1995, p. 128.

> ectly, with or without relays, for the will of all to form the fundamental authority of sovereignty, the disciplines provide, at the base, a guarantee of the submission of forces and bodies. The real, corporal disciplines constituted the foundation of the formal, juridical liberties.[454]

The similarities to Marx's metaphor of base and superstructure can hardly be overlooked. While Marx's materialism targeted the materiality of social relations, Foucault focuses on the practices of power inasmuch as they are exercised upon *bodies*.[455] *Dressage* methods leave traces on the body in the form of habitual behaviours; power targets everyday gestures and activities.[456] The human body enters a machinery of power, which penetrates, segments and puts it back together. Thus, in the seventeenth and eighteenth century a political anatomy and mechanics of power emerged.[457] This increases the economic usefulness of individuals and their bodily forces in order to make them compatible with the growth of the apparatus of production.[458] *Simultaneously* it reverses the course of their energy, the power that might result from it, and turns it into a relation of strict subjection.[459]

The disciplinary individual[460] is fabricated through procedures which distribute individuals, fix them in space, classify them, train their bodies, code their continuous behaviour, and maintain them in perfect visibility, surrounding them with an apparatus of observation and registration. Thus, they constitute a body of accumulated knowledge about them.[461] While this technology of power is totalising and creates a certain suspension of the law,[462] it is nonetheless less visible, violent and costly in comparison to the repressive, juridical technology of power.[463]

Foucault initially calls the effect of the disciplines 'normalisation', but eventually 'normation'.[464] Initially this term sets itself apart from the 'normativity'

454 Foucault 1995, p. 222.
455 Balibar 1992, p. 53.
456 Foucault 1995, p. 128.
457 Foucault 1995, p. 139.
458 Foucault 1995, p. 221.
459 Hardt and Negri very clearly follow this concept of the power of the many and the simultaneous regulation of its potential with their concept of 'immaterial labor' and the 'multitude' (Hardt and Negri 2000).
460 Foucault 1995, p. 308.
461 Foucault 1995, p. 231.
462 Foucault 1995, p. 223.
463 Foucault 1995, p. 102.
464 Foucault 2009, p. 57.

of the legal imperative, which expresses a normative expectation of individual behaviour. Normalisation and normation on the other hand are techniques. Normation divides through classification, *dressage* and permanent control the normal from the abnormal. It posits an optimal model and then tries to get people, gestures and micro-practices to actually, not only normatively, conform to this model. The normal is precisely that which can conform to this norm.[465]

At first Foucault 'discovered' the connection of discipline and law in the systemic correlations of the technologies of power. Here he still assumed that discipline was the dominant technology of power, so that discourses born of discipline are invading law and normalising procedures are increasingly 'colonising' its procedures.[466] Law and justice integrate more and more into a continuum of regulating apparatuses (from health to administration) which align the individual according to the norm. 'Continual and clamorous legislative activity' was merely the form which made an essentially normalising power acceptable.[467]

Accordingly, the fitting conclusion is that '[S]overeignty and discipline ... are in fact the two things that constitute – in an absolute sense – the general mechanisms of power in our society'.[468] And even when Foucault expands his technologies of power, the principle of this reasoning remains. When the technology of governmentality is asserted, it is now the turn of the disciplines to refuse to vanish: '... but nevertheless, discipline was never more important or more valorised than at the moment when it became important to manage a population'.[469]

That Foucault theorises disciplines and not government in the early 1970s as the dominant technology can certainly be read in line with Nancy Fraser's interpretation as an expression of the Keynesian welfare state of the time. Foucault grasped its inner logic, like the owl of Minerva, precisely in its moment of crisis.[470] He situates the origins of the disciplines in the eighteenth century, but in a genealogical reading of Foucault's texts the clinic and the prison appear as early and still isolated proving grounds for regulatory practices that only develop into a universal phenomenon with the advent of Fordism.[471] Here

465 Ibid.
466 Foucault 2003c, pp. 38–9.
467 Foucault 1978, p. 144.
468 Foucault 2003c, p. 39.
469 Foucault 1991, pp. 101–2.
470 Fraser 2003, p. 160.
471 Fraser 2003, p. 163.

they are the 'micro-political' counterpart of Fordist accumulation, the 'capillary' level of its regulatory method.[472]

One must, however, concur with Thomas Lemke in that Foucault recognised the limitation of his earlier analysis. Precisely in the crisis of the Fordist regulatory model one can note an increasing move away from the disciplinary approach, which appears now almost archaic to Foucault, in comparison to the new technologies.[473] The subjects, as he says in 1978, have become more and more varied, diverse and independent. More and more people are not subject to disciplinary coercion. Therefore it is evident that in future one has to say goodbye to 'today's' disciplinary society.[474] When he identifies the 'security *dispositifs*', even so-called panopticism suddenly appears to him as 'the oldest dream of the oldest sovereign: None of my subjects can escape and none of their actions is unknown to me'.[475] In *Discipline and Punish* he still opposed the disciplines with their institutionalisation in the 'carceral archipelago' to the concept of sovereignty.[476] Discipline thus shares a similar fate to law in the history of theory; it is colonised by other technologies in the system of correlations. Thus far this has not been taken into account in the 'dominant view' amongst legal theorists' critiquing Foucault.

2.3.2.3 *Biopolitical Security Technologies*

Although a clear-cut distinction between law and the disciplines was still possible, things become more complicated and contradictory with the 'newer' technologies of power. Foucault seems to permanently search for an ever more subtle form of power, and thus tends to continually decentre his old discoveries, going so far as to use formulations such as 'We have looked at all this'.[477] What is new now – biopower or government, security *dispositifs* or technologies of the self?

The next round of readjustments starts with *The Will to Knowledge*. Here Foucault develops the concept of 'biopower'. Initially he distinguishes this form of power in the usual way, delimiting it from the sovereign or juridical model of power, and in this regard he takes up the line of argument he set out in *Discipline and Punish*. The further development consists in the understanding of disciplines as only one of two moments of biopower. Biopower is on the whole

472 Fraser 2003, p. 162.
473 Lemke 2003, p. 268.
474 Foucault 2003a, p. 673.
475 Foucault 2009, p. 66.
476 Foucault 1995, p. 297.
477 Foucault 2009, pp. 5–6.

distinct from sovereignty in that it no longer takes place as a means of deduction, a subtraction mechanism, a right to appropriate a portion of the wealth – processes ultimately based on the right to '*take* life' – but by 'working to incite, reinforce, control, monitor, optimise, and organise the forces under it as managers of life and survival, of bodies and the race'. What matters now is thus to '*foster* life'.[478]

In this respect the argument remains in keeping with the disciplines. But now they are only one of two poles of development.[479] For while the disciplines were directed towards the individual body, the pole which Foucault alternately terms 'biopolitics of the population' or 'regulation of the population' centres on the species body.[480] The regulating controls target procreation, birth- and mortality rates. Biopower as an ensemble of disciplines and population regulation introduces the human species and its fundamental biological traits since the end of the eighteenth century as an object of politics.[481] The reason for this is that capitalist development at the time brought an increase in productivity and resources, which ended the basic threats of famine and devastating diseases in Western cities so that 'death was ceasing to torment life so directly'. In the space thus created, technologies of power could emerge, which took the processes of life in hand and no longer dealt with legal subjects, but with living beings.[482] In this respect one can speak for the Western world of a 'biological threshold of modernity'.

Foucault thus now combines the various elements of his analytics of power in the concept of biopower as a conflictual whole.[483] In doing so he adds a new

---

478 Foucault 1978, pp. 136 ff. (emphasis in original). In this regard Giorgio Agamben's interpretation contributes to an additional confusion, as it takes the opposite direction. He thus explicitly follows Foucault's approach of interrogating the relation of 'bare life and politics' (Agamben 1998, p. 4.) However, in his attempt to illuminate 'this hidden point of intersection between the juridico-institutional and the biopolitical models of power' (Agamben 1998, p. 6), he ends eventually, probably in particular because of his engagement with Carl Schmitt's theory of exception, with what is once again a purely juridical theory of power and the exaltation of the repressive state apparatus, which was precisely what Foucault had fought against. Biopolitics becomes in Agamben a juridical control of life and precisely not its administration. In contrast, the approach of Hardt and Negri of coupling biopolitics with immaterial production (Hardt and Negri 2000) moved rather more in the direction Foucault had prepared. Their difference to Foucault consists mainly in that they assessed the possibilities of repurposing the 'powers' of the subjects thus produced altogether more positively than Foucault himself did (Buckel and Wissel 2002).

479 Foucault 1978, p. 139.

480 Ibid.

481 Foucault 2009, p. 1.

482 Foucault 1978, p. 142.

483 Ott 1998, p. 48.

technology of power on the side of the law and the disciplines in the form of the biopolitical regulation of the population. 'Biopower' and 'life' are not conceived of substantively or biologically by Foucault.[484] With Foucault's nominalism no prior substance can be thought, no substratum beyond relational power. 'Life' corresponds rather to 'the totality of automatised abilities, the totality of behaviour, in short, the individual as "external unity"'.[485]

Contrary to Victor Tadros's assumption[486] biopolitics and the later concept of 'governmentality' do not describe the same phenomenon. While they have a common object of regulation, namely the population, biopolitics concentrates, as the term already shows, exclusively on the biological regulation of the population, while the control of behaviours which Foucault addresses with 'governmentality' has considerably wider effects.[487] The perspective Foucault pursues 1975–6 aims firstly at the differentiation between the juridical power to kill and the bio-political power of managing life. Here he encounters the issue of the population, which in turn led him to governmentality and thus the state, which from this perspective forms a crucial bio-political entity of regulation.

In the lecture of 17 March 1976, which he gives while working on the first volume of *The History of Sexuality*, Foucault furthermore introduces the 'security *dispositifs*', which, however, no longer appear in the volume itself.[488] Two years later, however, in the lectures of January 1978, they once again play such a central role that Foucault even asks if contemporary societies are developing into a domain of security, a society of security.[489] He asks whether the 'general economy of power'[490] in the system of correlation leads to the domination of the technology of security, which is based on juridical and disciplinary mechanisms and transforms them.[491] The *technologies* of security represent the least systematic moment in Foucault's analytics of power, for they are on the one hand introduced as technologies, but on the other as instruments or also as *dispositifs*. Those twists also occur because of the shared intersection of geo-

484 Balibar 1992, p. 55.
485 Charim 2002, p. 121.
486 Tadros 1998, pp. 78, 91.
487 The difference might not be all that unambiguous, but his 'Governmentality', which only exists as a lecture, shows that Foucault had moved his research interest and in order to investigate biopower – as was his declared project (Foucault 2009, p. 1) – had to take detours and situate biopower in the wider framework of governmentality. (Thus also Michel Sennelart, the editor of the lectures; see Foucault 2009, p. 369).
488 Thus also Michel Sennelart in the fifth note on the first lecture in Foucault 2009, p. 24.
489 Foucault 2009, pp. 10–11.
490 Ibid.
491 Foucault 2009, pp. 8–9.

politics and governmentality. In contrast to the disciplines – not to mention law – this is about the *regulation* and not the disciplining of 'life'.[492] Security mechanisms are regulatory mechanisms which seek to control the mass effects of a given population, not by individual drilling, but by the protection of 'the security of the whole from internal dangers'. A 'technology of security' is distinguished from a 'technology of drilling'.[493]

Biopolitics is a regulating technology of power which operates through the mode of security. The security *dispositif* leaves well enough alone, while discipline does not leave the smallest matters alone. They are not prevented, but seen as inevitable processes to rely on. While juridical power considers order as a residual category of that which is not forbidden, the disciplinary *dispositif* continually codes the permitted and the forbidden, and what matters are less the things that have to be refrained from than those that are to be done. The security *dispositif* on the other hand attempts to set things in motion, to control within 'elements of reality'.[494] Exemplary for this is the technology of vaccination. Thus a statistical analysis, a calculation of costs and an average (average rate of theft, mortality, etc.) are established, in order to subsequently keep conditions within a corridor of 'normality', in the sense of the average.[495] The target of this is the population in the sense of living beings and not people as legal subjects.[496] In his search for ever more subtle technologies, Foucault accordingly arrives at population policy, which works through biopolitical security mechanisms.

2.3.2.4 *Government*

However, the more Foucault turns to the regulation of the population, the more he has to shift the subject of his work. Already at the end of his third lecture on governmentality a 'far-reaching turning point' occurs when, 'in a sort of dramatic theoretical turn', a shift towards governmentality takes place.[497] With this term a new area of research opens up; the genealogy of the modern state, 'the entry of the question of the state into the field of analysis of micro-powers'.[498] Foucault arrives by way of biopolitics at security mechanisms and with them at the population. He now sums up himself: 'While I have been speaking about

492 Foucault 2003c, pp. 246–7.
493 Foucault 2003c, p. 249.
494 Foucault 2009, pp. 59ff.
495 Foucault 2009, pp. 4ff.
496 Foucault 2009, p. 21.
497 Sennelart in Foucault 2009, pp. 379–80.
498 Sennelart in Foucault 2009, p. 381.

population a word has constantly recurred ... and this is the word "government"'.[499] At the start of the fourth lecture he then says that he only wanted 'to make a bit of an inventory of this problem of government'.[500] In fact, however, he does nothing else from this point on. A 'bit of an inventory' turns into a reconstruction of political economy from the perspective of government.

Since engaging with the population, he appears to increasingly hold the view that there are predominately two 'economies of power': on the one hand the long since known sovereignty, which however he now defines as the exercise of power over the fine grain of individual behaviours,[501] that is, sovereignty now refers to legal *and* disciplinary power; and on the other hand the 'government of populations'.[502] Thus Foucault's shift already shows here, when he separates the two elements of brainpower and introduces two economies of power: one is sovereignty, which is directed towards individuals, and the other government, which targets the population. The terms 'biopower' and 'biopolitics' hardly appear any longer, and biopolitics is even limited to a local technology which inscribes itself in medical institutions.[503] Instead he speaks of 'government' and 'governmentality'.

A law cannot be imposed from above upon the population through 'legalistic voluntarism', but the population has to be managed according to its own quasi-natural laws by acting upon it through analysis and calculation.[504] From now on the question is thus no longer the safety of a territory, but the security of the population. It is not acted upon through laws and minute drills, but one allows circulations to take place and controls them,[505] that is, the economy is introduced into the political administration – this is the main activity that matters in governing. Economy in the original sense – the wise government of the house for the common welfare of the whole. What matters is therefore that the inhabitants, and the wealth and behaviour of each and all, are subject to attentive surveillance and control.[506] It is not a state or a territory that is governed, but people, individuals and groups.[507] Population is above all else the ultimate end of government.[508]

---

499 Foucault 2009, p. 76.
500 Foucault 2009, p. 88.
501 Foucault 2009, p. 66.
502 Ibid.
503 Foucault 2009, p. 120.
504 Foucault 2009, pp. 71ff.
505 Foucault 2009, p. 65.
506 Foucault 1991, p. 92.
507 Foucault 2009, p. 122.
508 Foucault 1991, p. 100.

But why is it especially population that plays such a decisive role in Foucault's argument since he began to deal with biopolitics? The threshold of modernity, he claims, is crossed at the moment when we are no longer dealing only with a territory that is ruled externally, but have discovered the population that lives in it as the basis of the state's wealth and power.[509] Here it is crucial that it is not treated as a group of juridical subjects, but according to its 'nature'. For this empirical surveys have to be undertaken to know the object of regulation in every detail. Here Foucault not only means procreation and mortality, but also economy and 'opinions'. Therefore biopolitics is no longer the appropriate term. The term 'public', which was such a crucial notion in the eighteenth century, 'is the population seen under the aspect of its opinions, ways of doing things, forms of behaviour, customs, fears, prejudices, and requirements; it is what one gets a hold on through education, campaigns, and convictions'.[510]

The perspective Foucault adopts here is in turn an implicit but harsh critique of liberalism. It is population – not the people. It is a question of regulating a productive multitude and not of legal subjects who rule themselves through democratic law. Once one leaves the juridical theory of power behind, one sees how in the niches of law the population has long since become an *object* of regulation, how it is being ruled, instead of being the one to rule. Nonetheless even the emergence of the concept of democratic self-legislation is an effect of constituting the population and the idea of self-government, which is expressed in juridical categories.

Now, Foucault holds the view that those practices for the leadership of people did not appear in one day, but developed over centuries, and finally transformed in the eighteenth century with the establishment of modern states into a specifically *political* form of power. Ever since the third century the prelude to this governing power was the Christian pastorate. Through its institutions it gradually 'gave rise to an art of conducting, directing, leading, guiding, taking in hand, and manipulating [human beings], an art of monitoring them and urging them on step by step, an art with the function of taking charge of [human beings] collectively and individually throughout their life and at every moment of their existence'.[511]

In pastoral power the ruler is imagined as a shepherd in relation to individuals. The salvation of the flock is its essential objective. The pastor guides the whole flock and does everything for the totality of his flock, and also for each

509 Foucault 2009, p. 61.
510 Foucault 2009, p. 75.
511 Foucault 2009, p. 165 (translation modified).

sheep of the flock.[512] The history of the pastorate has to be understood as the starting point of a particular type of power over people, as a 'matrix of procedures for the government of [human beings]'.[513] The Christian community, which constitutes itself as the institution of the church and claims to govern human beings in their daily life on the grounds of leading them to eternal life, developed and refined its technology in the course of fifteen centuries.

The struggles of the entire Western world from the thirteenth to the eighteenth century were fundamentally struggles around this pastoral power. At stake was who would actually have the right to govern human beings in their daily life. In the Reformation, for example, which was a great pastoral rather than doctrinal battle, what was at issue was actually the way in which pastoral power was exercised.[514] Here Foucault's materialism is again on show, as he situates materiality in practices, instead of writing a history of doctrinal ideas. Very much as Max Weber investigates in his *Protestant Ethic* the influence of religious 'ideas' on the conduct of life,[515] Foucault analyses how the Christian direction of conscience, the manner of salvation and the institution of pure obedience led to a particular worldly practice which constituted daily life.[516] Pastoral power was thus, exactly like the idea of 'predestination', which Weber had investigated, an earthly power, even it if was oriented towards the eternal life.[517]

From the end of the seventeenth century on the government begins to take responsibility for people's conduct.[518] Two intersecting processes were central in this transition: on the one hand the dismantling of feudal structures and the centralisation in the state, on the other hand the Reformation and Counter Reformation, which led to conflict about how one is spiritually directed here on earth for one's salvation, that is, to religious fragmentation.[519] Government secularises the previously religiously defined goals of happiness, salvation and prosperity and articulates them anew in the framework of the political question of the state.[520]

Foucault distinguishes three historical types of government: *raison d'état*, liberal and neoliberal government, although one can only speak of govern-

512 Foucault 2009, p. 128.
513 Foucault 2009, p. 147 (translation modified).
514 Foucault 2009, pp. 148 ff.
515 Weber 2001.
516 Foucault 2009, pp. 167–83.
517 Foucault 2009, p. 148.
518 Foucault 2009, p. 197.
519 Foucault 2009, pp. 88–9.
520 Lemke, Krasmann and Bröckling 2000, p. 11.

ment in the proper sense in the period following the liberal art of government, because it is only here that the population itself becomes central.[521] The liberal government manages instead of regulating, in that it does not prevent, but attempts to organise 'natural' phenomena in such way that they do not deviate from the desired trajectory.

At this point Foucault gets back to the security mechanisms as they are necessitated by this form of government. For now it is only possible to govern well under the condition that certain forms of freedom are truly respected (the freedom of the market, of speech, etc.).[522] However, this does not mean that this leads to a more tolerant or lenient government, for at the same time security mechanisms organise the conditions under which one can be free. Freedom is accordingly not an ideology, but a technique of government.[523] At the centre of liberal practice is also a problematic relationship between 'freedom' and that which creates and also threatens to limit and destroy it.[524]

The security mechanisms reformulate Foucault's idea that formal bourgeois freedom is bought by way of a corseting of bodies through disciplines, in such a way that now the security strategies are the 'other side of the coin' of liberalism. The interplay of freedom and security is at the centre of the new governmental reason.[525] At the very same moment that freedom is produced, limitations, controls, forms of coercion, and threats are established (such as the protectionism of tariffs). The disciplinary techniques also develop at the same time as the era of freedoms, and the Panopticon is practically the form of liberal government as a whole. Of course, a liberal government has to provide a space for natural mechanisms and must in no way exert an influence on them in any other way – 'at least in the first instance' – than through supervision. Only if it establishes that something irregular is taking place does it have to intervene.[526]

One sees clearly how Foucault redirects his system of correlation. Discipline is still the other side of democracy, although now as a moment of the security *dispositif*. While it did not disappear with the primacy of the 'governmental' kind of power[527] it is no longer, as was the case during his engagement with 'biopower', the other of population regulation. For to manage a

521 Foucault 2009, p. 352.
522 Foucault 2009, p. 353.
523 Foucault 2009, p. 49.
524 Foucault 2008, pp. 64 ff.
525 Foucault 2008, p. 66.
526 Foucault 2008, p. 67.
527 Foucault 1991b, pp. 101–2.

population means to do so just as much in its depths, subtleties, and details. Foucault describes the connection with his previous analytics of power as follows:

> Accordingly, we need to see things not in terms of the replacement of a society of sovereignty by a disciplinary society and the subsequent replacement of a disciplinary society by a society of government; in reality one has a triangle, sovereignty-discipline-government, which has as its primary target the population and as its essential mechanism the security *dispositif*.[528]

Governmental management or government is, precisely like the exercise of hegemony in Gramsci, not the same as ruling, commanding or laying down the law,[529] but instead refers to the way in which one directs the conduct of human beings[530] and manages them. Management does not take place by way of juridical order, but by encouraging technologies of self-management. 'To govern, in this sense, is to structure the possible field of action of others'.[531] The technology of government connects thus for the first time the relationship of the subjects to themselves (the technologies of the self) with the technologies of domination. The theory of governmentality appears therefore at the same time in Foucault as his research into technologies of the self, for it operates on the basis of other people's ability to self-regulate their behaviour. Governing is in this regard also an art of persuasion to behave in a certain way, the ability to affect the field of possible actions of others. It is based on a subject that is active or can be activated.[532] To rephrase this in a Gramscian manner, a consensus between governmental management techniques and the actions of subjects is produced.[533]

A frequent criticism of Foucault is that his capillary analysis does not make it possible to consider the material condensation of power relations in the state such as Poulantzas does, for example.[534] With governmentality Foucault belatedly provides this previously missing analysis, as he can no longer avoid the state apparatuses now that he is dealing with the population.

528 Foucault 1991b, p. 102.
529 Foucault 2009, p. 151.
530 Foucault 2008, p. 186 (translation modified).
531 Foucault 1982, p. 790.
532 Krasmann 2003, pp. 136–7.
533 Pieper and Gutierrez Rodriguez 2003, p. 11.
534 Hunt and Wickham 1994, p. 31; Lemke 2019, p. 120.

He continues nonetheless to object to the idea of the state as a prior substratum, which only has to be deciphered in its function. The totality of practices cannot be derived from the character of the state, because the state is not in itself an autonomous source of power.[535] Rather, Foucault states, very much like Poulantzas, it is also a praxis – 'a way of governing'.[536] The state has thus constituted itself through the practices of government, it is as it were the turning point of government. Hence it is not 'that kind of cold monster',[537] no 'thing' as Poulantzas would say, no 'state-thing' says Foucault.[538] Therefore it is necessary and possible to write a genealogy of the modern state and its apparatuses that is actually based on a history of governmental reason:[539]

> Why should one want to study this insubstantial and vague domain covered by a notion as problematic and artificial as that of 'governmentality'? ... in order to tackle the problem of the state and population.[540]

Governmentality as the technology of power whose main target is the population, whose major form of knowledge is political economy, and whose essential technical instruments are the *dispositifs* of security,[541] thus inscribes itself in the state apparatuses just as techniques of segregation do in psychiatry and techniques of discipline in prisons, schools or barracks.

2.3.3 Subjectivation

Until now it is mostly the perspective of power that has been adopted and not that of its effects. Relatively late, and surprisingly, Foucault explains that he is not at all concerned with an analysis of the phenomena of power: 'My objective, instead, has been to create a history of the different modes by which, in our culture, human beings are made subjects'.[542] On close examination all of his analyses in fact culminate in the production of the subject. This insight will become central for my concept of the legal form, and I will therefore now look into subjectivation in greater detail.

Foucault is clearly engaged with a similar set of questions as Gramsci, namely how the dominated come to participate in maintaining the social order that

535 Foucault 2008, p. 77.
536 Foucault 2009, pp. 283, 312.
537 Foucault 2009, p. 248.
538 Foucault 2009, p. 277.
539 Foucault 2009, p. 354.
540 Foucault 2009, p. 116.
541 Foucault 2009, p. 108.
542 Foucault 1982, p. 777.

dominates them. Here Gramsci mainly investigates how this consensus, understood as active assent, is organised. Foucault, on the other hand, starts at a more abstract level with the problem of the constitution of the subject as such. The specific form of the modern subject is according to him the central instrument of the subjection of human beings to the power relations of modern bourgeois-capitalist societies. *Dispositifs* from different discourses, practices and forms of knowledge constitute and organise the modern subject as a historical form of the human being.[543] Technologies of power thus not only inscribe themselves in institutions, but also take hold in the subjects.[544]

In line with the periods of his work Foucault initially researches in particular the moulding of the body and only then the more comprehensive process of subjectivation. The starting point for the subject analysis is in consistent, relational manner the recognition that the individual cannot be considered as an elementary core, upon which power is exercised and that it subjugates. 'In actual fact, one of the first effects of power is that it allows bodies, gestures, discourses, and desires to be identified and constituted as something individual'.[545] Just like the state, the subject also has to be reconstructed genealogically, in its becoming.

Subjection or subjectivation[546] is a paradoxical form of power. For it firstly forms the subjects, makes their agency possible and is at the same time what oppresses them. '"Subjection" signifies the process of becoming subordinated by power as well as the process of becoming a subject'.[547] Different technologies of power function through different forms of subjection:[548] as subject and object of discourses, by disciplining bodies, binding them to an identity, imposing laws of truth and managing through technologies of the self.

2.3.3.1 *The Subjected Individual*

The disciplines are processes that produce subjected individuals.[549] They weave a tight net of strict hierarchy around diversity's power of resistance. In doing so they increase the particular usefulness of every element: 'Hence, in order to extract from bodies the maximum time and force, the use of those overall methods known as time-tables, collective training, exercises, total and

543 Dreyfus and Rabinow 1983, p. 120, Ott 1998, p. 29.
544 Ott 1998, p. 49.
545 Foucault 2003c, pp. 29–30.
546 Butler 1997, p. 1.
547 Butler 1997, p. 2.
548 Lemke 2019, p. 273.
549 Foucault 1995, p. 138.

detailed surveillance'.[550] Foucault starts from the Marxian theory of the development of modern capitalism, which reconstructs the social production of the 'doubly free worker' as a process 'written in the annals of mankind in letters of blood and fire',[551] and which first creates the labour power that can then produce surplus value. Foucault concludes that this results in the replacement of those traditional, costly and violent forms of power by refined technologies of subjugation/subjection. Capitalism penetrates very deeply 'into our existence' by elaborating a set of political techniques, by which human beings are tied to something like labour, by which people's bodies and their time are transformed into labour power and labour time.[552]

The Panopticon becomes the abstract formula of the technology of individuals.[553] This technology produces the disciplined body in a twofold manner. Firstly the multiplicity of bodies has to become a diversity of individual bodies by isolating them in their positioning in space and by ranks. The disciplined body is isolated and hierarchised. The individual body thus produced subsequently also has to be analysed as such. Training disassembles it, in order to make it suitable and to produce capacities.[554] What is interesting about this idea is that power relations materially penetrate deeply into bodies, but are not taken up as concepts. Power is not internalised, as Poulantzas interprets Foucault,[555] but rather 'embodied'; knowledge is incorporated into and penetrates habits. 'These are the kind of capacities which training produces in the body, the behaviours of an automated aptitude'.[556] Subjectivity is formed in the practice of exercises, which create abilities, skills and capacities to carry something out. Subjectivity accordingly means 'the power to act' in the sense of being able to both carry out something and manage oneself.[557]

Here the isolated bodies become individuals, on the one hand by being related to a homogenous whole, and on the other by experiencing thus their specific difference according to a norm. 'The disciplinary individual is that which is "externally" nailed down by disciplinary power to its particularity, that is its individualising difference ...'[558] This technology of power organises the individual according to normalising categories, marks it with its individuality

550 Foucault 1995, p. 237.
551 Marx 1976, p. 875.
552 Foucault 2000, p. 86.
553 Foucault 1995, p. 225.
554 Charim 2002, p. 97.
555 Poulantzas 2000, p. 79.
556 Charim 2002, p. 98.
557 Krasmann 2003, p. 134.
558 Charim 2002, p. 99.

and chains it to its identity. Knowledge practices impose a law of truth (such as about its sexuality) upon it.[559] Individuals are thus subjects regulated by types of identities and specifically habituated through micro-practices.[560]

2.3.3.2 *Technologies of the Self*

Isolde Charim in turn objects that Foucault, at least in *Discipline and Punish*, understands by an individual nothing other than gestures, powers and energies brought together into an entity, but not the consciousness of the body. Disciplinary power turns it into some kind of machine,[561] rather than into an 'extended individual'. Foucault does not put any means into our hands to think about this extended access to an individual beyond the body as a machine.[562] Butler puts forth a similar argument and considers that Foucault's theory unjustly neglects the entire sphere of the psyche. She herself therefore attempts to pursue the question of the psychic form power takes.[563]

This may still apply to *Discipline and Punish*, but at the latest with the concept of governmentality this view is no longer convincing. The management of everyday behaviours through the art of government is simply not limited to the drilling of bodies. With this concept Foucault focuses on forms of subjection other than disciplinary subjugation.[564] At this point in time, the term subject has long since had a double meaning for Foucault: that of being subjected through control and dependence and at the same time of being rooted in its own identity through consciousness and self-awareness. Individuals no longer appear only as recipients of social constraints, but try to give themselves a form of existence.[565]

With the emergence of the modern state, subjection gains a new quality. State power as a new form of pastoral power is 'both an individualising and a totalising form of power',[566] that is at the same time both directed at the individual and at the population. Never before has there been such a tricky combination of the two. Foucault now positions the forms of subjection anew by giving priority – analogous to that of the power technologies – to the effects of government as the successor of pastoral power: 'What the history of the

559 Foucault 1982.
560 Hark 1999, pp. 26, 41.
561 Charim 2002, pp. 100 ff.
562 Charim 2002, p. 121.
563 Butler 1997, p. 2.
564 Thus also Lemke 2003, p. 269; Lemke, Krasmann and Bröckling 2000, p. 8.
565 Ott 1998, p. 33.
566 Foucault 1982, pp. 782–3.

pastorate involves, therefore, is the entire history of procedures of human individualization in the West. Let's say also that it involves the history of the subject'.[567]

Only the concept of the government, however, leads Foucault to recognise the necessity of engaging with the historical forms of relations to the self. In order to do so, he introduces in Volumes II and III of his *History of Sexuality* the 'technologies of the self'. Those are defined by the fact that they 'permit individuals to effect, by their own means, a certain number of operations on their own bodies, on their own souls, on their own thoughts, on their own conduct, and this in a manner so as to transform themselves, modify themselves …'[568] Power relations now include both technologies of domination and technologies of the self; and what matters is to analyse their connection:

> The contact point, where the way individuals are driven by others is tied to the way they conduct themselves, is what we can call, I think, government. Governing people, in the broad meaning of the word, is not a way to force people to do what the governor wants; it is always a versatile equilibrium, with complementarity and conflicts between techniques which assure coercion and processes through which the self is constructed or modified by himself.[569]

Technologies of the self are thus not per se self-chosen life plans, but can in fact be integrated into structures of domination or coupled with technologies of power. Moreover, they are also always attempts at self-mastery and of control over relationships to others.[570] An understanding of governmentality can certainly not do without an analysis of the subject, which is defined through its relation to itself, claims Foucault in his lectures on the *Hermeneutics of the Subject*.[571] The relation of the self to the self has to be its base, that is, what Foucault calls an 'ethics'.[572]

The technologies of power described thus produce 'regimes of subjection, those ensembles of forms of understanding, strategies of drilling and practices of the self, which turn human beings into subject and with which they have

567 Foucault 2009, p. 184.
568 Foucault 2016, p. 25.
569 Foucault 2016, pp. 25–6.
570 Ott 1998, p. 34.
571 Foucault 2005, p. 252.
572 Ibid.

and continue to make themselves subjects'. Subjection is thus always inscribed in strategies of control, understood as behaviour control.[573]

This has to be analysed, 'if we want to understand how we have been trapped in our own history'.[574] Accordingly the strategy of liberation means to promote new forms of subjectivity and to 'imagine and build up what we could be', 'through the refusal of this kind of individuality which has been imposed on us for several centuries'.[575]

2.3.4 Law

Those rather general reflections, although some of them seemingly lead away from the subject, have been necessary, because Foucault has not written a legal theory in the classic sense and his diverse statements on law have mainly been interpreted in the relevant literature as a dismissal of law. I have attempted to show that Foucault was in this respect rather concerned with a decentring of this technology of power.

Below I will sketch what can be gained from his reflections for an analytics of law. For his not-speaking about law occurred after all in a rather eloquent manner. Following the order of the three preceding sections, the focus will now be on the technology of the law itself.

2.3.4.1 *Law as Technology of Power*

Firstly, law has to be considered as one of the oldest technologies of power, which has undergone a substantial transformation in the course of its existence. It is in no way reducible to the law, and can therefore not be subsumed under a juridical theory of power, even if it has operated in such a way at some point in the past, which is something Foucault does not explicitly comment upon – for absolutist power has merely succeeded in presenting itself in this manner. Law is rather a practice or an ensemble of practices existing on many levels, from everyday ideas of the law and legal discourses about legislation up to jurisprudence and law enforcement. Those practices interlink to form larger legal formations and perpetuate through repetition, and thus generate family, commercial, criminal or administrative law. 'The law' can thus hardly form an instrument of a ruling elite, any more than it can in Poulantzas or Pashukanis, for the different strategies that employ the law consolidate into anonymous strategies. Legal practices also lead to a muddling of powers as this social practice becomes independent. Thus it follows no overall plan and can therefore

573 Bröckling 2003, pp. 80–1.

574 Foucault 1982, p. 780.

575 Foucault 1982, p. 785.

not exercise a 'function' for the reproduction of capitalist society or commodity production. At best it may produce an effect that enables this production.

Nor can the law be 'derived' from those basic structures; rather it emerges from the relationships of forces as their effect, albeit from relationships of forces in a wider sense; from the 'totality of the social network', that is, from gender relations no less than from struggles over the surplus product (Ritsert). However, this also means that law does not emerge from the state, but rather that it is governmentalised. With Foucault it is necessary, contrary to Boaventura de Sousa Santos' assumption,[576] to adopt a pluralist legal perspective: 'We adhere to a view that law is a complex of practices, discourses and institutions. Over this plurality of legal forms "state law" persistently, but never with complete success, seeks to impose a unity'.[577] Legal technology inscribes itself into the legal institutions and sets their direction. They in turn then develop their own dynamics and mechanisms of self-perpetuation.

2.3.4.2 *The Legal Code and the Monopoly on Violence*

Law is thus only *one* technology of power, if one follows Foucault: a moment of the correlation system which is determined by a dominant technology. Since the development of the modern state and of capitalist socialisation, which are both based upon the productive multitude, the population, this is the government. But what is then the specific characteristic of this independent practice in contradistinction to others? What is law's way of working? What is, in short, the specifically legal?

The difficulty consists in that Foucault mostly refers back to law only as a repressive model of power, but claims *at the same time* that legal practices also have to be thought of as themselves productive. Sovereignty is no longer the manner in which rule is exercised in bourgeois societies, but *at the same time* it persists through the transformations of power and is therefore an essential component in the triangle of governmentality.

According to Foucault, the rule of law develops with the emergence of the absolutist state as the prelude to the modern capitalist state. Law is here both a regulating power through its background of monopolised violence and the code in which power in Western societies has presented itself ever since the Middle Ages, and that reflects it (as legal theory). This is also the only form in which it is seen as legitimate since the advent of the modern state based on the rule of law. Since sovereignty thus still plays a role, Foucault also has to

576 Santos 1995b, p. 406.

577 Hunt and Wickham 1994, p. 39.

assume that its regulatory function, propped up by the monopoly on violence and the simultaneous representation of power as right, and the reflexive and by now democratised confrontation about the way in which power is exercised, are essential characteristics of law. Just as one cannot deny that the disciplines and the management of human beings have a certain repressive quality, this more strongly repressive aspect of law continues to play a central part in modern societies.

Juridical practices regulate the procedures by establishing legal and illegal behaviours (as criminal law is pre-eminent in Foucault's thought). At the same time, however, the legal code, in which power has to present itself, opens a discursive terrain of struggle, because the question of what law is cannot be answered in the final instance, and diverse legal discourses and practices compete precisely for this reason. Even the apparatuses of the state, which the law inscribes itself in, compete for the power of definition and enforcement. The positivity of the law has not changed anything about this, because written language is also open to iterability, that is, following Derrida, the form of repetition in which a sign can break free. It is moreover only this positivity that opens up the technical possibility of making the struggle over the legal code accessible for a range of strategies. Luhmann's paradox of the law reveals itself here as a strategic struggle about the representation of power. The code can be fixed only temporarily, according to the current relationship of forces. As such, however, it is then in contrast to moral practices which are again connected to the government's monopoly on violence. The legal serves as a code which enables formerly monarchic and now modern power to constitute itself, formalise its structure and reflect on its own working.[578]

But the legal system is precisely not only this discourse, 'it is armed'.[579] Because law remains the only representation of power in the urban centres, it contributes, following Neumann's understanding, not only to the pacification of conflicts, but also no less to their cover up. For it makes precisely all other categories of power invisible, and they can only become visible at all by presenting themselves in legal categories. The disciplining that takes place in the agency of socialisation that is school, for example, with all its micro-practices, only shows as power on the surface of the legally sanctioned obligation to attend school, the state's educational mission, and the intersection of state institutions and parental participation in their operations. Thus bourgeois society appears to be a realm of law.

578 Ewald 1991, p. 139.
579 Tadros 1998, p. 81.

Juridical practices, because of their genesis as repressive regulatory mechanisms and at the same time representations of power, have this double character of making power visible and invisible, constituting both repression and a legitimate form of power that can be changed. This double character has persisted throughout later developments and now articulates itself with the other technologies. Law thus primarily prohibits, while the disciplines produce the desired behaviours and the security technologies allow for them to take place. The three technologies are not connected in a cumulative manner, but the disciplines and the security technologies emerge in the niches and gaps of law, they guarantee on the level of the 'base' that the subjects which regulate their relations through the law can do so, because they are specifically habituated and competent in self-management.

According to Foucault this occurs precisely at the moment sovereignty is democratised and converted to the 'sovereignty of the people'. One could say that even the most rigorous 'organic intellectuals' (Gramsci) of this project, namely Kant and Rousseau, already address this in a way. In *Metaphysics of Morals* Kant bases his radically democratic concept on the bourgeois subject (the 'bourgeois personality'), which is meant to be characterised by 'independence', so that all apprentices, servants, 'minors' and in particular all 'women' are at first – until they gain independence – excluded.[580] Rousseau on the other hand does not undertake any exclusions of this kind, but assumes that the government has to undertake an educational activity, because the passions of human beings tend to dissolve the community. The precondition of freedom is the moral elevation of mankind.[581] Law, disciplines and security technology are thus intertwined and develop at the respective points of rupture.

What then does government's domination in the governmental correlation system mean for law? Governmentality targets the population, its main instrument are the security *dispositifs*. Foucault holds the view that here laws become tactics for the practice of government,[582] for its investigation, surveillance and intervention, when the security of the whole is in danger:

> However, once the governmental technology was put in place … the primary aim of law was no longer to prescribe general rules which defined a level of transgression, it was to intervene into the relationships between particular groups of people according to information carefully collected and analysed in the form of the economy … The 'positive' role of law, in

580 Kant 1991, p. 126.

581 Fetscher 1975, pp. 195–6.

582 Foucault 1991, p. 95; thus also Tadros 1998, p. 92.

the Foucauldian account, takes its place amongst a more general technical apparatus of governmental control which intervenes into the lives of individuals and groups in response to knowledge collected about those lives ... the way in which law operates has shifted to the regulation of the lives.[583]

2.3.4.3 *Subjectivation by Law*

Up to this point, what can be reconstructed for a legal theory on the basis of Foucault's statements on law remains relatively traditional. This is due to the fact that I have thus far concentrated on the repressive aspect of law. However, once one turns to its productive aspect, what is gained by a Foucauldian perspective becomes finally apparent (beyond recognising that law only purports to be *the* effect of power as such). While his entire theory really amounts to the analysis of the modern subject, he now states that amongst the social practices which contribute to the development of new subject formations, 'the most important ones are juridical practices'.[584] The modern subject, as a historical form of the human being whose history has been set in motion by pastoral power's processes of individualisation, is according to Foucault a social construction, an effect of power technologies. Subjection is the practice of constituting and co-originally subjugating modern man. It is constructed and organised by 'regimes of subjection' (Bröckling), which consist of discourses, practices (of the self), forms of knowledge and institutions. While the disciplines create the isolated body, habits and competencies, law as a part of the *dispositif* is very much essential in the constitution of knowledge, relation to the self and identity: 'The modern regulatory aspect of law, then, ought ... to be understood ... as intervening in the social construction and government of the modern subject'.[585]

Foucault already realised early on that social practices produce domains of knowledge and forms of subjects.[586] The juridical practices are here a central form 'by which our society defined types of subjectivity, forms of knowledge, and, consequently, relations between man and truth'.[587] The legal normalisations of subjectivity are thus no ideology, the legal subject is therefore not as

583 Tadros 1998, p. 93. The security legislation after the attacks on 11 September 2001 in the Western centres is a prominent example for this thesis. We have shown that what is taking place is practically a 'cartography of the population' (Buckel and Kannankulam 2002).
584 Foucault 2000 power, p. 4.
585 Tadros 1998, p. 93.
586 Foucault 2000, p. 4.
587 Ibid.

in Pashukanis an abstraction of 'real' human beings raised to the skies, but the medium that actually constitutes the subjects.[588] Social practices give rise to models of truth, power-knowledge. The disciplines, for example, create a knowledge 'characterised by supervision and examination, organised around the norm, through the supervisory control of individuals throughout their existence'.[589] Law makes a truth claim and exercises power through it – in its material effects (such as verdicts) as well as through its ability to disqualify other forms of knowledge and experiences, such as that of everyday reasoning. Those have to first be translated into another form before they can be processed through the legal system.[590]

Judith Butler, who follows Foucault in this respect, brings attention to the naturalising effect of legal subjection: 'Juridical power inevitably "produces" what it claims merely to represent. The law produces and then conceals the notion of 'a subject before the law' in order to invoke that discursive formation as a naturalised foundational premise that subsequently legitimates that law's own regulatory hegemony'.[591] The assumption that the subject logically precedes the law can be understood as a contemporary trace of the hypothesis of the state of nature: 'The performative invocation of a non-historical "before" becomes the foundational premise that guarantees a pre-social ontology of persons who freely consent to be governed and, thereby, constitute the legitimacy of the social contract'.[592] In this respect juridical practices are performative acts and the identities they produce are sustained performative repetitions. Identity is thus the product of 'a performance that is *repeated*'.[593] Performative acts conceal their productive effect through the logic of their staging of a supposedly pre-existing substance.[594]

Juridical practices as '*a regulated process of repetition*'[595] generate through naturalisation social power-knowledge about subjects, which, when in doubt, becomes enforceable through the law's repressive way of working. Juridical practices are a part of the subject-producing social *dispositifs*. Here the juridical laws do not simply face the individual any more than the moral ones, they are

---

588 Foucault 2000, p. 15.
589 Foucault 2000, p. 59.
590 Smart 1989, p. 11.
591 Butler 2002, p. 5. By 'law' Butler of course does not only mean the juridical law, but the separation between internal and external in general (Lorey 1996, pp. 32–3). This, however, also comprises the law in its juridical sense.
592 Butler 2002, p. 5.
593 Butler 2002, p. 178.
594 Butler 2002, pp. 44–5; Villa 2003, pp. 70–1.
595 Butler 2002, p. 185.

not mere codifications of behaviour, they also have to be wanted and lived to a certain extent, and reproduced as one's own identity.

Of course, the legal code differs from the moral one in that it can if necessary be imposed. But no modern society would function if subjection did not enter the technologies of the self. Foucault therefore concludes that the law is (even if only *one*) part of the history of techniques and technologies in the context of the subject's practices with regard to itself.[596] Legal practices generate identity concepts and norms of conduct in life, which themselves are results of relationships of forces, but precisely because of their potential for execution develop a particular impact. Thus even the most progressive anti-discriminatory prohibition still defines the forms of identity, which must not be discriminated against.

A society of nothing but legal subjects cannot exist according to Foucault. The modern, governmentalised state could never manage exclusively by way of such abstracting constructions, but always only with a population of living beings. However, it is nonetheless exactly this legal subjectivity that is very much crucially involved in the construction of the modern subject, which is ruled as such. All ideas of 'autonomous' rational actors, endowed with a 'will', who precisely because of their autonomy can enter into agreements and be found guilty, are in no other practice so very much presupposed and reproduced day by day as in law.

2.3.5 Critique

Confronting the Marxist concepts with those of Foucault proves to be a rich process, for Foucault's theory offers an alternative to the following difficulties identified thus far: He corrects a one-dimensional social theory, which is only developed according to one structuring principle; (1) he therefore by and large forgoes functionalist explanations; (2) takes the production of subjects as the starting point instead of always already assuming the previous existence of subjects; (3) he rigorously dissolves all 'condensations' in social relations; (4) opens up a perspective on other technologies of power beyond and within the 'niches' of the law; (5) and finally allows for another way of structuring the relationship of state and law with his proposed concept of governmentality (6).

Nevertheless his approach also has to be expanded, not least by looking at his own work again from the Marxist perspective that we have just subjected to critique.

596 Foucault 2005, p. 112.

2.3.5.1 *Extending the Concept of Power through Feminism*

What was called the 'isolation effect' in Poulantzas is in Foucault 'individualisation' or 'subjection'. At this point the two different theoretical approaches very obviously converge. Poulantzas even sees in this 'Foucault's original contribution', which he takes up in his own theory. Everything in Foucault leads to the analysis of the subject, and feminists can link up with this very point. No other author of the critical 'male'-stream offers such close proximity to the central themes of feminist theory. In particular the interest in the body, sexuality and the constructed character of perceptible entities [*scheinbarer Entitäten*] clearly offered many more linkages[597] than the previously discussed authors. Nonetheless, certain assumptions in his approach also have to be corrected or extended, because Foucault ultimately still systematically ignores the structuring category of gender and turns certain types of male subjection into absolutes.[598] Both the creation of the biological two-gender system through the 'gender *dispositif*' and the asymmetrical positioning of men and women within it are not taken into account, contrary to his own thesis that no form of subjectivity exists which is not the result of the historical conditions of its formation.[599] Also in the disciplinary society, subjects exist under different and contradictory disciplines. Foucault does not include this differentiation and thus turns a specific form of discipline, that which shapes individuals into workers for the production apparatuses, into an absolute. Thus the contradictory disciplining of women for domestic, family and in particular generative reproduction remains left out.[600] Foucault thus shares in the blind spot of those very Marxist theories which he seeks to correct with his analysis of the disciplines: 'One could say that he describes the disciplining of male-bodied subjects ... and thus the "production" of male bodies. It is therefore hardly surprising that when speaking of the body Foucault does not see that not only one body, but rather two different bodies are "produced"'.[601]

In particular Butler extends Foucault's approach with the analysis of gendered subjection. She points out that the modern subject is from the outset defined as male. The political system produces *gendered subjects* along a differential axis of domination.[602] Andrea Bührmann therefore proposes to systematically extend Foucault's theory with the concept of 'gendered forms of

597 Munro 2001, p. 550.
598 Bührmann 2004, p. 39.
599 Bührmann 2004, p. 40; Bublitz 2001, p. 257.
600 Bührmann 2004, p. 43; Ott 1998, p. 45.
601 Ott 1998, p. 45.
602 Butler 2002, pp. 4–5.

subjectivation', that is with 'how one experiences oneself as masculine or feminine, how certain behaviours are classified in a gendered manner and how bodies are experienced as either masculine or feminine, and also how they are seen as gendered by others'.[603] Those manners of subjectivation lead to the idea that one disposes of an unambiguous natural and unchangeable bodily sex. From this 'biological' body a certain gender identity can then be derived, which is endowed with certain ways of behaviour and feeling, and through which gendered human beings are integrated as women and men in a hierarchical gender relationship.[604] Gender relationships are regulated in the framework of the 'heterosexual matrix' and reified by naturalising bodies, gender identities and desire.[605] This leads to a 'metaphysics of substance' in the sense of a 'gender ontology'.[606]

This extension also has consequences for how the government of the population is conceived. Thus Hannelore Bublitz shows that the population as subject is constituted at the same time as the biological argument for gender appeared as an area of governing and regulating knowledge, which addresses health, care for life, reproduction, inheritance and hygiene concerns.[607] Gender is thus a central category in constituting and regulating the population since the nineteenth century, and thus in constituting and organising modern societies as such.[608] It is the intersection where individual ways of subjectivation and technologies for governing the population come together. Through the 'heterosexual matrix' the former are connected with precepts of reproduction, health, care for life and the normality of the population.[609]

For the subjectivation effect of law this means accordingly that regulating, performative legal practices produce as a moment of the gender *dispositif* in continuous repetition not *the* uniform modern subject, but hierarchically gendered subjects. Those subjects are disciplined in a contradictory manner and imitate those ways of subjection in their technologies of the self (Butler).

2.3.5.2 *Practice without Subjects*

As I have shown, Foucault very consistently starts from practices and their relations,[610] and tries to theoretically re-dissolve all congealed entities or to

603 Bührmann 2004, p. 242, note 6.
604 Bührmann 2004, p. 24.
605 Butler 2002, pp. 9, 194, note 6.
606 Butler 2002, p. 32.
607 Bublitz 2001, p. 257, note 2.
608 Bublitz 2001, p. 257.
609 Bublitz 2001, p. 270.
610 Thus also Lorey 1996, p. 60.

develop them genealogically as 'final forms'. In this regard he rightly defends himself against the accusation that he founds a new ontology of power. There is, however, a reason this accusation is brought up time and again, which cannot only be ascribed to a misunderstanding. Thus Rehmann, for instance, argues that there soon evaporates any trace of the promised diversity of power relations – for example in the context of his analysis of disciplinary society. Power is not really treated as a relational concept, but ends in a 'Neo-Nietzschean manner as a subject of almost infinite producer-status'.[611] Poulantzas' critique takes the same direction: the power relation is always only based upon itself. '[T]he question *what power* and *power to do what* appears as a mere obstacle'. This absolutisation of power leads, however hard one tries, irresistibly 'to the idea of a Power-Master ...'[612]

The accusation that power is always only based upon itself does not apply to Foucault, as it develops in his work, too, through social conditions. This is not the reason for the impression of many critics that Foucault describes power as a 'Power-Master'. It rather stems – or so I would contend – from the fact that Foucault begins at a certain level to abstract from the actors of those conditions in an inappropriate manner – very similar to the systems theory of law. This means that while they are logically assumed as those between whom the relationship of forces exists, they are within the conceptual logic subsumed under the 'relationship'. This is very similar to Luhmann, who presupposes communicating actors but leaves them unaddressed in the shadows, while the spotlight only shines on their effect – communication.

This does not mean the actors have to be considered the ultimate attributive subject; to the contrary, it is only an orientation towards practice and conditions that avoids ontologies. Conversely, however, this neither means that it is possible to abstract from those between whom the relationships exist, or from the materialisations of practices. Foucault himself very much focuses on addressing the effect of power on bodies, which always have to be someone's bodies. But his abstraction from the 'strategists' implies a common functionalism that shows, for instance, in what manner it is necessary for discipline to inscribe itself in the gaps of formal legal freedom in order to guarantee the production process. Yet again, some meta-subject appears to know already what is indispensable for reproduction. This means that Foucault, despite his finely detailed approach to micro-processes, also ultimately succumbs to a metaphysical 'grand narrative'.

611 Rehmann 2003, pp. 70–1.
612 Poulantzas 2000, p. 149 (emphasis in original).

Strictly speaking this reification starts with an abstraction on the level of power technologies. They ultimately become subjects in Foucault and this already shows in his language; they are 'omni-functional'.[613] This does not simply 'happen' to Foucault as he considers such an abstraction justified; and he does so because it expresses the described 'impermeability' of power relations from the perspective of individual actors. When diverse strategies link up and slip away from the subjects, when the subjects are governed by conditions and not vice-versa, is it then not simply consistent to also speak of anonymised technologies of power? His abstraction in the representation is meant to correspond to a 'real abstraction'.

The problem with this abstraction is, however, that here theory abstracts more comprehensively than 'the thing in itself' (Adorno). For Foucault ignores at the same time the unequal distribution of power in the relationship of forces. This is exactly what he makes disappear in theory and with it also the fact that, although relations become independent of *all* actors, there are those who because of their position in the relationship of forces can much more extensively penetrate the tangle of power and act upon it, in particular, however, to operate in the margins of the respective independent areas.

Poulantzas has shown this very fittingly for the relation of classes to each other: 'Power' means in this relationship the ability of one or more classes to realise their interests. This determines the scope of action of one class in relation to another. 'The capacity of one class to realise its interests is in opposition to the capacity (and interests) of other classes: *the field of power is therefore strictly relational*'.[614] The power of one class is at first an expression of its objective position within economic, political and ideological relations. This position comprises the unequal relations of domination and subjugation, which are rooted in the social division of labour. The position of every class and thus its power are thus limited, that is, determined and delineated through the positions of the other classes: 'Power is not then a quality attached to a class "in-itself", understood as a collection of agents, but depends on, and springs from, a relational system of material places occupied by particular agents'.[615] Political power expresses of course not only a class's level of organisation and its position in a given conjuncture. The political power of a class, that is, its capacity to realise its political interests, depends accordingly not only on its class position, but also on its position and strategy in relation to the other

613 Poulantzas 2000, p. 79.
614 Poulantzas 2000, p. 147 (emphasis in original).
615 Ibid.

classes.[616] The constituent field of power is thus an *unequal rapport* of force relationships and points towards a material system of distributing positions. This also explains the primacy of struggles in Poulantzas as well as his strategic orientation towards the state.[617] One therefore has to join with Jessop when he demands the development of a 'strategic-relational' approach following Poulantzas. After all, it makes a difference whether someone has the structurally mediated capacity to, for example, impose the value form upon a class[618] or not.

Any analysis therefore has to make the effort to extract the actors theoretically and empirically from the power tangle – without it ever being certain whether all or even the essential ones have been identified. This is simply the risk of speculation that critical theory cannot escape, if it wants to say something essential about society.[619] It is moreover the consequence of a genuine micro-political analysis. The concept of hegemony, as developed by Gramsci and applied by Poulantzas to the state, can represent a meaningful addition to Foucault. It can also be combined with the concept of government to conceive of how different power relations *somehow* combine into larger formations regulated by hegemonic projects; that government is not an anonymous process regulating a uniform population, but that it follows from the necessity of hegemonising particular interests. The 'positions' of the respective individual or collective subjects are the result of the crystallization or material condensation of past strategies.[620] A strategic-relation approach therefore 'must refer to real strategies, calculations, and calculating subjects'.[621] Of course strategies can fail or their interweaving with other strategies can result in unintended consequences; and of course the actors, because of the power tangle, do not have omnipotent abilities or an all-encompassing knowledge. Their strategies are in this respect exploratory movements.[622]

When Foucault's approach is thus completed with the analysis of concrete relationships of forces, and hence with calculating subjects, the question remains whether this is even possible with his concept of the subject. For, as Bröckling rightly notes, Foucault's subject only exists in the form of the gerund, 'as to be explored, to be normalised, to be optimised, to be aesthetically shaped,

616 Ibid.
617 Poulantzas 2000, p. 148.
618 Jessop 1985, p. 345.
619 Adorno 2008, p. 95.
620 Jessop 1985, p. 345.
621 Jessop 1985, p. 357.
622 Jessop 1985, p. 359.

and so on'. It is not the final stable point or an 'imaginary centre of the person', but rather 'the vanishing point of at the same time inevitable and unfinishable efforts at definition and control; not a submissive addressee, but neither a stubborn *point de résistance* against interventions of power, but always already their effect'.[623] The subject is accordingly an effect of power, but it has a materiality, it is temporarily fixed and acts as such, as a woman, for example, or as the owner of means of production, or both at once. It is an ensemble of subject positions, with over-determinations existing between them, a 'fundamental nodal point'.[624] As such it enacts strategic practices – even if its 'interests' do not result as such from its 'objective position', as Poulantzas thought, but only develop in political practice as advanced by Foucault.[625]

2.3.5.3 *Extending the Technology of Law*

The rather traditional aspect of Foucault's legal technology stems very much from his fixation on penal law, and hence his guiding distinction between what is permitted and what is forbidden. This has to be corrected with Luhmann's legal code, which is based upon the dualism of legal and illegal. Foucault's line of argument can be preserved, but at the same time even the technology of law would reveal itself to be less repressive than theorists of productive power imagine. The production of the modern subject is therefore less determined by the prevention of certain behaviours than it is by the (sanctioned) provision of (hegemonic) ways of subjection.

But a second correction is also necessary. His reduction of law to a tactic of governmentality in his late work fails to convince, as it ultimately reduces law again to something of an instrumental tool of government, thus falling back behind his previous insights. Moreover, legal technology has its own density and functions according to its own 'logic', as per Kelsen's historic insight. Of course Foucault also employs tactics in a repositioned manner, as tactics without tactician. However, as he does not describe any further how this serves the government of the population, what is to be understood by the tactics of the law remains at best a gap.

If one applies Foucault to himself, one would reach the conclusion that law functions through the constitution of the subject of the population itself. Again, this is no pre-existing being, which is always pregiven as an ensemble of biological elements and social practices, and only has to be regulated. It seems altogether fitting to combine Foucault at this point with Poulantzas' reflections

623 Bröckling 2003, p. 80.
624 Laclau and Mouffe 2001, p. 155.
625 Laclau and Mouffe 2001, p. 160.

on the state as a factor of cohesion. Foucault himself has noted that the modern state as successor of pastoral power individualises and totalises in the same breath. Poulantzas now attributes precisely this sanctioning of differences with their simultaneous homogenisation to the technique of the law inasmuch as it functions as a formal cohesive framework. Biopolitically regulated and governmentally ruled, the population is constituted as a unity of subjects as people and nation through the law. This also clarifies the connection between 'population' and 'people' again. The latter is the juridical construction of the subject that is to be politically governed. This could also explain why juridical theories of power limit themselves to this legal construction – because it is this construction that is presented in the official code of power, that is in the law.

PART 3

Reconstruction: Subjectivation and Cohesion

CHAPTER 8

Introduction to Part 3

Having described and critiqued central approaches in legal theory in part 2, I will now attempt to systematically develop elements of an updated materialist socio-legal theory. Here I do not intend to simply dismiss the critiqued theories, but instead to preserve those elements that have led to significant insights into the connection between law and capitalist society throughout my critique.

My argument here is that capitalist conditions produce in combination with modern law a particular technology of power, which on the one hand involves the production of subjects that are isolated in relation to each other (subjectivation), but on the other ties together those individuals in a precarious social whole (cohesion). Because this technology represents a specific independent form of social relations, I will call it, following form analysis, the *legal form*.

Thus I attempt to combine central insights of form analysis and of the Franco-Italian theory strand. However, in order to achieve this, some premises have to be clarified first.

I begin by reviewing the concept of the relationship of forces, so that from the beginning all statements can be traced back in a relational manner to the connections between social individuals. For only if history can be deciphered as one that is made by people, does the potential for its emancipatory change exist, and a resigned attitude with regard to social surplus objectivity can be avoided.

One of the main effects of capitalist conditions is the production of isolated, gendered and racialised subjects who are ruled in a particular manner. This modern subjectivation entails the problem that Habermas deals with under the heading 'integration': How are individuals who are subjectivated in relation to each other tied together in a social whole? For this it is necessary to make the power-theoretical concepts of hegemony and government productive for legal theory, in order to free the latter from subject-less mechanistic concepts which always already assume the form's functioning. In this analytical frame of reference the legal form then emerges as a particular technique of consensus, one which transforms the problem of hegemony in its own way and thus provides crucial support for social synthesis.

How the legal form works – not how it is derived – will then be reviewed with particular attention to its relative autonomy and following Marx's concept of the commodity form.

In order for such a theory not to run the risk of form analysis – of remaining at an abstract level and closed off from any empirical investigations of specific historic social formations – I will then conceive of the institutionalisation of the legal form understood as a historically and spatially concrete expression of a power technology.

The crucial question of the law's emancipatory potential will then be considered in the closing chapter (Part 4).

CHAPTER 9

Extended Relationships of Forces

Starting with the relationship of forces means an approach that is contrary to Luhmann's concept of the law, insofar as he understands it as a *system*. This is intended to avoid a situation where the autonomisation in a 'system' is always already assumed in the logic of the subject. Instead the fact that this autonomisation can only be thought *through* the practices of social actors needs to be acknowledged from the outset.

Despite their differences, the materialist theories presented all assume that legal theory must not start with final forms and effects of hegemony, but social relations and practices. In this respect they remain faithful to Marx's insight that the economy is not about things 'but the relationships between persons'.[1] Pashukanis speaks about the 'primacy of the legal relationship' in relation to the system of norms; Poulantzas, following Gramsci, assumes that the relations of production as the ensemble of political, economic and ideological practices form the basis of power; and Foucault finally refers to the moving substrate of force relations, which stems from the totality of the social net.

1 Totality

While Neumann, Gramsci, Poulantzas and Pashukanis construct something like a primacy of the relations of production, Foucault extends the concept of the relationship of forces to the entirety of social space without assuming one privileged location of power. For him the concept thus comprises both the relationships in the production process, as well as that between the sexes, the 'ethnicities', the 'normal' and 'abnormal', and so on.

I have described in detail that the 'primacy of being' marks the central materialist premise in relation to social totality. Totality here is identical to the process of social reproduction. This comprises production – that is, 'the very particular historical way in which in a society the materials and services that are necessary for the life of (physical and/or cultural) individuals are created and put to use'[2] – as well as circulation. Both always already exist within cer-

1 MECW, Volume 16, p. 476.

2 Ritsert 1988, p. 64.

tain relations of production, which have to be continuously produced anew, that is to say reproduced.

In order to sustain this primacy of being and *at the same* time take into account the plurality of principles of social structuring and the diversity of antagonisms, the material reproduction of society can only be at the centre of theory if it is itself conceived of as entirely overdetermined and therefore no particular location is theoretically *privileged* – neither production nor circulation, nor economic conditions as such. This means that there must be no naturalised idealisation according to which there is ultimately still one original hegemonic centre that determines all others. The 'first historical act', the production of material life, which Marx speaks of in *The German Ideology*,[3] cannot be defined, because it is overdetermined and in this work ultimately also only due the 'historically surpassed antagonism [*Frontstellung*]'[4] in the struggle against German idealism.[5] Even in production strictly speaking one has to assume an articulation of social relations. Thus wage labour, for instance, 'cannot be thought of as *ungendered*', as Ursula Beer notes, 'because it does not exist as such'.[6]

The question of totality is, as demonstrated in the *re*construction, one of the central questions for materialist legal theory. I therefore propose in sum to start from a *plural totality*, which can, however, produce a hegemonic centre as its effect: How people work, produce, and reproduce themselves and their conditions of production, is decisive for a reality-based analysis.

However, this does not lead to *any* analytical *primacy of socialisation dynamics*, in particular because material reproduction as an isolated, only economically understood process is already a bad abstraction. It is always a whole of economic, cultural, political and ideological moments. Law must therefore by no means be 'derived' from one moment, but instead, as Maihofer insists, it has to be connected to the plurality of social relations. Accordingly modern capitalist society has to be conceived as an incomplete, complex totality, which is therefore also the prerequisite of all individual phenomena. It can develop a 'centre' as an *effect*. However, this is then its product and not its pre-existing base. Such a hegemonic location can always only be determined historically as a result of struggles and hegemonic practices.[7] The unity of this incomplete

3 MECW, Volume 5, p. 42.
4 Reichelt 1973, p. 46.
5 Thus also Maihofer 1992, pp. 148 ff.
6 Beer 1990, p. 263.
7 I owe this insight to a discussion with Stephan Adolphs.

totality is external and not guaranteed by an underlying principle. Indeed, what has to be explained are its unifying mechanisms.

2 Relational Rights and Powers

In addition, a relation theory of power that starts from social conditions cannot assume a simple relationship of forces. Here one must agree with Poulantzas' critique of Foucault. The forces that are situated in relation to each other do not each have the same potential power, but dispose of rights and powers resulting from their respective social positions, or in Jessop's words: 'structurally-mediated abilit[ies]',[8] which are in turn embedded in the net of relations and struggles.

If there are no conditions prior to the relationships, but the relationships are at the same time mediated through the structure, then actions and structures cannot be thought of as two sets of phenomena that are independent of each other (as a dualism), but as a 'duality of the structure': structures are both the medium and result of the practices.[9] Structures only exist as phenomena in time and space if they are realised in reproduced practices.[10] This continually new production takes place through reproduction,[11] activities are undertaken in the same way every day:[12] 'day-to-day life' is repetitive.[13] Marx expressed this in the statement that men make their own history, but precisely not 'just as they please in circumstances they choose for themselves; rather they make it in present circumstances, given and inherited'.[14]

If rights and powers are unequally distributed, then this is the legacy of past struggles and thus a structurally inscribed 'strategic selectivity', which favours some struggles over others.[15] A structure is not equally limiting or enabling for all actors.[16] Jessop therefore proposes to understand structures as *strategic* (in their form, their content and their effects). Thus structure is considered from the outset in its relation to activity – and vice-versa.[17]

8 Jessop 1985, p. 345.
9 Giddens 1986, p. 25.
10 Giddens 1986, pp. 17, 170.
11 Lamla 2003, p. 260.
12 Giddens 1986, p. xiii.
13 Giddens 1986, p. 35.
14 Marx 2002, p. 19.
15 Jessop 1990, p. 309.
16 Jessop 2004, p. 209.
17 Ibid.

> This involves examining how a given structure may privilege some actors, some identities, some strategies, some spatial and temporal horizons, some actions over others; and the ways, if any, in which actors ... take account of this differential privileging through 'strategic-context' analysis when choosing a course of action.[18]

Structures are thus 'the crystallisation or material condensation of past strategies'.[19] They demarcate the strategic framework within relational power structures. The difference from Luhmann's systems theory, which operates through processes, is clearly slim in this respect, as structures are also understood as recursively produced here.

The key difference to this approach therefore lies in the emphasis on the reproduced strategic practice of subjects. The 'legal system' or the legal form, as I will call it, is perpetuated by those structurally mediated struggles and practices.

18 Jessop 2004, p. 209, similarly Jessop 1997, p. 91, Note 6.
19 Jessop 1985, p. 345.

CHAPTER 10

Subjectivation

However, starting from subjects and their practices does not mean to always already presuppose them as the elementary units of a legal theory, as Pashukanis does.[1] Rather, the social conditions first constitute those entities, which then appear as independent essentials. This is particularly valid for individuals, who are neither an origin, nor a unity, nor transparent for themselves as rational actors, but who are an 'ensemble of social relations' for materialist theory, as Marx already wrote in the sixth of his *Theses on Feuerbach*,[2] or in the language of Laclau and Mouffe, an 'ensemble of positions'.[3]

Foucault has shown that the different power relations do not only inscribe themselves in the institutions, but that they create in particular subjectivity – that the essential effect of power has to be situated in those procedures which transform people into subjects. Subjectivation is the process, in which plural relationships of forces culminate with serious consequences. The social totality's plurality thus corresponds to the diversity of subjectivation processes. The ensemble of subject positions is on closer inspection an ensemble of socially created and hierarchically organised differences.

The concept of difference serves on the one hand to take social construction into account, as distinct from any kind of pre-social 'natural' character, but on the other to consider that 'categorisations carry fundamental social consequences'.[4] Stressing difference is not intended to refer back to a 'multicultural coexistence',[5] but to the social hierarchisation of subject positions. Not all processes of differentiation develop in relations of oppression,[6] and thus in antagonistic contexts – but some crucial ones do.

The best known difference in the materialist tradition, namely that between *classes*, already makes this apparent: Classes constitute through the 'struggle over the surplus product' according to their structural position in the reproduction process,[7] that is, as owners of the means of production or on the other side as owners of labour power alone.

1 Thus also Maihofer 1992, p. 199.
2 MECW, Volume 5, p. 4.
3 Laclau and Mouffe 2001, p. 36.
4 Elsuni 2006, p. 181; Crenshaw 1989.
5 Engel, Schulz and Wedl 2005, p. 12.
6 Knapp 2005, p. 69.
7 Ritsert 1988, p. 74.

The second, long-since debated difference (and in the Marxist tradition often reductively only as a 'side contradiction') is the *gender binary* within a hierarchised gender order.[8] This gender order is at the same time constituted in the framework of the 'heterosexual matrix', that is in a grid that naturalises bodies, gender identities and desire.[9] A further hierarchised difference is therefore the one which is produced and regulated by *heteronormativity*.

Finally, national communitarisation produces *racialisation* as a further difference.[10] This can be understood as a process whereby people are constructed as a homogenous group and hierarchised according to ethnic characteristics.[11] Those racialised attributions combine with antisemitic and colonial elements in (neo)racist discourses.[12]

Myriad differences are thus articulated in individual and collective subjects. Those relations of domination permeate each other; they 'intersect', as first described by feminist legal theorists in the concept of 'intersectionality'.[13] No category can, however, be thought of independently of others, because it is co-constituted by them. Rather than adding them up, the multiple differences therefore have to be identified *within* the respective others.[14]

Between capitalism and sexuality, for example, a connection that mobilises heteronormativity can be observed. Heterosexuality is inscribed as a foundation in patriarchy, because it creates and enforces a gender binary and a hierarchical, binary order of sex and desire. This binary, hierarchical gender system secures in turn the reproduction of labour power in capitalism, with the naturalisation of sex and desire within the heterosexual matrix supporting the gendered division of labour.[15]

To consider subjectivation in the context of a materialist legal theory appears all the more necessary to me, because as I have shown most previous approaches have contented themselves with *one* structuring principle and therefore also with only *one* form of domination. However, when the process of subject production – subjectivation – comes into view, this leads to the question of how diverse relations create the modern subject, which is so central for law.

---

8 See for example Becker-Schmidt 1990; Beer 1990; Bührmann 2004; Butler 2002; Maihofer 1995 and 2004; Pühl Paulitz, Marx and Helduser 2004; Wetterer 2002.
9 Butler 2002, p. 194, Note 6.
10 Lenz 1996, p. 39.
11 Gutierrez Rodriguez 1999, p. 32.
12 Balibar and Wallerstein 1991.
13 For an overview see Elsuni 2006, pp. 180 ff.; Engel, Schulz and Wedl 2005; Knapp 2005.
14 Brunner 2005, p. 84.
15 Ibid.

On closer inspection, the modern subjectivation regime's various technologies of power culminate in isolated monads (1) with gendered, racialised, individualised bodies and differentiated identities (2). Those monads are politically regulated in their isolation (3), as they are conducted in their technologies of the self as formally equal and free legal subjects, endowed with subjective rights (4):

(1) Commodity owners: Balbus and Pashukanis already suggest the subjectivation effect created by the commodity form in showing that individuals cannot act as social ones under the capitalist division of labour, but only as competing commodity owners. They are opposed to society and remain structurally indifferent to the needs of others. Every other individual is not the condition of their own freedom, but its limit. They are seemingly isolated as individuals from the very social context that turns them into 'isolated monads', as Poulantzas writes, and have to be reconnected with each other first, associated[16] in their 'windowless isolation'.[17]

(2) Differentiated Bodies and Identities: Those isolated monads are bound to their identity by normalising practices and bodily disciplined through drilling, the production of behavioural skills and habits as automatic abilities – and thus also the ability to self-manage. This 'individuality' is then imprinted into their very corporeality in the form of hierarchised differences. It is thus not any originary and resistant core of subjectivity, but their 'flattering confidence in the subject's autarky' is itself already the result of the process of insulating individuals from the encompassing contexts.[18]

(3) Political Isolation: This isolated subject is politically regulated and ruled through its identity, down to the smallest gestures, and develops in its technologies of the self a relationship to this identity. Poulantzas speaks in this context of the 'isolation effect', which sanctions the socially drilled monads politically and juridically and institutionalises them.[19]

(4) Abstract Legal Subjects: Juridical subjectivation plays in this context a special role. It produces legal subjectivity in the regulated process of repetition and thus precisely that Robinsonade of the modern subject as isolated, rational, transparent for themselves, gender-neutral, classless and uniform that is seemingly presupposed in law. Peter Niesen aptly describes this process from the perspective of Habermas and Maus:

16 Derrida 1994, p. 193.

17 Adorno 2000, p. 219.

18 Ibid.

19 Poulantzas 2000, p. 69.

> Sovereign individuals 'are not "natural" individuals like moral persons, they are legally constituted actors, equipped with fundamental claims and separated from each other through the structure of law'.[20] Legal technology thus participates in producing individualised monads. At the same time this process of subjectivation is also the source of a second moment: Pashukanis and Balbus have pointed out that in the same way that products become commodities, individuals are transformed in law to legal subjects. Just as commodity-producing labour becomes abstract labour, 'labor sans phrase', concrete individuals become legal subjects. In the legal subject 'all concrete particularities which distinguish one representative of the genus homo sapiens from another dissolve into the abstraction of man in general'.[21] The subject, which is constituted as an ensemble of *differences*, becomes in law its opposite – *equal*.

Although the subjects are thus individuated and hierarchised with respect to each other, both in the process of reproduction, and through discipline and politically and juridically sanctioned isolation, they are at the same time homogenised through legal subjectivity. This process is very much decisive for the effects of the legal form. I will therefore come back to it below in the context of the legal form's effect of cohesion.

20 Niesen 2011, p. 141.
21 Pashukanis 2001, p. 113.

CHAPTER 11

Hegemony

1 Hegemonic Government

It would, however, be wrong to assume that the subjects, which are thus socially produced, are in any way also docile addressees, *because* they are socially constructed. Quite the opposite: modern subjects as historical forms of human beings, as 'autonomous' individuals and as such endowed with subjective rights, have the particular characteristic that they cannot be ruled directly.

The existence of stable relations of power in bourgeois society can, as Gramsci and Foucault insist, no longer be explained by a juridical model of power, or strictly speaking by the state. Liberal government rules through the consumption of freedom[1] and requires the consent, the active agreement, of the ruled. Hegemony is here, however, always also 'armoured with coercion', for purely hegemonic government is unlikely under conditions of a society permeated by multiple antagonisms. For this reason Foucault also points out that security *dispositifs* become central at the very moment bourgeois freedoms are established.

Habermas' social theory also focuses substantially on the production of social consensus. The difference appears, however, precisely in that Habermas does not conceive of social relations as relationships of forces, but as horizontal ones. Accordingly, his explanations on communicative action lack structural conflictuality from the outset.[2] Instead, this is added as a second element to action. While the danger of dissent is omnipresent, it is however only rooted in the possibility of different world views and not in structural asymmetries.

Systems theory as well as state theory, with its form analytical line of argument, always presuppose the 'functioning' of subjects, so that they do not have to deal with the reasons for this functioning. Although it already has all the necessary elements to do so, even Foucault's theory does not actually start any genuinely relational theory of power that has to foreground practice, because of its structuralist bent. And finally, the same problem in relation to systems is also evident in Habermas. All those approaches, because they are blind to practice, use subjects in a mechanistic way. I consider this one of the main limitations of

1 Foucault 2008, p. 64.

2 Similarly Mouffe 2005, p. 10.

their legal concept and will therefore extend it with the concept of hegemonic governmental practice.

If bourgeois government is characterised by the fact that it no longer functions in an essentially repressive manner, this opens up the field of hegemony. As Pashukanis adheres to a rather juridical theory of power, this question does not arise for him as such. Gramsci and Poulantzas consider hegemony as a practice of the ruling classes, who have to take other interests into account and integrate them in order to successfully defend their interests. Foucault theoretically extends the relationship of forces, but at the same time depersonalises it. He thus arrives at a power that is exercised as government of the population, biopolitical regulation and stimulation of technologies of the self.

'Government' in contrast to 'hegemony' is based upon a more general development, namely the consideration that the 'Western [individual]' has to firstly learn to be managed, 'to see [themselves] as a sheep in a flock',[3] a not at all self-evident process, but rather the effect of 'politics seen as a matter of the sheepfold'.[4] Governance is thus exercised in the tradition of the Christian pastorate over a 'multiplicity in movement',[5] which is in general not used to self-govern as a 'community of freely associated individuals' (Marx), but is instead governed or managed in its behaviour.

While Foucault can overcome a class-reductionist perspective thanks to this preliminary reflection, he nonetheless abstracts at the same time with the concept of 'population' and the government's subject-less technology of power from precisely those hierarchised differences. 'Population' can only be maintained as a category if it is conceived of as an ensemble of classes, genders, ethnicities and other unfixed social identities, as a 'multitude', which is entangled in a relational struggle for hegemony, *that is when government and hegemony are thus coupled.*

Government here stresses the modern management of the subjects' behaviour in their daily lives, while hegemony focuses on struggles for assent to this management. Struggles for hegemony target the procedures employed to manage others within a government project, they are conflicts about how the directing of conduct is carried out, who directs conduct, and their objectives, procedures and methods.[6] Beyond this there are, however, repeatedly forms of resistance against power as a form of conducting as such. Hegemonic projects

3 Foucault 2009, p. 130 (translation modified).
4 Ibid.
5 Foucault 2009, p. 125.
6 Foucault 2009, pp. 194–5, 201–2.

thus aim at the creation, reproduction and transformation of technologies of others and of the self. Hegemony thus becomes a problem for all social forces.

If Foucault's argument that there are no headquarters of power is taken seriously, and that accordingly social change cannot be conceptualised as the result of conscious actions or a conspiracy, yet at the same time the practice of social actors is supposed to be decisive, the temporary and process-like character of the hegemonic project has to be emphasised. There is no single such project that dominates the social context as a whole, but multiple competing projects that correspond to the diverse range of antagonistic differences.

Both Poulantzas and Foucault assume that with the emergence of the modern state the power technologies of civil society or the assent organised through civil society institutions are governmentalised. The practice of the state becomes the dominant form of government,[7] and thus of organising hegemony. Hegemonic projects thus have to become state projects in order to enter the government of the population, which is conducted and regulated by way of hegemonic ways of subjectivation, for example through abstract legal subjectivity. Hegemonic government is the art of persuasion. By contrast, the mechanisms of disciplining up to the smallest gestures and habits, control and orientation according to the norm and also the immediate exercise of violence remain in force as the 'downside' of formal freedom and as an expression of the problematic relationship of freedom and security at the centre of liberal government.[8] Disciplinary and legal drilling are over-determined and integrated in an art of conducting individuals, which depends on a consensus between governmental management techniques and the self-understanding of the subjects.

2 Routine Repetition

This form of domination, although it is no longer external to the subjects, is quite obviously also precarious, as it depends upon the assent of the ruled in their everyday lived practice and thus has to be created anew in a regulated process of repetition every hour of every day. Foucault has convincingly elaborated the argument that the great effects of hegemony have to implant themselves in micro-relations to become operative. A macro-theory of power such as the 'legal system' has to start from micrological mechanisms. 'The everyday

7 Foucault 2009, p. 248.
8 Foucault 2008, p. 64.

tasks, habits and routines which have become second nature represent a behaviour capital, a pool of self-evident practices, that seem to happen as though by themselves'.[9] Everyday actions are thus largely characterised by routinised repetitions as the dominant form of social everyday activity and thus 'routinised practices are the prime expression of the duality of the structure in respect of the continuity of social life'.[10]

This insight is decisive for considering legal theory from the perspective of the theory of democracy. For repetitions are, according to the insights of Derrida and Butler, always citations of previous practice, whose complete identical repetition the subject inevitably fails to bring about – there always exists the possibility of a shift.[11]

A hegemonic government has to inscribe itself in those everyday routines which form structures through reproduced practices and thus develop a certain continuity. Here the question of how competing hegemonic projects can assert themselves and actually enter the routines arises. Poulantzas holds the view that here the state apparatuses are decisive, as they make it possible to elaborate such projects. I concur with Poulantzas insofar as I share his reflection that a material base of a certain 'relative autonomy' is necessary to realise those projects. The strategic selectivity that favours certain projects has to express itself in a sedimentation into structures.

Contrary to Poulantzas, I am however of the opinion that this material base cannot only be found in state apparatuses or reduced to the state. There is instead a specific form of regulating routinised practice, which is characteristic for capitalist societies. It not only organises sustained regulated repetition, but reifies it in the same breath, so that any insight into social conditions is made particularly difficult. This is the moment when it is necessary to employ a reconfigured form analysis. The potential of those insights which, for law, begin with Pashukanis, can unfold in this context. For if governing practices succeed in inscribing themselves in social forms, they are – to an extent that must not be underestimated – 'removed' [*entlastet*] from everyday contestation.

Habermas' concept of systems and life world follows an altogether similar idea: different forms of behaviour (communicative/strategic) as well as mechanisms of consent (pre-categorical, conscious, and systemic) make 'integration' in society possible. However, he schematises the social in two worlds with different logics. From this point on, it becomes apparent that the dualism thus incurred would have to be overcome by refraining from a separation

9 Wetterer 2003, p. 300.
10 Giddens 1986, p. 282.
11 Butler 2002, p. 185.

into social *spheres*, with the analyst instead distinguishing the forms of *practice* and *consensus technologies*: political confrontations over hegemony orientated towards argumentative and communicative or strategic action, routinised action as well as finally reified routinised action. This also makes clear that it is not only the 'systems' which make the conditions for communication-oriented action harder, but also certain ways of naturalisation and essentialisation. At the same time it is also evident that even under those conditions the political struggle over hegemony – in the words of Habermas, 'the confrontation over criticisable validity claims' – is not brought to a halt, but constitutes also the 'moving substrate' of 'systemic' action.

CHAPTER 12

The Legal Form

Let us now look more closely into *how* hegemony inscribes itself into law. In doing so, we will see that the legal form is a technology for consensus and cohesion as Poulantzas already suspected. Material conditions for organising hegemony have to be relatively autonomous. The analysis of the legal form begun by Pashukanis lends itself very much as an explanatory model.

Pashukanis stresses that what matters for a materialist legal theory is not first and foremost a position that is critical of ideology and deciphers the *content* of the law in a manner critical of ideology, but rather the question of the *form*. It is this historic insight that theorists of the state-derivation debate developed later on. Below I will reformulate the insights of form analysis for legal theory. Here, instead of deriving the legal from the commodity form, my approach consists in generalising their *common way of working* following Foucault. This allows us to subsequently develop what is specific about the legal form.

1 Society – a Precarious Hegemonic Project

Karl Marx theoretically develops in his examination of the commodity form the social form of value as well as the forms of the commodity, of money and of capital. I follow – very much like Pashukanis – his analysis of the value form and attempt to reconstruct by retracing his line of argument a starting point for what the different forms have in common.

1.1 *Value as a Social Form*

Marx's critique of the political economy of his time is here the starting point:

> Political economy has indeed analysed value and its magnitude, however incompletely, and has uncovered the content concealed within these forms. But it has never once asked the question why this content has assumed that particular form ...[1]

1 Marx 1976, pp. 173–4 (emphasis S.B.).

Marx's charge is that the national economists despite all their insights have not reached any understanding of their actual scientific object.[2] This object can only be discovered when one asks why the sociality of labour under capitalism takes on the *form* of value. He thus leaves the terrain of economic theory in order to, according to Backhaus, '*demonstrate the social conditions* which make the existence of the value form necessary'.[3] He was thus not only concerned with introducing the mathematised market economy into sociology, but with demanding from the economy precisely that which it does not offer, 'namely the retranslation of the economic rules into congealed human relations'.[4]

What then are the social conditions of the social forms? Marx analysed the autonomisation of a very specific practice: what for him was the most immediate manifestation of *social activity*,[5] labour. Here he could turn to Hegel's reflections on abstract labour in the *Jena Lectures*,[6] which already clearly 'foreshadow' Marx's approach.[7]

Karl Marx was concerned with showing that value appears as a social quality of things 'when labour as a whole is *problematic* in a very specific way …'[8] This is the case under capitalist conditions because in the private organisation of production concrete, individual labour, unlike other production methods, does not already possess an immediate social form, but only acquires this form through exchange:[9]

> Because individuals expand their individual labour in the form of *mutually independent private labour*, they have to exchange their products. For this is the only possibility for their private labour to even operate as parts of the *social totality of labour*.[10]

With this the products of labour acquire the *social* quality of having value, which makes it possible to compare them to others and thus to exchange them. The sociality of private labour that is only performed for the sake of profit can thus only show itself as such through exchange. In this way, the producers create a social context which is the unconscious result of their actions. Marx there-

2 Brentel 1989, p. 12.
3 Backhaus 1980, p. 107 (emphasis S.B.).
4 Adorno 1993, p. 239.
5 Lukács 1975, p. 483.
6 Hegel 1983, p. 121.
7 Marcuse 1955, p. 78.
8 Brentel 1989, p. 155 (emphasis in original).
9 Ibid.
10 Heinrich 1999, p. 207 (emphasis in original).

fore poses with the analysis of the commodity form the 'fundamental question ... of how a coherent social context is produced in a society of *private* producers',[11] or in the words of Alfred Sohn-Rethel 'the network of relations forms by which society forms a coherent whole'.[12] 'Social synthesis'[13] 'holds together the multiplicity of links operating between [people] according to the division of labour'.[14]

This social synthesis is, however, not necessarily successful, and even if it is, it remains precarious and exists, in the words of Laclau and Mouffe, only as an effort to construct this impossible object.[15] In a field that is criss-crossed by multiple antagonisms, where hegemonic projects compete with each other, the social[16] cannot form a 'sutured space'.[17] Society is not understood as an objectively given totality, 'but as the complex and unstable result of multiple political articulations',[18] or in the words of Habermas as a network of ramifying communicative actions with diverse components,[19] or in terms of systems theory as the logic of sub-systems. Habermas hopes that the lifeworld forms a privileged vantage point in the fragmented space of capitalist societies, from which it is possible to rationally reflect upon society as a whole, while Luhmann and Teubner assume that 'integration' can only take place according to the logic of each respective 'sub-system'.[20]

With Marx one reaches an intermediary result. There is no longer a privileged location, from which it is possible to reflect about the whole, but instead there are carriers of social synthesis, which preserve a moment of the hope Habermas projects into the lifeworld: value is *one* such carrier, a 'form of *unity*

11 Heinrich 1999, p. 208.
12 Sohn-Rethel, Alfred 1978, p. 4.
13 With the term 'synthesis', Sohn-Rethel refers to Kantian epistemology: to how Kant linked the possibility of knowledge to the subjective ability for the synthesis of multiplicity, to that 'I think' that 'must be capable of accompanying all other presentations' (Kant 1996, p. 177).
14 Sohn-Rethel 1978, p. 4 (translation modified). As Holloway puts it: 'A world composed purely of particulars would be impossible to conceptualise and impossible to inhabit' (Holloway 2010, p. 63).
15 Laclau and Mouffe 2001, p. 112.
16 Laclau and Mouffe speak of the social (which means the same as discourse) and not of 'society.' However, their thesis of the 'impossibility of society' (Laclau and Mouffe 2001, p. 99) is only opposed to one particular concept of society, namely that of a transparent and self-reproducing unity (Stäheli 2000a, p. 36). In this regard the concept of society advanced here is compatible with that of discourse theory.
17 Laclau and Mouffe 2001, p. 96.
18 Müller and Christensen 2004, p. 175.
19 Habermas 1996, pp. 80–1.
20 Neves 2000, p. 47.

of social labour under the conditions of its *systematic divergence*'.[21] Thus the value form and subsequently also the legal form can be called a 'technology' in the language of Foucault. Technologies, as I have noted, develop as specific ways of working in concrete contexts and are answers to concrete problems, making their temporary 'solution' possible.

Whether a product has value, whether it is part of the social totality of labour, is in itself problematic and only ever becomes clear in retrospect. The unity thus gained is a unity that has been objectively and violently created with force through the capitalist mode of production.[22] Thus value as the carrier of social synthesis constitutes 'in an *irrational* mode of production and socialization the only "process," in which this society has an (although reified and alienated) "*rational*" form and a "consciousness", that is a limited possibility of assessing its overall context'.[23]

This systematic context constitutes the background of Balbus's comments about topsy-turvy sociability: for the always already social individuals their sociability becomes a second one, which develops behind their backs. The 'life of society as a whole', noted already *Max Horkheimer*, only emerges from commodity production 'at the cost of excessive friction', and as something of an accident.[24]

1.2 *Law as a Technique of Cohesion*

Pashukanis and his successors then observe that 'value' is not the only carrier of social synthesis, not the only possibility for individuals to obtain through a limited process insight into their overall context. Poulantzas, for example, elaborates on how the state constitutes an essential apparatus for cohesion. Joachim Hirsch similarly argues that

> … what holds for the sociality of labour also holds for political sociality: it too cannot be immediately realised in a society shaped by the division of labour, mediated by competition and marked by material class antagonisms, but has to take on an equally reified-objectified form – the political form that confronts individuals as an external context of coercion or the bourgeois-capitalist state.[25]

---

21 Brentel 1989, p. 160 (emphasis in original).
22 Brentel 1989, p. 161.
23 Ibid.
24 Horkheimer, 1972, p. 203.
25 Hirsch 1994, p. 164.

This equally applies to law. As the mark of bourgeois society is precisely that it creates subjects as mutually isolated monads, the question is how those subjects are at all articulated into the whole, which Foucault calls 'population' and Poulantzas 'people-nation'. Poulantzas calls both the state and the political community, as well as law, 'techniques of cohesion'.

As I already pointed out in the passage on subjectivation above, the legal form does not only have a subjecting, but also a homogenising effect. I will now pursue this line of argument: Legal practices do not negate subjectivation and its isolating and hierarchising aspects, but they tie the subjects together in an external unity. Concluding contracts, settling conflicts in court, as well as punitive and administrative acts are ways in which subjects practice their sociality. *The legal form thus produces subjectivation and cohesion.*

In sum, the legal form not only serves to make commodity exchange possible, as considered hitherto in the tradition of Pashukanis, but touches a much more comprehensive question, that of the outline of socialisation. Here, social cohesion as such is precarious and can only develop through naturally emerging techniques of cohesion, whose own functioning remains uncertain. When socialisation can no longer be conceived as starting from one principle and the social therefore is no sutured space either, the unity of the ensemble itself becomes a hegemonic project[26] that has to be reasserted time and again – but which can rely on techniques such as law to regulate this unification.

2 The Concept of Form

My central critique of the form analytical approach consists in that it derives forms from their 'function' in capitalist commodity production. Instead I believe that it is crucial to analyse *how* the forms *operate*, as this can potentially affect commodity production later on.

From this perspective I will analyse below the techniques of cohesion or social forms. Here Joachim Hirsch's definition points the way:

> Social forms are reified and fetishised shapes that can only be deciphered through theoretical critique. They are the shapes that the mutual relation of social individuals takes on, in a manner that has become alienated from their conscious will and actions. Those forms shape their immediate perceptions and behavioural orientations: commodity, money, capital, law

26 Laclau and Mouffe 2001, p. 64; Jessop 1990, p. 291.

> and state. By guiding the behaviour of individuals and classes in a manner that is not immediately transparent for them, they make it possible to 'process' fundamental social antagonisms, i.e. they ensure that society maintains and reproduces itself despite and because of its contradictions, without, however, abolishing them. A 'form analytical' social theory is thus in clear contrast to a 'functionalist' one.[27]

The significance of the legal *form* shall unfold in the following sections, each illuminated by the social form Marx analysed: the value form.

2.1 *Value and Value Form*

How then does value function as a social form? Commodities, as the elementary forms of capitalist socialisation, have the peculiar characteristic of possessing value. This only seemingly inherent property of theirs can be deciphered, following Marx, as the *sociality of labour* in bourgeois society – as abstract-general labour. Thus one of the dimensions of social forms as defined by Brentel (*'form I'*) is already named:[28] The equality of private labour in the act of exchange is not a quality it has in and of itself. It is 'instead a specific social relation to all other private labour. And only because of this equality, which is not natural, but specifically social, can one speak of abstract labour'.[29] This particular labour of the private individual has to present itself as its direct opposite, as abstract, general labour, in order to have a social effect.

Although 'value' is a social relation, it appears to be a property of the products of labour.[30] This property firstly belongs to commodities in their dual character (use value and exchange value), but as Esser notes (see part 2), it has to take on a 'truly independent' form of existence in the natural form of another commodity. Value thus exists only in a specific form of value, form of appearance or form of existence. We have thus arrived at the second dimension of the value form (*'form II'*).[31] For the transformation of commodities into value signs takes place in the head through simple abstraction, 'but in the real exchange process a real *mediation* is required, a means to accomplish this abstraction'.[32]

---

27 Hirsch 1994, p. 161.

28 Brentel 1989, p. 13. Helmut Brentel distinguishes three form-dimensions (I–III), with the 'social form' presented in 1.1 (*'form III'*) (Brentel 1989, p. 154). Or, in the words of Krahl, 'the materialist idea of the general form' (Krahl 1985, p. 348.), determining the other two dimensions.

29 Heinrich 1999, p. 209.

30 Brentel 1989, p. 13.

31 Brentel 1989, p. 14.

32 Marx 1993, p. 142.

The unity produced in one's mind has a 'merely imaginary existence', 'in actual exchange this abstraction in turn must be objectified, must be symbolised, realised in a symbol'.[33]

Forms I and II, value and value form, are thus sensual and transcendent, both relation and thing: on the one hand purely social, but on the other always also reified existence.[34] While the commodity is dual, its body only appears as its use value. Value can thus only appear as a social quality in the social relation to another commodity and requires its own value form.[35] 'The problem of the value form, of the independent representation of value in exchange value', thus Krahl, 'is therefore its reified self-representation'.[36] Exchange value remains an inherent quality of commodities, while simultaneously existing outside of them. In money he confronts the commodity as something different. 'The inner opposition enveloped in the commodity ... here becomes represented by an external opposition'.[37] Accordingly the commodity is not solely an object of use, but also the embodiment of social relations.[38]

2.2 *Real Abstraction*

How then is this immanent contradiction resolved in the independent existence or appearance of the social form? The transformation of products into commodities is, as has been shown, only possible by reducing them to the same. This takes place by way of abstraction. The actors in the commodity exchange ignore both the concrete qualities of the labour they create and also the personal qualities of the buyers and sellers. They abstract from the particularities of the production process and from the use values of the products.

Abstraction is at first not a practice that is only immanent in those conditions, but, as Ritsert notes, abstraction as the disregarding of attributes that could actually be identified exists in each experience, as concrete as it may be. Abstraction from other possibilities of proceeding characterises every action. 'There can be no complete experience ... of any situation we face, no matter how concrete'.[39]

Abstractions are intellectual activities, conceptual operations. Marx's specific discovery, which is in particular emphasised by Sohn-Rethel and Adorno,

33 Marx 1993, pp. 143–4.
34 Marx 1993, p. 144.
35 Heinrich 1999, p. 222.
36 Krahl 1985, p. 36.
37 Marx quoted in Backhaus 1980, p. 111.
38 Postone 1986, p. 208; Krahl 1985, p. 348.
39 Ritsert 1998, p. 333.

is, however, that 'conceptuality lies not only in the minds of the philosophers but also in the reality of the object itself …'[40] Abstraction takes place in *real* society as 'real abstraction'.[41] An element of conceptuality enters the exchange process, it is an objective reduction to the same, regardless of whether human beings reflect on it or not:[42]

> The first, objective abstraction takes place not so much in scientific thought as in the universal development of the exchange system itself, which happens independently of the qualitative attitudes of producer and consumer, of the mode of production, even of need, which the social mechanism tends to satisfy as a kind of secondary by-product. Profit comes first.[43]

With real abstraction Marx deviates from Hegel in such a way that abstraction is no longer only exclusively a privilege of thought:[44]

> The essence of commodity abstraction, however, is that it is not thought-induced; it does not originate in [people's] minds but in their actions … While the concepts of natural science are thought abstractions, the economic concept of value is a real one. It exists nowhere other than in the human mind but it does not spring from it. Rather it is purely social in character, arising in the spatio-temporal sphere of human interrelations. It is not people who originate these abstractions but their actions.[45]

The processes of abstraction are carried out by the actors themselves in the course of their actual exchange activities, and do not have to be constructed only from the observer's position.[46] The abstraction takes place as an unconscious routine, it is 'a lack of awareness within awareness itself':[47] '… by equating their different products to each other in exchange as values, they equate their different kinds of labour as human labour. They do this without being aware of it'.[48]

40 Adorno 2018, p. 156.
41 Sohn-Rethel 1978, p. 21.
42 Adorno 2018, p. 156.
43 Adorno 1989, p. 148.
44 Sohn-Rethel 1978, p. 18.
45 Sohn-Rethel 1978, p. 20 (translation modified).
46 Ritsert 1998, p. 335.
47 Reichelt 2007, p. 16.
48 Marx 1976, pp. 166–7.

Equalisation, which plays such a crucial role for the value as well as for the legal form, remains opaque for those involved themselves, it is not at all an intellectual process of abstraction; instead abstraction takes place through the activities of those involved in the exchange.[49] Independently of the significance of this conclusion for the theory of knowledge, it also constitutes a theory of the autonomisation of human actions which prevents an immediate understanding of social conditions. Routinised activities are indeed fundamentally characterised by taking place 'as if by themselves' on the basis of 'practical consciousness' (Giddens). Form-directed routinised activities are, however, in addition, not directly accessible for 'discursive consciousness', because they first have to be theoretically deciphered, potentially even using 'counter-intuitive' theoretical knowledge, as Habermas put it.

Social forms therefore require a theory of the fetish: They are nothing but congealed human relations, but hide this at the same time. Legal systems theory expresses on closer examination a similar idea – its 'fetish theory' appears as the concept of the 'paradox'. Fundamental indeterminacy introduces politics into the system and is ultimately the expression of an only precariously successful reification. Different techniques have to disguise the fact that also the system, the social form, is ultimately nothing but congealed and reproduced social relations.

This is neither the result of a metaphysical subject nor of the strategic actions of powerful actors – even they are subjected to those forms. Fetishism is therefore the core of Marx's discussion of power[50] and cannot be reduced to the commodity and money fetish. In particular Georg Lukács, with his terminology of 'reification', points out early on that the relationships between people take on the character of objects and thus a 'ghostlike objectivity', which in its strict, seemingly completely closed internal dynamic covers up any trace of their character as a relation between human beings.[51] Axel Honneth reframes this idea for the relationship between the subjects as 'forgetfulness of recognition', a process wherein, in the knowledge and cognition of other persons, as well as in their recognition, consciousness is lost 'of the degree' to which this is owed 'to an antecedent stance of empathetic engagement and recognition'.[52]

Jacques Derrida frames his analysis of the fetish chapter as a 'spectral theory': The character of the fetish is its 'spectrality', the production of the *revenant*.[53]

49 Heinrich 1999, p. 209.
50 Holloway 2010, p. 43.
51 Lukács 1971, p. 100.
52 Honneth 2008, p. 56.
53 Derrida 1994, pp. 165–6.

The *revenant* does not simply signify spiritualisation, as in the autonomisation of the spirit following Hegel, but it refers to an autonomisation that is *effected* by gaining a body, i.e. becoming a spectre.[54] The merely imaginary abstraction in the mind, as Marx said above, is mediated by the embodiment of the spectre. In particular the enlightened, capitalist society of extended reproduction cannot do away with the religious moment and is instead dominated by 'occultism, obscurantism, lack of maturity before Englightenment' and turns into a 'childish or primitive humanity'[55] subjected to spectres.[56] This autonomisation is the irreducibly specific character of the spectre.[57]

Habermas' and Luhmann's concepts of the system take precisely this objectified mechanism into account, but then accommodate it, either resignedly or affirmatively. They are right to the extent that social forms represent – particularly due to reification – especially stubborn techniques of consensus. They are, however, wrong in inferring from this that even those resistant impermeabilities have to be produced in everyday routines.

2.3 *The Autonomisation of Social Relations: Reification, Naturalisation and Co.*

Honneth pointed out that there are signs that the concept of 'reification', which is a leitmotiv of social critique in the 1920s and 1930s, could experience a renaissance.[58] While Marx traces reification back to the social forms, Foucault and Derrida suggest a more comprehensive social process. While both start from theoretical premises that differ from Marx's, that is, not with commodity production but with language, discourse, or power relations, they also conclude with the autonomisation of social relations. In Foucault, as has been shown, the idea of 'entangled' power relations that develop in every corner of society and link up into larger formations leads him to start from a social anonymity independent of any possible abstraction processes of social forms. Thus, the underlying idea is very similar to Marx's.

Derrida, however, argues that Marx attributes spectrality solely to commodity production, so that it would disappear with a change in the mode of production.[59] He assumes in contrast that socialisation as such brings forth spectres and haunting. He explains this with the difference between exchange and

54 Derrida 1994, p. 157.
55 Derrida 1994, p. 191.
56 Derrida 1994, pp. 193–4.
57 Derrida 1994, p. 185.
58 Honneth 2008, p. 17.
59 Derrida 1994, pp. 205–6.

use value. Use value is seemingly unproblematic in Marx, it is intact, before exchange value comes on stage – pure and simple, without mysterious properties,[60] self-same. Derrida rejects this origin of the spectre[61] as use value is socially determined as well. There is no pure use, its meaning is socially overdetermined and historically contingent. The fetish of social forms is not autonomisation alone. Language, for one, always confronts social subjects already as a system that functions according to its own rules. Discourses also develop '*their own momentum of semantic and cultural processes*'.[62] In this respect Derrida wants to speak of hauntology[63] instead of ontology.[64]

The two approaches are, however, only seemingly in contradiction, for the society where power strategies link up in myriad ways to form a social haunting, is in principle nothing other than Marx's fetish. The modern capitalist society Derrida and Foucault refer to is the 'first genuinely global type of societal organization in history …',[65] and thus the first to give its meaning to the term 'socialisation', which casts its spell over more and more sectors and cannot exist without 'constantly revolutionising … the relations of production, and with them the whole relations of society'.[66] Surplus objectivity is its particular distinguishing feature. Adorno speaks in this context, following Emile Durkheim, of an 'impenetrability' through which one is made to experience society as an autonomous objectivity, which has an element of inaccessibility.[67] The *specifically social* consists in the imbalance of institutions over people.[68]

Social forms are thus no longer the only 'impenetrabilities' and in this respect Derrida and Foucault are right.[69] What is special about social forms and could strictly speaking be called spectral consists, however, precisely in that relations are not only complex and therefore hard to see through, but cover up that they are social relations and *become reified* in that sense. This can be shown with Derrida's example of use value: although it is overdetermined, as there is no unmediated pre-social use, there is actually nothing 'mysterious' about the

60 Derrida 1994, p. 188.
61 Derrida 1994, p. 200.
62 Bublitz 2003, p. 7 (emphasis in original).
63 'Hauntology' refers to the study of haunting, to Spuk. In French 'hauntology' is pronounced similarly to ontology. Thus Derrida wants to show that it is already inscribed in the term itself that any theory of being is always already one of non-being, of ghosts.
64 Derrida 1994, p. 202.
65 Giddens 1986, p. 183; see also Adorno 1989, p. 144.
66 MECW, Volume 6, p. 488.
67 Adorno 2000, pp. 36, 38.
68 Adorno 1989, p. 144.
69 Thus also – critical of Lukács – Honneth 2008, p. 80.

commodity as use value to the extent that it remains obviously natural matter that has been changed through human activity.[70] In exchange value this is no longer visible, as it can only present itself in another commodity and is hence reified.

A theory that focuses on the autonomisation of human activity has to pursue this phenomenon more extensively, beginning with autonomisation in general and how it arises from modern capitalist society and subsequently its specific manners of reification or naturalisation. A striking parallel with the gender binary exists, for instance, which is hardly less fittingly described as an 'embodiment of social relations' than the social labour of the commodity. The insight into its social construction is here accomplished by another mechanism: that of biologising the social relation, which remains just as impenetrable for everyday behaviour as the commodity fetish. All the autonomisations suggest that modern bourgeois society has no or only very rudimentary procedures for enlightening and collectively governing itself.

Below I will turn to the specifically juridical manner of autonomisation, the fascination with legal theory, which owes its effects to the hybrid character of its normative factuality. In the represented theories it has thus far been explored through the concepts of 'relative autonomy' or 'relative independence', and 'internal-external-dialectic'. I will show that this appearance of impenetrability, similarly to exchange value, can be dissolved in a social relation.

2.4 *The Legal Form*

2.4.1 Subjectivation and Cohesion

The value or commodity form describes a *social* form in the Marxian tradition. It processes the satisfaction of needs through social labour in capitalist society, which is based upon private and surplus value production. With the legal form Pashukanis then identifies a further social form. For this assumption to hold true, the legal form also has to represent a social relation that becomes autonomous through abstraction and develops its own form. As a form it has to have an independent object-like quality that is removed from the immediate grasp of everyday behaviour, but guides it, thus becoming a technology of cohesion.

I have attempted to show that law plays a crucial role in subjectivation. Here a mechanism similar to that of equating the products of labour takes place. Balbus calls this 'the common mode of substitution'. The equality of different kinds of labour can only persist by abstracting from their real inequal-

70 Marx 1976, p. 163.

ity,[71] that is 'if we reduce them to the characteristic they have in common, that of being the expenditure of human labour-power, of human labour in the abstract'.

Legal subjects are also placed in relation to each other as abstract equals. Equality that is socially produced through abstraction is, one can conclude, the central mode of making the incommensurable commensurable. From this perspective it becomes clear that not only economic (class) differences and antagonisms are processed, as was suggested through the narrow debate about the spheres of production and circulation, but differences as such. Moreover, the legal form thus does not fulfil a 'function', but produces a result. That this also turns commodity owners into legal subjects and allows for the exchange of commodities is one effect.

Their division makes the social monads incommensurable with each other. While legal practices create their own divisions, they *simultaneously* organise the recombination of the social body. The equality of legal subjectivity is a way to allow for the connection of respectively individuated members of society, be it through contracts, through laws or through court rulings. 'Abstract and equal subjects, the atoms of the legal relationship, cannot relate to each other according to principles of "traditional" privilege, but do so by means of *contract*, which is the *formalisation of mutual recognition of equal subjects*', writes China Mieville in the tradition of Pashukanis.[72]

Thus law not only provides a forum for engaging in conflicts – 'disputes', as Pashukanis thought – but constitutes more widely a formal cohesive framework for the individuated monads. What is formal and abstract is in this sense actually closely related to the real fractures of the social division of labour and of individualisation.[73] In civil proceedings, for example, *social* moments, which the dispute of two legal parties is embedded in, are procedurally placed on the agenda, such as questions of minority, legal responsibility, questions of 'good faith', of error and of liability. In constitutional processes the relation of the individual and society is made operational and 'assessed' according to formal examination criteria. Pashukanis' statement, that the legal fabric is 'the succession of subjects linked together by claims on each other ...',[74] can also be reinterpreted accordingly. Through formalised procedures and abstracting norms society is retrospectively brought into social relationships, and diverging

71 Marx 1976, p. 166.
72 Mieville 2005, p. 88 (emphasis in original).
73 Poulantzas 2000, p. 64.
74 Pashukanis 2003, p. 99.

individuals are woven together into a social fabric. They can, however, only be bound together through the abstract equality of legal subjectivity.

It is also possible to understand Luhmann's dictum that law is exclusively about normativity from this perspective. Individuals are only normatively placed in relation to each other as equals. Normativity is possible because of processes that abstract from the here and now. Form abstractions make it possible to process social contradictions. Marx has shown this with the example of the exchange process, which functions although the contradictions remain. 'The further development of the commodity does not abolish these contradictions, but rather provides *the form within which they have room to move. This is, in general, the way in which real contradictions are resolved*'.[75] Contradictions move within the form; a contradiction without synthesis, that is to say – a paradox.

In the mode of the legal subject the subjects treat each other actually as equals amongst equals, those who are 'free' to enter into contracts. No matter, whether the contract concerns employment, marriage, rental or sales, in practice abstractly equal parties to the contract have to be counterfactually assumed. In the marriage contract, for example, the hierarchical gender relationship is juridically transformed into one of equals. 'Capitalist' and 'worker' treat each other as equals in their legal practices, even if they remain unaware of this at the moment of their actions. Buying bread, for instance, takes place as part of everyday routine activity as a simple exchange of a product of labour against money. Neither do the subjects think about how labour is equated in the money form, nor are they even aware that this creates a contract based on two equal legal subjects. They do not know it, but they are doing it. Their actions are real abstractions or performative acts, which produce the equality of the subjects at this very moment. If the purchase takes place without problem, this is not addressed. Only when this contractual relation is disturbed, is the relationship legally codified. With contracts, which are required to be in writing, the legal coding is present from the outset, but not the performative production of legal subjectivity. This subjectivity is most readily apparent in the case of company forms that are treated as 'juridical persons' in private law[76] and thus only acquire subject character through the law.

This mechanism does not only work in private law. Thus the legal practices of penal law, which centre on the relationship of the individual subject and the authority of the state, assume a responsible, autonomous subject. Or when, for

75 Marx 1976, p. 198 (emphasis S.B.).
76 See §§ 21–89 of the BGB (civil code of Germany).

example, a lack of responsibility is established, this is explicitly substantiated as a deviation from the norm through an exception rule. The legal subject in its double existence as an empirical, real and imaginary one also constitutes a real abstraction.[77] It is also apparent at this point of the analysis that the legal abstractions of, for example, class and gender differences or of the 'hidden abode of production' (Marx), the 'veiling function' of the law Franz Neumann noted, are expressions of this 'mode of encoding reality' (Balbus) and thus a product of those social structures rather than a conspiratorial strategy. Elements of social differentiation are for the law 'virtually inconceivable'.[78]

Furthermore, precisely the common mode of abstraction that makes concrete, different individuals compatible is a prerequisite for qualitative antagonisms. Only *because* everyday agents can encounter each other in law as formally equal and free, do their differences remain structurally covered, and thus unaddressed. Law succeeds, moreover, in presenting itself as an exclusive code of power, as the code of organised public violence, as Foucault shows. *At the same time*, however – and this has created difficulties for materialist legal theory thus far – as the flipside of abstraction, subjects *can* also encounter each other as equal and free. Abstraction is a condition for making society possible in its *dual meaning*. Therefore Andrea Maihofer aptly notes that the abstraction of modern law is *both* its strength *and also* its structural limit.[79]

2.4.2 Reification through Procedures

When the sociality of subjects is expressed in law, it nevertheless remains a purely social imaginary just like the value abstraction. How does this imaginary enter social practice? How is this managed and symbolised? Law gains a material existence (Maihofer) in legal form II,[80] that is, in juridical procedures. There only certain juridical arguments can be presented by a body of specialised legal practitioners. Modern law develops co-originally with modern officialdom, that is, a specialised intellectual labour force which is highly qualified and technically trained through long years of preparatory education.[81] Court cases, legislative and administrative procedures do not leave law to the everyday activities of the subjects, they code those practices juridically. They interpret social reality according to certain rules as legal, as legal communication as

77 Thus also Harms 2000, p. 123, note 625.
78 Adler 1964, p. 36.
79 Maihofer 1992, p. 205.
80 From a discourse-theoretical background one could here also speak of a 'legal discourse'. 'Legal form II' refers to the classification of forms by Brentel; see above.
81 Weber 1978, p. 958.

understood by Luhmann. The individual actors are no longer able to grasp their own conditions, once they have entered those procedures. They include both a specific language and technical knowledge, but potentially also architectural peculiarities, mechanisms of social exclusion, their own time frames and so on, thus leading a 'life of their own'.[82]

In engaging with Habermas the central significance of those processes for the modern legal form has become apparent: They sort out 'issues and contributions, information and reasons in such a way'[83] that only such arguments can pass the 'filters' of the procedures – these are on the one hand juridical and on the other hand can claim hegemonic validity. They exclude the subalterns and are the classic terrain of legal intellectuals, who master the techniques of legal argument and are juridically disciplined. Poulantzas and Foucault concur that the relationship of intellectual labour and political domination, of knowledge and power, culminates in the capitalist state or the secularised form of pastoral power.[84] The political as well as the legal form are on the side of intellectual labour, organise hegemony through it and rule the population.

That juridical procedures require arguments to be put forward makes, according to Habermas's insight, the communicative contradiction permanent. This thereby transforms that contradiction into a productive force,[85] which can lead to social integration. In light of the insights of Gramsci and Foucault, this idea has to be reformulated so that the procedures are technologies of consensus which create consensus in a procedural manner through communicative action. It has to be possible to generalise every argument and to relate it to the context of other arguments.

I had argued with systems theory against Habermas that law is also systemic, or, in the terminology employed here, that it functions in a legal form, but that this does not mean that action is therefore brought to a halt. It only shows what this means concretely: the communicative actors are forced into particular procedures in which their own social relations slip away from them. Not they themselves, but juridical intellectuals argue according to particular techniques. Thus communicative action is not brought to a halt in general, but particular subjects are excluded, although always only on the basis that they accept those exclusionary procedures as well as their rules in their everyday practices and behave accordingly. Indeed, the opposing parties in a civil case can interrupt the procedure and settle according to other considerations

82 Luhmann 1969, p. 47.
83 Habermas 1996, p. 462.
84 Wissel 2007, p. 77.
85 Habermas 1996, p. 38.

of fairness or of a pragmatic character 'out of court'. However, in doing so the production of recursive legal operations is cut short. Nor can judges in penal cases ignore the rules of court and close the proceedings, because the accused appears 'innocent' to them according to their own moral concepts. Legal form II is also ultimately reproduced by the practice of subjects, if they let themselves be ruled just as they get up every morning, go to work or school, accept the traffic regulations, participate in elections or start families of origin.

Those procedures result in the transformation of original social relations through court decisions, acts, legal codes, street signs (as a specific form of the administrative act), and even deportations and incarcerations. The procedures, which Kirchheimer dismisses as merely 'technical law', in which decisions are in fact wrested from the respective social distribution of power and transferred into the legal sphere as well as juridically coded, are here revealed as by no means the end of the legal form, but as its essence. The legal form creates a new reality with its own realm: a counterfactual factuality (Brunkhorst) that seals itself off against direct access. The social relation represented by legal form I is that of subjects to each other. In legal form II it becomes independent in the legal procedures as an ensemble of practices and institutions. The initial social relation is dissolved and reshaped by the processes of the legal form, in which participants become entangled as though in a spider web. Procedures thus become normalising procedures, in which the opposing parties in defending their legal affairs experience the abstraction from their subjectivity: 'of being written into the relevant doctrinal script, the erasure of their subjectivity in order to become the necessary kind of legal subjects ... Legal subjects are thus locked in the house of law ...'[86]

The legal subject created in the procedures appears in consequence as though it precedes the law and is merely regulated by it. Its qualities (equality, freedom, autonomy, responsibility) appear as natural qualities. A legal fetishism emerges, which prevents both the awareness of its constructed character and concepts of a society that can reproduce itself without the legal (form). Law no longer appears as a social relation and becomes instead an eternal, quasi-anthropological medium of socialisation. This is how it is reified – by becoming a quality of society as such. What remains invisible here is that this actually corresponds instead to a (form of) socialisation that produces itself surreptitiously.

86 Hunter 2006, p. 40.

2.4.3 Relational Autonomy

The autonomisation of social relations is at the same time the condition of their 'relative autonomy'. The specific socialisation under capitalism creates social forms, 'economic' no less than legal or political ones. It is the autonomisation and fetishisation of those relations that make possible a materiality of those forms themselves. For then they can no longer be mere 'appearance', 'insofar as human beings in fact become dependent on those objectivities, which are obscure to them'.[87] They are 'not only false consciousness, but also simultaneously reality ... That the categories of illusion are in truth also categories of reality, this is dialectic',[88] and it already shows in that seeing through this 'appearance' changes nothing materially. Thus convicted offenders cannot save themselves from punishment through their awareness of the legal form; contracts have to be followed, even if they are nothing but the reified form of human sociality.

The self-referentiality of law, which in Luhmann differentiates itself into a legal system, is in principle the same discovery. When he claims that the differentiation of an 'operatively closed legal system' takes place through the recursive reference of legal operations to legal operations, and accordingly calls it an intentional tautology,[89] or when Kelsen anticipates systems theory in evoking the 'autonomy' of normative systems,[90] they describe the fetishised autonomisation of the legal *form*.

Form analysis makes clear that social 'subsystems' do not have to be 'derived' in a functionalist way. The law does not exist *in order to* fulfil a social function (be that the exchange of commodities, the stabilising of expectations or the production of a united power bloc). It is rather possible to genealogically trace how social forms develop as a result of the autonomisation of social conditions, as they gain a certain stability over a particular period and are initially removed from immediate action and thus also change through their fetishised form. That they also process social contradictions in the course of this and thus provide the form those contradictions can move within, is the result of a process of searching and the condition for their continued existence, but not their assigned performance.

This autonomy is, however, *relative*. Autonomy and relativity initially appear as irreconcilable contradictions. That is indeed the case, but only for a non-dialectical theory. The dialectic thinks the presence of the different up to the

---

87 Adorno 2018, p. 160.
88 Ibid.
89 Luhmann 2004, p. 90.
90 Kelsen 1981, p. 80.

opposite in the respectively other or the unity of the opposed.[91] The autonomy of the law is historically specific, the result of the autonomisation of social conditions. As such it is, however, always already an element of the social totality. The law is only autonomous in abstraction from this totality, but relative *in relation* to the other practices and conditions or power technologies and in particular to the social context. 'Relative' is time and again misunderstood as 'some shaded concept of autonomy',[92] that is, as one that discusses a greater or lesser degree of autonomy. This is then at the same time rejected in a dualist manner as a logical contradiction. Even Luhmann is ultimately defeated by this concept and remains committed to a Kantian idea of dialectics, that is, a negatively connoted one of antinomies, where there is nothing but either/or. The dialectics that go back to Hegel, on the other hand, start from the 'absolutely mediated nature of every existing thing',[93] – a pure autonomy, no matter how much it might be backed up by autopoiesis,[94] is accordingly a mere function – a 'stop to reflection'. However, in order to prevent the possibility of biased misunderstandings, I will in what follows no longer talk about relative, but about *relational* autonomy.[95]

It is also its own density that is central for the question of whether a social norm is part of the legal technology or whether it is only 'a mock-up of legality'. *Only if* the legal form is present in its relational autonomy, which makes direct access even for powerful social actors impossible or at least much harder, can one speak in bourgeois-capitalist societies with regards to social norms of 'law'. Precisely this is the basis for the distinction conceptualised by Franz Neumann. The legal form is always already, as Foucault has shown, embedded in a correlation system of power technologies. Other technologies insert themselves into its niches and overdetermine it. But it retains nonetheless a relational autonomy with regard to those techniques. Only when this is no longer the case, for instance when immediate relations of power, in the form of the old, repressive form of power, let it implode, is its 'autonomy' destroyed and this technology of power eroded. The concrete conditions for generating relational autonomy all have to be researched in their historic specificity. The decisive question is whether a certain right has the possibility to develop according to

91 See Daniel 1983, pp. 139–40.
92 Luhmann 1994, p. 96.
93 Adorno 2001, p. 181.
94 Luhmann 1994, p. 97.
95 Katrina Blindow gave me this idea during the *block seminar* 'Zur Aktualität von Gramscis Staats- und Hegemonietheorie' [On the contemporary relevance of Gramsci's state and hegemony theory] in the summer of 2004.

its own internal logic without permanent challenge to its independent reproduction. A third entity outside the parties in conflict (ordinarily a court) is a conditio sine qua non. However, the monopoly on coercive force cannot be held responsible for autonomisation a priori. It is *one central* condition for making it possible, but not the only one. It is even more decisive that the law is socially practised, as Maihofer rightly stresses.

Furthermore, the autonomisation of the legal institutions explains why law according to Neumann's conclusions has 'two sides' as it offers at least legal possibilities to the weak.[96] It is a *material* condensation of the relationship of forces. For Poulantzas' problem of founding relational autonomy, this means also that precisely this fetishised, reified independence of the social forms brings its own logic and resistance to social power relations with it. Even the most powerful actors do not dispose of the social forms, but also have to move within them.

2.4.4 Out of the Legal Form

If the understanding of Luhmann's systems theory advanced in Part 1 is correct, which is that, although affirmative, it is an altogether appropriate description of the reification of social relations, it can as an immanent description help here to represent the *concrete mechanisms* of law's own density. It thus provides an answer to the question of *how* autonomisation is actually operationalised, and how it prevents as legal form a transparent and immediately accessible law.

2.4.4.1 *Self-reproduction*

Firstly 'operative closedness' – understood as a quasi-systemic isolation of the legal form – is a mode of impermeability. In contrast to the normative-democratic concepts of Habermas and Maus, who envisage an internal hierarchy of legal acts with the democratic legislature at the top, the really existing autonomisation of the legal form is marked by the circular ('hyper-cyclical') interlinking of legal acts with each other. This leads to a creation of legislation internally within law, which itself brings forth law respectively through binary coding, executing programmes and legal validity.

In doing so, it independently produces, articulates and reflects the components of the legal form, so that the sovereignty of the people is thwarted and at most still serves as a self-description for enabling new linkages within the legal. The practice of law-producing actors has only little in common with the everyday understanding of a self-organised society. Permanent shifts in the exercise

96 Neumann 1957, p. 75.

of applying law and of jurisprudence occur that are almost euphemistically described by the term 'legal development'. Thus the constitutional ties of state apparatuses to 'programming through the base' (Maus) fall victim to this autonomisation. The structural reason for modern law's resistance to the rule of law and democracy lies in the autonomisation that characterises social forms and at the same time makes this process invisible. For legal discourses become inaccessible for extra-legal moments. When it is legally coded, the extra-legal world is incorporated in legal practice. 'Untamed thinking outside the law cannot claim any relevance', Luhmann aptly writes.[97] Only through filters can it find its way into law, and always at the price that legally incompatible moments are selected.

Here the second effect of autonomisation also already shows itself: The legal form provides a deferral, a delay and additional difficulty for asserting immediate claims to power.[98] This duality is the reason for the ambivalent character of law, the 'intersection of emancipation and violence'.[99]

At the same time this is how abstraction from socially produced and hierarchised differences functions *in actu*. Only the legal construction of the legal subject as formally equal, free and autonomous is processed in the legal form, not the differences. If the attempt is made to nonetheless include them in law, this can only take place incompletely and again with legal mechanisms, such as the reverse onus clause in favour of the materially weaker litigant,[100] or the 'Third Party Effect of Fundamental Rights', for example as 'shining through' sub-constitutional general clauses, so that they can also be applied against powerful private parties to a dispute and no longer only asserted against the state. Thus contracts, for one, are considered immoral, if a structural inequality is exploited in their conclusion.[101]

2.4.4.2 *Dogma*

Within the process of autonomisation the juridical method, called dogmatics in the legal system of continental Europe, plays a decisive role. This 'self-description' only made self-referentiality and the construction of an order possible, as Teubner has shown. Moreover, individual cases are thus situated in the

97 Luhmann 2004, p. 327.
98 Fischer-Lescano and Christensen 2012, p. 112.
99 Negt 1975, p. 31.
100 Thus for example in the 'chicken-pest decision' of the Federal Court of Justice: BGHZ 51, pp. 91 ff.
101 An example for this is the Federal Constitutional Court's 1993 ruling on bank guarantees – BVerfGE 89, pp. 214 ff. NJW 1994, 36. See, however, for a critique of the justification Teubner 2000.

context of previous and subsequent distinctions. It assumes that cases have been decided before and that others will follow after.[102] For this recursive network to be recognised and a coordination of decisions to become possible, a certain redundancy is necessary, a formulaic character and reproducibility. Dogmatics provides for relative consistency in the relations of myriad decisions to each other. Thus the risk of disintegration through the sheer number of individual decisions that have nothing to say to each other – and this could make the paradox of the legal form visible – is normalised:

> With the technique of subsumption, the style of expert opinion, the establishment of a 'prevailing view' and the disciplining of the juridical subjects.[103] From the eighteenth and nineteenth century on this structural framework, this web of points of view, developed.[104]

Robert Alexy describes the way dogmatics works in the following way: First it has a stabilising effect, that is, certain solutions, once found, are fixed over long periods and thus rendered reproducible: 'If one were to reopen the discussion at any time the possibility would arise that … one might arrive at different outcomes'.[105] Furthermore it has a burden-reducing effect: unless there is some special ground, fresh testing of the legal form is unnecessary,[106] it can be used in routinised activity. Moreover it makes possible ever-increasing differentiation and a simplified, systematic presentation of legal norms according to the relationships of dependency between them.[107] Finally, it saves multiple models of solutions, which would not occur to those beginning anew.[108] Thus it seals itself off from independent and unlimited (legal policy) questioning and functions as a 'rule of limitation for reasoning in its quest for reasons'.[109]

2.4.4.3 *Hegemonic Deparadoxification*

At this point one encounters within the legal form its paradox, the contradiction it processes: The juridical argumentation is a deparadoxifying regulation. The autonomous character of the legal form rests on uncertain ground. What is legal and thus conversely illegal, is not predetermined by the legal *form* itself,

102 Luhmann 2004, p. 314.
103 Buckel 2002.
104 Luhmann 2004, p. 327.
105 Alexy 1989, p. 267.
106 Alexy 1989, p. 269.
107 Alexy 1989, pp. 268, 271.
108 Alexy 1989, p. 272.
109 Luhmann 2004, p. 342.

but the result of hegemonic struggles, which are however normalised through the formal coercion of dogmatics. Hegemonic leadership is inscribed in this form of argument. In particular when one asks why precisely this *specific* argument prevails in jurisprudence and not another one, for instance how a 'right to the enterprise' can be argued for, but not a 'right to work', the political character of the legal form is revealed. The decisions based upon power, which are ultimately secured by figures of argumentation, are by no means arbitrary. They follow on the one hand the dogmatic requirements of the legal form and secondly the hegemonic projects which can be universalised. Thus they are anything but the arbitrary decisions of individual agents of the state.

Formally the inscription of hegemony shows in that the consistency of the dogmatic arguments always only exists in relation, according to the relational autonomy of the legal form. For the arguments are essentially based on their repetition of previous arguments – an identical repetition is, however, impossible. Here hegemonic shifts can thus already take place. The questioning cannot be stopped in the radical manner envisaged by Luhmann, who stopped at a 'literalness of communication theory'[110] and postulated the explanation as the correct exegesis of a text in Old-European style. Dogmatic justifications rather give birth to texts, and texts increase the opportunity to say 'no'.[111] Hegemonic decisions only solve the paradox *temporarily*. In antagonistic struggles a network of social actors thus manages to consensually universalise a particular world view, which can inscribe itself in the legal form. Yet, due to the antagonistic structure of the decision the counter-hegemonic project is always already being planned: 'Every hegemonic order is susceptible of being challenged by counter-hegemonic practices, i.e. practices which will attempt to disarticulate the existing order so as to install another form of hegemony'.[112]

Hegemonic projects can thus draw on the legal form to the extent that here projects are developed by juridical knowledge workers in particular legal argumentation. The law thus allows for a unification of divergent projects. It provides virtually the ideal type of a formal cohesion framework, because it is designed for universality in its own structure, its abstraction and reliance on formalised justification.[113]

110 Stäheli 2000b, p. 284.
111 Fischer-Lescano and Christensen 2012, p. 103.
112 Mouffe 2005, p. 18.
113 See in greater detail Buckel and Fischer-Lescano 2009.

2.4.4.4 *The Material Support of Autonomisation*

In Luhmann's view, compulsory decision-making and legal force – institutionalised in courts – justifiably support the autonomisation of law. That courts ultimately have to make decisions and at least temporarily actually 'free' those decisions from permanent questioning, stems from the fact that the legal form can only prevail if it succeeds in *the individual case*. For it is only then that the recursive network of legal operations reaches closure. An unapplied law would leave the circle at some point. Therefore jurisdiction did not gain a special position within the legal system only with Luhmann, but already for Hans Kelsen. He rightly emphasised that 'one should not overlook the important fact that in the last analysis the law is not what the legislator more or less clearly sets forth or what the rule of custom more or less comprehensibly implies. The law is what the court finally decides'.[114] Indeed many, if not most, legal communications take place outside of juridical institutions; however, this occurs only in the material context that ensures that they could always also be accessible to juridical procedures. The legally binding decision ends 'in the last instance' – a possibly infinite regress which would destroy the connections between legal discourses and thus make autonomisation impossible.

Obviously those decisions are again new texts, the meaning of which cannot be fixed once and for all but is open to hegemonic practice. However, the decision in the last instance fixes, at least for a historical moment, a particular meaning, so that it can become effective. It 'freezes' social relations for a particular moment in time and thus allows for decisions following from it to be developed. A shift in meaning is at first postponed. The prohibition of the denial of justice coupled with legal force is truly the pillar of the legal form. The courts as its institutionalisation are therefore especially significant for the relational autonomy of the law. Without a strong juridical institutionalisation (including extensive rights to sue and jurisdictions) this cannot develop. Powerful actors can instead occupy the meaning of what is 'legal' and trigger something of a law of fables [*Legendenrecht*].

2.4.4.5 *Fetish and Paradox*

Managing the paradox of the social forms has the effect of processing social contradictions. The contradiction (the foundational paradox) is precisely not resolved, but maintained. The 'windowless monads' are connected without a master plan or steering subject, decentralised through anonymous, autonomised mechanisms. The paradox is accordingly included in the process as a permanent risk.

---

114 Kelsen 1941, p. 575.

Luhmann now argues that this has to be rendered invisible. Form analysis shows that this is very crucially produced by the fetish character of the social forms, that is, through their reification. Thus the legal form does not even appear as a social relation to begin with. This lends the foundational paradox its stability. However, as the debate about the paradoxology of systems theory has also shown, subversion lurks in the very heart of the legal form itself: that some day the connection of legal operations will fail. Precisely because the legal form is politically overdetermined and does not constitute a reversible principle, and because it has to be developed in their daily practices by actors who cannot initially understand it as their own practice – precisely for this reason its validity is deeply uncertain.

CHAPTER 13

The Institutionalisation of the Legal Form

In order to take the previous chapter's insight that form analysis must not remain at this abstract level into account, it is firstly necessary to look into the historical possibility of change through practice using a dual structural theory. For this allows us to arrive at a lower level of abstraction that makes it methodologically possible to research concrete social formations or institutional ensembles.

Social forms constitute a central *structuring principle* of capitalist socialisation. Structuring principles are the structural elements which have the greatest time-space extensions.[1] They are the organising principles that specify types of societies by constituting an institutional fabric. Those interwoven institutional ensembles are in turn, following Anthony Giddens, the most fundamental identifying characteristics of a society.[2] Christoph Görg has pointed out that in this concept Giddens omits precisely social forms as a specific type of the autonomisation of structural moments.[3] Indeed, Giddens specifies that the distinguishing structural principle of class societies under modern capitalism is the disembedding of state and economic institutions, although they remain interconnected.[4] On closer inspection, he thus begins one abstraction level too low, namely already on that of institutions. Analytically it would rather be appropriate to speak of political, economic and legal forms. Following this shift, it is now possible to examine the relationship of structural principles and institutions.

1 Institutions – a Lower Level of Abstraction

Institutions are concrete historical and temporal formations of structural principles. Foucault insists that what matters are power technologies and that institutions form something of an external framework, an apparatus with its own rules and mechanisms of self-preservation. Technologies of power are thus continually maintained and gain a certain stability: 'What is institutional about

1 Giddens 1986, p. 17.
2 Giddens 1986, pp. 170, 164.
3 Görg 1994, p. 54.
4 Giddens 1986, p. 183.

institutions is always concerned with stability'.[5] Joachim Hirsch therefore says that social forms *materialise* in institutions.[6] One could also phrase this following Maihofer as the former gaining a 'material existence' in the latter: The form requires an institutional base for its realisation, although it can oppose this base through the antagonisms embedded within it.[7] For the procedures of the legal form this means that they materialise in various different temporal and spatial ways in the institutions of the specific social formations: in the German Federal Constitutional Court unlike the European Court of Justice or the US Supreme Court. In addition, the various sub-disciplines of private and public law are historical expressions of the general legal form. Social forms thus depend on the concrete manner of their institutionalisation and only exist in the institutional apparatuses, form-analytically speaking as 'form II'.

1.1 *The Intersection of Different Structural Principles*

Social forms are structural principles *specific to capitalism*. They in no way explain the entire institutional system of those societies. If one wants to do justice to the diversity of modern technologies of domination, one has to acknowledge that modern societies 'were not constructed on a political *tabula rasa* but on the historically variable foundations of past social forms and discourses'.[8] Thus, for example, 'an inherited patriarchal context'[9] exists which is reconfigured within capitalism. In the institutions the legal form links up with other structural principles, that is, with other social forms, power technologies and ways of subjectivation, which also inscribe themselves in the apparatuses. Therefore it is no accident that Pashukanis addresses the close connection of law and commodity production. Civil law contracts are always a combination of the legal and the commodity form. At the same time the legal form is institutionally entangled with the political form in a particular manner. But also the gender binary and heteronormativity articulate themselves through legal practice. It is only in bourgeois society that nature and society are to such an extent – and with such subtlety – subjected to a binary gendering and at the same time naturalised; and as such it is only here that the traces of social construction are entirely eliminated.[10] The hierarchical gender binary is thus the way in which patriarchal and heterosexist relations of dom-

---

5 Göhler quoted after Brodocz 2003, p. 38.
6 Hirsch 1994, p. 173.
7 Hirsch 1994, p. 175.
8 Jessop 2004, p. 220.
9 Ibid.
10 Wetterer 2002, p. 113.

ination are inscribed in modern institutions and systematically interlink in them with the legal form. This connection could mainly emerge in a process of searching, because the legal form operates simultaneously in an individualising and a totalising manner. On the one hand it sanctions existing social ways of subjectivation, on the other it brings them together into a hegemonic whole through the very abstraction it performs, and thus also processes its antagonistic position. Broadening the perspective to not only examine the materialisation of the legal form in the institutions, but also in the totality of socially dispersed legal practices, one can speak of legal *dispositifs*. Those encompass more than the condensation of the legal form in the institutions alone; they also articulate discourses about law that are not yet institutionalised, attempts to make a certain discourse hegemonic, and everyday practices.

The totality of social *dispositifs* forms a historical block, that is, a coherent ensemble of techniques of coercive force and consensus that reproduces itself over a longer period of time. The perspective of analysis depends on which phenomena one seeks to investigate. All that matters is to reflect carefully on which level of abstraction to argue at; on that of the legal form, the historical block, the *dispositif* or the institution.

1.2 *Institutions and Everyday Behaviour*

The further structural principles can extend across institutions in space and time, the more resistant they can become to attempts to change them.[11] For institutions gradually develop a 'longue durée', which both pre-exists the lives of individuals born into a particular society and also outlasts them.[12] We are, as John Holloway put it, born into a world that is always already pre-shaped 'before we begin to reflect critically'.[13] As they are institutionalised, structural principles are therefore immanent to everyday actions in a way that marks its 'immediate perceptions and behavioural orientation' (Hirsch). Angelika Wetterer accordingly also speaks in the context of the construction of gender of a 'relationship of concealment'[14] whereby the construction remains *systematically* hidden from those who develop it. For in routine everyday behaviour, relevant knowledge for activities, practical consciousness, is immune to the institutionalising structural principles that are already given from the outset.[15] Due to the longue durée those become plausible in the world of everyday life. Here the

11 Giddens 1986, p. 171.
12 Giddens, p. 170.
13 Holloway 2010, p. 49.
14 Wetterer 2002, p. 159.
15 Wetterer 2002, p. 160.

connection of the overall 'spectrality' of social conditions and their continual recreation in everyday behaviour – until they are 'unburdened' through their sedimentation in institutions – becomes clear.

1.3 *Apparatuses*

In addition to social forms and other technologies of power, there still remains to be examined materiality. The concept of the 'apparatus' allows both Poulantzas and Foucault, following Althusser, to describe the materiality and the external unity of certain practices. It appears therefore appropriate to follow Foucault and separate institutions analytically into apparatuses on the one hand and power technologies on the other. Here power technologies thus describe the respective effects of power (subjectivation, discipline, social cohesion, etc.), while the apparatuses represent the mechanisms of the internal momentum required. Ultimately institutions are also nothing other than social practices, but they temporarily fix those practices. For example, as the processes of the legal form reproduce and thus institutionalise themselves permanently through routinised practices, as they develop a differentiated court system, specialised jurists, a plurality of codified legal norms, a specific practice of legal argumentation and of filtering non-juridical 'reality', norm projections, legality and illegality etc., a legal world of its own emerges and gives rise to an interest in its own perpetuation, which is then articulated in the social practices of the legal actors, and most notably in bureaucracy.

That historically and spatially diverse legal apparatuses can come into conflict with each other and are marked by social contradictions, is plausibly described by Poulantzas. An interconnected ensemble of diverse apparatuses can only be created through a hegemonic project; it then shapes a specific social formation. It is, however, always possible to act in opposition to institutions, because their materiality is neither eternal nor insurmountable. There always remains 'scope for actions to overflow or circumvent structural constraints'.[16] Their success is nonetheless less likely and significantly harder, in particular for those who are disadvantaged by strategic selectivity. Moreover strategic and even routinised action can fail: '[b]ecause subjects are never unitary, never fully aware of the conditions of strategic action, never fully equipped to realise their preferred strategies, and always face possible opposition from actors pursuing other strategies or tactics'.[17]

16 Jessop 2004, p. 210.
17 Ibid.

2 On the Relationship of Law and State

The legal form is not only relationally autonomous with regard to the economic, but also to the political form. As can be seen especially in Blanke et. al., law's own density is recognised in the first, but not in the second case. It is therefore nothing but the medium through which the state can act upon society. Poulantzas' theory is similarly characterised by something of a 'state-surplus'. The reason is easy to see: modern, rational law and the modern nation state are deeply interwoven. Thus all legal institutions are organised by the state and the necessary enforceability of the law, the repressive side of legal technology, is tied to an extra-economic coercive force. At the same time the legal form limits the immediate coercive force of the state.[18] Luhmann holds that it is the obvious mutual dependence of the two systems, politics and law, that makes it difficult to discover their functional differentiation.[19] It is this institutional symbiosis that also leads to a legal-theoretical dilemma for materialist theory, namely to the inadequate analysis of the legal form. The impression is created that law is always implicitly included in the context of state-theoretical reflections. However, this actually negates its own materiality, which cannot be reduced to that of the state.

In order to make this 'differentiation' visible, I propose to distinguish between the necessary articulation of political form and legal form on the most abstract analytical level, that of *structural principles*, on the one hand, and the historically and spatially specific *institutional* form of law and nation state on the other. Those levels of analysis must not be mixed with each other, because then historical forms would be taken for structural principles.

Already on the level of the structural principles of *capitalist* societies it must be noted that both forms function independently, but at the same time refer to each other. The legal form is always also a process of reflection, in which every practice develops a relationship to itself. In specialist legal literature and comments or in court decisions, for example, questions of the attribution of actions to subject artefacts or collisions of social norms are discussed. Law is here a specific technology for reflection, which captures and legally encloses concrete social practices in the autonomous procedures of legal arguments. Law thus brings those practices together in a hegemonic order, and formalises them. It thus allows one to define a position that can then be again politically contested.[20] In terms of its content, the political form processes the art of beha-

18 Thus also Habermas 2006, p. 116.

19 Luhmann 2004, p. 162.

20 Similarly Puntscher Riekmann 1998, p. 139.

viour management and of governing the population. As Pashukanis shows, its formal democratic procedures reflect legal norms *publicly*. While the legal form thus codifies social practices and the norms arising from them juridically and brings them into a certain operationalisable form, the political form confronts in its processes the norms thus developed, with hegemonic struggles taking place in relation to the modalities of governance. Hegemony is inherent in different ways in both of the two forms.

In essence, juridical and political form refer to each other as structural principles of capitalist society, because in this mode of production legal technology is governmentalised. The political form functions not only in a hegemonic way, but is protected by the armour of coercion, as stressed in particular by Gramsci and Poulantzas. It forms together with coercive mechanisms *a possible* material support to make legal norms enforceable. This must, however, not obscure the fact that other technologies of power, such as – very clearly – discipline, are also involved in this enforcement. The political form thus includes a large pool of governmentalised power technologies, each of which the legal form is specifically coupled with.

The two forms can finally develop in different directions, for instance when the social structure of a society changes and political developments can no longer keep up due to a crisis, as Neumann and Kirchheimer emphasise. As such the political process is, as long as it is formally democratically organised, slower than the juridical one, which can start with the individual case. Under such conditions, struggles over the modalities of governance can shift predominately to fractures in the legal form's doctrinal reasoning, so that politically defined norms may retain the exact same wording even though their facticity has long since shifted.

On the institutional level, the historically specific connection of law and politics can be shown more clearly. Foucault demonstrates that the unity of state and law is a *historic* result. He highlights that the symbiosis of law and state only begins to take shape in the second half of the European Middle Ages with the concentration of legal power in the hands of the feudal lords. At this time one cannot yet speak of states in the modern sense. Therefore, for instance, Germanic law does not know any institutionalised political form, that is, no public entity that intervenes in legal disputes, 'there was no one – representing society, the group, authority, or the holder of power – charged with bringing accusations against individuals'.[21] Only in the twelfth and thirteenth

21 Foucault 2000, p. 34.

century does a legal form develop[22] that the powerful can resort to. As the circulation of goods, which occurred mainly through theft and war, is codified in legal disputes,[23] the powerful try to bring those legal disputes under their control in order to prevent those affected from managing their own affairs. Only now individuals have to submit to an external power. 'We thus see how state power appropriated the entire judicial procedure, the entire mechanism of interindividual settlement of disputes in the early Middle Ages'.[24]

As Max Weber shows, this institutionalisation process of the legal and political form reaches its peak in the modern state, which finally monopolises jurisprudence and physical violence. This means that since the developmental period of capitalist societies, when both the political and the legal form become key pillars of the social system, their evolution has been interconnected.[25] The institutionalisation of the legal form takes place in the institutional framework of the nation state as a historically specific shape of the political form.

Furthermore, the divergence of the two forms can be shown through the institutions: a good example for this is for instance the German Civil Code, which came into force in 1900, outlasted changing political regimes relatively unchanged, and whose most dynamic part, the law of obligations, was only altered a hundred years later. In the intervening century, however, jurisprudence had long since adapted the significance of the norms to the realities of the respective social structures.[26]

22 Foucault understands by 'legal form' not the form analytical category, but rather traditionally the form of the law.

23 Foucault 2000, p. 40.

24 Foucault 2000, p. 43.

25 Weber 1978, p. 1394.

26 See for example Knieper 1996.

PART 4

Self-government

CHAPTER 14

Introduction to Part 4

Revolution not only consummates evolution, but also corrects its course.[1]

∵

In the preceding chapters I have tried to demonstrate the insights a social-theoretically argued, reformulated materialist theory can contribute to analysing law. Understanding modern law as a technology of both subjectivation and cohesion makes it possible to reconnect forgotten Marxist approaches to contemporary debates in legal theory.

However, my research cannot end at this point. For, if the aim of a theory in the tradition of Karl Marx – as I noted in the introduction – is in fact a 'global constitution' beyond the dichotomy of materialism and idealism, wherein human beings make their own history, then the question of the emancipatory potential of the law becomes all the more urgent in light of current results.

I want to conclude by turning to this question. My answer will have to be cursory, as a comprehensive alternative concept would go beyond the scope of this work. Therefore, the concluding theses have a preliminary character and are mainly intended to underscore the consequences of the findings to date.

Law and emancipation are closely connected in the history of ideas. Rousseau already states that 'Obedience to a self-prescribed law is freedom'.[2] Kant rephrases this concept in such a way that only the people's lawgiving force can be the source of all law and not do anybody wrong, because all decide the same about everyone.[3] The democratic principle of theory and practice in the eighteenth century, to bring social conditions completely under the control of the social base, is a decisive change, a truly new matrix of the social imaginary.[4] This idea develops precisely at the moment when secularised pastoral power begins to rule the 'multitude' in its everyday practices as a 'population'.

1 Brunkhorst 2005, p. 6.
2 Rousseau 2002, p. 167.
3 Kant 1991, p. 125.
4 Laclau and Mouffe 200, p. 155.

Faced with this, eighteenth-century revolutionaries develop a radical concept of democracy which assumes that 'another world is possible',[5] a world in which, as Marx pointedly describes, those who are socialised are not *governed* but *govern themselves* in an association of free producers This concept of a self-organised society is from the outset described in the juridical code of power. The core of utopia is accordingly called *'popular sovereignty', which means the same as 'the social competence of self-legislation'*.[6] Here, the concept of the 'people' is a purely constitutional one. By juridically producing the 'people' it constitutes at the same time the democratic sovereign. 'People' is synonymous with the legal community and precisely an abstraction from descendance and soil, while in the twentieth century 'the National-Socialist abuse of the concept has won the day'.[7]

The advance of capitalist socialisation, as Habermas shows, makes the hope for an intentionally created and continuously sustained association gradually come to appear unrealistic.[8] Today, the radically democratic concepts of the eighteenth century are only measured against a criterion of political particip-ation which is already adapted to the bad reality.[9] The field of the political is limited to the administration of this social positivity. 'Now, without "utopia", without the possibility of negating an order beyond the point that we are able to threaten it', Laclau and Mouffe aptly write, 'there is no possibility at all of the constitution of a radical imaginary ...'[10] Therefore normative theories of law and Teubner's self-regulation approach also cling to the possibility of the 'democratic self-organization of a legal community',[11] in contrast to Luhmann's systems theory.

This normative telos of democratic social self-organisation also forms the basis of the present work: The association of free human beings is no liberal utopia, as Laclau and Mouffe think,[12] but the basic normative premise of a social theory following Marx. On that basis it is significant that people are not 'governed' in the social organisation of their lives, but that they can access the 'potential of an agreement between people and things'.[13]

---

5 Hardt and Negri 2004, p. 307.
6 Maus 1992b, p. 36.
7 Maus 2006, p. 475.
8 Habermas 1996, p. 46.
9 Maus 1992a, p. 8, similarly Hardt and Negri 2004, p. 307.
10 Laclau and Mouffe 2000, p. 190.
11 Habermas 1996, p. xli.
12 Laclau and Mouffe 2000, p. 145.
13 Adorno 1985, pp. 499–500.

Following the above findings, the concept of democratisation through law has to be shifted towards a democracy of law, or of the legal form. For the analysis of the legal form has shown that systems theory remains correct with regards to discourse theory insofar as law conceived of as a medium of self-organisation slips away from its authors.

The legal form becomes independent with respect to its producers just like the organisation of satisfying social needs does in the commodity, so that the emancipation of the subalterns, their capacity for self-government, is basically prevented.[14]

In concluding my research I will therefore attempt to develop on the final pages some considerations that such a shift would have to start with. Firstly, however, I want to look into the emancipatory potential of the legal form under current conditions, in order to afterwards look for a potential that exceeds this. This chapter is therefore about the 'possibilities for emancipatory politics both through law and against law'.[15]

---

14 Demirović 1997, p. 152.

15 Cutler 2005, p. 528.

CHAPTER 15

The Emancipatory Potential of Law

The 'mode of social self-programming'[1] *over* law, in the sense of a programming at the social base[2] that is afterwards realised by the state apparatuses, and which can only take on the form of machines of subsumption, is structurally undermined by the legal form. This, however, means nothing less than that the constitutional state and democracy truly belong under current conditions to Luhmann's hard to bear 'self-misunderstandings' of modernity. Franz Neumann and Otto Kirchheimer identified this structural deficit already early on, and at the same time showed with great clarity that its final consequence can be the instauration of a terror regime during the secular crises of capitalism.

Although the law cannot itself satisfy the demands for the legitimation of its own self-description in capitalist societies, it nonetheless produces three effects that must not be underestimated:

1 Formal Recognition

As has been shown, the legal form contributes significantly to subjectivation. In the abstract generalisation that is the legal subject, it produces the ambivalent effect of formally recognising individuals as equal and free. Maihofer stresses that this at least formally reciprocal recognition takes place as lived practice, and is therefore no 'mere ideology', but has a material existence.[3] Even if the legal form only connects 'windowless monads', and thus exclusively recognises them according to the 'principle of singularity',[4] 'the law's minimal guarantees of recognition' allow at least for the personal characteristics of each subject to be taken into consideration.[5] That this is not a matter of course can be seen in the struggles of the first and also the second wave of the women's movement, which had to fight for this status for women in the first place.[6] This also

1 Frankenberg 2003, p. 8.
2 Maus 1992a, p. 178.
3 Maihofer 1992, p. 195.
4 Honneth 1989.
5 Honneth 2008, p. 80.
6 See Dackweiler 1995; Holland-Cunz 2003.

demonstrates that while the legal form produces legal subjectivity, its enforcement nonetheless always depends on social struggles.

The obverse, however, consists in that this formal form of recognising the particularity of subjects is abstracted and at the same time solidifies the fiction of the sovereign, uniform individual and thus 'a specifically masculinist discourse of rights'. From a feminist perspective the law is thus a deeply paradoxical medium: 'rights secure our standing as individuals even as they obscure the treacherous ways that standing is achieved and regulated'.[7]

2 A Technology of Knowledge

I have attempted to show that capitalist socialisation disposes only of rudimentary procedures for its self-enlightenment. The legal form is such a procedure, in which the individuals can begin to dispose of limited knowledge about their own social context. Even if this knowledge presents itself in the juridical code and is potentially only accessible for a small elite of knowledge workers, the legal form nonetheless, on the one hand, preserves a given society's current level of reflection and, on the other, offers a procedure for developing it further.

Legal argumentation far beyond the current social formation, such as for instance Roman legal instruments, can be followed in legal history and reflected in legal theory. They thus offer a reservoir of insights from contemporary and past societies, which includes their respective antagonistic conflicts and hegemonic projects. However, positions which have not become hegemonic are thus coded as illegal. Antagonistic de-paradoxification produces as its effect the legal and the illegal and thus 'subjugated knowledges'.[8]

3 Deferral of Power

The legal form's most important effect is its deferral of power, which reveals time and again its inherent ambivalence beneath its reified procedures. A direct result of its processes of abstraction and autonomisation, this at the same time prevents social self-organisation. When antagonisms can be processed through the social forms, they leave power relations intact, but *simultaneously* transcend their immediate potential for violence. They force confrontations

7 Brown 2002, pp. 430–1.
8 Foucault 2003, p. 7.

into a formal procedure, which blocks or delays the immediate exercise of domination, such as the 'law' of the stronger. Those processes require argument and reason, and also predefine lines of argument in terms of their sequence and form. Furthermore, social mechanisms of protection are sedimented within them, such as the principle of legality in penal law, or that decisions can be challenged across several instances.

At the same time, the autonomisation and the relational 'life of its own' of the legal form also represent a shift in those power relations. As an independent technique of consensus, the legal form thus provides for the functioning of hegemony a lever to generalise interests. In consequence, weaker forces can also always draw upon the legal form. Social relations of forces therefore inscribe themselves in the legal form in a *relational manner* only to the extent that a certain norm can become hegemonic.

The rights that are realised and materialised in the legal form, in particular due to their independent existence, cannot simply be circumvented; they therefore do indeed constitute 'weapons' in social conflicts – ones that are also available to the weaker positions.

In particular the double character of the legal form, of representing on the one hand a structural obstacle to social emancipation, and on the other at least a postponement of, if not even protection from immediate violence, constitutes its complexity, which cannot be theoretically resolved in one way.

Attempts by lawyers to shift political power relations by strategic reference to law are numerous: they are based on precisely the legal form's 'inner logic of its own'. Especially in the US, there is a successful political practice in the tradition of the civil rights movement, which uses, for example, the courts as a forum for protests. As elements of a political campaign, court cases allow one to draw upon the inherently political content of all juridical procedures. Along the cracks of juridical legal figures, a politicising practice of translation can reveal their political character. Meanwhile various legal think tanks have also been founded in Europe that employ the particular logic of law in order, by means of strategic court procedures, to shift political relations of domination. These include the European Center for Constitutional and Human Rights in Berlin or the AIRE Centre (Advice on Individual Rights in Europe) in London. The Hungarian Helsinki Committee in Budapest is even under political attack due to its legal success. Their goal is not limited to victories in court, but aims to mobilise a social movement, making it possible to have a 'success without victory' – a political success without a legal victory.[9]

9 Lobel 2004.

Compared to immediate relations of force, the legal form also has to be interpreted as a social achievement as understood by Franz Neumann. Oskar Negt insists that 'whenever merely formal justice is overcome, but this does not surpass and lead beyond its limited level of emancipation …' this represents 'a historic relapse'.[10] This is also the issue raised in critiques of Pashukanis' 'withering away' thesis, as it is seen to underestimate the proactive dimension of law. A withering away then necessarily leads to a return of the power of the stronger and to lynch law. Regardless of other issues with the withering away thesis, this critique, however, misses its mark. A withering away of the legal form *under capitalism* would effectively lead to those processes. Neumann had described National Socialism precisely as such a capitalist society under a state of exception, and thus as one with neither legal nor political form. This, however, must not lead to an eternal perpetuation of the legal form, including its 'negative side', for all future social formations.

10 Negt 1975, p. 44.

CHAPTER 16

The Extension of Democracy

1 Exiting the Juridical Concept of Democracy

Following the above considerations, the consequences for a democratisation of social conditions are obvious. It is very much crucial to leave the *juridical concept of democracy* behind, for two interconnected reasons.

The first follows immediately from the above reflections. In capitalist societies law is not a neutral medium of mediation between self-legislation and political implementation, but an independent technology of cohesion. It thus slips away from the grasp of those who produce it day-by-day and confronts them as a technology of power. Those reified and naturalised forms of social conditions signal that modern bourgeois society has no or only very rudimentary procedures of self-enlightenment and collective self-government. When engaging with Habermas' theory I already reached the conclusion that this presents a central barrier for democratic organisation, and that this must not be tolerated in an expertocratic fashion.

The second reason follows from Foucault's critique. The legal form is 'only' the official code of power and hides the other technologies of power in its operations: disciplines, biopolitical regulation through security *dispositifs*, governmental control. Subjectivation does not only take place through the law, but very crucially through the whole of the modern subjectivation regime. One can already see similar concerns in discourses of the 1920s and 30s which demand an extension of democracy to the factories, or in the women's movements' assertion that the personal is political. A democratization of official politics alone is based on the misunderstanding that a juridical theory of power consists in situating power relations not within society, but solely in the 'political system'. This is itself already an effect of power.

Taken together, the reification of social relations as well as the plurality of power technologies both show what is at stake in leaving behind the paradigm of juridical democratic theory – a fundamental extension of the concept of democracy. This means that what matters is to develop procedures that make subjects not only the authors of their own laws, but of the network of political conditions that surround them. The idea of 'self-legislation' is thus transferred to plural social spaces: '*Democracy then ceases* here *to be only a political condition and becomes the condition of society as a whole* …'[1] This corresponds

1 Abendroth 1968, p. 139.

to a shift in the concept of 'democratic positivism',[2] namely the idea that an 'adequate constitutional theory' can today

> hardly be anything but an extension of this procedural principle [the correctness of the decision is inferred from its democratic organizational form] to the context of the social totality, as self-determination understood as 'total'.[3]

The 'profound subversive power of the democratic discourse' lies, as Laclau and Mouffe rightly note, precisely in the extension of equality and freedom to increasingly wider domains. 'It can act as a fermenting agent upon the different forms of struggle against subordination'.[4] An emancipatory project therefore has to situate itself entirely on the terrain of democratic revolution: 'It is not in the abandonment of the democratic terrain, but, on the contrary, in the extension of the field of democratic struggles to the whole of civil society and the state, that the possibility resides for a hegemonic strategy of the Left'.[5]

2 A Counter-Hegemonic Democratic Project

The question as to how a society without social forms and other objectifications, a society without discipline, or the abolition of all relations of subjugation would be possible, leads necessarily to antinomies, as all ideas about another socialisation are burdened by the ways of thinking and the practices of contemporary society. One can only speculate 'on the state of reconciliation',[6] that is, one can make somewhat general statements based on a negation of present conditions.

A good example for this is, for instance, a question from a discussion shared by Isaac D. Balbus[7] about how conflicts are to be resolved at all after a 'withering away' of the law. The problem with this question lies in the fact that it extends today's conflicts into the future. It presupposes an ontology of antagonisms as given, similarly to Chantal Mouffe's theory of democracy, which, in explaining

2 Niesen and Eberl 2006.
3 Maus 1976, p. 17.
4 Laclau and Mouffe 2000, p. 155.
5 Laclau and Mouffe 1985, p. 176.
6 Adorno 1985, p. 499.
7 Balbus 1977, p. 583.

this idea, tellingly follows Carl Schmitt's *Concept of the Political*. She opposes the 'ineradicable character of antagonism' that shows itself in the 'inescapable moment of decision', to Habermas' concept of a rational consensus.[8] In doing so, however, she neither does Habermas justice – who after all founds the conditions for the possibility of a rational consensus on language – nor does she succeed in conceptualising antagonistic relations as a *historically contingent* form of human relations.

The second problem with this line of argument consists in that law is here essentially described as an entity for conflict resolution. Against this Luhmann already rightly raised the objection that there are many social equivalents for this. Moreover, one can further note with Foucault that all technologies of subjectivation contribute to the containment and production of social conflicts. However, if one seriously holds that, aside from its way of subjectivation, the legal form is above all a technology of cohesion, then the question as to the significance of the law's withering away has to focus less on conflicts than on social cohesion beyond law.

The third difficulty resides in the fact that this viewpoint is not oriented towards process. To ask in the here and now how a socialisation without social forms, and thus also without the legal form, can be thought, poses this question from a perspective that only considers abolition, but not the path towards it. This is in principle based on a 'Jacobine' concept of revolution, which implies that the revolutionary act has a foundational character, and that power is concentrated at one point from which society can be reorganised.[9] This would, however, mean that all the various technologies of power and all relations of oppression would have to be eroded at the same time, which is ultimately only possible if they can all be attributed to a common cause. But this assumption has been rejected as reductionist in the present study.

What has to be considered instead is democracy as a process, that is to say democratisation. This is the possible content of an emancipatory, counter-hegemonic project that organises alternative practices in all social spaces. As a counter-hegemonic project its essential features are themselves already democratic, because it has to be oriented towards articulating multiple struggles against different types of oppression.

At the centre is the question of alternative forms of subjectivation and cohesion which can oppose governmental control. That is, which ways of subjectivation can be imagined that would bring forth *social* subjects, and through what

8 Mouffe 2005, pp. 10–1.

9 Laclau and Mouffe 2000, p. 177.

mechanisms would the social itself have to be produced – the 'common', in the language of Hardt and Negri?[10]

As I have argued, juridical and political technologies of cohesion unify the social monads in the people-as-nation. How could forms of collective life and the composition of public life instead be organised as the work of an irreducible plurality? Paolo Virno suggests that we once again make methodologically productive Spinoza's concept of the multitudo, which was once opposed to the concept of 'people'. While 'people' stands precisely for unification, the term multitude encompasses the political form of existence of the many as many,[11] a non-representative form of democracy, a 'republic of the multitude'.[12]

This republic of associated individuals above all has to 'place the still natural capitalist division of labour … itself at the disposal of collective self-determination. Only this would make it possible to rationalise processes of collective will formation and procedures of generalization and to develop a new type of general will, making control and governance unnecessary'.[13]

Michael Hardt and Antonio Negri assume, like Virno, that post-Fordist socialisation requires a level of self-organisation that subjectifies producers in a paradoxical manner: on the one hand communicative, relationship-intensive, cooperative and inventive abilities become a component of labour power.[14] Thus the means of production in immaterial labour are transferred into the subjects; that is, into knowledge, communication, affects and information.[15] At the same time, however, those abilities are demanded in an authoritarian manner as technologies of the self: 'Become subjects!'[16] Those engaged in immaterial labour 'must consult and engage in discussion; they must be able to express themselves and listen; they must be ready to question their own assumptions, to learn, and to develop continually'.[17]

Hardt und Negri then assume that it is possible to take this subjectivation as the starting point for another socialisation, because individuals develop with it 'cooperative autonomy', although under current relations of domination this is regulated and controlled.[18] They thus suggest a potential for self-government in the area of production and reach the conclusion that

10 Hardt and Negri 2004, pp. 196–7.
11 Virno 2004, p. 21.
12 Virno 2004, p. 69.
13 Demirović 1997, p. 163.
14 Thus also Gorz 1999, pp. 61–2.
15 Hardt and Negri 1994, p. 13.
16 Lazzarato 1996, p. 35.
17 Gorz 1999, p. 30.
18 Hardt and Negri 2000, p. 392.

> What the multitude produces is not just goods or services; the multitude also and most importantly produces cooperation, communication, forms of life, and social relationships. The economic production of the multitude, in other words, is not only a *model* for political decision-making but also tends itself to *become* decision-making.[19]

This concept is not unproblematic, because its precondition is authoritarian subjectivation. On the other hand, relations of domination are as such hardly likely to produce a better starting point. This approach points at least methodologically in the direction of an alternative production of the 'common'. It abandons juridical concepts of democracy and asks for possibilities of 'self-legislation' beyond the law, for alternative forms of subjectivation. For only social subjectivation can lead to the 'withering away' of social forms, in which subjects, as Hegel already writes, can understand other subjects not as the limit, but the condition of their own freedom, in the 'association of free individuals'.[20]

The changing social division of labour is, however, only one aspect of a counter-hegemonic project 'as it is necessary to put an end to capitalist relations of production, which are at the root of numerous relations of subordination; but socialism is *one* of the components of a project for radical democracy, not vice versa'.[21]

In addition to an alternative practice of cohesion or as its second dimension, new forms of subjectivity have to be developed, as Foucault demanded, 'through the refusal of this kind of individuality which has been imposed on us for several centuries', and to 'imagine and to build up what we could be'.[22] This would mean a reworking of the constituting matrix of power. Following Foucault, Butler sees the potential for this in that the subject is never completely constituted, but has to be subjected and produced time and again. There is therefore the 'permanent possibility of a certain resignifying process'.[23]

John Holloway pursues a similar strategy by insisting that social forms are not unalterable facts, but 'raging, bloody battlefields'.[24] It has become clear that the legal form has to be produced in everyday routines, that its structure is one of sedimented practices, and that paradox lurks within the it. 'The existence of forms of social relations, in other words, cannot be separated from their con-

19 Hardt and Negri 2004, p. 339 (emphasis in original).
20 See also Becker and Brakemeuer 2004.
21 Laclau and Mouffe 2000, p. 178.
22 Foucault 1982, p. 785.
23 Butler 1992, p. 13.
24 Holloway 2010, p. 90.

stitution. Their existence is their constitution, a constantly renewed struggle against the forces that subvert them'.[25] Holloway makes this clear for the value form in the everyday behaviours of the actors:

> Every time a small child takes sweets from a shop without realising that money has to be given in exchange for them, every time workers refuse to accept that the market dictates that their place of work should be closed or jobs lost, every time that the shopkeepers of São Paulo promote the killing of street children to protect their property, every time that we lock our bicycles, cars or houses – value as a form of relating to one another is at issue, constantly the object of struggle, constantly in process of being disrupted, reconstituted and disrupted again.[26]

In parallel to alternative forms of collectively producing the social, what matters are thus counter-hegemonic everyday routines. The daily, micro-political technologies of the self that create social forms, genders, sexualities, madness and so on, have to be accessible to procedures, which allow us to reflect on and collectively 'reinterpret' them.

Therefore, a counter-hegemonic project that can gradually shift the conditions of mutually isolated subjects would be crucial in order for them to be able to leave their 'habitually ossified perspective', which prevents them from empathetically engaging with other persons and occurrences.[27] This could make superfluous mediations such as that of the legal form. The articulation of different struggles for recognition in one counter-hegemonic project would be the 'attempt to establish, institutionally and culturally, expanded forms of reciprocal recognition'.[28] In doing so, those collective struggles at the same time have to anticipate the recognition they are denied under prevailing conditions.[29]

3 The Democratisation of the Law

In conclusion, the question of the role of the legal form in this project remains. It will not be possible to give it up overnight. The social forms would have to be

25 Holloway 2010, p. 91.
26 Holloway 2010, p. 90.
27 Honneth 2008, p. 53.
28 Honneth 1995, p. 93.
29 Honneth 1995, p. 164.

gradually framed by democratic procedures that consciously deal with those forms. For the legal form this means that procedures have to be created that use its limited character as a process for reflection and recognition, and at the same time lift it out of its sphere of a secret science.

Poulantzas has pointed out that the legal knowledge demanded of every citizen is not even covered in a special class in school. This makes subjects dependent on and subordinated to a small elite of legal experts: 'Modern law is a *state secret* which grounds a form of knowledge monopolised for reasons of State'.[30]

First of all, therefore – and by no means only through the discipline of the school – the knowledge stored up in the legal form as well as the procedures of its production would have to be democratised, so that the subaltern gain the ability to use strategic selectivity and thus at the same time shift it. This depends upon exposing the autonomisation mechanisms of the legal form, that is, the procedures of juridical argumentation. This would amount to 'demystifying the legal world', as Rudolf Wiethölter demanded already in 1968, and to effectively demythologise the legal juggling with systematics and dogmatics[31] in a 'decoding' of legal fetishism as envisioned by Balbus.

Only once comprehensive legal knowledge circulates in society such that it can be used strategically, only then could there begin a social debate about the meaning of such a technology for cohesion, which today mainly takes place behind the backs of the individuals. Legal procedures therefore have to be changed so that their results can be verified by everyone and their hegemonic decisions exposed. Then those are really 'just-ifications' [*'Recht-Fertigungen'*].[32]

Yet, once again, this is no plea for some kind of 'lawyers' socialism', but merely the first step towards a democratisation of the legal form. Without parallel emancipatory subjectivation and alternative social cohesion, such a transformation would lead nowhere.

30 Poulantzas 2000, p. 90.
31 Wiethölter 1968, p. 26.
32 Wiethölter 2005, p. 75.

Bibliography

Abendroth, Wolfgang 1968, 'Zum Begriff des demokratischen und sozialen Rechtsstaates im Grundgesetz der Bundesrepublik Deutschland', in *Rechtsstaatlichkeit und Sozialstaatlichkeit*, edited by Ernst Forsthoff, Darmstadt: Wissenschaftliche Buchgesellschaft.

Adler, Max 1964 [1922], *Die Staatsauffassung des Marxismus. Ein Beitrag zur Unterscheidung von soziologischer und juristischer Methode*, Darmstadt: Wissenschaftliche Buchgesellschaft.

Adolphs, Stefan 2003, *Der Staat nach der Krise des Fordismus – Nicos Poulantzas und Michel Foucault im Vergleich*, Frankfurt am Main: Goethe-University (unpublished PhD dissertation).

Adolphs, Stefan 2007, 'Biopolitik und die anti-passive Revolution der Multitude', in *Empire und die biopolitische Wende*, edited by Marianne Pieper, Thomas Atzert et al., Frankfurt am Main: Campus.

Adolphs, Stefan, Wolfgang Hörbe and Alexandra Rau 2002, 'Der Begriff des politischen Subjekts hat seinen Gehalt verändert', *Subtropen*, 16/08, 8 August 2002.

Adorno, Theodor W. 1974, *Philosophische Terminologie II*, Frankfurt am Main: Suhrkamp.

Adorno, Theodor W. 1985, 'Subject and Object', *The Essential Frankfurt School Reader*, edited by Andrew Arato and Heike Gebhardt, New York: Continuum.

Adorno, Theodore W. 1989, 'Society', in *Critical Theory and Society: A Reader*, edited by Stephen Eric Bronner and Douglas MacKay, translated by F.R. Jameson, London and New York: Routledge.

Adorno, Theodore W. 2000a, *Introduction to Sociology*, edited by Christoph Gödde, translated by Edmund Jephcot, Stanford, CA: Stanford University Press.

Adorno, Theodore W. 2000b [1973], *Negative Dialectics*, translated by E.B. Ashton, London and New York: Routledge.

Adorno, Theodor W. 2001, *Kant's Critique of Pure Reason*, edited by Rolf Tiedemann, translated by Rodney Livingstone, Stanford, CA: Stanford University Press.

Adorno, Theodor W. 2008, *Lectures on Negative Dialectics. Fragments of a Lecture Course 1965/1966*, edited by Rolf Tiedemann, translated by Rodney Livingstone, Cambridge: Polity Press.

Adorno, Theodor W. 2018 [1960/61], Ontology and Dialectics, edited by Rolf Tiedemann, translated by Nicholas Walker, Cambridge: Polity Press.

Adorno, Theodore W., Verena Erlenbusch-Anderson and Chris O'Kane 2018, 'Marx and the Basic Concepts of Sociological Theory. From a Seminar Transcript in the Summer Semester of 1962', *Historical Materialism*, 26, 1: 154–64.

Agamben, Giorgio 1998, *Homo Sacer: Sovereign Power and Bare Life*, translated by Daniel Heller-Roazen, Stanford, CA: Stanford University Press.

Alexy, Robert 1989, *A Theory of Legal Argumentation. The Theory of Rational Discourse as Theory of Legal Justification*, translated by Ruth Adler and Neil MacCormick, Oxford: Oxford University Press.

Althusser, Louis 2005 [1969], *For Marx*, translated by Ben Brewster, London and New York: Verso.

Althusser, Louis 1984 [1970], 'Ideology and Ideological State Apparatuses (Notes towards an Investigation)', in *Essays on Ideology*, London: Verso.

Althusser, Louis 1978, 'The Crisis of Marxism', *Marxism Today*, July 1978, 215–220, 227.

Anderson, Perry 1976, 'The Antinomies of Antonio Gramsci', *New Left Review*, I, 100: 5–78.

Arthur, Chris 1978, 'Introduction', in *Law and Marxism: A General Theory*, by Evgeny Pashukanis, Ink Links: London.

Backhaus, Hans-Georg 1980, 'On the Dialectics of the Value-Form', *Thesis Eleven*, 1, 1: 99–120.

Backhaus, Hans-Georg 1997, 'Zuvor: Die Anfänge der neuen Marx-Lektüre', in *Dialektik der Wertform: Untersuchungen zur Marxschen Ökonomiekritik*, Freiburg, Ça ira.

Bader, Veith-Michael 1977, 'Kritik an Burkhard Tuschling: Rechtsform und Produktionsverhältnisse. Zur materialistischen Theorie des Rechtsstaats', in *Abendroth Forum: Marburger Gespräche aus Anlaß des 70. Geburtstages von Wolfgang Abendroth*, edited by Frank Deppe et al., Marburg: Arbeiterbewegung und Gesellschaftswissenschaft.

Balbus, Isaac D. 1977, 'Commodity Form and Legal Form: an Essay on the "Relative Autonomy" of the Law', *Law and Society Review*, 11: 571–88.

Balibar, Étienne 1992, 'Foucault and Marx: the Question of Nominalism', in *Michel Foucault: Philosopher*, edited by Timothy J. Armstrong, Hemel Hempstead: Harvester Wheatsheaf.

Balibar, Étienne and Immanuel Wallerstein 1991, *Race, Nation, Class: Ambiguous Identities*, translation of Étienne Balibar by Chris Turner, London and New York: Verso.

Bast, Jürgen 1999, *Totalitärer Pluralismus. Zu Franz L. Neumanns Analysen der politischen und rechtlichen Struktur der NS-Herrschaft*, Tübingen: Mohr Siebeck.

Becker, Jens and Heinz Brakemeier (eds.) 2004, *Vereinigung freier Individuen. Kritik der Tauschgesellschaft und gesellschaftliches Gesamtsubjekt bei Theodor W. Adorno*, Hamburg: VSA.

Becker-Schmidt, Regina 1990, 'Individuum, Klasse und Geschlecht aus der Perspektive der Kritischen Theorie', in *Die Modernisierung moderner Gesellschaften. Verhandlungen des 25. Deutschen Soziologentages in Frankfurt am Main 1990*, edited by Wolfgang Zapf, Frankfurt am Main: Campus.

Beer, Ursula 1990, *Geschlecht, Struktur, Geschichte. Soziale Konstituierung des Geschlechterverhältnisses*, Frankfurt am Main: Campus.

Benhabib, Seyla 1988, 'Feminism and Postmodernism: An Uneasy Alliance', in *Feminist*

Contentions. A Philosophical Exchange, by Seyla Benhabib, Judith Butler et al., London and New York: Routledge.

Biebricher, Thomas 2006, 'Macht und Recht: Foucault', in *Neue Theorien des Rechts*, edited by Sonja Buckel, Ralph Christensen and Andreas Fischer-Lescano, Stuttgart: Lucius & Lucius.

Bieling, Hans Jürgen 2001, 'Sozialstruktur und gesellschaftliche Entwicklung: zwischen funktionaler Differenzierung und kapitalistischer Organisationsstruktur', in *Komplexität und Emanzipation. Kritische Gesellschaftstheorie und die Herausforderung der Systemtheorie Niklas Luhmanns*, edited by Alex Demirović, Münster: Westfälisches Dampfboot.

Bieling, Hans-Jürgen and Jochen Steinhilber 2000, 'Hegemoniale Projekte im Prozess der europäischen Integration', in *Die Konfiguration Europas. Dimensionen einer kritischen Integrationstheorie*, edited by Hans-Jürgen Bieling and Jochen Steinhilber, Münster: Westfälisches Dampfboot.

Blanke, Bernhard 1975, 'Theorien zum Verhältnis von Staat und Gesellschaft', in *Kritik der Politischen Wissenschaft. Analysen von Politik und Ökonomie in der bürgerlichen Gesellschaft*, edited by Bernhard Blanke, Ulrich Jürgens and Hans Kastendiek, Frankfurt am Main: Campus.

Blanke, Bernhard, Ulrich Jürgens and Hans Kastendiek 1974, 'Zur neueren marxistischen Diskussion über die Analyse von Form und Funktion des bürgerlichen Staates, Überlegungen zum Verhältnis von Politik und Ökonomie', *Prokla*, 14/15: 51–102.

Blanke, Thomas 1984, 'Kirchheimer, Neumann, Preuß: Die Radikalisierung der Rechtstheorie', in *Recht, Demokratie und Kapitalismus. Aktualität und Probleme der Theorie Franz L. Neumanns*, edited by Joachim Perels, Baden-Baden: Nomos.

Bolsinger, Eckard 2001, 'Autonomie des Rechts? Niklas Luhmann's soziologischer Rechtspositivsmus – Eine kritische Rekonstruktion', *Politische Vierteljahresschrift*, 42: 1: 3–29.

Bommes, Michael 1999, *Migration und nationaler Wohlfahrtsstaat. Ein differenzierungstheoretischer Entwurf*, Opladen: Westdeutscher Verlag.

Brand, Ulrich and Christoph Görg 2003, *Postfordistische Naturverhältnisse. Konflikte um genetische Ressourcen und die Internationalisierung des Staates*. Münster: Westfälisches Dampfboot.

Brentel, Helmut 1989, *Soziale Form und ökonomisches Objekt: Studien zum Gegenstands- und Methodenverständnis der Kritik der politischen Ökonomie*. Opladen: Westdeutscher Verlag.

Bröckling, Ulrich 2003, 'Das demokratisierte Panopticon. Subjektivierung und Kontrolle im 360°-Feedback', in *Michel Foucault. Zwischenbilanz einer Rezeption. Frankfurter Foucault-Konferenz 2001*, edited by Axel Honneth and Martin Saar, Frankfurt am Main: Suhrkamp.

Brodocz, Andre 2003, *Die symbolische Dimension der Verfassung. Ein Beitrag zur Institutionentheorie*, Wiesbaden: Westdeutscher Verlag.

Brown, Wendy 2002, 'Suffering the Paradoxes of Rights', in *Left Legalism/Left Critique*, edited by Wendy Brown and Janet Halley, Durham, NC and London: Duke University Press.

Brunkhorst, Hauke 2005, *Solidarity. From Civic Friendship to a Global Legal Community*, translated by Jeffrey Flynn, Boston, MA: The MIT Press.

Brunkhorst, Hauke 2005, 'Demokratie in der globalen Rechtsgenossenschaft. Einige Überlegungen zur poststaatlichen Verfassung der Weltgesellschaft', in *Zeitschrift für Soziologie*; special issue *'Weltgesellschaft'*, 34: 330–47.

Brunner, Georg 2005, 'Sexualität und Spätkapitalismus – revisited? Queer-politische Praktiken im Kontext neoliberaler Verhältnisse', in *femina politica*, 1: 82–92.

Bublitz, Hannelore 2001, 'Geschlecht als historisch singuläres Ereignis: Foucaults poststrukturalistischer Beitrag zu einer Gesellschafts-Theorie der Geschlechterverhältnisse', in *Soziale Verortung der Geschlechter. Gesellschaftstheorie und feministische Kritik*, edited by Gudrun-Axeli Knapp and Angelika Wetterer, Münster: Westfälisches Dampfboot.

Bublitz, Hannelore 2003, *Diskurs*, Bielefeld: Transcript.

Buci-Glucksmann, Christine 1980, *Gramsci and the State*, translated by David Fernbach, London: Lawrence and Wishart.

Buci-Glucksmann, Christine and Göran Therborn 1982, *Der sozialdemokratische Staat. Die 'Keynesianisierung' der Gesellschaft*, Hamburg: VSA.

Buckel, Sonja 2002, 'Die Mechanik der Macht in der juristischen Ausbildung', in *Kritische Justiz*, 35, 1: 111–4.

Buckel, Sonja, 2003, 'Global None-State. Ansätze für eine materialistische Theorie des globalen Rechts', in *Formen und Felder politischer Intervention. Zur Relevanz von Staat und Steuerung*, edited by Sonja Buckel, Regina-Maria Dackweiler and Ronald Noppe, Münster: Westfälisches Dampfboot.

Buckel, Sonja 2006, 'Neo-materialistische Rechtstheorie', in *Neue Theorien des Rechts*, edited by Sonja Buckel, Ralph Christensen and Andreas Fischer-Lescano, Stuttgart: Lucius & Lucius.

Buckel, Sonja 2007, '"Judge without a legislator" – Transnationalisierung der Rechtsform', in *Völkerrechtspolitik. Hans Kelsens Staatsverständnis*, edited by Hauke Brunkhorst and Rüdiger Voigt, Baden-Baden: Nomos.

Buckel, Sonja and Fischer-Lescano Andreas (eds.) 2007, *Hegemonie gepanzert mit Zwang. Politik und Zivilgesellschaft im Staatsverständnis Antonio Gramscis*, Baden-Baden: Nomos.

Buckel, Sonja and Fischer-Lescano Andreas 2009, 'Gramsci Reconsidered: Hegemony in Global Law', *Leiden Journal of International Law*, 22, 3: 437–54.

Buckel, Sonja, Ralph Christensen and Andreas Fischer-Lescano (eds.) 2006, *Neue Theorien des Rechts*, Stuttgart: Lucius & Lucius.

Buckel, Sonja and John Kannankulam 2002, 'Zur Kritik der Anti-Terror-Gesetze nach dem "11. Septembers". "Sicherheit" im postfordistischen Präventionsstaat', *Das Argument*, 244, 1: 34–50.

Buckel, Sonja and Jens Wissel 2002, 'Im Namen des Empire: Sie sind Biomacht!', *ak analyse & kritik*, 462.

Bührmann, Andrea 2004, *Der Kampf um weibliche Individualität. Zur Transformation moderner Subjektivierungsweisen in Deutschland um 1900*, Münster: Westfälisches Dampfboot.

Butler, Judith 1992, 'Contingent Foundations: Feminism and the Question of "Postmodernism"', in *Feminists Theorise the Political*, edited by Judith Butler and Jean W. Scott, London and New York: Routledge.

Butler, Judith 2002 [1990], *Gender Trouble. Feminism and the Subversion of Identity*, London and New York: Routledge.

Butler, Judith 1997, *The Psychic Life of Power. Theories in Subjection*, Stanford, CA: Stanford University Press.

Calliess, Gralf-Peter 2006, 'Systemtheorie. Luhmann/Teubner', in *Neue Theorien des Rechts*, edited by Sonja Buckel, Ralph Christensen, Andreas Fischer-Lescano, Stuttgart: Lucius & Lucius.

Charim, Isolde 2002, *Der Althusser-Effekt. Entwurf einer Ideologietheorie*, Wien: Passagen.

Cohen, Jean L. 1995, 'Critical Social Theory and Feminist Critiques: The Debate with Jürgen Habermas', in *Feminists read Habermas. Gendering tbe Subject of Discourse*, edited by Johanna Meehan, London and New York: Routledge.

Cox, Robert W. 1983, 'Gramsci, Hegemony and International Relations: An Essay in Method', *Millenium: Journal of International Studies*, Volume 12, 2: 162–75.

Crenshaw, Kimberlé 1989, 'Demarginalising the Intersection of Race and Sex: A Black Feminist Critique of Anti-Discrimination Doctrine, Feminist Theory and Antiracist Politics', in *Feminist Theory and Antiracist Politics, University of Chicago Legal Forum*, 1989: 139–67.

Cutler, A. Claire 2005, 'Gramsci, Law, and the Culture of Global Capitalism', in *Critical Review of International Social and Political Philosophy*, 8, 4: 527–42.

Dackweiler, Regina 1995, *Ausgegrenzt und Eingemeindet. Die neue Frauenbewegung im Blick der Sozialwissenschaften*, Münster: Westfälisches Dampfboot.

Dackweiler, Regina-Maria 2002, 'Staatliche Rechtspolitik als geschlechterpolitische Handlungs- und Diskursarena. Zum Verrechtlichungsprozess von Vergewaltigung in der Ehe', in *Gewalt-Verhältnisse. Feministische Perspektiven auf Geschlecht und Gewalt*, edited by Regina-Maria Dackweiler and Reihild Schäfer, Frankfurt am Main: Campus.

Dackweiler, Regina-Maria 2003, 'Zur Analyse wohlfahrtsstaatlicher Geschlechterregime', in *Formen und Felder politischer Intervention. Zur Relevanz von Staat und*

Steuerung, edited by Sonja Buckel, Regina-Maria Dackweiler and Ronald Noppe, Münster: Westfälisches Dampfboot.

Daniel, Claus 1983, *Hegel verstehen. Eine Einführung in sein Denken*. Frankfurt am Main: Campus.

Demirović, Alex 1987, *Nicos Poulantzas. Eine kritische Auseinandersetzung*. Berlin: Argument.

Demirović, Alex 1997, 'Zivilgesellschaft, Öffentlichkeit, Demokratie', in *Demokratie und Herrschaft. Aspekte kritischer Gesellschaftstheorie*, edited by Alex Demirović, Münster: Westfälisches Dampfboot.

Demirović, Alex 2001a, 'Hegemoniale Projekte und die Rolle der Intellektuellen', *Das Argument*, 239: 59–65.

Demirović, Alex 2001b, 'Komplexität und Emanzipation', in *Komplexität und Emanzipation. Kritische Gesellschaftstheorie und die Herausforderung der Systemtheorie Niklas Luhmans*, edited by Alex Demirović, Münster: Westfälisches Dampfboot.

Demirović, Alex 2003, 'Demokratie, Politik und Staat in der transformistischen Gesellschaft. Vergleichende Anmerkungen zu den Gesellschaftstheorien Niklas Luhmanns und Jürgen Habermas', in *Das System der Politik. Niklas Luhmanns politische Theorie*, edited by Kai-Uwe Hellmann, Karsten Fischer and Harald Bluhm, Wiesbaden: Westdeutscher Verlag.

Derrida, Jacques 1991, 'Force of Law: "The Mystical Foundation of Authority"', *Cardozo Law Review*, 11, 5/6: 920–1045.

Derrida, Jacques 1994, *Specters of Marx. The State of the Debt, the Work of Mourning and the New International*, translated by Peggy Kamuf, New York and London: Routledge.

Dosse, François 1998a, *History of Structuralism I. The Rising Sign. 1945–1966*, translated by Deborah Glassman, Volume 1, London and Minneapolis: University of Minnesota Press.

Dosse, François 1998b, *History of Structuralism II. The Sign Sets. 1967-Present*, translated by Deborah Glassman, Volume 2, London and Minneapolis: University of Minnesota Press.

Dreier, Ralf 2002, 'Niklas Luhmanns Rechtsbegriff', *Archiv für Rechts- und Sozialphilosophie*, 88, 3: 305–22.

Dreyfus, Hubert L. and Paul Rabinow 1983, *Michel Foucault: Beyond Structuralism and Hermeneutics*, Chicago: The University of Chicago Press.

Düx, Henry 1972, 'Zur Subjekt-Objekt Dialektik in der Rechts- und Staatstheorie der DDR', in *Kritische Justiz*, 5, 4: 349–60.

Ehrlich, Eugen 2009 [1936], *Fundamental Principles of the Sociology of Law*, translated by Walter L. Moll, New Brunswick and London: Transaction Publishers.

Elsuni, Sarah 2006, 'Feministische Rechtstheorie', in *Neue Theorien des Rechts*, edited by Sonja Buckel, Ralph Christensen, Andreas Fischer-Lescano, Stuttgart: Lucius & Lucius.

Engel, Antke, Nina Schulz and Juliette Wedl 2005, 'Queere Politik: Analysen, Kritik, Perspektiven. Kreuzweise queer: Eine Einleitung', in *femina politica*, 14, 1: 9–23.

Esser, Josef 1975, *Einführung in die materialistische Staatsanalyse*, Frankfurt am Main: Campus.

Esser, Josef 1999, 'Der kooperative Nationalstaat im Zeitalter der "Globalisierung"', in *Sozialstaat in der Globalisierung*, edited by Diether Döring, Frankfurt am Main: Suhrkamp.

Esser, Josef, Wolfgang Fach and Werner Väth 1983, *Krisenregulierung. Zur politischen Durchsetzung ökonomischer Zwänge*, Frankfurt am Main: Suhrkamp.

Esser, Josef, Joachim Hirsch and Christoph Görg 1994, *Politik, Institutionen und Staat. Zur Kritik der Regulationstheorie*. Hamburg: VSA.

Ewald, Francois 1991, 'Norms, Discipline, and the Law', in *Law and the Order of Culture*, edited by Robert Post, Berkeley: University of California Press.

Fetscher, Iring 1975, *Rousseaus politische Philosophie. Zur Geschichte des demokratischen Freiheitsbegriffs*, Frankfurt am Main: Suhrkamp.

Fisahn, Andreas 1993, *Eine Kritische Theorie des Rechts – Zur Diskussion der Staats- und Rechtstheorie von Franz L. Neumann*, Aachen: Shaker.

Fischer-Lescano, Andreas 2003, 'Die Emergenz der Globalverfassung', *Zeitschrift für ausländisches öffentliches Recht und Völkerrecht*, 63, 3: 717–60.

Fischer-Lescano, Andreas 2005, *Globalverfassung. Die Geltungsbegründung der Menschenrechte*, Weilerswist: Velbrück.

Fischer-Lescano, Andreas and Ralph Christensen 2012, 'Auctoritatis Interpositio: How Systems Theory Deconstructs Decisionism', *Social & Legal Studies*, 21, 1: 93–119.

Fischer-Lescano, Andreas and Gunther Teubner 2004, 'Regime-Collisions: The Vain Search for Legal Unity in the Fragmentation of Global Law', *Michigan Journal of International Law*, 25, 4: 999–1046.

Fischer-Lescano, Andreas and Gunther Teubner 2006, 'Prozedurale Rechtstheorie: Wiethölter', in *Neue Theorien des Rechts*, edited by Sonja Buckel, Ralph Christensen, Andreas Fischer-Lescano, Stuttgart: Lucius & Lucius.

Foucault, Michel 1977, 'Prison Talk', *Radical Philosophy*, 16: 10–15.

Foucault, Michel 1978, *The History of Sexuality. Volume 1: An Introduction*, translated by Robert Hurley, New York: Pantheon Books.

Foucault, Michel 1980, *Power/Knowledge. Selected Interviews and Other Writings 1972–1977*, edited by Colin Gordon, translated by Colin Gordon, Leo Marshall et al., Pantheon Books, New York.

Foucault, Michel 1982, 'The Subject and Power', *Critical Inquiry*, 8, 4: 777–95.

Foucault, Michel 1985, 'An Interview with Michel Foucault', interviewed by Jean-Louis Ezine, translated by Renée Morel, History of the Present, 1: 2–3, 14.

Foucault, Michel 1991a [1987], 'An Ethic of Care for the Self as a Practice of Freedom. An Interview with Michel Foucault on January 24, 1984', in *The Final Foucault*, edited by James Bernauer and David Rasmussen, Cambridge, MA: The MIT Press.

Foucault, Michel 1991b, 'Governmentality', in *The Foucault Effect: Studies in Governmentality*, edited by Graham Burchell, Colin Gordon and Peter Miller, Chicago: The University of Chicago Press.

Foucault, Michel 1995 [1977], *Discipline and Punish: The Birth of the Prison*, translated by Allan Sheridan.

Foucault, Michel 2000 [1974], *Truth and Juridical Forms, in Essential Works of Foucault 1954–1984. Volume 3: Power*, edited by James D. Faubion, translated by Robert Hurley et al., New York: The New Press.

Foucault, Michel 2003a [1978], 'Die Disziplinargesellschaft in der Krise', in Schriften in vier Bänden. Dits et Ecrits. *Band III. 1976–1979*, edited by Daniel Defert and François Ewald, Frankfurt am Main: Suhrkamp.

Foucault, Michel 2003b [1978], 'Methodologie zur Erkenntnis der Welt: Wie man sich vom Marxismus befreien kann', in *Schriften in vier Bänden. Dits et Ecrits. Band III. 1976–1979*, edited by Daniel Defert and François Ewald, Frankfurt am Main: Suhrkamp.

Foucault, Michel 2003c, *'Society Must Be Defended': Lectures at the College de France, 1975–76*, edited by Mauro Bertani and Alessandro Fontana, translated by David Macey, New York: Picador.

Foucault, Michel 2005a, *The Hermeneutics of the Subject. Lectures at the* Collège *de France 1981–1982*, edited by Frédéric Gross, translated by Graham Burchell, New York: Palgrave Macmillan.

Foucault, Michel 2005b [1970], *The Order of Things. An archaeology of the human sciences*, London and New York: Routledge.

Foucault, Michel 2008, *The Birth of Biopolitics. Lectures at the* Collège *de France 1978–79*, edited by Michel Senellart, translated by Graham Burchell, New York: Palgrave Macmillan.

Foucault, Michel 2009 [2007], *Security, Territory, Population. Lectures at the Collège de France 1977–1978*, edited by Michel Senellart, translated by Graham Burchell, London, New York: Palgrave Macmillan.

Foucault, Michel 2016, *About the Beginning of the Hermeneutics of the Self: Lectures at Dartmouth College, 1980*, translated by Graham Burchell, Chicago and London: University of Chicago Press.

Frankenberg, Günter 2003, *Autorität und Integration. Zur Grammatik von Recht und Verfassung*, Frankfurt am Main: Suhrkamp.

Frankenberg, Günter 2006, 'Partisanen der Rechtskritik. Critical Legal Studies etc.', in *Neue Theorien des Rechts*, edited by Sonja Buckel, Ralph Christensen, Andreas Fischer-Lescano, Stuttgart: Lucius & Lucius.

Fraser, Nancy 1989, *Unruly Practices. Power, Discourse, and Gender in Contemporary Social Theory*, Minneapolis: University of Minnesota Press.

Fraser, Nancy 2003, 'From Discipline to Flexibilisation? Rereading Foucault in the Shadow of Globalization', *Constellations*, 10, 2, 160–71.

Giddens, Anthony 1986 [1984], *The Constitution of Society: Outline of the Theory of Structuration*, Cambridge: Polity Press.

Gill, Stephen (ed.) 1999, *Gramsci, Historical Materialism and International Relations*, Cambridge: Cambridge University Press.

Görg, Christoph 1994, 'Der Institutionenbegriff in der "Theorie der Strukturierung"', in *Politik, Institutionen und Staat. Zur Kritik der Regulationstheorie*, edited by Josef Esser, Christoph Görg and Joachim Hirsch, Hamburg: VSA.

Gorz, Andre 1999, *Reclaiming Work. Beyond the Wage-Based Society*, translated by Chris Turner, Cambridge: Polity Press.

Gramsci, Antonio 1967, *Philosophie der Praxis*, edited by Christian Riechers, Frankfurt am Main: Fischer.

Gramsci, Antonio 1991 (1971), *Selections from the Prison Notebooks of Antonio Gramsci*, edited and translated by Quintin Hoare and Geoffrey Nowell Smith, New York: International Publishers.

Gramsci, Antonio 1996, *Prison Notebooks, Volume 2*, translated by Joseph A. Buttigieg, New York: Columbia University Press.

Gramsci, Antonio 2011 [1992], *Prison Notebooks, Volume 1*, translated by Joseph A. Buttigieg and Antonio Callari, New York: Columbia University Press.

Gramsci, Antonio 2011, *Prison Notebooks, Volume 3*, translated by Joseph A. Buttigieg, New York: Columbia University Press.

Günther, Klaus 1992, 'Ohne weiteres und ganz automatisch. Zur Wiederentdeckung der Privatrechtsgesellschaft', *Rechtshistorisches Journal*, 11: 473–500.

Günther, Klaus 1994, 'Diskurstheorie des Rechts oder liberales Naturrecht in diskurstheoretischem Gewände?', *Kritische Justiz*, 27, 4: 470–87.

Gutierrez Rodriguez, Encarnacion 1999, *Intellektuelle Migrantinnen – Subjektivitäten im Zeitalter von Globalisierung. Eine postkoloniale dekonstruktive Analyse von Biographien im Spannungsverhältnis von Ethnisierung und Vergeschlechtlichung*, Opladen: Leske und Budrich.

Habermas, Jürgen 1971, 'Theorie der Gesellschaft oder Sozialtechnologie? Eine Auseinandersetzung mit Niklas Luhmann', in *Theorie der Gesellschaft oder Sozialtechnologie*, edited by Jürgen Habermas and Niklas Luhmann, Frankfurt am Main: Suhrkamp.

Habermas, Jürgen 1979, 'Historical Materialism and the Development of Normative Structures', in *Communication and the Evolution of Society*, translated by Thomas McCarthy, Boston: Beacon Press.

Habermas, Jürgen 1984, *The Theory of Communicative Action Volume 1: Reason and the Rationalization of Society*, translated by Thomas McCarthy, Boston: Beacon Press.

Habermas, Jürgen 1987, *The Theory of Communicative Action Volume 2: Lifeworld and System: A Critique of Functionalist Reason*, translated by Thomas McCarthy, Boston: Beacon Press.

Habermas, Jürgen 1996, *Between Facts and Norms. Contributions to a Discourse Theory of Law and Democracy*, translated by William Rehg, Cambridge, MA: The MIT Press.

Habermas, Jürgen 1998, 'What is Universal Pragmatics', in *On the Pragmatics of Communication*, edited by Maeve Cooke, Cambridge, MA: The MIT Press.

Habermas, Jürgen 2006, *The Divided West*, Cambridge: Polity Press.

Hardt, Michael and Antonio Negri 1994, *Labor of Dionysus: A Critique of the State-Form*, Minneapolis: University of Minnesota Press.

Hardt, Michael and Antonio Negri 2000, *Empire*, Cambridge, MA: Harvard University Press.

Hardt, Michael and Antonio Negri 2004, *Multitude. War and Democracy in the Age of Empire*, New York: The Penguin Press.

Hark, Sabine 1999, *Deviante Subjekte. Die paradoxe Politik der Identität*, Opladen: Leske + Budrich.

Harms, Andreas 2000, *Warenform und Rechtsform. Zur Rechtstheorie von Eugen Paschukanis*, Baden-Baden: Nomos.

Hartmann, Eva 2006, *Zur Rolle der UNESCO in der globalen Wissensökonomie*, Kassel: University of Kassel (unpublished PhD dissertation).

Hegel, Georg Wilhelm Friedrich 1991, *Elements of the Philosophy of Right*, edited by Allen W. Wood, translated by H.B. Nisbet, Cambridge: Cambridge University Press.

Hegel, Georg Wilhelm Friedrich 1983, *Hegel and the Human Spirit: a translation of the Jena Lectures on the Philosophy of Spirit (1805–6) with commentary*, translated by Leo Rauch, Detroit: Wayne State University Press.

Heinrich, Michael 1999, *Die Wissenschaft vom Wert. Die Marxsche Kritik der politischen Ökonomie zwischen wissenschaftlicher Revolution und klassischer Tradition*, Münster: Westfälisches Dampfboot.

Helduser, Urte et al. 2004, 'Einführung', in *under construction? Konstruktivistische Perspektiven in feministischer Theorie und Forschungspraxis*, edited by Urte Helduser et al., Frankfurt am Main: Campus.

Hellmann, Kai-Uwe 2004, '1988 – und was nun? Eine Zwischenbilanz zum Verhältnis von Systemtheorie und Gender Studies', in *Gender Studies und Systemtheorie. Studien zu einem Theorietransfer*, edited by Sabine Kampmann, Alexandra Karentzos and Thomas Küpper, Bielefeld: Transcript.

Hirsch, Joachim 1976, 'Bemerkungen zum theoretischen Ansatz einer Analyse des bürgerlichen Staates', in *Gesellschaft. Beiträge zur Marxschen Theorie 8/9*, edited by Hans-Georg Backhaus et al., Frankfurt am Main: Suhrkamp.

Hirsch, Joachim 1994, 'Politische Form, politische Institutionen und Staat', in *Politik, Institutionen und Staat*, edited by Josef Esser, Christoph Görg and Joachim Hirsch, Hamburg: VSA.

Hirsch, Joachim 1995, *Der nationale Wettbewerbsstaat. Staat, Demokratie und Politik im globalen Kapitalismus*, Berlin: Edition ID-Archiv.

Hirsch, Joachim 2005, *Materialistische Staatstheorie. Transformationsprozesse des kapitalistischen Staatensystems*, Hamburg: VSA.

Holland-Cunz, Barbara 2003, *Die alte neue Frauenfrage*, Frankfurt am Main: Suhrkamp.

Holloway, John 2010 [2002], *Change the World without Taking Power: The Meaning of Revolution Today*, London and New York: Pluto Press.

Holloway, John and Sol Picciotto 1978, 'Introduction: Towards a Materialist Theory of the State', in *State and Capital. A Marxist Debate*, edited by John Holloway and Sol Picciotto, Austin: University of Texas Press.

Honneth, Axel 1989, 'Moralische Entwicklung und sozialer Kampf. Sozialphilosophische Lehren aus dem Frühwerk Hegels', in *Zwischenbetrachtungen im Prozeß der Aufklärung. Festschrift für Jürgen Habermas*, edited by Axel Honneth et al., Frankfurt am Main: Suhrkamp.

Honneth, Axel 1995, *The Struggle for Recognition: The Moral Grammar of Social Conflicts*, translated by Joel Anderson, Cambridge, MA: The MIT Press.

Honneth, Axel 2008, *Reification: A New Look at an Old Idea*, Oxford: Oxford University Press.

Horkheimer, Max 2002 [1972], 'Traditional and Critical Theory', in *Critical Theory. Selected Essays*, Max Horkheimer, translated by Matthew J. O'Connell et al., New York: Continuum.

Horster, Detlef 1992, *Habermas: An Introduction*, translated by Heidi Thompson, Philadelphia: Pennbridge Books.

Hunt, Alan and Gary Wickham 1994, *Foucault and Law. Towards a Sociology of Law as Governance*, London: Pluto Press.

Hunter, Rosemary 2006, 'Law's (Masculine) Violence: Reshaping Jurisprudence', *Law and Critique*, 17, 1: 27–46.

Hutchinson, Allan C. and Patrick J. Monahan 1984, 'Law, Politics, and the Critical Legal Scholars: The Unfolding Drama of American Legal Thought', *Stanford Law Review*, 36, 1: 199–245.

Jessop, Bob 1985, *Nicos Poulantzas: Marxist Theory and Political Strategy*, London: Macmillan.

Jessop, Bob 1990, *State Theory. Putting the Capitalist State in its Place*, Cambridge: Polity Press.

Jessop, Bob 2004. 'The Gender Selectivities of the State', *Journal of Critical Realism*, 3, 2: 207–37.

Joerges, Christian and David M. Trubek 1989, *Critical Legal Thought: An American-German Debate*, Baden-Baden: Nomos.

Jour fixe initiative berlin 1999, 'Einleitung', *Das Argument*, special issue, 271: 5–12.

Kampmann, Sabine, Alexandra Karentzos, and Thomas Küpper (eds.) 2004, *Gender Studies und Systemtheorie. Studien zu einem Theorietransfer*, Bielefeld: Transcript.

Kannankulam, John 2000, *Zwischen Staatsableitung und strukturalem Marxismus. Zur*

Rekonstruktion der staatstheoretischen Debatten der siebziger Jahre, Frankfurt am Main: Goethe-University (unpublished MA dissertation).

Kannankulam, John 2006, *Autoritärer Neoliberalismus*, Frankfurt am Main: Goethe-University (unpublished PhD dissertation).

Kant, Immanuel 1991, *The Metaphysics of Morals*, translated by Mary J. Gregor, Cambridge: Cambridge University Press.

Kant, Immanuel 1996, *Critique of Pure Reason*, translated by Werner S. Pluhar, Indianapolis: Hackett.

Kaufmann, Erich 1911, *Das Wesen des Völkerrechts und die Clausula rebus sic stantibus. Rechtsphilosophische Studie zum Rechts-, Staats- und Vertragsbegriff*, Tübingen: J.C.B. Mohr (Paul Siebeck).

Kelsen, Hans 1915, *'Eine Grundlegung der Rechtssoziologie'*, Archiv für Sozialwissenschaft und Sozialpolitik, 39: 839–76.

Kelsen, Hans 1941, 'International Peace – By Court or Government?', *The American Journal of Sociology*, 46, 4: 571–81.

Kelsen, Hans 1955, *The Communist Theory of Law*, New York: Praeger.

Kelsen, Hans 1967, *Allgemeine Rechtslehre im Lichte materialistischer Geschichtsauffassung*, in *Demokratie und Sozialismus. Ausgewählte Aufsätze*, Wien: Wiener Volksbuchhandlung.

Kelsen, Hans 1981 [1922], *Der soziologische und der juristische Staatsbegriff*, Aalen: Scientia.

Kelsen, Hans 2005, *Pure Theory of Law*, translated by Max Knight, Clark, NJ: Lawbook Exchange.

Kennedy, Duncan 1982, 'Antonio Gramsci and the Legal System', *American Legal Studies Association (ALSA) Forum*, 6, 1: 32–7.

Kirchheimer, Otto 1969a [1928], 'The Socialist and Bolshevik Theory of the State', in *Politics, Law, and Social Change. Selected Essays of Otto Kirchheimer*, edited by Frederic S. Burin and Kurt L. Shell, New York: Columbia University Press.

Kirchheimer, Otto 1969b [1930], 'Weimar – and What Then? An Analysis of a Constitution', in *Politics, Law, and Social Change. Selected Essays of Otto Kirchheimer*, edited by Frederic S. Burin and Kurt L. Shell, New York: Columbia University Press.

Kirchheimer, Otto 1976a [1930], 'Artikel 48 und die Wandlungen des Verfassungssystems. Auch ein Beitrag zum Verfassungsstag', in *Von der Weimarer Republik zum Faschismus: Die Auflösung der demokratischen Rechtsordnung*, Frankfurt am Main: Suhrkamp.

Kirchheimer, Otto 1976b [1932], 'Die Verfassungsreform', in *Von der Weimarer Republik zum Faschismus: Die Auflösung der demokratischen Rechtsordnung*, Frankfurt am Main: Suhrkamp.

Klenner, Hermann 1972, *Rechtsleere. Verurteilung der reinen Rechtslehre*, Frankfurt am Main: Marxistische Blätter.

Knapp, Gudrun-Axeli 1992, 'Macht und Geschlecht. Neuere Entwicklungen in der feministischen Macht- und Herrschaftsdiskussion', in *Traditionen Brüche. Entwicklungen feministischer Theorie*, edited by Gudrun-Axeli Knapp and Angelika Wetterer, Freiburg: Kore.

Knapp, Gudrun-Axeli 2004, *'Grundlagenkritik und stille Post. Zur Debatte um einen Bedeutungsverlust der Kategorie Geschlecht'*, in *Strukturierung von Wissen und der symbolischen Ordnung der Geschlechter. Gender Tagung Bamberg 2003*, edited by Marianne Heimbach-Steins et al., Münster: LIT.

Knapp, Gudrun-Axeli 2005, '"Intersectionality" – ein neues Paradigma feministischer Theorie? Zur transatlantischen Reise von "Race, Class, Gender"', *Feministische Studien*, 1: 68–81.

Knapp, Gudrun-Axeli and Angelika Wetterer 2003, 'Vorwort', in *Achsen der Differenz. Gesellschaftstheorie und feministische Kritik II.*, edited by Gudrun-Axeli Knapp and Angelika Wetterer, Münster: Westfälisches Dampfboot.

Kneer Georg and Armin Nassehi 2000 [1993], *Niklas Luhmanns Theorie sozialer Systeme*, München: Fink.

Knieper, Rolf 1996, *Gesetz und Geschichte. Ein Beitrag zu Bestand und Veränderung des Bürgerlichen Gesetzbuches*, Baden-Baden: Nomos.

Kohlmorgen, Lars 2004, *Regulation, Klasse, Geschlecht. Die Konstituierung der Sozialstruktur im Fordismus und Postfordismus*, Münster: Westfälisches Dampfboot.

Korsch, Karl 1970 [1930], 'Einleitung', in *Allgemeine Rechtslehre und Marxismus*, Eugen Paschukanis, Frankfurt am Main: Neue Kritik.

Krahl, Hans-Jürgen 1985 [1971], 'Zur Wesenslogik der Marxschen Warenanalyse', in *Konstitution und Klassenkampf. Schriften und Reden 1966–1970*, Frankfurt am Main: Neue Kritik.

Kramer, Annegret 1975, 'Gramscis Interpretation des Marxismus', in *Gesellschaft. Beiträge zur Marxschen Theorie 4*, edited by Hans-Georg Backhaus, Frankfurt am Main: Suhrkamp.

Krasmann, Susanne 2003, *Die Kriminalität der Gesellschaft. Zur Gouvernementalität der Gegenwart*, Konstanz: UVK Universitätsverlag Konstanz.

Laclau, Ernesto 1982, 'Diskurs, Hegemonie und Politik', *Das Argument*, special issue, 78: 6–22.

Laclau, Ernesto and Chantal Mouffe 2001 [1985], *Hegemony and Socialist Strategy*, Towards a Radical Democratic Politics, London: Verso.

Lamla, Jörn 2003, 'Kopplung versus Dualität. Ein Vergleich der Strukturbegriffe von Niklas Luhmann und Athony Giddens', in *Das System der Politik. Niklas Luhmanns politische Theorie*, edited by Kai-Uwe Hellmann, Wiesbaden: Westdeutscher Verlag.

Lazzarato, Maurizio 1996, 'Immaterial Labour', in *Radical Thought in Italy. A Potential Politics*, edited by Paolo Virno and Michael Hardt, Minneapolis: University of Minnesota Press.

Lemke, Thomas 2019, *A Critique of Political Reason. Foucault's Analysis of Modern Governmentality*, London: Verso.

Lemke, Thomas 2003, 'Andere Affirmationen. Gesellschaftsanalyse und Kritik im Postfordismus', in *Michel Foucault. Zwischenbilanz einer Rezeption. Frankfurter Foucault-Konferenz 2001*, edited by Axel Honneth and Martin Saar, Frankfurt am Main: Suhrkamp.

Lemke, Thomas, Susanne Krasmann and Ulrich Bröckling 2000, 'Gouvernementalität, Neoliberalismus und Selbsttechnologien. Eine Einleitung', in *Gouvernementalität der Gegenwart. Studien zur Ökonomisierung der Sozialen*, edited by Thomas Lemke, Susanne Krasmann and Ulrich Bröckling, Frankfurt am Main: Suhrkamp.

Lenin, V.I. 2014 [1964], *State and Revolution*, Chicago: Haymarket.

Lenz, Ilse 1996, 'Grenzziehung und Öffnungen: Zum Verhältnis von Geschlecht und Ethnizität zu Zeiten der Globalisierung', in *Wechselnde Blicke. Frauenforschung in internationaler Perspektive*, edited by Ilse Lenz, Andrea Germer and Brigitte Hasenjürgen, Opladen: Leske + Budrich.

Lipietz, Alain 1993, 'From Althusserianism to "Regulation Theory"', in *The Althusserian Legacy*, edited by E. Ann Kaplan and Michael Sprinker, London: Verso.

Lipietz, Alain 1997, 'Warp, Woof and Regulation: A Tool for Social Science' in *Space and Social Theory: Interpreting Modernity and Postmodernity*, edited by Georges Benko and Ulf Strohmayer, Walden/MA: Wiley-Blackwell.

Litowitz, Douglas 1997, *Postmodern Philosophy and Law. Rorty, Nietzsche, Lyotard, Derrida, Foucault*, Lawrence, KS: University Press of Kansas.

Litowitz, Douglas 2000, 'Gramsci, Hegemony, and the Law', *Brigham Young University Law Review*, 2: 515–51.

Lobel, Jules 2004, 'Courts as Forums for Protest', *bepress Legal Series*, Working Paper 213, available at: http://law.bepress.com/expresso/eps/213.

Löwenthal, Richard 1977 [1946], *Jenseits des Kapitalismus: Ein Beitrag zur sozialistischen Neuorientierung*, Berlin: Dietz.

Lorey, Isabell 1996, *Immer Ärger mit dem Subjekt. Theoretische und politische Konsequenzen eines juridischen Machtmodells: Judith Butler*, Tübingen: Edition Diskord.

Luhmann, Niklas 1969, *Legitimation durch Verfahren*, Neuwied am Rhein: Luchterhand.

Luhmann, Niklas 1974, *Grundrechte als Institution. Ein Beitrag zur politischen Soziologie*, Berlin: Duncker & Humblot.

Luhmann, Niklas 2003 [1988], 'Frauen, Männer und George Spencer Brown', in *Frauen, Männer, Gender Trouble. Systemtheoretische Essays*, edited by Ursula Pasero and Christine Weinbach, Frankfurt am Main: Suhrkamp.

Luhmann, Niklas 2004, *Law as a Social System*, Oxford: Oxford University Press.

Luhmann, Niklas 2012, *Theory of Society*, Volume 1, translated by Rhodes Barrett, Stanford, CA: Stanford University Press.

Lukács, Georg 1971, *History and Class Consciousness. Studies in Marxist Dialectics*, translated by Rodney Livingstone, Cambridge, MA: The MIT Press.

Lukács, Georg 1975, *The Young Hegel: Studies in the Relations between Dialectics and Economics*, translated by Rodney Livingstone, London: Merlin Press.

Luthardt, Wolfgang 1976, 'Bemerkungen zu Otto Kirchheimers Arbeiten bis 1933', in *Von der Weimarer Republik zum Faschismus: Die Auflösung der demokratischen Rechtsordnung*, Otto Kirchheimer, Frankfurt am Main: Suhrkamp.

MacKinnon, Catharine A. 1989, *Towards a Feminist Theory of the State*, Cambridge, MA: Harvard University Press.

Maihofer, Andrea 1992, *Das Recht bei Marx: zur dialektischen Struktur von Gerechtigkeit, Menschenrechten und Recht*, Baden-Baden: Nomos.

Maihofer, Andrea 1995, *Geschlecht als Existenzweise. Macht, Moral, Recht und Geschlechterdifferenz*, Frankfurt am Main: Helmer.

Maihofer, Andrea 2004, 'Geschlecht als soziale Konstruktion – eine Zwischenbetrachtung', in *Under construction? Konstruktivistische Perspektiven in feministischer Theorie und Forschungspraxis*, edited by Katharina Pühl et al., Frankfurt am Main: Campus.

Marcuse, Herbert 1955, *Reason and Revolution: Hegel and the Rise of Social Theory*, London: Routledge & Kegan Paul.

Marx, Karl 1976, *Capital. A Critique of Economy*, Volume One, translated by Ben Fowkes, London: Penguin Books.

Marx, Karl 1981, *Capital. A Critique of Economy*, Volume Three, translated by David Fernbach, London: Penguin Books.

Marx, Karl 1993 [1973], *Grundrisse. Foundations of the Critique of Political Economy (Rough Draft)*, translated by Martin Nicolaus, London: Penguin Books.

Marx, Karl 2002 [1996], 'The Eighteenth Brumaire of Louis Bonaparte', translated by Terrell Carver, in Marx's *Eighteenth Brumaire. (Post)modern Interpretations*, edited by Mark Cowling and James Martin, London: Pluto Press.

Marx, Karl 2009, *Critique of the Gotha Programme*, Gloucester: Dodo Press.

Marx, Karl and Friedrich Engels 1958, *Marx-Engels-Werke* (*MEW*), 40 volumes, Berlin: Dietz.

Marx, Karl and Friedrich Engels 1975–2005 [1835–95], *Collected Works* (*MECW*), 50 volumes, London: Lawrence & Wishart.

Maus, Ingeborg 1976, *Bürgerliche Rechtstheorie und Faschismus. Zur sozialen Funktion und aktuellen Wirkung der Theorie Carl Schmitts*, München: Fink.

Maus, Ingeborg 1986a, 'Entwicklung und Funktionswandel der Theorie des bürgerlichen Rechtsstaats', in *Rechtstheorie und politische Theorie im Industriekapitalismus*, München: Fink.

Maus, Ingeborg 1986b, 'Hermann Heller und die Staatsrechtslehre der Bundesrepublik', in *Rechtstheorie und politische Theorie im Industriekapitalismus*, München: Fink.

Maus, Ingeborg 1986c, 'Verrechtlichung, Entrechtlichung und der Funktionswandel von Institutionen', in *Rechtstheorie und politische Theorie im Industriekapitalismus*, München: Fink.

Maus, Ingeborg 1992a, 'Von der Metaphysik des Widerstandsrechts zum nachmetaphysischen Prinzip der Volkssouveränität: die Demokratietheorie Kants', in *Zur Aufklärung der Demokratietheorie*, Frankfurt am Main: Suhrkamp.

Maus, Ingeborg 1992b, *Zur Aufklärung der Demokratietheorie*, Frankfurt am Main: Suhrkamp.

Maus, Ingeborg 1995, 'Liberties and Popular Sovereignty: On Jurgen Habermas's Reconstruction of the System of Rights', *Cardozo Law Review*, 17: 825–82.

Maus, Ingeborg 2006, 'From Nation-State to Global State, or the Decline of Democracy', *Constellations*, 13, 4: 465–84.

Mieville, China 2005, *Between Equal Rights. A Marxist Theory of International Law*, Leiden: Brill.

Mouffe, Chantal 2005, *On the Political*, London: Routledge.

Müller, Friedrich and Ralph Christensen 2004, *Juristische Methodik, Band 1, Grundlagen Öffentliches Recht*, Berlin: Duncker & Humblot.

Müller, Wolfgang and Christel Neusüß 1970, 'Die Sozialstaatsillusion und der Widerspruch von Lohnarbeit und Kapital', *Sozialistische Politik*, 2, 6/7: 4–67.

Müller-Tuckfeld, Jens Christian 1994, 'Gesetz ist Gesetz. Anmerkungen zu einer Theorie der juridischen Anrufung', in *Das Argument*, special issue, 228: 182–205.

Munro, Vanessa E. 2001, 'Legal Feminism and Foucault – A Critique of the Expulsion of Law', *Journal of Law and Society*, 28, 4: 546–67.

Nassehi, Armin 2003a, 'Geschlecht im System. Die Ontologisierung des Körpers und die Asymmetrie der Geschlechter', in *Frauen, Männer, Gender Trouble. Systemtheoretische Essays*, edited by Ursula Pasero and Christine Weinbach, Frankfurt am Main: Suhrkamp.

Nassehi, Armin 2003b, 'Die Differenz der Kommunikation und die Kommunikation der Differenz', in *Beobachter der Moderne. Beiträge zu Niklas Luhmanns 'Die Gesellschaft der Gesellschaft'*, edited by Hans-Joachim Giegel and Uwe Schimank, Frankfurt am Main: Suhrkamp.

Negri, Antonio 2017, 'Rereading Pashukanis: Discussion Notes', *Stasis*, 5, 2: 8–49.

Negt, Oskar 1975, '10 Thesen zur marxistischen Rechtstheorie', in *Probleme der marxistischen Rechtstheorie*, edited by Hubert Rottleuthner, Frankfurt am Main: Suhrkamp.

Neumann, Franz 1936, *The governance of the rule of law: an investigation into the relationship between the political theories, the legal system, and the social background in competitive society*. London: The London School of Economics and Political Science (unpublished PhD dissertation), available at: http://etheses.lse.ac.uk/668/.

Neumann, Franz 1957, 'The Change in the Function of Law in Modern Society', in *The*

Democratic and the Authoritarian State: Essays in Political and Legal Theory, Glencoe, IL: Free Press.

Neumann, Franz 1978, 'Zur marxistischen Staatstheorie', in *Wirtschaft, Staat, Demokratie. Aufsätze 1930–1954*, edited by Alfons Söllner, Frankfurt am Main: Suhrkamp.

Neumann, Franz 2009 [1942], *Behemoth. The Structure and Practice of National Socialism 1933–1944*, Chicago: Ivan R. Dee.

Neves, Marcelo 2000, *Zwischen Themis und Leviathan: eine schwierige Beziehung. Eine Rekonstruktion des demokratischen Rechtsstaates in Auseinandersetzung mit Luhmann und Habermas*, Baden-Baden: Nomos.

Neves, Marcelo 2001, 'From the Autopoiesis to the Allopoisesis of Law', *Journal of Law and Society*, 28, 2: 242–64.

Niesen, Peter 2011, *'Legitimacy without Morality. Habermas and Maus on the Relationship between Law and Morality', in* Jürgen Habermas, *Volume 1, edited by Camil Ungureanu, Klaus Günther and Christian Joerges*, Farnham: Ashgate.

Niesen, Peter and Oliver Eberl 2006, 'Demokratischer Positivismus: Habermas und Maus', in *Neue Theorien des Rechts*, edited by Sonja Buckel, Ralph Christensen, Andreas Fischer-Lescano, Stuttgart: Lucius & Lucius.

Niesen, Peter and von Schömberg, Rene 2002, 'Einleitung', in *Zwischen Recht und Moral. Neuere Ansätze der Rechts- und Demokratietheorie*, edited by Peter Niesen and Rene von Schömberg, Münster: LIT.

Ott, Cornelia 1998, *Die Spur der Lüste. Sexualität, Geschlecht und Macht*, Opladen: Leske + Budrich.

Pashukanis, Evgeny 1972 [1931], 'Für eine marxistisch-leninistische Staats- und Rechtstheorie', in *Marxistische und sozialistische Rechtstheorie*, edited by Norbert Reich, Frankfurt am Main: Athenäum Fischer.

Pashukanis, Evgeny 2003 [1978], *The General Theory of Law and Marxism*, translation by Barbara Einhorn, introduction and editorial notes by Chris Arthur, New Brunswich, NJ: Transaction Publishers.

Pasero, Ursula 2003, 'Gender, Individualität, Diversity', in *Frauen, Männer, Gender Trouble. Systemtheoretische Esssays*, Frankfurt am Main: Suhrkamp.

Pasero, Ursula and Christine Weinbach (eds.) 2003, *Frauen, Männer, Gender Trouble. Systemtheoretische Esssays*, Frankfurt am Main: Suhrkamp.

Perels Joachim et al. (eds.) 1971, *Kritische Justiz*, 4, 2: 133–240.

Perels, Joachim 1973, *Kapitalismus und politische Demokratie. Privatrechtssystem und Gesellschaftsstruktur in der Weimarer Republik*, Frankfurt am Main: Europäische Verlagsanstalt.

Picciotto, Sol 1982, 'The Theory of the State, Class Struggle and the Rule of Law', in *Marxism and Law*, edited by Piers Beirne and Richard Quinney, New York: Wiley.

Pieper, Marianne and Encarnacion Gutierrez Rodriguez 2003, 'Einleitung', in *Gouvernementalität. Ein sozialwissenschaftliches Konzept in Anschluss an Foucault*, edited by

Marianne Pieper and Encarnacion Gutierrez Rodriguez, Frankfurt am Main: Campus.

Postone, Moishe 1986, 'Anti-Semitism and National Socialism', in *Germans and Jews Since the Holocaust*, edited by Anson Rabinbach and Jack Zipes, New York: Holmes and Meier.

Postone, Moishe 1993, *Time, Labor, and Social Domination. A Reinterpretation of Marx's Critical Theory*, Cambridge: Cambridge University Press.

Poulantzas, Nicos 1964, 'L'examen marxiste de l'état et du droit actuels et la question de l'alternative', in *Les Temps Modernes*, 219–20: 274–302.

Poulantzas, Nicos 1972, 'Aus Anlass der marxistischen Rechtstheorie', in *Marxistische und sozialistische Rechtstheorie*, edited by Norbert Reich, Frankfurt am Main: Athenaeum Fischer.

Poulantzas, Nicos 1978 [1973], *Political Power and Social Classes*, translated by Timothy O'Hagan, London: Verso.

Poulantzas, Nicos 1979 [1974], *Fascism and Dictatorship: The Third International and the Problem of Fascism*, translated by Judith White, London: Verso.

Poulantzas, Nicos 2000 [1978], *State, Power, Socialism*, translated by Patrick Camiller, London: Verso.

Priester, Karin 1981, *Studien zur Staatstheorie des italienischen Marxismus: Gramsci und Deila Volpe*, Frankfurt am Main: Campus.

Pühl, Katharina and Birgit Sauer 2004, 'Geschlechterverhältnisse im Neoliberalismus. Konstruktion, Transformation und feministisch-politische Perspektiven', in *under construction? Konstruktivistische Perspektiven in feministischer Theorie und Forschungspraxis*, edited by Urte Helduser et al., Frankfurt am Main: Campus.

Puntscher Riekmann, Sonja 1998, *Die kommissarische Neuordnung Europas. Das Dispositiv der Integration*, New York: Springer.

Rehmann, Jan 2003, 'Vom Gefängnis zur modernen Seele. Foucaults "Überwachen und Strafen" neu besichtigt', in *Das Argument*, 249: 63–81.

Reich, Norbert 1972a, 'Marxistische und sozialistische Rechtstheorie – Subjekt und Objekt von Wissenschaft', in *Marxistische und sozialistische Rechtstheorie*, edited by Norbert Reich, Frankfurt am Main: Athenaeum Fischer.

Reich Norbert 1972b, 'Marxistische Rechtstheorie zwischen Revolution und Stalinismus. Das Beispiel Paschukanis', *Kritische Justiz*, 2: 154–62.

Reich, Norbert (ed.) 1972c, *Marxistische und sozialistische Rechtstheorie*, Frankfurt am Main: Athenäum Fischer.

Reich, Norbert 1973, 'Marxistische Rechtstheorie', in *Recht und Staat in Geschichte und Gegenwart*, Volume 420/421, Tübingen: Mohr.

Reichelt, Helmut 1973, *Zur logischen Struktur des Kapitalbegriffs bei Karl Marx*, Frankfurt am Main: Europäische Verlagsanstalt.

Reichelt, Helmut 2007, 'Marx's Critique of Economic Categories: Reflections on the

Problem of Validity in the Dialectical Method of Presentation in Capital', *Historical Materialism*, 15, 4: 3–52.

Ritsert, Jürgen 1988, *Der Kampf um das Surplusprodukt. Einführung in den klassischen Klassenbegriff*, Frankfurt am Main: Campus.

Ritsert, Jürgen 1998, 'Realabstraktion. Ein zu Recht abgewertetes Thema der kritischen Theorie?', in *Kein Staat zu machen. Zur Kritik der Sozialwissenschaften*, edited by Christoph Görg and Roland Roth, Münster: Westfälisches Dampfboot.

Rödel, Ulrich, Günter Frankenberg and Helmut Dubiel 1989, *Die demokratische Frage*, Frankfurt am Main: Suhrkamp.

Rottleuthner, Hubert (ed.) 1975, *Probleme der marxitischen Rechtstheorie*, Frankfurt am Main: Suhrkamp.

Rousseau, Jean-Jacques 2002, 'The Social Contract', translated by Susan Dunn, in *The Social Contract and The First and Second Discourses*, edited by Susan Dunn, New Haven: Yale University Press.

Rüthers, Bernd 2005, *Die unbegrenzte Auslegung. Zum Wandel der Privatrechtsordnung im Nationalsozialismus*, Tübingen: Mohr Siebeck.

Santos, Boaventura de Sousa 1995a, 'The Postmodern Transition: Law and Politics', in *The Fate of Law*, edited by Austin Sarat and Thomas R. Kearns, Ann Arbor: University of Michigan Press.

Santos, Boaventura de Sousa 1995b, *Toward a New Common Sense. Law, Science and Politics in the Paradigmatic Transition*, New York: Routledge.

Scherrer, Christoph 2003, 'Das Ende von Bretton Woods – Strategisches Handeln und weltwirtschaftliche Strukturen', *in Formen und Felder politischer Intervention. Zur Relevanz von Staat und Steuerung*, edited by Sonja Buckel, Regina-Maria Dackweiler and Ronald Noppe, Münster: Westfälisches Dampfboot.

Scheuerman, William E. 1997, *Between the Norm and the Exception. The Frankfurt School and the Rule of Law*, Cambridge, MA: The MIT Press.

Scheuerman, William E. 2002, 'Franz Neumann – Legal Theorist of Globalization?', *Kritische Justiz*, 1: 79–89.

Schmidt, Alfred 1971, *The Concept of Nature in Marx*, translated by Ben Fowkes, London: NLB.

Schmitt, Carl 1996, *The Concept of the Political*, translated by Georg Schwab, Chicago: The University of Chicago Press.

Schmitt, Carl 2004, *Legality and Legitimacy*, translated by Jeffrey Seitzer, Durham, NC: Duke University Press.

Schneider, Wolfgang Ludwig 2003, 'Handlung – Motiv – Interesse – Situation', in *Beobachter der Moderne. Beiträge zu Niklas Lubmanns 'Die Gesellschaft der Gesellschaft'*, edited by Hans-Joachim Giegel and Uwe Schimank, Frankfurt am Main: Suhrkamp.

Seifert, Jürgen 1984, 'Einführung', in *Recht, Demokratie und Kapitalismus. Aktualität und*

Probleme der Theorie Franz L. Neumanns, edited by Joachim Perels, Baden-Baden: Nomos.

Shaw, Martin 2000, *Theory of the Global State. Globality as Unfinished Revolution*, Cambridge: Cambridge University Press.

Smart, Carol 1989, *Feminism and the Power of Law*, London: Routledge.

Sohn-Rethel, Alfred 1978, *Intellectual and Manual Labour. A Critique of Epistemology*, translated by Martin Sohn-Rethel, London: MacMillan.

Söllner, Alfons 1978, 'Franz L. Neumann – Skizzen zu einer intellektuellen und politischen Biographie', in *Wirtschaft, Staat, Demokratie. Aufsätze 1930–1954*, Franz L. Neumann, Frankfurt am Main: Suhrkamp.

Söllner, Alfons 1980, 'Franz Neumanns "Die Herrschaft des Gesetzes". Versuch einer wissenschaftsgeschichtlichen und wissenschaftspolitischen Einordnung. Nachwort', in *Die Herrschaft des Gesetzes*, Franz L. Neumann, translated by Alfons Söllner, Frankfurt am Main: Suhrkamp.

Staff, Ilse 1985, *'Staatslehre in der Weimarer Republik. Herman Heller zu* Ehren', in *Staatslehre in der Weimarer Republik*, edited by Christoph Müller and Ilse Staff, Frankfurt am Main: Suhrkamp.

Stäheli, Urs 2000a, *Poststrukturalistische Soziologien*, Bielefeld: Transcript.

Stäheli, Urs 2000b, *Sinnzusammenbrüche. Eine dekonstruktive Lektüre von Niklas Luhmanns Systemtheorie*, Weilerswist: Velbrück Wissenschaft.

Stäheli, Urs 2001, 'Die politische Theorie der Hegemonie: Ernesto Laclau und Chantal Mouffe', in *Politische Theorien der Gegenwart II*, edited by André Brodocz and Gary S. Schaal, Opladen: Leske + Budrich.

Strecker, David and Gary S. Schaal 2001, 'Die politische Theorie der Deliberation: Jürgen Habermas', in *Politische Theorien der Gegenwart II*, edited by André Brodocz and Gary S. Schaal, Opladen: Leske + Budrich.

Tadros, Victor 1998, 'Between Governance and Discipline: The Law and Michel Foucault', *Oxford Journal of Legal Studies*, 18: 75–103.

Teubner, Gunther 1983, 'Substantive and Reflexive Elements in Modern Law', *Law and Society Review*, 17: 239–85.

Teubner, Gunther 1993a, *Law as an Autopoietic System*, translated by Anne Bankowska and Ruth Adler, Oxford: Blackwell.

Teubner, Gunther 1993b, '"Man schritt auf allen Gebieten zur Verrechtlichung". Rechtssoziologische Theorie im Werk Otto Kirchheimers', in *Der Einfluss deutscher Emigranten auf die Rechtsentwicklung in den USA und in Deutschland*, edited by Marcus Lutter, Ernst C. Stiefel and Michael H. Hoeflich, Tübingen: Mohr Siebeck.

Teubner, Gunther 1997a, 'Global Bukowina: Legal Pluralism in the World Society', in *Global Law Without a State*, edited by Gunther Teubner, Aldershot: Dartmouth.

Teubner, Gunther 1997b, *Global Law Without a State*, edited by Gunther Teubner, Aldershot: Dartmouth.

Teubner, Gunther 2000a, 'Contracting Worlds: The Many Autonomies of Private Law', *Social and Legal Studies*, 9, 3: 399–417.

Teubner, Gunther 2000b, 'Ein Fall von struktureller Korruption? Die Familienbürg schaft in der Kollision unverträglicher Handlungslogiken (BVerfGE 89. 214 ff.)', *Kritische Vierteljahreschrift für Gesetzgebung und Rechtswissenschaft*, 83, 3/4: 388–404.

Teubner, Gunther 2002, 'Breaking Frames. Economic Globalization and the Emergence of lex mercatoria', *European Journal of Social Theory*, 5, 2: 199–217.

Teubner, Gunther 2004, 'Global Private Regimes: Neo-Spontaneous Law and Dual Constitution of Autonomous Sectors?', in *Public Governance in the Age of Globalization*, edited by Karl-Heinz Ladeur, Aldershot: Dartmouth.

Teubner, Gunther 2006a, 'Dealing with Paradoxes of Law: Derrida, Luhmann, Wiethölter', in *Paradoxes and Inconsistencies in the Law*, edited by Oren Perez and Gunther Teubner, Oxford: Hart.

Teubner, Gunther 2006b, 'Die anonyme Matrix: Zu Menschenrechtsverletzungen durch "private" transnationale Akteure', *Der Staat*, 45, 2: 161–87.

Teubner, Ulrike 2001, 'Soziale Ungleichheit zwischen den Geschlechtern – kein Thema innerhalb der Systemtheorie?', in *Soziale Verortung der Geschlechter: Gesellschaftstheorie und feministische Kritik*, edited by Gudrun-Axeli Knapp and Angelika Wetterer, Münster: Westfälisches Dampfboot.

Tuschling, Burkhard 1976, *Rechtsform und Produktionsverhältnisse: Zur materialistischen Theorie des Rechtstaates*, Köln: Europäische Verlagsanstalt.

Tuschling, Burkhard 1977, 'Aspekte einer materialistischen Theorie des Rechts und des Staats', in Abendroth Forum: Marburger Gespräche aus Anlaß des 70. Geburtstages von Wolfgang Abendroth, edited by Frank Deppe et al., Marburg: Verlag Arbeiterbewegung und Gesellschaftswissenschaft.

Villa, Paula-Irene 2003, *Judith Butler*, Frankfurt am Main: Campus.

Virno, Paolo 2004, *A Grammar of the Multitude. For an Analysis of Contemporary Forms of Life*, translated by Isabella Bertoletti, James Cascaito, and Andrea Casson, Los Angeles: Semiotext(e).

Wassermann, Rudolf 1969, *Erziehung zum Establishment. Juristenausbildung in kritischer Sicht*, Karlsruhe: C.F. Müller.

Weber, Andreas 2005, *Subjektlos. Zur Kritik der Systemtheorie*, Konstanz: UVK.

Weber, Max 1978 [1976], *Economy and Society. An Outline of Interpretive Sociology*, edited by Guenther Roth and Claus Wittic, Berkeley: University of California Press.

Weber, Max 2001, *The Protestant Ethic and the Spirit of Capitalism*, translated by Talcott Parsons, London: Routledge.

Weinbach, Christine 2003, 'Die systemtheoretische Alternative zum Sex-Gender-Konzept: Gender als geschlechtsstereotypisierte Form der "Person"', in *Frauen, Männer, Gender Trouble. Systemtheoretische Essays*, edited by Ursula Pasero and Christine Weinbach, Frankfurt am Main: Suhrkamp.

Weinbach, Christine 2004a, *Systemtheorie und Gender. Das Geschlecht im Netz der Systeme*, Wiesbaden: VS.

Weinbach, Christine 2004b, 'Systemtheorie und Gender: Geschlechtliche Ungleichheit in der funktional differenzierten Gesellschaft', in *Gender Studies und Systemtheorie. Studien zu einem Theorietransfer*, edited by Sabine Kampmann, Alexandra Karentzos and Thomas Küpper, Bielefeld: Transcript.

Weingarten, Michael 2001, 'System – Entwicklung – Evolution. Warum Luhmanns Theorie sozialer Systeme keine Entwicklungstheorie ist', in *Komplexität und Emanzipation. Kritische Gesellschaftstheorie und die Herausforderung der Systemtheorie Niklas Luhmanns*, edited by Alex Demirović, Münster: Westfälisches Dampfboot.

Wetterer, Angelika 2002, *Arbeitsteilung und Geschlechterkonstruktion. 'Gender at Work' in theoretischer und historischer Perspektive*, Konstanz: UVK.

Wetterer, Angelika 2003, 'Rhetorische Modernisierung: Das Verschwinden der Ungleichheit aus dem zeitgenössischen Differenzwissen', in *Achsen der Differenz. Gesellschaftstheorie und feministische Kritik*, edited by Gudrun-Axeli Knapp and Angelika Wetterer, Münster: Westfälisches Dampfboot.

Whitehead, Jason E. 1999, 'From Criticism to Critique: Preserving the Radical Potential of Critical Legal Studies Through a Reexamination of Frankfurt School Critical Theory', *Florida State University Law Review*, 26: 701–42.

Wiethölter, Rudolf 1968, *Rechtswissenschaft*, Frankfurt am Main: Fischer.

Wiethölter, Rudolf 1970, 'Zur politischen Funktion des Rechts am eingerichteten und ausgeübten Gewerbebetrieb', *Kritische Justiz*, 3: 121–39.

Wiethölter, Rudolf 2005, 'Just-ifications of a Law of Society', in *Paradoxes and Inconsistencies in the Law*, edited by Oren Perez und Gunther Teubner, Oxford: Hart.

Wiggershaus, Rolf 1995, *The Frankfurt School. Its History, Theories, and Political Significance*, translated by Michael Robertson, Cambridge/MA: The MIT Press.

Wissel, Jens 2002, 'Naming the Beast. Nicos Poulantzas und das Empire', *Das Argument*, 248: 791–801.

Wissel, Jens 2007, *Die Transnationalisierung der Herrschaftsverhältnisse. Zur Aktualität von Nicos Poulantzas' Staatstheorie*, Baden-Baden: Nomos.

Young, Iris Marion 1990, *Justice and the Politics of Difference*, Princeton, New Jersey: Princeton University Press.

Young, Iris Marion 2003, 'Europa, leerer Mittelpunkt – Widerstand gegen die US-Politik kann nur eine Dezentrierung der Demokratie leisten', *Frankfurter Rundschau*, 22 July.

Name Index

Subject Index

CPSIA information can be obtained
at www.ICGtesting.com
Printed in the USA
JSHW052239100921
18558JS00005B/5

9 781642 595949